THE ABYSS OF RL

THE ABYSS OF REPRESENTATION

MARXISM AND THE POSTMODERN

SUBLIME **GEORGE HARTLEY** DUKE

UNIVERSITY PRESS DURHAM AND LONDON 2003

POST-CONTEMPORARY INTERVENTIONS: SERIES

EDITORS: STANLEY FISH AND FREDRIC JAMESON

© 2003 Duke University Press

All rights reserved

Printed in the United States of

America on acid-free paper ∞

Designed by Amy Ruth Buchanan

Typeset in Minion by Keystone

Typesetting, Inc. Library of Congress

Cataloging-in-Publication Data appear

on the last printed page of this book.

For Barry Watten—comrade, inspiration, friend

CONTENTS

Acknowledgments, ix

Abbreviations for Works Cited, xi

O N E   Representation and the Abyss of Subjectivity, 1

T W O   Presentation beyond Representation: Kant and the Limits of Discursive Understanding, 22

T H R E E   The Speculative Proposition: Hegel and the Drama of Presentation, 53

F O U R   Marx's Key Concept? Althusser and the *Darstellung* Question, 84

F I V E   Figuration and the Sublime Logic of the Real: Jameson's Libidinal Apparatuses, 127

S I X   The Theater of Figural Space, 182

S E V E N   Can the Symptom Speak? Hegemony and the Problem of Cultural Representation, 235

Notes, 295

Bibliography, 319

Index, 327

ACKNOWLEDGMENTS

For a variety of reasons, this book has been long in coming. And there are three people who are most responsible for seeing me through the process: Fredric Jameson, who gave me encouragement and support early on as well as throughout; Reynolds Smith, executive editor at Duke University Press, who also supported me with great enthusiasm and greater patience since the day I first contacted him in 1995; and most importantly, Barrett Watten, who has been a supporter of my project from its earliest and who for almost twenty years has provided me with an intellectual companionship and lively friendship that have kept me relatively sane and honest through good times and bad.

I thank all of the editorial staff at Duke University Press, including Fred Kameny, Katie Courtland, and Rebecca Johns-Danes. I received time off for this project at Ohio State and Ohio University.

There are many other great friends and scholars whom I also wish to thank for seeing me through this project and through my life and career as well. My tenure review team was the answer to my dreams: Charles Altieri, Charles Bernstein, Fredric Jameson, Hank Lazer, Jerome McGann, Marjorie Perloff, and Barrett Watten. My professors: Lee Bartlett, Michael Fischer, George Huaco, Grant Keener, and Hugh Witemeyer. My many colleagues and friends at Ohio State: Murray Beja, Roger Cherry, Tom Cooley, Chris Daniggelis, Matt Dingo, Jeff Gabel, Kay Halesek, Ethan Knapp, Barbara Rigney, and most of all, Clifford Vaida and Steve Yao. At the University of Kansas: Jesse Aleman, Byron Caminero-Santangelo, Marta Caminero-Santangelo, Tony Tyeeme Clark, Joe Harrington, Ken Irby, Stan Lombardo, Jonathan Mayhew, Jeff Moran, Judy Roitman, Tony Rosenthal, and Rochelle Vota. And now at Ohio University: Marilyn Atlas, Ken Daley, Pepo Delgado, Andy Escobedo, Whitney Huber, David Lazar, Bob Miklitsch, Betsy Partyka, Beth Quitslund, Mark Rollins, Carey Snyder, Tom Walker, and Johnnie Wilcox. And other friends have helped me from afar: Francisco Alarcón, Wilton Azevedo, Rodolfo "Corky" Gonzales, Juan Felipe Herrera, Nathaniel Mackey, Demetria Martínez, Mez, and Regina Cecilia Pinto.

Many thanks again to my others close to me: my children, Dylan and Katy

Hartley; my siblings, Gail Boudreault and Eric Hartley; my parents, George Hartley (senior) and Helen Zadrozny; my in-laws, John and Virginia Mendoza; my dear friends, Donna Baker, Matt Richardson, and John Tritica; and my wonderful wife and soulmate, Valerie Mendoza. And to St. Jude, patron saint of hopeless causes.

Portions of this book have previously appeared in *Journal of the Kafka Society of America* and *Poetics Journal.*

ABBREVIATIONS FOR WORKS CITED

A: CR Pierre Vilar. "Marxist History, a History in the Making: Towards a Dialogue with Althusser." In *Althusser: Critical Readings.*

BL John Sallis. *Being and Logos: Dialog and the Platonic Way.*

BT Friedrich Nietzsche. *The Birth of Tragedy and the Case of Wagner*

C1, C2, C3 Karl Marx. *Capital.* 3 vols.

CI Terry Eagleton. *Criticism and Ideology.*

CHPR Karl Marx. *Critique of Hegel's Philosophy of Right.*

CJ Immanuel Kant. *Critique of Judgment.*

CM Fredric Jameson. "Cognitive Mapping." In *Marxism and the Interpretation of Culture.*

CPCR Gayatri Chakravorty Spivak. *Critique of Postcolonial Reason.*

CPR Immanuel Kant. *Critique of Pure Reason.*

CS Franz Kafka. *Collected Stories.*

CSV Leerom Medovoi, Shankar Raman, and Benjamin Robinson. "Can the Subaltern Vote?" *Socialist Review.*

D Georg Wilhelm Friedrich Hegel. *The Difference between the Fichtean and Schellingian Systems of Philosophy*

E Georg Wilhelm Friedrich Hegel. *The Encyclopedia.*

EB Karl Marx. *The Eighteenth Brumaire of Louis Bonaparte.*

EYS Slavoj Žižek. *Enjoy Your Symptom.*

FA Fredric Jameson. *Fables of Aggression: Wyndham Lewis, the Modernist as Fascist*

FFC	Jacques Lacan. *The Four Fundamental Concepts of Psycho-Analysis.*
FM	Louis Althusser. *For Marx.*
FTK	Slavoj Žižek. *For They Know Not What They Do.*
G	Karl Marx. *Grundrisse.*
GI	Karl Marx and Friedrich Engels. *The German Ideology.*
GPA	Fredric Jameson. *The Geo-Political Aesthetic.*
HC	Néstor García Canelini. *Hybrid Cultures: Strategies for Entering and Leaving Modernity.*
HCS	Gillian Rose. *Hegel contra Sociology.*
HD	John Ashbery. "Syringa." In *Houseboat Days.*
HSS	Ernesto Laclau and Chantal Mouffe. *Hegemony and Socialist Strategy.*
IOW	Gayatri Chakravorty Spivak. *In Other Worlds.*
IR	Michael Sprinker. *Imaginary Relations: Aesthetics and Ideology in the Theory of Historical Materialism*
IT1, IT2	Fredric Jameson. *Ideologies of Theory.* 2 vols.
LA	Slavoj Žižek. *Looking Awry: An Introduction to Jacques Lacan Through Popular Culture.*
LC	Louis Althusser et al. *Lire le capital.*
LOC	Homi Bhabha. *The Location of Culture.*
LP	Louis Althusser. "Ideology and Ideological State Apparatuses." In *Lenin and Philosophy.*
LPR	Georg Wilhelm Friedrich Hegel. *Lectures on the Philosophy of Religion.*
MC	Antony Cutler, Barry Hindess, Paul Hirst, Athar Hussein. *Marx's Capital and Capitalism Today.*
ME	Slavoj Žižek. *The Metastases of Enjoyment.*
PS	Georg Wilhelm Friedrich Hegel. *Phenomenology of Spirit.*

PM	Fredric Jameson. *Postmodernism, or, the Cultural Logic of Late Capitalism.*
PMPV	Gayatri Chakravorty Spivak. "Poststructuralism, Marginality, Postcoloniality, and Value."
PR	Georg Wilhelm Friedrich Hegel. *Elements of the Philosophy of Right.*
PU	Fredric Jameson. *The Political Unconscious.*
R	Plato. *The Republic of Plato.*
RC	Louis Althusser and Etienne Balibar. *Reading Capital.*
RD	Thomas E. Lewis. "Reference and Dissemination: Althusser after Derrida."
SL	Georg Wilhelm Friedrich Hegel. *Science of Logic.*
SK	Johann Gottlieb Fichte. *Science of Knowledge.*
SOI	Slavoj Žižek. *The Sublime Object of Ideology.*
SS	Ranajit Guha, editor. *Subaltern Studies.*
SSS	Ranajit Guha, editor. *Selected Subaltern Studies.*
SV	Fredric Jameson. *Signatures of the Visible.*
TS	Slavoj Žižek. *The Ticklish Subject.*
TWN	Slavoj Žižek. *Tarrying with the Negative.*
U	Louis Marin. *Utopics: Spatial Play.*

ONE REPRESENTATION AND THE ABYSS OF SUBJECTIVITY

In his poem "Syringa," John Ashbery stages a double writing of loss. The initial loss is Orpheus' loss of his love, Eurydice. This loss—this irruption of death and disappearance into the fantasy field of love—throws Orpheus out of his customary, everyday existence, characterized by the Imaginary fusion of lover and beloved, into the Dionysian abyss of music. Orpheus' world is rent apart. Curiously, it is not the loss as such that rends his world but his own sorrowful lament in response to that loss:

> Orpheus liked the glad personal quality
> Of the things beneath the sky. Of course, Eurydice was a part
> Of this. Then one day, everything changed. He rends
> Rocks into fissures with lament. Gullies, hummocks
> Can't withstand it. The sky shudders from one horizon
> To the other, almost ready to give up wholeness.
>
> (HD 69, ll. 1–6)

The once comforting, sheltering sky now shudders and threatens to be swallowed up by the abyss opened up by this elegiac voice, the sky ready to give up its wholeness.[1] What the spacing of the poem prepares us for, however, is the fact that this whole was already fragmented, that Eurydice was already "a part / . . . ." The line break suggests what Apollo, the second voice of the poem, then tells us explicitly:

All other things must change too.
The seasons are no longer what they once were,
But it is the nature of things to be seen only once,
As they happen along, bumping into other things, getting along
Somehow. That's where Orpheus made his mistake.
Of course Eurydice vanished into the shade;
She would have even if he hadn't turned around.

(ll. 11–17)

The Orphic song attempts to freeze the moment of loss eternally through its lament; the Apollonian voice of "reality," on the other hand, continually, even obsessively reminds Orpheus that death and loss are in the nature of things—that nature being one of continuous process and change. The whole is always already a part. What the reader doesn't yet realize, though, is that Apollo's own distanced stance on the eternal round of things is itself the unacknowledged attempt to paste over the abyss opened up through his own loss. This loss, lying "frozen and out of touch," only accidentally comes to consciousness when "an arbitrary chorus / Speaks of a totally different incident with a similar name / In whose tale are hidden syllables / Of what happened so long before that / In some small town, one indifferent summer" (ll. 84–88).

What the poem ultimately records is the breakdown of representation itself: the Orphic song outdistances the "matter," the poem streaking by, "its tail afire, a bad/Comet screaming hate and disaster, but so turned inward/That the meaning, good or other, can never/Become known" (ll. 68–71); at the same time, the Apollonian vision depends on the repression of the traumatic event, which functions in its very repression as the ground for the dispassionate, merely careful, "scholarly setting down of/Unquestioned facts, a record of pebbles along the way" (ll. 62–63). When we attempt to eternalize the traumatic moment of the loss in time and to memorialize its emotional fury, to render it by rending the world that now embodies its absence, we end up streaking right past it all aflame into utter meaninglessness. But when we attempt to explain this loss, to rationalize it, to submit it to the symbolic structure that is meant to domesticate it, this loss only breaks through under the mask of some other body, some other long-forgotten name which, merely in its structural similarity as a forgotten and repressed name, shatters that symbolic structure itself. We go too far, we don't go far enough. Either way, the irruption of this trauma into our Imaginary stabilized existence (the "glad, personal quality" of the sky) sets representation into its own ultimately self-destroying motion.

At such a moment we are faced with the beyond of representation: the point at which the representational apparatus turns in on itself and collapses in its inability to flesh out some adequate embodiment of the loss. But it is this loss itself that is the constitutive element of representation. The beyond as the mirage erected in the place of the always-already lost object is in this sense internal to representation as its condition of possibility. But there is another crucial sense in which these Orphic and Apollonian attempts to confront the loss present the beyond of representation: the beyond as the original Thing behind the surface appearance that representation provides. Or, in other words, the distinction between appearance and its underlying reality, between phenomena and noumena, between image and concept, between the representation and the Thing-in-itself.

I begin with this particular poem because it stages the setting in motion of a metaphor that continues to lie behind contemporary Marxism's response to the postmodern sublime—that abyss as the figure for the breakdown of representation. Any theory of ideology has to come to terms with the problem of representation—a problem that itself has a figurative history. This is the case with Louis Althusser's conceptions of structural causality and ideological interpellation. This is also true of Fredric Jameson's notion of the political unconscious. And this is equally so with Gayatri Chakravorty Spivak's conception of the subaltern. The figure of the abyss in one way or another imposes itself in these and other Marxist formulations of ideology. This book is an attempt, then, to lay out the terms of the history of this figure as it undergoes various transformations from Immanuel Kant's theory of the sublime to G. W. F. Hegel's speculative reversal to Karl Marx's scientific inversion on up to the Althusserian moment (which I believe we still are coming to terms with despite the forty years that have passed since Althusser's writings on the significance of the passage from the young Marx to the mature one).

Another related figure to the abyss is the beyond—the figure that seems to be pointing to a dimension existing on the other side of the abyss. The key point is that the beyond of representation is representation's own beyond. That is, the beyond is nothing but the effect of the limit internal to representation itself. I stress this in order to avoid the compelling urge to read the "beyond" of representation as that space or operation or adequation that somehow completes or surpasses the limits of representation. It is in this light that the representation/presentation distinction referred to throughout this book (which in German idealism is written as the *Vorstellung/Darstellung** distinction) should precisely *not* be seen as that which somehow poses Darstellung as the more adequate mode of doing justice to the concept (*Begriff*) to be fleshed out. Presentation is not the better mode of developing or elaborating on the concept in the sense of doing something distinct from representation; presentation—at least as Hegel uses the term—is the operative moment at which representation represents its own failure: since no representation, because of its abstract and seemingly immediate nature, can adequately present its concept, representation must mediate itself, must set itself in motion by staging its own failure arising from its own subjection to time. What this means is that, strictly speaking, *there is no beyond of representation*. Yet the space of incommensurability opened up in the heart of representation—in, for example, the experience of the sublime— projects just such a beyond both as the more adequate operation and as the Thing beyond appearance. This space of incommensurability—the gap or abyss opened up between the figure and the concept—this space of impossibility, is at the same time the space of possibility of representation as such. Without such an immanent limitation, representation could not operate at all.

What this means, in effect, is that the beyond is on *this* side of appearance. The opposition appearance/essence or sensible/supersensible is the constitutive illusion of appearance itself. As Hegel argues in the *Phenomenology of Spirit*, "The supersensible is the sensuous and the perceived posited as it is *in truth*; but the *truth* of the sensuous and the perceived is to be *appearance*. The supersensible is therefore appearance* qua *appearance*" (PS 89). The abyss is thus not a problem of the subject—as the result of the subject's limited capacity for knowledge beyond sensory experience—but the very ground of the subject: this paradox of a grounding abyss means nothing more than that the subject *is this space* of incommensurability as such, the problem residing rather on the side of substance (the network of unreflective relationships and activities against which we pose ourselves as active subjects—for instance, society). The subject is nothing but the gap, the space of negativity, inherent in substance itself. The problem of the political subject's relationship to the social substance, for example, is therefore the problem of the impossibility of society itself: society is impossible in the sense that the social can never be reduced to a given organic being but is rather the scene of antagonism, as Ernesto Laclau and Chantal

*Foreign terms are italicized at first mention only.

Mouffe have suggested.[2] In the words of Slavoj Žižek, "The Hegelian 'subject' is ultimately nothing but a name for the externality of the Substance to itself, for the 'crack' by way of which the Substance becomes 'alien' to itself, (mis)perceiving itself through human eyes as the inaccessible-reified Otherness."[3]

It is in this sense that the Apollonian commentary on Eurydice should be taken. The point isn't simply that all things change in time; rather, the Thing that made Eurydice "Eurydice," that intimate kernel "in Eurydice more than Eurydice" (as Jacques Lacan would say), is nothing but a fantasy construct, yet this fantasy is a constitutive one. Orpheus' entire symbolic field of reference is determined by the placement of this Eurydice-Thing in the gap at the heart of the symbolic. Eurydice is the Thing that gives Orpheus' symbolic order consistency. This Thing occupying the abyss of representation is Hegel's transformation of the Kantian sublime (which itself refers to the abyss and its beyond). Once the absolute negativity of death and disappearance intervenes, however, Orpheus' own identity disintegrates, and he is desubjectivized in the process. That is, in his descent into Hades, Orpheus confronts Eurydice in the space between the two deaths: Eurydice's actual physical death and her subsequent symbolic one. In such a state of subjective destitution, Orpheus can no longer allow himself the fantasy of representation: no mere image can survive the irruption of the Real, the point at which representation fails. Yet "Syringa" presents this failure as such: once both the Orphic and Apollonian responses to loss either exhaust themselves or are forced to confront their repressed loss, the poem itself rises up as the record of this failure. Here we have the presentation beyond representation. It is only at this point, with the loss of the loss that the poem enacts, that the initial loss no longer functions as the avoidance of the Real. For the initial loss, in both Orpheus and Apollo, functions as the node or kernel around which their symbolizations organize themselves in order to repress, each in its own way, the radical negativity of the Real. Eurydice vanishes into the shade, the beyond of representation, not in the sense of entering another world (Hades) but in the sense that the fantasy construct that was Eurydice from the start can no longer function since it was nothing more than the split internal to the field of representation in the first place. Eurydice and the lost summer love were nothing but the retroactive embodiments of the negative space of desire itself.

The question of representation and its beyond, then, has to do with a complex of themes that grow out of and receive varying inflections from the seemingly differing theoretical practices of a certain Hegelianism, psychoanalysis, and Marxism. These themes work together in different ways in the (re)turn to Kant, Hegel, Marx, and Lacan as exemplified (in distinct ways) in the works of Jameson and Žižek. And for both Jameson and Žižek, this return functions as a clarification and extension of questions raised by Althusser and the various Althusserians and post-Althusserians in his wake. The key problem or obsession motivating this return to figures who seemed safely interred in the aftermath of the poststructuralist moment (which was defined in large part as a rejection of "Hegel," "Freud," and "Marx") is that which obsessed the poststructuralisms as well—representation. But as Hamlet still testifies, the dead have a habit of returning from the grave. The figure of Eurydice still had some work to do in the psychic economy of Orpheus before she would (or could) disappear, traumatically, into her second, symbolic death.

Hence, this book may appear to be somewhat anachronistic. Hasn't time bid farewell to Althusser already, not to mention Kant, Hegel, and Marx (what about 1989?)? But time is by nature out of joint. Representation is by nature a problem of this condition of being out of joint. For if all were immediately and satisfactorily put in place and done with, there would be no need for representation—indeed, there would be no representation. If the concept were ever capable of immediate and successful psychic inhumation, there would be no need for the figure, that material excess that clings like putrid flesh to the sacred soul of thought. Yet the figure is the scene of the concept: the concept is nothing but the retroactive staging of an always incomplete series of figures or images. The Socratic philosopher could discern the Idea as it shines forth in its manifestations among the many; but it is precisely those manifestations that through their constitutive incompletion or corruption project the illusion of the Idea in the beyond of representation. Had we intellectual intuition, Kant mused, we would have no need for representation—for we would be God. But we are not God, and we are thereby free. We are not God, and we are thereby subject to the glories and sufferings of this pathological excess, this human condition whereby every reduction to some pure form is dependent on an excess of desire for its very existence.

THE SUBJECT VERSUS SUBJECTIVIZATION

The problem of representation is that of the subject. This is the point at which Žižek differs most dramatically from Althusser and the various Foucauldian and poststructuralist moves to locate the position of the subject in the display of various subject-positions. As Žižek rightly argues, the subject and the subject-position must be seen as two quite different moments in the process of ideological construction. The notion of subject-position is related to Althusser's theory of interpellation. As is well known, for Althusser ideology is not a question of false consciousness, at least not in the sense of a simple misunderstanding or conceptual inversion of what should appear as true—that is, nonideological. For Althusser, we are always in ideology. "Ideology," Althusser contends, "is a 'representation' of the imaginary relationship of individuals to their real conditions of existence."[4] He elaborates on this definition on several counts. First, it is not "the real conditions of their existence" that ideology represents for individuals. We do not have a one-to-one correspondence between "reality" on one side and its representation on the other. What is in fact represented is the *relationship* between the individuals and their real conditions of existence. Again, this is not the "existing" relations—that is, the material relations of production that govern human existence—but the "imaginary" ones.[5] "If this is the case," Althusser continues, "the question of the 'cause' of the imaginary distortion of the real conditions in ideology disappears and must be replaced by a different question: why is the representation given to individuals of their (individual) relation to the social relations which govern their collective and individual life necessarily an imaginary relation? And what is the nature of this imaginariness?" (LP 165).

The more immediate question to be answered, however, is: What is the nature of this representation? Ideology as representation takes place not on a spiritual (*Geistige*) but a material level. Representation is a material practice whereby ideology comes into being. According to the usual ("ideological") conception of the relationship between belief and practice, belief precedes practice. We kneel in church because we believe in God. In such a view, every subject is endowed with a consciousness, believes in certain ideas and not in others, and freely acts according to his or her ideas. But Althusser is on this question Pascalian: *we believe because we kneel*. This ritual of kneeling is one of many that make up the material practice of what Althusser refers to as an ideological apparatus. In this way "ideas" have disappeared as a thing of the beyond while "their existence is inscribed in the actions of practices governed by rituals defined in the last instance by an ideological apparatus" (LP 170). Here is one way of elaborating on the claim that ideas are already on the side of representation: there is no ideology (representation) without the category of the subject:

> I say: the category of the subject is constitutive of all ideology, but at the same time and immediately I add that *the category of the subject is constitutive of all ideology insofar as all ideology has the function (which defines it) of "constituting" concrete individuals as subjects*. In the interaction of this double constitution exists the functioning of all ideology, ideology being nothing but its functioning in the material forms of existence of that functioning. (LP 171)

Althusser fails to develop the full nature of this "double constitution," though, as he presents his theory of interpellation. According to his theory, subjects are produced through interpellation, which is precisely the function of ideology: the injunction for us to take upon ourselves our symbolic mandate, to assume the subject-position provided for us by the ideological call. Representation (the material practice of ideology) constitutes the representing subject; that is, representation represents the subject as the representing subject. Althusser describes this ideological hailing of the subject as follows:

> I shall then suggest that ideology "acts" or "functions" in such a way that it "recruits" subjects among the individuals (it recruits them all), or "transforms" the individuals into subjects (it transforms them all) by that very precise operation which I have called *interpellation* or hailing, and which can be imagined along the lines of the most commonplace everyday police (or other) hailing: "Hey, you there!"
>
> Assuming that the theoretical scene I have imagined takes place in the street, the hailed individual will turn round. By this mere one-hundred-and-eighty-degree physical conversion, he becomes a *subject*. Why? Because he has recognized that the hail was "really" addressed to him, and that "it was *really him* who was hailed" (and not someone else). Experience shows that the practical telecommunication of hailings is such that they hardly ever miss their man: verbal call or whistle, the one hailed always recognizes that it is really him who is being hailed. And yet it is a strange phenomenon, and one which cannot be explained solely by "guilt feelings," despite the large numbers who "have something on their consciences."
>
> Naturally for the convenience and clarity of my theoretical theater I have had to present things in the form of a sequence, with a before and an after, and thus in the form of a temporal succession. (LP 174)[6]

Rather than a temporal succession, however, Althusser asserts that interpellation has always-already produced individuals as subjects: "Before its birth, the child is therefore always-already a subject, appointed as a subject in and by the specific ideological configuration in which it is 'expected' once it has been conceived" (LP 176). Yet how is this interpellation into subjects, this allotting of subject-positions, maintained? Through what Althusser refers to as a "duplicate mirror-system." We are subjects only through our subjection to the Subject— the Unique, Absolute, Other Subject, what Lacan refers to as the Master Signifier. Without this radically contingent externalized Other excluded from the round of subjectivity, the subjects cannot be "subjectivized." What Althusser nevertheless doesn't recognize here is that this excluded Subject is—to borrow again from Žižek's reading of Hegel—nothing but a stupid, senseless thing filling the crack of the social, the radical negativity of the split internal to Substance. Althusser does point to a Subject distinct from the subject-position, but that Subject is very different from Hegel's (although it is dependent on Hegel's discussion of, among other things, the role of the monarch in a constitutional monarchy). Althusser describes the Subject in these terms: "God thus defines himself as the Subject par excellence, he who is through himself and for himself ('I am that I am'), and he who interpellates the subject, the individual subjected to him by this very interpellation" (LP 179). The subject-Subject relationship is a double-mirror relationship, according to Althusser, in the sense that the subject needs the Subject (interpellation occurs through the Subject, Moses is called by God to do His bidding, Moses recognizes himself as "Moses" through this call) and the Subject needs the subjects (people were made in the image of God, even in their debauchery when they function as the "terrible inversion of his image in them"—the subjects are the Subject's reflections). What Althusser does not acknowledge is the Hegelian inflection of the Subject's self-relation in the claim "I am that I am." What we have here in this Fichtean Subject (I = I) is the tautological relationship of what Hegel refers to as the infinite judgment: this statement of pure identity folds in on itself and opens up the abyss, the radical negativity that characterizes the (Hegelian) subject, for the reduplication of the I as subject in the I as predicate illustrates that this Fichtean identity is nonidentical in that it cannot be both subject and its opposite, predicate.[7] I = I becomes I = not-I through this very proposition of identity. The empty name of the subject is fleshed out with nothing but its own empty name as its predicate. The Subject as such, then, can never function as the point of self-reflection for the subjects, for they can only become subjectivized-reflected (take up their subject-positions) when the Subject-position is filled with some excluded, stupid object (for example, the king's body, the broken body of Christ, or the commodity functioning as the money-form). Thus, Althusser's conception of interpellation provides a theory of subjectivization, but not of its prior moment as subject-as-radical-negativity. Subjectivization-interpellation is nothing but the attempt to cover over the traumatic recognition of the abyss of subjectivity as such. The Subject *is* thus identical in form to the infinite judgment or speculative proposition "I am that I am," yet precisely through the nonidentity that constitutes both.[8]

As Žižek observes, the subject's congruency with the speculative proposition (which negates the statement of identity) is also behind Lacan's conception of the subject—a conception that distinguishes Lacan from the poststructuralist notion of the subject-position whereby in the latter the "subject" is an effect of a nonsubjective process. For Lacan, in Žižek's view, the subject is instead the empty place to be filled by subjectivization:

> To put it simply: if we make an abstraction, if we subtract all the richness of the different modes of subjectivization, all the fullness of experience present in the way the individuals are "living" their subject-positions, what remains is an empty place which was filled out with this richness; this original void, this lack of symbolic structure, *is* the subject, the subject of the signifier. The *subject* is therefore to be strictly opposed to the effect of *subjectivization*: what the subjectivization masks is not a pre- or trans-subjective process of writing but a lack in the structure, a lack which is the subject. (*SOI* 175)

What cannot be accounted for in Althusser's depiction of interpellation is the failure of subjectivization (since, according to his account, interpellation occurs prior to birth). This failure is not just absolute in the sense of individuals who refuse to heed the interpellative call (Althusser's "bad subjects" who provoke the intervention of the Repressive State Apparatus when the Ideological State Apparatuses fail); even in the seemingly successful examples of interpellated subjects there remains a traumatic, antagonistic kernel that resists symbolization. The point is not that this failure refutes the theory of interpellation; quite the opposite. This failure, this little leftover of the Real, is interpellation's condition of possibility. As such, this failure is a necessary one, for without this point of negativity in the midst of the symbolic, the space for the subject-position could never open up. This negativity, this radical split of the social-symbolic, is subjectivity itself. The subject, then, opens up the space for subjectivization. The surplus object resisting symbolization is the materialization of the abyss of subjectivity, the subject that is internally split in relation to its own incommensurable surplus object (the formula for which is Lacan's $\$\lozenge a$). This surplus is the hook upon which the symbolic fastens itself in the process of identification or interpellation.[9] Žižek notes that "the process of interpellation-subjectivization is precisely an attempt to avoid this traumatic kernel through identification: in assuming a symbolic mandate, in recognizing himself in the interpellation, the subject evades the dimension of the Thing" (*sor* 181). Without this little piece of the Real, that thing in me more than me, the symbolic is desubjectivized: thrown into the abyss of subjectivity, caught in the vicious circle of radical negativity.

One of the key motifs of my book, then, is the relationship between the vicious circle and the stupid Thing. In the terms established above, the vicious circle is the traumatic confrontation with the negativity of subjectivity, while the stupid Thing is the contingent little piece of the Real that occupies the space of negativity itself at the heart of the symbolic, and that anchors and stabilizes the circulation of this negativity by functioning as its embodiment, its positivization. The object that occupies this place of the Thing both domesticates the Thing by embodying it while at the same time taking on the sublime qualities of the Thing itself. This anchoring point of the object in the place of the Thing is necessary for the fantasy construction that provides consistency to the symbolic. This vicious circle operates across many registers of life. In political terms, the vicious circle equates with the notion of democracy as pure negativity, as the refusal to fill in the space of power with any particular body, for any body that occupies this gap is by definition an impostor, a usurper. It was in this light that Hegel analyzed the Terror of the French Revolution: the Terror was the manifestation of pure reason, and as a consequence of this he proposed that the choice of the body to occupy this space must, in its very irrationality, embody the negativity of the social and in the process subjectivize the "subjects." This irrational response, as we will see in chapter 3, is the monarch, the figure chosen strictly through the irrational quality of the accident of birth. In this way the monarch embodies the stupidity of any thing that occupies the space of political power, serving as a reminder of the paradoxical nature of the Thing as both necessary and impossible, as internally split precisely through its function as the subject that subjectivizes the polis. The monarch is the equivalent of the speculative proposition. The contradictory figure of the stupid body of the king was thus a compromise formation for Hegel, a figure who at once embodied the impossibility of the subject while at the same time providing the function of subjectivization—of keeping the radical negativity of the

Real before our view while providing us with the benefits of avoiding such a confrontation with the Real. I will return to the question of such a politics in the final chapters.

HYSTERIA PRECEDES INTERPELLATION

Successful interpellation indicates that we have accepted our symbolic mandate: we have taken on the identity presented to us by the big Other. What is passed over in Althusser's theory, however, is the hystericization of the subject that is at one and the same time the necessary condition for and the reminder of the impossibility of interpellation or subjectivization. The hysteric is both the precondition for and the resistance to successful interpellation.

The initial moment of hystericization is the provocation of the feeling of guilt. The symbolic order, the big Other, poses the questions, What were you doing? What is the meaning of this? Who is responsible for this? The response of the addressee of these questions is guilt and shame for, even though the individual may be "innocent" and "ignorant," the form of the question itself produces the scene of guilt. We are guilty even if we have done nothing; in fact, we are guilty precisely because we can do nothing. The question from the Other, then, is basically obscene in the way it exposes the degree to which such questions are unanswerable. Such is the real purpose of such questions: not to elicit a "true" answer but to reveal the impossibility of the subject in relation to the Other as interrogator. The only answer to these questions is the subject itself, the subject as, in Žižek's words, "the void of the impossibility of answering the question of the Other" (*soi* 178). The subject does not *have* the answer; the subject *is* the answer to this questioning—the answer of the Real. The question points to that object within the subject, that innermost point of intimacy that Lacan refers to as *objet petit a*. The question confronts us with the Thing inside us, the object to which the big Other draws our attention but that can never be symbolized, the object to which the Other draws our attention *because* it cannot be symbolized, because the object itself is nothing but the remainder or leftover of the signifying process itself, the horrifying object that embodies our *jouissance*, and thus both attracts and repels us at the same time, thereby producing guilt. This attraction/repulsion relationship to the object inside us splits us: such is the constitution of the split subject of desire as the answer of the Real to the question of the Other:

> The question as such produces in its addressee an effect of shame and guilt, it
> divides, it hystericizes him, and this hystericization is the constitution of the
> subject: the status of the subject as such is hysterical. The subject is con-
> stituted through his own division, splitting, as to the object in him; this
> object, this traumatic kernel, is the dimension that we have already named as
> that of a "death drive," of a traumatic imbalance, a rooting out. Man as such
> is "nature sick unto death," derailed, run off the rails through a fascination
> with a lethal Thing. (*SOI* 180–181)

This confrontation with the traumatic Thing is the subject as such. Interpellation, on the other hand, is the attempt to avoid exactly this confrontation.
This is the difference between subject and subjectivization: the subject is constituted by the negativity of the traumatic Thing that is the remainder of
symbolization; subjectivization-interpellation is the avoidance mechanism in
response to this Thing of the Real, our attempt to outstrip our guilt. Interpellation functions as the identification of the subject with the Law as symbolic
order, the superego function that maintains the illusion of social cohesion;
hystericization functions as the identification with the obscene side of the
superego, the side that demands that we "Enjoy!" and that constitutes both
subjectivization as such (as the avoidance of just this impossible demand) and
the impossibility of subjectivization (as the irreducible kernel of the Real at the
heart of the Symbolic that frustrates the illusion of symbolic totalization).[10]

The hysteric, as we have seen, is the subject constitutive of interpellation. But
the hysteric who remains despite this subjectivization is the one who refuses
this symbolic mandate, who refuses to be subjectivized or interpellated. The
hysteric, above all, seeks to maintain his or her desire by continually deferring
its satisfaction (at which point it would no longer be desire). The hysterical
response to any potential solution to the deadlock of the subject caught between the attraction to and repulsion from the Thing is to say, "No, that is
not it!" The symbolic mandate conferred on the hysteric would be such a resolution and must, therefore, be resisted in deference to the object within, which
this mandate seeks to displace from view. As the inverse of the symbolic mandate, however, the hysteric's act remains tied to the Symbolic (unlike the psychotic whose total lack of identification dissolves any tie with the Symbolic
whatsoever).

The hysteric's basic act is the transformation or conversion of this deadlock
into its own embodiment, the symptom. The hysteric thus stages what Žižek

refers to as "hysterical theater": the hysterical symptom gives body to the dead-lock that cannot be symbolized. That which cannot be spoken is converted into body language—just think of a nervous twitch or an inexplicable paralysis whereby an unacknowledged psychic deadlock seeks resolution through this body language: "What we have here is quite literally a 'conversion': the *figuration* ('acting out') of a theoretical impasse (of the 'unthought' of a theoretical position) and at the same time the *inversion* best rendered by one of Hegel's constant rhetorical figures: when, for example, Hegel deals with the ascetic's position, he says that the ascetic converts the *denial of the body* into the *embodied denial*" (FTK 143). Žižek explains the drive behind this inversion:

> According to Lacan, the fundamental experience of man qua being-of-language is that his desire is impeded, constitutively dissatisfied: he "doesn't know what he really wants." What the hysterical "conversion" accomplishes is precisely an inversion of this impediment: by means of it, the impeded desire converts into a *desire for impediment*; the unsatisfied desire converts into a *desire for unsatisfaction*; a desire to keep our desire "open"; the fact that we "don't know what we really want"—what to desire—converts into a *desire not to know*, a desire for ignorance. . . . Therein consists the basic paradox of the hysteric's desire: what he desires is above all that his desire itself should remain unsatisfied, hindered—in other words: alive as a desire. (FTK 143–44)

There are four points I wish to make concerning this passage on hysterical conversion:

First, this is another example of the beyond of representation functioning not as some transcendent principle or moment but as an inversion internal to appearance itself. The solution to the mystery of the appearance of the hysterical symptom "is to be sought not *beyond* its appearance but in the very *appearance of mystery*" (FTK 107). This suggests, then, that representation itself is a form of this hysterical theater.

Second, the hysterical subject who "does not know what he wants" desires the desire of the Other. That is, the hysteric identifies with the gaze of the Other, the point in the symbolic order from which the hysteric sees himself as desirable. The hysteric does not identify with a subject-position in the sense of taking on that particular symbolic mandate as the point of his own desire (subjectivization) but as that of the Other's desire. It is the conflict between these two points of desire that produces the anxiety of the hysteric: "How is what you (the Other) say I am not what I thought I was?" The job of ideology criticism, then, is to identify the position in the Other that functions as the desire that the hysteric desires to please.

Third, hysterical conversion as the staging or acting out of an inexpressible conceptual deadlock in bodily terms is the primary mechanism of *figuration* that Jameson identifies in his theory of the political unconscious. What Jameson undertakes to lay out is exactly this hysterical theater (as we will see in chapter 5).

Finally, hysterical conversion as the production of the other as symptom is where the question of cultural representation, for example, comes to the fore. As a given culture elaborates its hysterical conversion, it does so by expelling to the margins or the outside its other, its excluded element that figures as the embodiment of the radical negativity at the core of the social substance. The correlative of the Subject at the center of the big Other, then, is the excluded other at the margins. This excluded other becomes the object of the concept of hegemony. (This is the topic of chapter 7.)

THE SUBLIME AND THE STAGING OF THE BEYOND

Orpheus sang into the abyss. Such an abyss was beyond the limits of poetic representation and could only be sounded with song, with lamentation. Had Orpheus been a Kantian, his exhaustion at the failure of his song would have provided for a moment when, in utter pain and despair, a newfound pleasure would rise up in their place—a pleasure based on the Idea that beyond this loss and breakdown of representation there was the immortality of the soul and the wisdom and power of a God, an intuitive intellect to whom all of this would make perfect sense, the Almighty to whom death could pose no threat. Orpheus could have taken solace in the experience of the Kantian sublime, in accordance with which pain would give way to pleasure. The impossibility of representation could have been converted into the presentation of impossibility. Such is the hysterical conversion of the Kantian theater of the sublime.

In a sense, though, while Orpheus himself may have collapsed in impotence and despair and Apollo may have frozen in the recognition of a long-buried loss now thrust into his consciousness, the poem itself, "Syringa," combines the Apollonian understanding (that Eurydice was always already to have vanished) with the Orphic plunge into sublime despair and song. The poem itself embodies the sublime crossing of the loss of the Idea (Eurydice) with the Idea of loss (Apollo's recognition). And in this crossing, it opens up the hysterical space for the conversion of the sublime from the breakdown of art to the art of the breakdown. For Orpheus, Eurydice was nothing but a moment of art from the start, a moment of the fleshing out of Orpheus' desire that in order to remain as desire, had to have vanished to open up into the abyss that is the constitutive opening of the space of desire as such. Orpheus' rending of rock and sky converted the loss of the object into the objectification of loss. And this is the Hegelian sublime.

To be more accurate, Kant's theater of the sublime is a particular species of hysteria—obsessive compulsion. Hegel's own theater of the sublime, on the other hand, is the hysterical as such. Žižek describes the turn from Kantian obsession to Hegelian hysteria by drawing attention to "the Kantian postponement of the encounter with the Thing—for the Kantian gap dividing forever the Thing from the world of phenomena: it conceals a foreboding that perhaps this Thing is itself nothing but a lack, an empty place; that beyond the phenomenal appearance there is only a certain negative self-relationship because of which the positively given phenomenal world is perceived as 'mere appearance'—in other words, that 'The supersensible is therefore appearance *qua* appearance' " (*SOI* 192–93). The obsessional's self-punishment for the realization of desire (through postponement of the encounter with the desired object—which is horrifying in that it offers too much enjoyment) is in this light actually the hysterical sense that no object can in fact live up to and take the place of the object of desire.

In this book the question of the sublime will serve as shorthand for and the stage upon which will be played out the question of the abysmal limits of representation and the beyond that rises up out of this experience of limitation. I will explore this problem in Kant's work by examining his look at the limits of what he calls the discursive understanding. In light of this belief that human understanding is limited because of its discursive (rather than intuitive) nature, Kant's critical philosophy is one of the key places where the limits of representation, as well as the sublime nature of its beyond, gets articulated. But as we have seen above, Hegel is not content to give Kant the last word. Hegel's conception of the relationship between representation and presentation (Vorstellung and Darstellung), then, will be seen as the dialectical (hysterical) conversion of the Kantian problem. The question of the relationship between Hegel and Marx, then, underlies my analysis of Althusser's "anti-Hegelian" reading of Marx's *Capital*, in which Marx's "key concept" of Darstellung holds out the tool for moving from the "ideological" Hegelian problematic to the "scientific" Marxist conception of structural causality. One might wonder at this point, however, whether Althusser has retreated to a pre-Hegelian figure of abstract negativity that cannot do justice to Marx's conception of the presentation of value—a conception that returns us to the problem of the vicious circle (value as such) and the stupid Thing (the money form). From this vantage point, Marx's conception of the money form repeats the Hegelian move of converting the Kantian sublime of the gap into the Hegelian (Lacanian) sublime object that occupies the place of the gap.

All of this affords a critical apparatus with which to undertake an analysis of Jameson's theory of figuration and the political unconscious. Jameson's work represents one of the most significant attempts to elaborate on what could be seen as a Marxist theory of the postmodern sublime; and what makes his work all the more appropriate in the present context is his attempt to extend Althusser's project (especially the concepts of structural causality and ideological interpellation) while, like Žižek, pointing to the limitations of the Althusserian theory of interpellation. Unlike Žižek, though, Jameson does not see in Althusser's theory an overemphasis of the Symbolic (which for Žižek masks a refusal to confront the real of our desire). In fact, for Jameson, Althusser's problem was to have left out the Symbolic altogether. How do these differing views of Althusser's work come about? Part of the difficulty is that Jameson takes Althusser literally when he defines ideology as "the representation of the subject's *Imaginary* relationship to his or her *Real* conditions of existence" (*PM* 51). According to Jameson, this definition suggests that Althusser is concerned with Lacan's Imaginary and Real, but not the Symbolic. Ideology is seen, then, as an Imaginary relationship to the Real. But there are two problems here. First, the "Real" that Althusser indicates is what Lacan would refer to as "reality." Reality in this sense is a compromise formation that keeps us from confronting the Real of our desire (the primary illustration being Lacan's reference to Sigmund Freud's story of the father's dream of the burning son).[11] Second, as we have seen above in terms of the distinction between the subject and subjectivization, this "reality" is thoroughly Symbolic. The moment of symbolic interpellation in Althusser's definition of ideology comes in the term "representation." The conditions of the Real that Althusser refers to above (our real conditions of existence—that is, our class determination) are social-symbolic conditions that themselves are the result of such a representation. For this representation, as we have seen, occurs at the level of material practice, the point at which ideological interpellation produces its performative dimension: representation takes place when we kneel and, therefore, believe.

Yet Jameson translates the Althusserian definition of ideology into the concept of cognitive mapping. With such a move, Jameson hopes to "renew the analysis of representation on a higher and much more complex level" by working out a framework that would "enable a situational representation on the part of the individual subject to that vaster and properly unrepresentable totality which is the ensemble of society's structures as a whole" (*PM* 51). The unrepresentable: here is where I return to the question of the sublime. In Žižek's Lacanian scheme, there are several different ways of approaching the sublime (object), as we have seen in the discussion of hysteria and subjectivization. But the psychoanalytic ethic urges one to identify with the kernel of the Real, the object at the heart of the subject, to work through one's fantasy in order to identify with the Thing that organizes one's enjoyment. Jameson's more properly Marxist project, on the other hand, defines the sublime as a problem to be resolved. (One question to pursue later, then, is whether Jameson's sublime is Kantian as opposed to Žižek's Hegelian sublime.) With Kant the sublime was a problem, but one that yielded the Idea upon its conversion. For Jameson, however, the characteristic trait of late capitalist, postmodern life is the impossibility of such an Idea; the injunction to cognitive mapping nevertheless commits us to the mapping of this impossible space beyond representation. Such is the topic of chapter 5. Suffice it to say here that such a project appears obsessional.[12] That is to say, this mapping approach to "the Real" beyond representation seems to be a detour away from the Real as such, and it is in this manner that I return to the hysterical theater.

Theater as metaphor, metaphor as theatricalization: with this topic I bring the various theorists I have discussed so far into concert by examining the way certain theatrical models of subjects in social space operate in the works of Althusser, Friedrich Nietzsche, Franz Kafka, and Jameson. Here is one place where the question of politics arises in the form of a politics of representation and its beyond. This figure of the theater brings together the theater in its usual sense as a dramatic art of the stage as well as in its figurative sense as a stage for the performance of various modes of subjectivity, various calls or interpellations that transform the spectator into an actor. Hence, performativity will be used in its dramatic sense as well as its Hegelian, Lacanian, and Analytical senses.

Performativity is a tropic-concept that attempts to represent the process of presentation itself. That is, "performativity" functions as a representation or Vorstellung that stages the elaboration of presentation or Darstellung. Darstellung as staging and performance, then, ventures onto the field of the political.

This point leads into the final chapter, "Can the Symptom Speak? Hegemony and the Problem of Cultural Representation." As we saw, the moment of hysterical conversion brings into being the symptom of the social-symbolic order. One question that arises here, however, is how we are to think (that is, represent) this other of the social. What mode of access do we have, given the abysmal character of representation itself? This becomes the problem driving Spivak's infamous subaltern. According to the terms of Spivak's construction of the subaltern as sheer heterogeneity, whatever itineraries of the subject we might imagine capable of offering themselves up as objects of intellectual seduction, we must, it seems, content ourselves with the impossible demand to continue on the quest to represent the unrepresentable. The subaltern thus functions for Spivak as the postmodern sublime object continually effaced from view under Western(ized) eyes. Laclau and Mouffe, on the other hand, offer a productive mode of entry into this impossible space through their notion of hegemony—a notion that Žižek modifies in his Lacanian model of the symptom. The question still remains, When we say that we cannot represent the subaltern, who is this "we"? And what happens when the symptom or the subaltern occupies the position of the subject of the sentence? To put this in terms of American cultural politics, we can say that Anglo-Americans, as they rose to dominance in the nineteenth century, depended on the production of a variety of symptoms that would serve as the foundation of Anglo-American identity itself. The figure of the Mexican-American, following the Treaty of Guadalupe-Hidalgo in 1848, became one such symptom, one such embodiment of the radical impossibility at the heart of Anglo-American identity as the placeholder for "American" identity as such. There had to be a species of American, in other words, that could never quite be American enough—an American whose own identity included otherness, who was to be perceived at once as citizen and foreigner. But what happens when the symptom speaks? What happens when the sublime object itself rises up as the Chicano—the self-articulated other of Anglo-America? This becomes the focus of the latter half of chapter 7 and one index, it would seem, of the current historical condition of American identity as it hovers over the abyss of representation.

EXPOSITION, EXPLICATION, CRITIQUE: A NOTE ON METHOD

The language of postmodern discourse has achieved a certain currency, if not a life of its own. This is no doubt a good thing. But this very currency is at times deceptive in that certain terms and phrases and slogans appear in very different contexts and do very different work in some of these contexts. This is certainly what Hegel had in mind as an inevitable outcome of the dialectical development of concepts as they outstrip themselves (or, in his terms, become true to their Notion). What this means in practice, however, is that the same term—such as "subject" or "subject-effect" or "essentialism"—used by two different writers can refer to two very different concepts. This is no less true for proper nouns. The name Kant operates in the world differently in different contexts. One person's Hegel may even appear to be the complete opposite of another's. Hegel is the Great Satan of much poststructuralism and yet the Savior of certain postexistential Marxisms, such as Žižek's.

I am quite aware that this is so with several of the terms and proper names I put to work in this book (not the least being "Hegel"). For this reason, among others, at certain points I have chosen a writing mode that resembles exposition. Another reason is that as a teacher of graduate students—who often feel as though they each have to recreate the wheel just to read a book of contemporary theory—I have found that there can never be too much explication simply because few graduate students have twenty years of practice at reading theory. And such exposition has gone a long way in helping me sort out the mass of codes and signals that makes up theoretical discourse. But my primary reason for engaging in an expository process is that my argument itself concerns particular fundamental starting points that provide points of continuity and contrast between the people I discuss. The Kant that I expose, in other words, is fundamental to my own readings of Marx, Jameson, and Spivak.

No explication or exposition is ever innocent. Every explication is the result of selection and critique and, therefore, ideological containment. Every explication is the putting to work, in a specific way and for specific critical ends, of various strands of the text under question. Every explication is, at the same time, the omission (conscious or not) of other strands of the text. The word "explication" itself implies this process: this mode of rewriting the text depends on the bringing to the surface of certain strands or layers (the "-plies" of "explication"), of bringing those plies out from the immanent dormancy of the text. If this notion of inside and outside seems troubling in this now thoroughly postmodern age, it should; that is precisely my contention and the object of my book. What is at stake these days in the notion of representation? What is the relationship between the uses of the word "representation" in epistemology, aesthetics, ideology critique, and cultural-political discourse? What is the relationship between the sentences "The image represents the concept" and "Western European male intellectuals represent non-Western female subalterns"? And is the form of the sentence itself somehow implicit (or complicit) in this relationship, as my reading of Hegel suggests?

My argument is that one can come closer to answering these questions by looking at a history of the term "representation" as it has passed down from Kant through Hegel to Marx and then on to contemporary Late Marxism. Within that assertion is a methodological assumption: to repeat, that the names Kant, Hegel, Marx, Althusser, Jameson, Žižek, or Spivak do not necessarily represent the same things in all contexts. I take the word "exposition" quite literally in that my goal is to position these names in specific ways and for specific purposes. ("Exposition" is itself etymologically and methodologically related to two other words signifying modes of positioning: Vorstellung and Darstellung.) As any reader of Žižek can attest, the name Hegel seems to stand in for a different textual operation than it does for, say, Georg Lukács, Jean-Paul Sartre, or Althusser, not to mention its more conservative applications in bourgeois academic philosophy. I often wonder whether Žižek and I are reading the same Hegel, and—as will be obvious to many readers—my reading of Hegel has certainly to some extent come under the sway of Žižek's. But my purpose for discussing Hegel in this book is to ask how his method—summed up in my reading of the speculative proposition—both inverts Kant's own propositional understandings of discursive understanding and foreshadows certain methods of Western avant-garde poetics. More specifically, I trace the intricate dialectical interplay of the terms "representation" and "presentation," or Vorstellung and Darstellung, from Kant to Spivak. This dialectical interplay is what is at stake, ultimately, in Jameson's own notion of figuration, which underlies his conceptions of the political unconscious and cognitive mapping as he creates his own dialectical image by fusing Lukácsian homologism and Frankfurt School estrangement.

My rationalization for resorting to exposition, then, is to position these figures into a particular constellation that might be of some use in the attempt to move Marxism into the culturally complex network of global relations in the twenty-first century.

TWO PRESENTATION BEYOND REPRESENTATION: KANT AND THE LIMITS OF DISCURSIVE UNDERSTANDING

A funny thing happened on the way to ideology critique: Western Theoretical Marxism, which since Lukács had hoped to pose Marxism as at least two steps beyond Kant and his bourgeois antinomies (having passed through the fortunate fall of Hegelianism), continued to find itself—even if by negation—bogged down in its Kantian mire.[1] I would argue, in fact, that however materialist contemporary Marxist theory may or may not be, it remains indebted to the basic terms of German Idealism—and particularly as the latter develops out of Kant—on at least two scores. Ideology theory since Althusser remains grafted to the theoretics of the sublime, while scientific practice since Althusser (if the word "science" still carries any weight after Althusser) remains trapped within the dynamics of Kantian teleological aesthetics (as developed in the second half of the *Critique of Judgment*).[2] These two moments can be seen, for example, in Jameson's theory of postmodernism. Jameson's emphasis on scientific practice (or what in more humanistic terms used to be called "praxis") as embodied by his call for a new cognitive mapping remains bound by the limitations on thought characteristic of the sublime. To be sure, this is a postmodern sublime, as distinct from the Enlightenment sublime of Kant's time during the advent of the capitalist order. But my argument is that while the historical character of the sublime has changed in the past two centuries, the essential problem (albeit equally historicized) marked out by that term has not.[3]

In order to appreciate the stakes involved in the question of the sublime as a problem for Marxism in the postmodern era, one must keep in mind what was at stake when that problem was definitively outlined by Kant. For in many ways Kant's take on the problem of the sublime—which at root is a problem of and for representation—continues to frame the way we conceive of the sublime today. This is so not only in the way we frame the problem in terms of the breakdown of the faculty of Imagination in the face of the sublime in nature; this is also so in the way Kant converts a problem of spatial apprehension into one of language. Or to reverse the terms of this formulation, our experience of the sublime as a spatial problem is due to our being at base creatures of discourse. We are, in Kant's view, discursive animals. The abyss that opens up and threatens to swallow us in our experience of the sublime is nothing but the abyss of discourse itself. Our primary mode of relating to the world is through representation, and representation itself must operate within the limits of our discursive understanding. If one agrees with Jameson that the sublime object for us in this postmodern age is no longer nature—which, he argues, has by now been thoroughly colonized—but the vast network of global capital, this in no way changes the fundamental structure of the experience of the sublime as Kant outlines it in the *Critique of Judgment*.

Kant's *Critique of Judgment* stages a drama—the drama of the abyss. The abyss is a space—or rather a series of spaces—of incommensurability, limitation, and discord. As such, the *Critique of Judgment* gestures toward the construction of a space of commensurability, infinitude, and harmony. This abyss is that which stretches between the realms of the understanding and reason in the territory of knowledge as well as between this sensible territory of knowledge and its supersensible beyond (*cj* intro., 12–13). What Kant gestures toward, yet insists is ultimately futile given the discursive nature of our faculties of knowledge, is the analogical appropriation of the faculty of judgment as a bridge that spans this abyss and joins the two realms in a new, purely hypothetical territory—one in which the sensible and the intelligible can function according to the same law.[4] That law is *purposiveness*, the key concept of the *Critique of Judgment*. The problem, however, is that purposiveness is an intellectual concept, an Idea of reason, and as such cannot operate according to the same law that rules over the concepts of the understanding.

Kant explains that "it is possible for us to think without contradiction of both these jurisdictions, and their appropriate faculties, as coexisting in the same subject" (*cj* intro., 13). Still, despite this noncontradictory coexistence within the same subject, these jurisdictions never meet:

Between the realm of the natural concept [which rules over the understanding], as the sensible, and the realm of the concept of freedom [which rules over reason], as the supersensible, there is a great gulf fixed, so that it is not possible to pass from the former to the latter (by means of the theoretical employment of reason), just as if they were so many separate worlds, the first of which is powerless to exercise influence on the second: still the latter is *meant* to influence the former—that is to say, the concept of freedom is meant to actualize in the sensible world the end proposed by its laws; and nature must consequently also be capable of being regarded in such a way that in the conformity to law of its form it at least harmonizes with the possibility of the ends to be effectuated in it according to the laws of freedom.—There must, therefore, be a ground of the *unity* of the supersensible that lies at the basis of nature, with what the concept of freedom contains in a practical way, and although the concept of this ground neither theoretically nor practically attains to a knowledge of it, and so has no peculiar realm of its own, still it renders possible the transition from the mode of thought according to the principles of the one to that according to the principles of the other. (*CJ* intro., 14)

The difficulty of providing such a rendering, though, is that the question of rendering itself is what is at stake here: concepts of the understanding, in order to become objects of knowledge, must be rendered sensible, must be *presented* by means of a sensible intuition or representation; in order to be presented, they must be *represented*. But concepts of reason are by definition incapable of such a rendering or presentation, for they can never be represented, they can never be aligned with a given intuition, since Ideas are beyond the sensible and can never refer to the sensible world in any determinate way. "In a literal sense and according to their logical import, ideas cannot be presented" (*CJ* general remark, 119). Nevertheless, we have different types of experiences that seem to mimic such a presentation of the supersensible. The sublime, for instance, can be seen as "an object (of nature) the *representation* [*Vorstellung*] *of which determines the mind to regard the inaccessibility of nature as the presentation* [*Darstellung*] *of ideas*" (*CJ* general remark, 119; translation modified). What makes an experience like the sublime so important for Kant, then, is the feeling it renders, which suggests that the presentation of ideas in nature could in some way be possible, that through aesthetic experiences we somehow tap into a supersensible substrate common both to nature and to ourselves as moral beings: "Now, reason is further interested in ideas (for which in our moral feeling it brings about an immediate interest,) having also objective reality" (*CJ* §42: 159).

Kant's discussion of the sublime is one of the best-known moments in his *Critique of Judgment*. And while the concept of the sublime proves to be a critical turning point in that work as a whole, it is nevertheless important to identify its relationship to other key moments in the *Third Critique*. For the sublime's importance lies predominantly in its function as a mode of presentation or Darstellung. It is also the question of the possibility and effectivity of Darstellung that becomes key to Kant's goal of determining the importance of judgment as a faculty. The sublime is only one such mode of presentation, and its importance becomes clearer when one can see how other modes of presentation operate in Kant's system. It is the possibility of system itself that is at stake here, or, more precisely, the possibility of determining a principle that would serve to unify the various transcendental functions Kant identified in all three of his *Critiques* into a systematic and coherent unity of reason. The problem, however, is that such a system can only operate within the limits of discursive understanding, within the limits of language. Presentation, while gesturing beyond these limits, can only take place within them.

The urgency behind this search for a unifying principle does not just grow out of Kant's search for philosophical consistency but also his project of enlightenment, his attempt to ground human knowledge and action in reason. A problem arises, first of all, in that reason's role in the *First Critique*, or the *Critique of Pure Reason*, appears to be quite different from its role in the *Second Critique*, the *Critique of Practical Reason*. In the *First Critique*—the goal of which is the determination of the limits of reason in producing knowledge of sensible nature—reason, being a faculty of the supersensible, has a limited role to play in the sensible realm. Kant bases his critique precisely on this need to limit reason's ambitions in producing knowledge (which in its technical sense can only be knowledge of the sensible world) because ideas—the objects of reason—while they can and must be thought and employed in the production of knowledge, cannot be known since their realm is the supersensible, which by definition is beyond the realm proper to knowledge—the sensible. This distinction between what we can think and what we can know is crucial here. In the *Second Critique*, the question no longer centers on knowledge but on freedom—that is, on humans as autonomous beings; here reason rightly legislates in the supersensible realm of moral (or practical) ideas. The problem, put crudely, is how to present human beings as both natural (and therefore naturally determined) and supernatural (autonomous). The stake in this problem is the possibility of free and rational action in a world of natural causality. If we are indeed heteronomous beings—operating according to discrete and possibly conflicting systems of causality—then there can be no guarantee that our free will and our bodily drives and limitations can ever be harmonized; there can be no guarantee that we, though free beings, can ever bring into existence the world that ought to exist, right here, but does not in fact exist now. Kant needs to discover a principle that bridges the abyss separating the realms of the sensible and the supersensible, a terrain of articulation into unity. Such a principle—itself a supersensible object—must be capable of being presented at the same time as a sensible object. The question, then, comes down to presentation.

REPRESENTATION AND PRESENTATION

The English word "presentation" is a translation of the German "Darstellung." As we will see in my chapter on Hegel and presentation, the concept of Darstellung has a rich and varied history in philosophy and aesthetics, so we should identify the particular way Kant uses the term. At one point in the *Third Critique*, Kant writes: "*Concepts of the Understanding* must, as such, always be demonstrable (if, as in anatomy, demonstration is understood in the sense merely of *presentation*). In other words, the object answering to such concepts must always be capable of being given in intuition (pure or empirical); for only in this way can they become cognitions" (*CJ* §57, Remark I:210). The job of presentation, then, is the production of intuitions, which means that it is an activity of the imagination, the source of our intuitions. Imagination is the faculty of presentation and as such, is responsible for the demonstration or exhibition of concepts of the understanding or of reason; its job, then, when the goal is cognition, is the staging of examples (or empirical intuitions) that illustrate and verify the concepts of the understanding—the understanding being the legislative faculty of cognition. This process is what Kant calls schematism in the *First Critique*. In a determining judgment, this schema serves as the mediation between concepts (or universals) and intuitions (or particulars). In the *First Critique*, Kant explains that since "no representation [Vorstellung], save when it is an intuition, is in immediate relation to an object, no concept is ever related to an object immediately, but to some other representation of it, be that representation an intuition, or itself a concept. Judgment is therefore the mediate knowledge of an object, that is, the representation of a representation of it" (CPR A68/B93). "The modality of judgments," Kant continues, "is a quite peculiar function. Its distinguishing characteristic is that it contributes nothing to the content of the judgment (for, besides quantity, quality, and relation, there is nothing that constitutes the content of a judgment), but concerns only the value of the copula in relation to thought in general" (CPR A74/B99–100). The value of the copula, Kant's exploration of the possibilities of judgment, promises to distinguish the relationship between subject and predicate in relation to thought in general; that is, a critique of judgment should supply the transcendental grounds for predication. But such is not the job of the *First Critique*, for such grounds lie beyond human experience and are therefore beyond the limits of cognition.

The question, then, is what role presentation plays in the *Third Critique*—that is, when cognition is no longer the goal. The mode of judgment at issue here is no longer determining but reflective; in other words, this process is no longer deductive—the demonstration or exemplification of a concept—but inductive. How are we to judge when we are faced with particulars for which no universal lies ready to hand? What is the value of the copula when the relationship between subject and predicate appears indeterminate? How can this situation still be considered as presentation when no concepts are present? These questions lie behind Kant's turn to the question of reflective judgment, and particularly that species of reflection that Kant calls aesthetic judgment:

> But I have already said that an aesthetical judgment is quite unique, and affords absolutely no, (not even a confused), knowledge of the Object. It is only through a logical judgment that we get knowledge. The aesthetic judgment, on the other hand, refers the representation, by which an Object is given, solely to the Subject, and brings to our notice no quality of the object, but only the final [*zweckmäßige*, purposive] form in the determination of the powers of representation. (CJ §15: 71)

Reflective judgment begins with an intuition or the formal representation of the object. The difference between the two kinds of reflective judgments, aesthetic and teleological, lies in the direction toward which we refer the intuition. In an aesthetic judgment, as Kant explains above, this referral is to the subject—that is, to the powers of the subjective faculties themselves as they operate—whereas in teleological judgment it is to the object. What is important to note here is that imagination—the faculty of presentation—plays the major (though not legislative) role in these judgments. In a comparison of the beautiful and the sublime, Kant observes that they agree "on the point of pleasing on their own account" (*cj* §23: 90). That is, the pleasure we have in the two is not due to mere agreeable sensation or any definite concept of the good (both of which would lead us to take an interest in the existence of the object). Rather, "the delight is connected with the mere presentation or faculty of presentation, and is thus taken to express the accord, in a given intuition, of the faculty of presentation, or the imagination, with the faculty of concepts that belongs to understanding or reason, in the sense of the former assisting the latter" (ibid.). Unlike logical judgments, then, in aesthetic judgments nothing is immediately presented; the importance in aesthetic judgment lies in the work of presentation itself, in the accord of the faculties of presentation. Here lies the importance of aesthetic disinterestedness: if we take no interest in the presentation of the concept of the object before us, what we get is the unity of presentation itself. What is presented indirectly in this pure presentation is the value of the copula, the value of this accord of the faculties, which is what Kant calls purposiveness. Purposiveness, in ways we will soon see, is the principle that grounds that higher synthesis, that supreme copula that Kant posits as the supersensible substrate of aesthetic and teleological judgments, and through a further analogical final (purposive) extension, phenomena and noumena.

Presentation, then, is not merely a mechanical psychological reflex; it is, rather, subjectively or transcendentally reflex*ive*—the spontaneous and autonomous concert of the faculties that characterizes subjective purposiveness. In aesthetic judgment, subjective purposiveness presents itself *as such*—as purposiveness without purpose or finality without end—as the purposive ground of aesthetic pleasure and, by extension, of cognition as well. Kant defines purposiveness (or finality: *Zweckmäßigkeit*) and purpose (*Zweck*: purpose, end, goal) as follows: "An end [or purpose] is the object of a concept so far as this concept is regarded as the cause [*Ursache*] of the object (the real ground of its possibility); and the causality of a *concept* in respect of its *Object* is finality [or purposiveness] (*forma finalis*)" (*cj* §10: 61). The object, Kant has just written, is an effect and the concept is its cause: purposiveness is the process whereby the concept determines the object as representation. In the *First Critique*, Kant made a similar claim that clarifies this causal relationship: "Representation in itself does not produce its object in so far as existence is concerned, for we are not here speaking of its causality by means of the will. Nonetheless the representation is *a priori* determinant of the object, if it be the case that only through the representation is it possible to know anything *as an object*" (CPR A92/B125). Such is Kant's Copernican revolution and his response to the empiricist insistence on the sole priority of experience for the production of concepts. What seemed never to have occurred to David Hume, Kant supposes, was that "the understanding might itself, perhaps, through these concepts, be the author of the experience in which its objects are found" (CPR B127). But this conceptual causality is not enough in itself to determine an object as an end or a purpose, for this conceptual causality is true of all objects. So what singles out a certain object as purpose? In the *Critique of Judgment*, Kant adds: "Where, then, not the cognition of an object merely, but the object itself (its form or real existence) as an effect, is thought to be possible only through a concept of it, there we imagine an end. The representation of the effect [the object] is here the determining ground of its cause [the concept] and takes the lead of it" (CJ §10: 61).

The purposive object is the one which, in the mere apprehension of it as representation, prior to any cognition of it as an object, produces in us the feeling of pleasure. For purposiveness is not really, or at least not immediately, in the object but in ourselves—purposiveness referring to a subjective process that seems to the cause of those objects that cannot be explained according to some blind, accidental cause.[5] When the indeterminate object we come upon appears as design, as artifact, as the result of someone's activity—a planned and deliberate activity necessarily preceded by a concept of the object as an end to have been produced—what we don't recognize is that by a certain imposition, or what Kant calls an objective subreption, we read into the object what is in fact the activity of our own faculties in response to the object's mental representation. When a rational concept such as purposiveness is seen as relating to our cognitive faculties, it is employed in its correct, immanent or transcendental sense; but if it is referred to the object, it is then employed in a transcendent, and therefore illegitimate, sense. "All errors of subreption," Kant explains in the *First Critique*, "are to be ascribed to a defect of judgment, never to understanding or to reason. Reason is never in immediate relation to an object, but only to the understanding; . . . It does not, therefore, *create* concepts (of objects) but only *orders* them, and gives them that unity which they can have only if they be employed in their widest possible application, that is, with a view to obtaining totality in the various series" (CPR A643/B671). Purposiveness functions as a *regulative* concept if we impute it to an object simply as an aid to understanding ("This object appears as if it had been created according to some design"); it functions as a *constitutive* concept if we attribute it to the object as such ("This object is itself purposive"), for purposiveness is a concept we can never *know* because we can never represent it as embodied by a determinate intuition. We can *feel* it, however, and thereby experience pleasure in our simple apprehension of the supposedly purposive object: "The consciousness," Kant explains, "of the causality of a representation in respect of the state of the Subject as one tending *to preserve a continuance* of that state, may here be said to denote in a general way what is called pleasure" (*CJ* §10: 61).

The mere apprehension of formal subjective purposiveness as the source of pleasure: this is, of course, Kant's definition of the beautiful as a judgment of taste. And it is his critique of the judgment of taste concerning the beautiful that allows Kant to develop his concept of purposiveness and render it analogous to other types of presentation. The question of presentation for the *Third Critique*, grounded in aesthetic judgment and extended to teleology, is the role of nature. Gilles Deleuze has formulated that concern in the following outline:

> We should not confuse the various ways in which, according to Kant, the Ideas of reason can be presented in sensible nature. In the sublime the presentation is direct but negative, and done by projection; in natural symbolism or in the interest of the beautiful the presentation is positive but indirect, and is achieved by reflection; in genius or in artistic symbolism the presentation is positive but secondary, and is achieved through the creation of another nature. We will see later that the Idea is capable of a fourth mode of presentation, the most perfect, in nature as a system of ends.

He goes on to describe that fourth mode more fully:

> In nature we find no divine, intentional ends; on the contrary, we start from ends which are initially those of nature, and add to them the Idea of a divine intentional cause as condition of their comprehension. We do not impose ends on nature "violently and dictatorially"; on the contrary, we reflect on the final natural unity, which is empirically known in diversity, in order to raise us to the Idea of a supreme cause determined by analogy. . . . The combination of these two movements constitutes a new way of presenting the Idea; the final way which is distinct from those we have analyzed above.[6]

THE BEAUTIFUL

For Kant, the beautiful refers to the mere formal appearance of a particular object. Kant's analysis of the judgment of an object as beautiful is made up of four moments: quality, quantity, relation, and modality. In terms of quality (judgments of affirmation, negation, or infinite extension), the intuition is referred not to the logical function of our faculties but merely to their aesthetic function. This means that we do not come to a judgment of taste through thinking but rather feeling—in particular, the feeling of pleasure in the mere contemplation of the form of the object apart from any concept of (or interest in) it—and it is in terms of feeling that Kant will be able to extend the concept of purposiveness beyond the mere reference to our subjective response. In terms of *quantity* (judgments on singularity, particularity, and universality), Kant's point is that the judgment of the beautiful is a universal one, for it depends on the universal human subjective faculties which we employ in cognition and reflection. Third, in terms of *relation* (judgments of category, hypothesis, and disjunction), Kant pursues the relationship between foundations and ends (purposes) of judgments of taste, and concludes that "*beauty* is the form of *purposiveness* in an object, so far as perceived in it *apart from the representation of a purpose*" (*CJ* §17: 80). The beautiful object must be perceived, that is, as purposive in form yet without any particular or determinate purpose; we must perceive the purposiveness of its form—"How could such a beautiful object in nature have occurred randomly?"—but have no concept of what purpose its beautiful form might serve. Once we conceive of a purpose, we have applied a concept to the representation and have thereby imposed an interest into our judgment of it, and have passed from a simple aesthetic judgment to a logical one. The purposiveness of the object will engage our faculties in free play, free of the necessity to add a concept to the representation. What the object engages, then, is our own subjective purposiveness through the appearance of the object's purposiveness. And finally, in terms of modality (judgments concerning possibility, reality, and necessity), Kant asserts that "the beautiful is that which, apart from a concept, is cognized as object of a necessary delight" (*CJ* §22: 85).

We have arrived at an interesting problem here—one that will have important consequences for my exploration of Kant's conception of presentation. The key principle operating in the judgment of taste is the aesthetic experience of subjective purposiveness—the way our faculties work together in order to present a concept, in order to relate a representation or intuition of the imagination with a concept of the understanding. What the experience of the beautiful presents is presentation itself, the pure presentational activity of the imagination. But there are places in the *Critique of Judgment* where Kant appears to refer purposiveness to the object itself, in the form of objective purposiveness. To do so, however, is to engage in objective subreption, which, as we have seen, is "the tendency to ascribe to the object itself the property which entailed beauty, even though according to Kant beauty resides in the response of the subject, i.e., in subjective formal purposiveness."[7] For instance, in discussing the judgment of taste concerning beauty in nature, Kant remarks, "There the purposiveness has its foundation in the Object and in its outward form—although it does not signify the reference of this to other objects according to concepts (for the purpose of cognitive judgments), but is merely concerned in general with the apprehension of this form so far as it proves accordant in the mind with the faculty of concepts as well as with that of their presentation (which is identical with that of apprehension)" (*CJ* §30: 133). This seems to say that beauty—the feeling of pleasure in the mere apprehension of purposive form without purpose—has its foundation in the form of the object, which is in accord with the faculties of presentation. This implication is even stronger when, in his contrast between the beautiful and sublime, Kant writes that "we express ourselves on the whole inaccurately if we term any Object of nature sublime, although we may with perfect propriety call many such objects beautiful. For how can that which is apprehended as inherently anti-purposive be noted with an expression of approval? All that we can say is that the object lends itself to the presentation of a sublimity discoverable in the mind" (*CJ* §23: 91–92). But does the object that we experience as beautiful do more than lend itself to its own subjective purposiveness? And does the objective status of the sublime or the beautiful really depend on our expression of approval?

In the introduction to the *Critique of Judgment*, Kant goes to great length to distinguish between subjective and objective purposiveness. Aesthetic judgments refer to subjective purposiveness, while teleological judgments refer to objective purposiveness: "*Natural beauty* may, therefore, be looked on as the *presentation* of the concept of formal, i.e. merely subjective, finality and *natural ends* as the presentation of the concept of a real, i.e. objective, finality" (*CJ* intro., VIII:34). The question of objective purposiveness depends on the concept of the "technic of nature," the analogy between nature and art, the sense that certain objects of nature are formed like objects of art and thus "lend themselves" to the speculation that there may be some final end to nature that serves as the principle behind the appearance of objective purposiveness: "But it is only judgment that, without being itself possessed a priori of a principle in that behalf, in actually occurring cases (of certain products) contains the rule for making use of the concept of ends in the interest of reason, after that the above transcendental principle has already prepared understanding to apply to nature the concept of an end (at least in respect of its form)" (*CJ* intro., VIII:35). Yet such speculation has obviously moved beyond the terms that delimit a critique of aesthetic judgment—namely the requirement of disinterestedness— for here we have attached an interest to the apprehension of the object. The position Kant would have to take, then, in order to be consistent with his demand for disinterestedness and in order to avoid objective subreption would be the one he actually does take in the following: "In a judgment of taste, the pleasure felt by us is exacted from every one else as necessary, just as if, when we call something beautiful, beauty was to be regarded as a quality of the object forming part of its inherent determination according to concepts [that is, as if the beautiful object was the result of purposive activity]; although beauty is for itself, apart from any reference to the feeling of the Subject, nothing" (*CJ* §9: 59). Nevertheless, as I will show in my discussion of teleological presentation, this flirtation with subreption has a crucial role to play in the final use of judgment.

Now to return to the question of presentation and the beautiful. In concluding his *Critique of Aesthetic Judgment*, Kant clarifies the connection between judgments of taste and presentation in the claim that

> taste is, at its base, a faculty that judges the rendering sensible [*Versinn-lichung*] of moral ideas (through the mediation of a certain analogy of reflection on both); and it is this rendering also, and the increased sensibility, founded upon it, for the feeling which these ideas evoke (termed moral sense), that are the origin of that pleasure which taste declares valid for mankind in general and not merely for the private feeling of each individual. (*CJ* §60: 227; translation modified)

The key term here is Versinnlichung, a rendering in terms of sense, the rendering of an idea so as to evoke a feeling in us. In the *Critique of Judgment*, Kant identifies presentation as Versinnlichung, a form of hypotyposis: "All *hypotyposis* (presentation [Darstellung], *subjectio sub adspectum*) as a rendering sensible [Versinnlichung], is twofold. Either it is *schematic*, as where the intuition corresponding to a concept comprehended by the understanding is given a priori, or else it is *symbolic*, as where the concept is one which only reason can think, and to which no sensible intuition is adequate" (*cj* §59: 221). Darstellung is the concrete presentation or Versinnlichung (either schematic and direct or symbolic and indirect) of pure concepts of the understanding or reason (themselves representations) through the production of a mediating concrete representation (Vorstellung). These two types of hypotyposis are related only in terms of a formal analogy, not in terms of content. "Intuitions are always required," Kant maintains, "to verify the reality of our concepts. If the concepts are empirical their intuitions are called *examples*: if they are pure concepts of the understanding the intuitions go by the name of *schemata*. But to call for the objective reality of rational concepts, i.e. of ideas, and, what is more, on behalf of the theoretical cognition of such a reality, is to demand an impossibility" (ibid.). Rational concepts, which include moral ideas, can only pose as intuitions by analogy; the analogy does not apply to the intuition itself, however, but to *the schematic process*, "the rules of reflection upon both and their causality" (ibid., 223) of the intuitive mode of representation. Both processes of intuitive representation, the schematic and the symbolic, are "hypotyposes, i.e. presentations (*exhibitiones*), not mere *marks*" (ibid., 222). Marks [*Charakterismen*], such as words or visible algebraic or mimetic signs, are mere discursive designations for concepts, "sensible signs devoid of any intrinsic connexion with the intuition of the Object." Schemata or symbols, on the other hand, embody presentations or *Darstellungen* of the concept.

THE SUBLIME AS NEGATIVE PRESENTATION

The sublime, Kant claims, involves negative presentation. It involves the experience of the breakdown of the accord between the imagination and the understanding. It is the imagination's job to produce a representation that unifies the sensible attributes of the object and to present this intuition to the understanding, whose job is then to supply a concept. But the problem for the imagination is that there are some objects in nature that exceed our capacity for sensible comprehension; while the imagination can *apprehend* the multiple sensible attributes of the object, the object's vastness confounds our ability to *comprehend* it—that is, to join all of these apprehended moments into a unified image. We are still concerned here with a purely aesthetic experience—we have no concept in mind when we experience the sublime—yet the feeling we experience is not pleasure but now pain. The imagination is pained by its failure.

The sublime is that "*in comparison with which all else is small*" (*CJ* §25: 97). This greatness is not that of the object, however. While the object is great, either in terms of magnitude or power, we can always imagine a greater object. The earth is great, for example, but we can imagine climbing aboard a spacecraft and viewing it from a vantage point in space. The sublime, though, is absolutely great, which no sensible object, no matter its size or strength, could claim. Reason demands absolute totality, but the inability to produce the image of this totality "is the awakening of a feeling of a supersensible faculty within us; and it is the use to which judgment naturally puts particular objects on behalf of this latter feeling, and not the object of sense, that is absolutely great" (ibid.). The supersensible employment, not the sensible object, is the source of one's feeling of the sublime. As we saw in my earlier discussion of objective subreption, to call any object sublime is to impute a subjective response onto an object. It is the disposition of spirit (*Geistesstimmung*) that is in reality sublime (ibid., 98).[8]

While the sublime is initially painful, it nevertheless engenders a feeling of pleasure, albeit a negative pleasure: respect. This negative pleasure comes about through the presentation of the limits of every standard of sensibility when viewed in comparison with the supersensible. The imagination feels pain at its inability to attain to a unified intuition, but then feels respect for that which outstrips any possible phenomenon—the ideas of reason, products of our own magnificent faculty, which the impossibility of representation presents to one in the experience of the sublime. But what exactly is presented here? "This effort [to render the sensible representation adequate to the totality demanded by reason], and the feeling of the unattainability of the idea by means of imagination, is itself a presentation of the subjective purposiveness of our mind in the employment of the imagination in the interests of the mind's supersensible province, and compels us to *think* nature itself in its totality as a presentation of something supersensible, without our being able to effectuate this presentation *objectively*" (*CJ* General Remark, 119). It is in the negative space opened up by the failure of representation that this negative presentation takes place; it is through the breakdown of representation, the point at which our representative faculties are confronted with their immanent limit, that the realm of the supersensible is opened up as the beyond of representation itself.[9]

Žižek remarks on the negative possibilities of this limitation:

> This priority of limitation over transcendence also sheds a new (Hegelian) light on the Kantian sublime: what we experience as the positive sublime

content (the moral law in ourselves, the dignity of the free will) is of a strictly secondary nature; it is something which merely fills out the original void opened up by the breakdown of the field of representations. In other words, the Sublime does not involve the breakdown of the field of phenomena, i.e., the experience of how no phenomenon, even the mightiest one, can appropriately express the suprasensible Idea. This notion—that, in the experience of the Sublime, phenomena prove unfit to render the Idea—results from a kind of perspective-illusion. What actually breaks down in the experience of the Sublime is the very notion that, behind the field of phenomena, lies some inaccessible positive, substantial Thing. In other words, this experience demonstrates that phenomena and noumena are not to be conceived as two positive domains separated by a frontier: the field of phenomena as such is limited, yet this limitation is its inherent determination, so that there is nothing "beyond" this limit. The limit ontologically *precedes* its Beyond: the object we experience as "sublime," its elevated glitter, *Schein*, is a mere secondary positivization of the "nothing," the void, beyond the limit. (*TWN* 37–38)

I will return to this question of limitation at the end of the current chapter. But for now, it is helpful to look at Kant's discussion of §23, in which Kant discusses the difference between the beautiful and the sublime:

The most important and vital distinction between the sublime and the beautiful is certainly this: that if, as is allowable, we here confine our attention in the first instance to the sublime in Objects of nature, (that of art being restricted by the conditions of an agreement with nature), we observe that whereas natural beauty (such as is self-subsisting) conveys a purposiveness in its form making the object appear, as it were preadapted to our power of judgment, so that it thus forms itself an object of our delight, that which, without our indulging in any refinements of thought, but, simply in our apprehension of it, excites the feeling of the sublime, may appear, indeed, as regards its form, as anti-purposive [*zweckwidrig*] in relation to our power of judgment, to be ill-adapted to our faculty of *Darstellung*, and to be, as it were, an outrage on the imagination, and yet it is judged all the more sublime on that account. (*CJ* §23: 91: translation modified)

The beautiful appears to be zweckmäßig or purposive, whereas the sublime appears to be zweckwidrig or antipurposive, contrafinal. Our faculties—

namely, the imagination and the understanding—are at cross-purposes when confronted with the antipurposive. Apprehension is one of the jobs of the imagination, which is simply the immediate formalization of units of intuitive material. But the imagination's other job is its role as the agent of Darstellung, and that is *com*prehension. It must unify these apprehended moments into a single representation in preparation for that representation's relationship to a concept. Versinnlichung, or sensory objectification, as we have seen, is an aspect of this comprehensive moment of the imagination, the fleshing out or making concrete (*in concreto*) of a concept. The sublime, however, is the experience of being confronted with an object that cannot be comprehended, an object that keeps the scanning movement of apprehension continuously in motion. The sublime object seems to frustrate any sense of purposiveness and therefore causes pain. Judgment is a comparative faculty, but the sublime object is that which is great beyond all comparison: "It is a greatness comparable to itself alone. Hence it comes that the sublime is not to be looked for in the things of nature, but only in our own ideas" (*CJ* §25: 97). Which means, then, that the sublime is to be looked for in reason, our faculty of ideas. And this is the source of the contradiction the sublime presents: the imagination is bound to the sensible world while reason is bound to the supersensible. There is no way for the imagination to present an idea such as infinity—that which is absolutely great—in any immediately concrete form. Infinity can be thought, but it cannot be pictured. Reason demands totality, and under normal circumstances, imagination can produce the appropriate image for the job. Yet the sublime is an infinite totality, and only reason can offer the infinite. There is a point, then, when the imagination defers to reason's supersensible power, and as a result, its initial pain is transformed into pleasure, although this pleasure is a negative one: respect.[10] In terms of the question of Darstellung, the sublime has been transformed from the frustration of Darstellung in the face of the unpresentable to the negative Darstellung of the idea of reason. The sublime can only be presented negatively, as the experience of a lack as the nonplace of the idea—a necessary absence that summons the presence-through-absence of the power of reason. The infinitely possible is called up in the space of impossibility. Kant assures us that:

> We have no reason to fear that the feeling of the sublime will suffer from an abstract mode of presentation like this, which is altogether negative as to what is sensuous. For though the imagination, no doubt, finds nothing

beyond the sensible world to which it can lay hold, still this thrusting aside of the sensible barriers gives a feeling of being unbounded; and that removal is thus a presentation of the infinite. As such it can never be anything more than a negative presentation—but still it expands the soul [*die Seele*]. Perhaps there is no more sublime passage in the Jewish Law than the commandment: Thou shalt not make unto thee any graven image, or any likeness of any thing that is in heaven or on earth, or under the earth, &c. (*CJ* General Remark, 127)

This "negative presentation" can now be related to the presentation of purposiveness in the judgment of the beautiful. Purposiveness, as we have seen, involves the powers of the faculties involved in producing a schema for the understanding. The beautiful is therefore a presentation of the pleasure involved in the experience of the free play of the schematic process itself. The sublime, then, is painful in that it confounds this schematic process. In being presented with an object of nature that induces in us a feeling of the sublime, our imagination finds itself incapable of producing a schema that could adequately unify the various sensible features of the object into a single intuition. It is only with the breakdown of our schematic apparatus that the negative pleasure of the sublime experience takes hold, when we realize how much more magnificent our own faculty of reason is in the objects it produces when compared with even the grandest or most outrageous objects of nature with which the imagination and the understanding have to work. Thus the breakdown of presentation brings about the negative presentation of the ideas of reason, or as Žižek puts it, "The paradox of the Sublime . . . is in the conversion of the impossibility of presentation into the presentation of impossibility" (*FTK* 144).

NATURAL SYMBOLISM

One way to introduce the difference, in terms of presentation, between the sublime and the beautiful is to focus again on the question of schematism. For the sublime, there is what could be referred to as a *schematic deficit*, meaning that no matter how hard the imagination works, it cannot take in all of the information before it and present it as an intuition for the understanding. But as we have seen, this deficit leads to the negative presentation not of a concept of the understanding but of an idea of reason. In symbolism, on the other hand, which for Kant is manifested in the beautiful (either in art or nature), we have a *schematic surplus*. Now we are confronted with an intuition whose attributes far outstrip the understanding's ability to provide a unifying concept. It is in this schematic surplus of the symbol that the presentation of ideas takes place. There is another distinction to contend with in terms of presentation, and that is Kant's distinction between natural and artistic beauty. While both, as symbolic modes, operate in similar ways, the artistic symbol must add a concept of the object to its otherwise purposeless display. "A beauty of nature is a *beautiful thing*," Kant observes; "beauty of art is a *beautiful representation of a thing*" (cj §48: 172). But before exploring the significance of this difference, I want to examine what they have in common: beauty as a symbol of the good.

In order to understand this claim that beauty is a symbol of the good, I first have to examine how symbolic analogy works for Kant. To return to a quotation cited earlier: "All *hypotyposis*," he writes:

> (*Darstellung, subjectio sub adspectum*) as *Versinnlichung*, is twofold. Either it is *schematic*, as where the intuition corresponding to a concept comprehended by way of understanding is given *a priori*, or else it is *symbolic*, as where the concept is one which only reason can think, and to which no sensible intuition can be adequate. In the latter case the concept is supplied with an intuition such that the procedure of judgment in dealing with it is merely analogous to that which it observes in schematism. In other words, what agrees with the concept is merely the rule of this procedure, and not the intuition itself. Hence the agreement is merely in the form of reflection, and not in the content. (*cj* §59: 222–23)

Analogy works with the rule or form of reflection. In the case of the analogous relationship between beauty and the good, the point is that our apprehension of both is purely formal and is registered in the feeling resulting from this reflective procedure. The feeling we experience in the face of beauty is akin to the feeling we experience in reflecting on the form of the good. Aesthetic and moral judgments produce analogous feelings. As in the sublime, however, this first stage in a judgment of taste is not enough for the presentation of an idea and depends on a "symbolic" turn as a second stage. This turn involves the "awakening" that results from our reflection on the surplus of the symbol that poses the object as the expression of an aesthetic idea.

By an aesthetic idea, Kant explains, "I mean that representation of the imagination which induces much thought, yet without the possibility of any definite thought whatever, i.e. *concept*, being adequate to it, and which languages, consequently, can never get quite on level terms with or render completely intelligible.—It is easily seen, that an aesthetic idea is the counterpart (pendant) of a rational idea, which, conversely, is a concept, to which no *intuition* (representation of the imagination) can be adequate" (*CJ* §49: 175–76). The fine art, so Kant claims, that best expresses this aesthetic idea is poetry: "*Poetry* (which owes its origin almost entirely to genius and is least willing to be led by precepts and examples) holds the first rank among all the arts. It expands the mind by giving freedom to the imagination and by offering, from among the boundless multiplicity of possible forms accordant with a given concept, to whose bounds it is restricted, that one which couples with the presentation of the concept a wealth of thought to which no verbal expression is completely adequate, and by thus rising aesthetically to ideas" (*CJ* §53: 191). This wealth of thought to which no verbal expression is completely adequate is what Kant refers to as aesthetic attributes, those "forms which do not constitute the presentation of a given concept itself, but which, as secondary representations of the imagination, express the derivatives connected with it, and its kinship with other concepts" (*CJ* §49: 177). The presentation of natural symbolism (an intellectual interest in the beautiful), then, is both positive and secondary (depending as it does on what could be referred to as the "symbolic turn").

This shift from schema to symbol is key to Kant's later turn to teleology, and thus to the purpose of the *Critique of Judgment* as a whole, with its distinction between discursive understanding and expressive reason. Schematism is a discursive procedure that depends on *Ausführung*, the working out or execution of the concept through the presentation of illustrative examples. Symbolism, on the other hand, depends on expression or *Ausdruck*, which like the English word etymologically means to squeeze or push outward. While discursivity is a process of working out or constructing the links between concept and intuition in the field of the sensible, expression is the intimation or trace of a unifying ground common to both the sensible and the supersensible. Kant explains this in the *Critique of Teleological Judgment*, which forms the second volume of the *Third Critique*. Judgment is the subsumption of the particular under the universal. But the human mode of understanding can never assure the absolute validity of determinant (that is, theoretical) judgments. "Our understanding is a faculty of conceptions," he writes. "This means that it is a discursive understanding for which the character and variety to be found in the particular given to it in nature and capable of being brought under its conceptions must certainly be contingent. . . . But it is just this contingency that makes it so difficult for our understanding to reduce the multiplicity of nature to the unity of knowledge. Our understanding can only accomplish this task through the harmonizing of natural features with our faculty of conceptions—a most contingent accord" (*cj* §77: 62). Nevertheless, we have an idea of such harmony as possible, if not for *our* understanding, then at least for an *intuitive understanding*, which only a divine being could have. *For us* intellectual intuition is impossible; but that does not mean it is absolutely impossible, which is another way of saying that it *is* possible for an absolute being. This intuitive understanding thus serves as a regulative principle for our own limited understanding and assures, though in a negative way, that our efforts are not, absolutely speaking, futile. It underscores the necessity of images for human understanding, but intimates a supersensible ground that itself suggests (but can never guarantee) an accord that is not merely contingent. "It is sufficient to show," Kant contends, "that we are led to this idea of an *intellectus archetypus* by contrasting with it our discursive understanding that has need of images (*intellectus ectypus*) and noting the contingent character of a faculty of this form, and that this idea involves nothing self-contradictory" (ibid., 65).

This lack of guarantee is only a problem for obtaining absolute guarantees for the theoretical (rather than reflective) employment of reason. Symbolism, on the other hand, as opposed to schematism or discursivity, through the establishment of a kinship between aesthetic and moral feeling, expresses the idea of just such a unity of the sensible and the supersensible, but for practical rather than speculative reason. The harmonious accord between the form of the beautiful object and our faculties of taste expands, extends, and lifts up our thoughts from the merely sensible nature of the intuition to the supersensible substrate of nature and humanity. Kant draws these points together:

> Now, I say, the beautiful is the symbol of the morally good, and only in this light (a point of view natural to every one, and one which every one exacts from others as a duty) does it give us pleasure with an attendant claim to the agreement of every one else, whereupon the mind becomes conscious of a certain ennoblement and elevation above mere sensibility to pleasure from impressions of sense, and also appraises the worth of others on the score of a like maxim of their judgment. This is that *intelligible* to which taste . . . extends its view. It is, that is to say, what brings our higher cognitive faculties

into common accord, and is that apart from which sheer contradiction would arise between their nature and the claims put forward by taste. In this faculty judgment does not find itself subjected to a heteronomy of laws of experience as it does in the empirical estimate of things—in respect of the objects of such a pure delight it gives the law to itself, just as reason does in respect of the faculty of desire. (*cj* §59: 224)

This "extended view" brought about by natural symbolism is the prize won by analogical presentation according to the rule or relation of reflection. The symbolic turn this involves could be described as follows:

— We first establish, according to the analogies of reflection, the kinship (in terms of a common *rule*) between aesthetic and moral feeling.

— We then posit the symbol as the expression of the aesthetic idea (the trace of the supersensible accord between nature and practical reason).

In this turn, we have moved beyond the terms of mere schematic *representation* to symbolic *expression*. At this point, then, Kant's basically neoclassical aesthetic in terms of form points the way toward a nascent romanticism that will see its greatest elaboration in Kant's theory of genius.

GENIUS AND THE ARTISTIC TURN

Genius, Kant explains, "is the innate mental aptitude (*ingenium*) *through which* nature gives the rule to art" (*cj* §46: 168). Whatever the inherent merits of this definition, it must be seen in addition as serving a certain function in Kant's general discussion of fine art and the beautiful. Since the beautiful, whether of art or nature, cannot be judged according to a concept, we cannot establish rules of taste. The beautiful must occur naturally. But how can we say that a work produced by a human being is natural? And how can the fine arts be excluded from the demand common to all other arts, that its pursuit be guided by certain rules and learned techniques? Kant's answer is that genius, the natural gift for the expression of aesthetic ideas, is a talent rather than a learned activity and is always original in its source. It is in this way that nature can be seen as giving the rule to art, yet this rule itself cannot be the result of cognition but must be a pure expression of the imagination. "Hence, where an author owes a product to his genius, he does not himself know how the ideas for it have entered his head, nor has he it in his power to invent the like at pleasure, or methodically, and communicate the same to others in such precepts as would put them in a position to produce similar products" (*cj* §46: 169).

The product of genius is the aesthetic idea, "that representation of the imagination which induces much thought, yet without the possibility of any definite thought whatever, i.e. *concept*, being adequate to it, and which language, consequently can never get quite on level terms with or render completely intelligible" (*cj* §49: 174–75). As we have seen, the intuition is too rich, too overflowing with what Kant refers to as aesthetic attributes, for the concept it is associated with, and it is this richness that stimulates the rational movement that produces the feeling Kant associates with the aesthetic idea. The sublime pushes the imagination to its negative limit whereas the symbol pushes the understanding to its negative limit, thus passing over to that faculty that can think beyond the limits of the understanding—reason. And whereas the sublime produces an accord between the imagination and reason through forcing the imagination's breakdown and its subsequent respect for reason, the symbol induces such an accord through the expressive power of the imagination in its production of "a wealth of thought as would never admit of comprehension in any definite concept, and, as a consequence, giving aesthetically an unbounded expansion to the concept itself" (ibid., 177).

The "extended view" that we saw resulting from natural symbolism has its correlate in an "extension of thought" resulting from aesthetic symbolism through the production of an aesthetic idea. The aesthetic idea is another way of presenting an idea, though this time the idea is not rational but purely aesthetic. It nevertheless puts the rational faculty in motion, just as the beautiful puts the imagination in motion in its free play. As Kant describes this process:

> If, now, we attach to a concept a representation of the imagination belonging to its presentation, but inducing solely on its own account such wealth of thought as would never admit of comprehension in a definite concept, and, as a consequence, giving aesthetically an unbounded expansion to the concept itself, then the imagination here displays a creative activity, and it puts the faculty of intellectual ideas (reason) into motion—a motion, at the instance of a representation, towards an extension of thought, that, while germane, no doubt, to the concept of the object, exceeds what can be laid hold of in that representation or clearly expressed. (ibid.)

From this passage one can infer another "turn"—the correlate to the symbolic turn discussed above—which could be called the "artistic turn." The turn or double function of artistic symbolism as expressed through genius, then, could be presented as follows:

— We first encounter the presentation of a concept plus a wealth of thought beyond the adequacy of language (aesthetic attributes).

— This is then followed by our rising (expanding the soul) to aesthetic ideas.

In distinguishing between aesthetic and rational ideas, Kant offers one sense of what is involved in his concept of presentation. " 'Ideas,' in the most comprehensive sense of the word, are representations referred to an object according to a certain principle (subjective or objective), in so far as they can still never become a cognition of it" (cj §57, Remark I:209–10). We can break this down into five key components: presentation is a process of referring; this process begins with a particular kind of representation (an idea); this representation is referred to an object (which one discovers in Kant's following sentence is either an intuition or a concept); the referring operates according to a certain principle (either subjective or objective); and this process can never become a cognition of the object. Presentation is this process of referring an idea to either an intuition or a concept.

In the production of the aesthetic idea, the work of artistic presentation, we arrive at a quickening supplement:

> In a word, the aesthetic idea is a representation of the imagination, annexed to a given concept, with which, in the free employment of the imagination, such a multiplicity of partial representations are bound up, that no expression [Ausdruck] indicating a definite concept can be found for it—one which on that account allows a concept to be supplemented in thought by much that is indefinable in words, and the feeling of which quickens [belebt] the cognitive faculties, and with language, as a mere thing of the letter, binds up the spirit (soul) also [mit der Sprache, als bloßem Buchstaben, Geist verbindet]. (cj §49: 179)

The feeling of the supplement quickens (enlivens) the cognitive faculties and binds the *Geist* with language. Thus, the limits internal to discursive understanding turn in on themselves through the production of the supplement as the embodiment of the negative space of precisely these limits. The artistic turn in its relationship to the sublime could be rewritten, then, as follows:

— We stumble on the impossibility of adequate (discursive) expression.

— Nevertheless, we then encounter the (symbolic) expression of adequation.

TELEOLOGY: THE PURPOSIVE WAY

As we have seen, when Kant defines purpose and purposiveness (end and finality) in transcendental terms in the *Critique of Judgment,* he writes: "A purpose is the object of a concept so far as this concept is regarded as the cause [Ursache] of the object (the real ground of its possibility); and the causality of a *concept* in respect of its *Object* is purposiveness (forma finalis)" (*CJ* §10: 61). He then goes on to elaborate on this sense of purposiveness by arguing that in our judgment of the beautiful we apprehend a purposiveness without purpose, an appearance of causality in the form of an object without the comprehension of its concept-cause. In a judgment of taste, we will recall, we are simply concerned with subjective formal purposiveness as a process, not in a concept of its end or purpose. But in teleological judgment, which is the extension of the principle of purposiveness into its logical and not merely aesthetic employment, we are now precisely concerned with ends or purposes and their causality. This concern can never be determining—we can never extend our knowledge as a result of this employment—but it will function as a regulative principle for making sense of (but not knowing) nature as a whole. Nature appears as a purposive system. Yet whatever understanding may be producing the concepts that function as the cause of this systematicity will forever remain a mystery. It cannot be a human understanding, for such a superhuman understanding would have insight into things in themselves; but since our own understanding is all that we know, we must model our concept of such an understanding on our own. That is, we must extend our reflective judgment, based on the principles of human thought, out into the supersensible realm lying at the base of nature as a system of ends.

"Now we are always obliged," Kant tells us, "to look with the eye of reason into what we observe (i.e., to consider it in its possibility)" (*CJ* §10: 62). As such, when we observe purposiveness in nature, reason prods us on to ask how such could be possible, to search out the cause behind the object. Again, this goal of reason's is incapable of direct, schematic presentation. And while reflection will remain the key principle at work here, we have taken an interesting turn—a teleological one. Reflection is no longer simply the process whereby we come up with a mode of presenting a concept of reason; it is now *the concept of reflection itself* that allows us to present the objective purposiveness that appears to be at work in nature (keeping in mind all the while that any real ascription of such objective purposiveness would be a case of subreption). The teleological turn thus involves the following:

— Through the critique of aesthetic judgment we arrive at the concept of reflection, a type of judgment that refers to itself when a universal is not available for a given particular.

— In our teleological judgment, we then apply this concept of reflection to the purposive objects of nature, and thereby impute an intelligent cause (another reflective being) behind objective purposiveness.

As Deleuze puts it, " 'Reflection' therefore changes its meaning: it is no longer the formal reflection of the object without the concept, but the concept of reflection through which the content of the object is reflected on. In this concept our faculties are freely and harmoniously exercised. But here the free accord of the faculties is still contained within the contingent accord of Nature and the faculties themselves."[11]

A key distinction operating in Kant's teleological critique is that between mechanical and teleological causality. For many objects in nature, a merely mechanical explanation of their cause is adequate. Sand is caused by friction produced by wind and rain; rain is produced by the condensation of moisture in the air brought about through a change in temperature; a change in temperature is brought about by . . . ; and so on. This relationship of causality does not immediately send us out in search of a supersensible principle as the ordering principle of these phenomena. The question of ends rarely occurs to us in these cases. Yet there are other natural objects that cannot be accounted for in terms of purely mechanical causality but appear as though designed—that is, created by some intelligent cause, some reflective being whose concept served as the cause of the object: "Who or what could have created such a thing? Why?" The objects of this second type are those that exhibit what Kant refers to as *intrinsic finality*. While we can talk about sand and wind and rain in terms of *relative finality*—in terms of how each serves a particular purpose in relation to one another ("grass is for cows to eat; cows are for humans to eat . . .")—organic beings, organisms, in themselves must be explained otherwise. An organism exhibits an internally constituted system of purposiveness apart from any other purposive relation it may have with another object. The cow, for example, is not only a relative end in terms of food for us but is also an intrinsic end in terms of its organicity. Now how could such a complex organism just happen?

We can turn to genetics, evolution, or whatever, but we ultimately extend back to some original cause. This original cause must serve as a regulative principle for teleological judgment in its attempt to get to the bottom of the purposiveness of nature as a whole. We can infer the purposive organization of an individual organism, but how do we explain the multiplicity of organic and inorganic objects in their relation to one another as nature? How did nature come about? Why? To what end? And assuming we have answers to these questions, how can we present such a purpose that can only be supersensible in origin?[12] Kant suggests that

> once we have discovered a capacity in nature for bringing forth products that can only be thought by us according to the conception of final causes, we advance a step farther. Even products which do not (either as to themselves or to the relation, however final, in which they stand) make it necessarily incumbent upon us to go beyond the mechanism of blind efficient causes and seek out some other principle on which they are possible, may nevertheless be justly estimated as forming part of a system of ends. For the idea from which we started is one which, when we consider its foundation, already leads beyond the world of sense, and then the unity of the supersensible principle must be treated, not valid merely for certain species of natural beings, but as similarly valid for the whole of nature as a system. (*CJ* §67: 30–31)

Here, yet again, is a symbolic or analogical mode of presentation: "Our only intention is to designate in this way a kind of natural causality on an analogy with our own causality in the technical employment of reason, for the purpose of keeping in view the rule upon which certain natural products are to be investigated" (*CJ* §68: 34). The analogous rule: the contents of the analogy are not to be compared but simply the relationship present in each, the rule that appears to regulate each process. As we have seen above, that relationship is reflection itself as its own principle of analogy. Since we ourselves are purposive beings and operate reflectively in the world, moving from the contingent myriad of individual facts of nature to some overarching principle uniting these individuals, we can only assume that some such being operates according to the same rule. But we must be careful to keep in mind, Kant reminds us, that "it proves no more than this, that by the constitution of our cognitive faculties, and, therefore, in bringing experience into touch with the highest principles of reason, we are absolutely incapable of forming any conception of the possibility of such a world unless we imagine a highest cause operating designedly" (*CJ* §75: 52). We can never intuit such a process but must present it through analogy, for "strictly speaking, we do not *observe* the ends in nature as designed. We only *read* this conception *into* the facts as a guide to judgment in its reflection upon the products of nature" (ibid., 53).

THE LIMITS OF THE DISCURSIVE UNDERSTANDING

In the terms of human understanding we cannot even explain the purposive origin of a simple blade of grass. But we can come up with the projection of the negative embodiment of the limits of human understanding. And it is this question of the negative limits of our own understanding that comes into view as that which underlies Kant's entire critical project. The purpose of critique, after all, is to pose limits, to recognize the points at which knowledge ends and pure thinking continues. And the question of presentation is the question of how we can engage our discursive understanding with reason, which outstrips our discursive limits. This outstripping of limits nevertheless takes place within the limits of the discursive since the question of symbolism and other modes of extradiscursive presentation operate within the limits of the question of the discursive. Symbolism is nothing but the negative extension of the operation of schematism.

In §77 of the *Critique of Judgment*, Kant distinguishes between human, discursive understanding and a superhuman, intuitive understanding. The discursive understanding is ectypal, meaning that it "has need of images" in order to unite the individual, particular, and universal. The intuitive understanding, on the other hand, is archetypal, meaning that the relationship between concept and intuition is immediate and spontaneous. As the name implies, the discursive understanding is bound to the progressive linearity of time, and thus, can never obtain an immediate relationship between intuition and concept or any immediate access to the supersensible. The discursive is contingent—that is, the relationship between particular image and universal concept depends on experience, on what sensible intuitions are available at a given moment— whereas the archetypal understanding has no experience in this sense since knowledge and intuition are immediate. This distinction also occurs in the *Critique of Pure Reason* in Kant's elaboration on the distinction between phenomena and noumena. The concept of noumena, in fact, functions as a purely negative term in the way I am speaking of here: "The doctrine of sensibility is . . . the doctrine of the noumenon in the negative sense, that is, of things which the understanding must think without this reference to our mode of intuition, therefore not merely as appearances but as things in themselves" (*CPR* B307). Only a being possessed of intellectual intuition could experience noumena in the positive sense.

But what leads Kant to speculate on the possibility (but not the actuality) of such an intuitive understanding? Purposiveness. Because our reflective judgment leads us to posit—even if only for the purposes of reflection—a purposive ground for certain objects in nature, we must have an idea of an understanding whose concepts would function as the cause of such objects, an understanding outside the limits of ours, limited as ours is to the phenomenal realm in the determination of objects. Because such a purposive source lies beyond our understanding, we can neither affirm nor deny its existence, but we must nevertheless form an idea of it in order to reflect on purposiveness in general. But we can only reflect on this understanding *negatively*, "or simply as not discursive" (*CJ* §77: 62), as the reflection of *reflection's own negative limit*. Such an understanding would have no need for reflective judgment for, as the cause of the unity in nature, it would have no trouble associating the contingent, multiple particulars of nature with its own ordering principle. But much like the sublime, this idea of an understanding beyond the discursive is nothing but the fleshing out of the space of negativity of the discursive itself, the projection of a beyond of the limits of human understanding that is made possible only by the negative space of the limit. The extradiscursive, then, remains within the circle of intelligibility of the discursive as its own immanent negation. Presentation beyond representation remains bound to the circle of representation as *its* immanent negation.

Our discursive understanding, in its causality, in its production of an object, "moves from the *analytic universal* to the particular, or, in other words, from conceptions to given empirical intuitions." Yet the intuitive understanding would move from the synthetic universal, "or intuition of whole as a whole, to the particular—that is to say, from the whole to the parts" (ibid., 63). So to what use can we put the concept of an intuitive understanding in order to better our own understanding? None, if by use one means a determining application of the principle of purposiveness to the production of wholes (the whole of nature as a purposive system):

> The very peculiarity of our understanding in question prevents this being done in such a way that the whole contains the source of the possibility of the nexus of the parts. This would be self-contradictory in knowledge of the discursive type. But the *representation* of a whole may contain the source of the possibility of the form of that whole and of the nexus of the parts which that form involves. This is our only road. But, now, the whole would in that case be an effect or product the representation of which is looked on as the cause of its possibility. But the product of a cause whose determining ground is merely the representation of its effect is determined an end. Hence it follows that it is simply a consequence flowing from the particular character of our understanding that we should figure [*vorstellen*] to our minds products of nature as possible according to a different type of causality from that of the physical laws of matter, that is, as only possible according to ends and final causes. . . . Here it is also quite unnecessary to prove that an intellectus archetypus like this is possible. It is sufficient to show that we are led to this idea of an *intellectus archetypus* by contrasting with it our discursive understanding that has need of images (*intellectus ectypus*) and noting the contingent character of a faculty of this form, and that this idea involves nothing self-contradictory. (ibid., 64–65)

So we see that the presentation of the beyond of discursivity can only come about by *contrasting* it "with our discursive understanding that has need of images." The result is the negative projection of an *intellectual intuition*—a concept that Johann Fichte and Friedrich Schelling ran with and that led Hegel to write, among other things, his preface to the *Phenomenology of Spirit* in reaction to the use of such a concept as immediate intuitive knowledge. For Hegel, as we will see, just as for Kant, knowledge is only possible discursively. The difference will be that while for Kant the image and therefore the symbol will remain necessary for higher modes of thinking, for Hegel thinking as such will depend on a passing through the image and the symbol to the pure concrete concept or Notion (Begriff).

Kant's conception of the negativity of the symbol nevertheless prepares the way for Hegel's project of dialectical negation. What is presented in the symbol, ultimately, is the rule, the relation: symbolism is a mode of thinking the limits of thinking itself, of the negative relationship between discursive understanding and its own discursive limits. The symbol, to repeat yet again, is the embodiment of the space of negativity immanent to discursivity itself as it reflects on its own limits. Cathy Caruth presents Kant's conception of the symbol in this way:

> Since knowledge of relation is . . . always a knowledge of knowledge, the symbolic representation of the supersensible will also be a reflection on the very establishing of the symbol, a symbol of symbolic thinking. To think a symbolic relation is thus to represent the supersensible in terms of the very act of thinking which makes this representation possible. The symbol, that is, always remembers that it is, only, a symbol. It knows, one could say, that it posits. The symbol thus mediates between thinking and knowing, or the negativity of knowledge and the knowledge of that negativity.[13]

Symbolism, then, is not really about the world or God or whatever else, but, as Kant tells us, about "language only and not the object itself."[14] Philosophical language itself, even when it strives to present its most basic concepts, records this discursive limitation in such symbolic expressions as "*ground* (support, basis), to *depend* (to be held up from above), to *flow* from (instead of to follow), *substance* (as Locke puts it: the support of accidents), and numberless others, which are not schematic, but rather symbolic hypotyposes" (*CJ* §59: 223). Because of the limits of discourse, language can never give a pure presentation of supersensible objects; its symbolic presentations always carry an excessive element within them, an unintelligible thing at the heart of the presentation of the supersensible that prevents language from ever becoming a closed symbolic system. The *Critique of Judgment*, the immanent discourse on the limits of the discursive, thus marks its own limitations in relation to its own limits as it projects the narrative of purposiveness onto the beyond of discursive knowledge, installing this beyond in terms of a temporal ordering (causes and ends) that which analogically attempts to "ground" our concepts in terms which we can know. Yet temporality contains its own excess and announces the impossibility of the immediate, the intellectual intuition, the archetypal understanding that would fuse intuition and concept in a single, nontemporal instant. To cite Caruth once more:

> We might think of this nonclosure in terms of the difference between the symbol and its concept, or the symbol and its representation as an analogy. If the symbol represents the thinking relation of the sensible to the supersensi-

ble, the concept of the symbol—the definition of the symbol in critical discourse—enacts a kind of positing that cannot be recuperated symbolically. This nonrecuperation would be marked by the proliferation of examples, not "empirical" examples, but examples in the argument, linguistic examples, which would eventually take the form of a narrative. The concept of the limit which structures the system would thus be made possible by the symbol and impossible by its concept. The articulation of parts of the system by the symbol would be made possible and impossible by the disarticulation of the symbol with itself. The limit, we might say then, is divided between the structure which the symbol symbolizes, and the story which its example tells.[15]

In her provocative discussion of Hegel's writings on politics and religion, Gillian Rose suggests an unusual reading of Hegel's famous sentence from the preface to the *Philosophy of Right*, "What is rational is actual; and what is actual is rational" (PR 20). If this sentence is read as an "ordinary" proposition, then Hegel's point is missed completely. We should instead read this and other propositions from Hegel's works as "speculative propositions." As an ordinary proposition, according to which the subject functions as a static ground to which the predicate is added as a merely external accident, the claim that the rational is actual must be read as a proposition of identity, a tautology that claims that two separate things are identical, this being especially so for a proposition that reverses subject and predicate as this one does ("and the actual is rational"). But as a speculative proposition, Hegel's statement must be seen as expressing the lack of identity between subject and predicate—"lack of identity" referring not to the obvious difference between subject and predicate as two distinct things or concepts but instead to the proposition as a whole in its failure "to correspond to the state of affairs or object to which it should correspond" (HCS 49). It is precisely in the reader's experience of this failure-to-correspond that the proposition acquires its speculative meaning.[1]

A similar statement of Hegel's that Rose claims has been almost uniformly misread is the following from *Lectures on the Philosophy of Religion*: "In general religion and the foundation of the state is [*sic*] one and the same thing; they are identical in and for themselves" (LPR 16: 236). "The *speculative* proposition that

religion and the state are identical," Rose contends, "implies the *experience* of a
bad religion and a bad state, where the state and religion are in opposition, not
identical. The experience of the disunion of the state and religion reoccurs in the
realm of religion, in the medium of representation [Vorstellung]" (HCS 93). So
the claim that religion and the state are identical must be read as meaning that
they are so only in their nonidentity with their Notions. The clue to this reading,
according to Rose, comes in our experience of such a claim to identity as pure
nonsense. For our ordinary consciousness—the state of mind, presumably, in
which the written text—such a claim is patently absurd: it should be obvious to
anyone that in early-nineteenth-century Prussia, religion and the state were not
identical. But it seems that for Rose this is exactly the reaction Hegel hopes for in
his readers, for it is only from this experience of the failure of identity that this
approach to the speculative identity between the subject and predicate of the
proposition can be attained. It is only when everyday consciousness comes up
against complete absurdity, in other words, that we are projected into a speculative frame of mind, in terms of which the previously absurd claim to identity can
then be read as identical in the nonidentity of the two terms with themselves.
Religion and the state, the actual and the rational, are identical to the extent that
they both fail to actualize their Notions—fail, that is, to develop completely
through history according to their ideal (but as yet unrealizable) potential.

But if Hegel's ultimate point is that church and state are identical in their
nonidentity, then why doesn't he just say so? Why leave it up to the reader to go
through the elaborate stages necessary in moving from "the actual is the rational" to the speculative conclusion that neither the actual nor the rational has
attained its Notion, and that it is through this selfsame "nonidentity" that they
have become identical? Why leave such a crucial process up to the contingencies
of the audience, which (as the history of the reception to Hegel's work has
shown) will most likely read such propositions in light of ordinary consciousness? Perhaps this risk and loss is as crucial an element of the speculative as
whatever positive content we end up arriving at after our long labor of the
negative. For it is only in terms of the Understanding, the ruling faculty of
"ordinary consciousness," that a positive statement is simply a positive statement. In terms of speculative Reason, on the other hand, the Notion is only ever
actualized after the fact, the actual is only ever rational after the owl of Minerva
has taken flight at dusk, after the nonidentity of subject and predicate has
propelled the proposition through the experience of the negative movement
that a single proposition can never contain.

The main question at stake here, then, is what mode of presentation is adequate to the speculative. I would further claim that this question is at the heart of the entire Hegelian project: How can we best present the dialectical movement of the negative? One way to approach this question of presentation is by exploring the issues involved in a key passage from Hegel's preface to the *Phenomenology of Spirit*, which I quote at length:

> The need to represent [*vorzustellen*] the Absolute as *Subject* has found expression in the propositions: God is the eternal, the moral world-order, love, and so on. In such propositions, the True is only posited [*gezetzt*] immediately as Subject, but is not presented [*dargestellt*] as the movement of reflecting itself into itself. In a proposition of this kind one begins with the word "God." This by itself is a senseless [*sinnlose*] sound, a mere name; it is only the predicate that says *what God is*, gives Him content and meaning [*Erfüllung und Bedeutung*, or fulfillment and signification]. Only in the end of the proposition does the empty beginning become actual knowledge. This being so, it is not clear why one does not speak merely of the eternal, of the moral world-order, and so on, or, as the ancients did, of pure notions like "being," "the One," and so on, in short, of that which gives the meaning without adding the *senseless* sound as well. But it is just this word that indicates that what is posited is not a being, or essence, or a universal in general, but rather something that is reflected into itself, a Subject. But at the same time this is only anticipated. The Subject is assumed as a fixed point to which, as their support, the predicates are affixed by a movement belonging to the knower of this Subject, and which is not regarded as belonging to the fixed point itself; yet it is only through this movement that the content [*Inhalt*] could be presented [*dargestellt*: A. V. Miller translates this as "represented"] as Subject. The way in which this movement has been brought about is such that it cannot belong to the fixed point; yet, after this point has been presupposed [*Voraussetzung*], the nature of the movement cannot really be other than what it is, it can only be external. Hence, the mere anticipation that the Absolute is Subject is not only *not* the actuality of this Notion, but it even makes the actuality impossible; for the anticipation posits the subject as an insert point, whereas the actuality is self-movement. (PS §23: 15–16, 12–13)

I would maintain that this dense passage is key to understanding Hegel's conception of presentation (Darstellung) and its relationship to the question of the proposition. For that reason, I will examine this passage one part at a time. To begin: "The need to represent [*vorzustellen*] the Absolute as *Subject*." In this phrase, there are three important concepts that underlie Hegel's entire project: representation (Vorstellung), the Absolute, and the Subject. Most important, however, is the relationship between them. Prior to this passage, Hegel had been criticizing current approaches to the question of scientific presentation—in particular, those of Fichte and Schelling. While their systems vary in quite fundamental ways (as Hegel's own *The Difference between the Fichtean and Schellingian Systems of Philosophy* makes clear), both philosophers posit the possibility of intellectual intuition. For Kant, as we have seen, human consciousness is only capable of empirical, sensory-based intuition; his *Critique of Pure Reason* was devoted to arguing against any such possibility as an intellectual or rational intuition. Reason plays a regulative rather than a constitutive role in what the subject does with its intuitions, but it is just such a constitutive role that Fichte and Schelling attribute to intellectual intuition. Like Kant, Hegel denies the possibility (or even the desirability) of intellectual intuition, the immediate presentation of an Idea of Reason to the Imagination. Any Idea in its immediacy is an abstract universality devoid of concrete content; Reason, Hegel claims, demands that the Idea be made concrete, that it present itself as the actualization and sublation of the Notion.

A = A: FICHTE ON POSITING AND THE ABSOLUTE

Fichte opens his *Science of Knowledge* [*Wissenschaftslehre*] with the assertion that "our task is to *discover* the primordial, absolutely unconditioned first principle of all human knowledge. This can be neither *proved* nor *defined*, if it is to be an absolutely primary principle" (sk 91, 93). The absolute by definition cannot be defined: this paradox (that which is defined as that which cannot be defined) was not lost on Hegel. Nor was it lost on Fichte himself, I should add; the rest of the *Science of Knowledge* is devoted to laying out dialectically how that which is undefined defines itself as both undefined (the subjective principle, the free Act) *and* defined (the objective principle, Nature—all that which is posited as the antithesis of subjective freedom). The infinite I, the Absolute, posits itself both as that which posits and that which is posited. The Absolute determines itself as indeterminate.

Determination, Fichte argued, is a form of subjection, a limitation of absolute freedom that must itself be beyond all determination. The Absolute can thus be represented in the proposition A is A, or A = A: the first A (the subject of the proposition, the active principle, the ground of the predication) posits the second A (its predicate, its determinations), which is none other than itself as the object of itself. A posits itself as identical to itself; its determinations are its own self-determinations—it determines itself as self-determining. What unites the two As is an unstated X, "the *necessary connection* between the two that is posited *absolutely*, and *without any other ground*" (sK 93, 95). The X is the groundless ground, or the I, the self that posits. This groundless ground can be represented as I = I, the infinitely self-identical self, the ultimate proposition of identity that underlies all other identities, the unconditioned primordial Act of positing. This "I am" is the self that posits itself and is therefore pure activity [*die reine Thätigkeit*]: "The *self posits itself*, and by virtue of this mere self-positing it *exists*; and conversely, the self *exists* and *posits* its own existence by virtue of merely existing. It is at once agent and the product of action . . . , and hence the 'I am' expresses an Act, and the only one possible," writes Fichte (96, 97).

The form of the proposition itself appears to support Fichte's claims:

> In the proposition "A = A," the first A is that which is posited in the self, either absolutely, like the self itself, or on some other ground, like any given not-self. In this matter the self behaves as absolute subject; and hence the first A is called the subject. The second A designates what the self, reflecting upon itself, discovers to be present in itself, because it has first set this within itself. The judging self predicates something, not really of A, but of itself, namely that there is an A in it; and hence the second A is called the predicate.—Thus in the proposition "A = B," A designates what is now being posited; B what is already encountered as posited.—*Is* expresses the passage of the *self* from positing to reflection on what has been posited. (ibid.)

For Hegel, however, this refusal to accept determinacy as an attribute or condition of the Absolute results in a "monochromatic formalism" (PS §15; 9) in which this empty representation (Vorstellung) of monotonous abstract universality hurls all determinate entities into "the abyss of vacuity" (PS §16; 9):

> Dealing with something from the perspective of the Absolute [for Fichte as well as Schelling] consists merely in declaring that, although one has just been speaking of it just now as something definite, yet in the Absolute, the A = A, there is nothing of the kind, for there all is one. To pit this single insight,

that in the Absolute everything is the same, against the full body of articulated cognition, which at least seeks and demands such fulfillment [Erfüllung], to palm off its Absolute as the night in which, as the saying goes, all cows are black—this is cognition naively reduced to vacuity." (ibid.)

Mere vacuity versus full-bodied articulation: such is the opposition at work in Hegel's response to Fichte's subjective idealism. The reflective moment that Fichte refers to above in his discussion of the proposition—the predicate as the moment of reflection—is submerged in immediate, unmoved substantiality in the reduction of cognition to intellectual intuition. Reflection, the movement of mediation, must be seen as substance-become-subject; the Subject is nothing but the simple negativity of reflection, the bifurcation (*Entzweiung*) of the simple, the "doubling which sets up opposition, and then again the negation of this indifferent diversity and of its antithesis. Only this self-*restoring* sameness, or this reflection in otherness within itself—not an *original* or *immediate* unity as such—is the True" (PS §18; 10). The "I" is therefore not the inertia of "I am" but the pure negativity of the "I am becoming" of reflection, the "unrest that is the self" (PS §22; 10). In *Difference*, Hegel writes:

> To the extent that reflection makes itself into its object, its highest law, which is given to it by Reason and through which it becomes Reason, is its annihilation. It exists, like everything, only in the Absolute, but as reflection it is opposed to it. Thus, in order to exist, it must give itself the law of self-destruction. The immanent law by which it constitutes itself as absolute out of its own power would be the law of contradiction, namely, that its posited-being would be and would persist. (D 28, 17).

Now to return to the Hegel passage above: "The need to represent [vorzustellen] the Absolute as *Subject* has found expression in the propositions: God is the eternal, the moral world-order, love, and so on. In such propositions, the True is only posited [gezetzt] *immediately* as Subject, but is not presented [dargestellt] as the movement of reflecting itself into itself." The major question here is the ability of the proposition to represent the Absolute; ultimately, it is a question about the efficacy of representation itself, of Vorstellung. The proposition functions, According to Hegel's analysis here, as a species of Vorstellung (representation through an image or picture-thought), which immediately posits the relationship between subject and predicate; still, what Hegel is looking for is a mode of exposition that not only *represents* the

Absolute but *presents* it: Hegel is demanding a presentation or Darstellung that is adequate to the negative reflective movement of dialectical becoming, a mode in which the True is "presented [dargestellt] as the movement of reflecting itself into itself"—presented, that is, as Subject. The speculative proposition, on the other hand, enacts this negative movement by contradicting the immediate sense of the representation and thereby setting the whole dialectical system itself into motion. In light of this, one should be especially careful of translations such as Miller's that conflate the terms *Vorstellung* and *Darstellung* as in §23. It is precisely the sublation of representation through presentation that is at issue here. Before continuing with my analysis of §23, then, I need to contextualize Hegel's conception of Vorstellung and its relationship to the word, the proposition, and speculative method as a whole.

REPRESENTATION AND SIGNIFICATION

For Hegel, humans are by nature thinking animals. Logos is our element, which is another way of saying that an exposition of logic cannot be true to its content without taking into account the transformations wrought by language. Thinking itself is the product of these linguistic transformations; thinking is dialectical movement systematized and realized by language. But if thinking is to be posed as the result of a transformation, what exactly has been transformed? Hegel's answer is: all that which becomes something inward, Vorstellung or figuration in general, which humans thereby make their own. The dialectical transformation of these prelinguistic moments—taking the form of intuitions, images, and symbols—supplies the sign, word, name, or external product that bears the stamp of its own inward productive force. The word thus brings about the process that at once depends on and destroys the word as such. The word brings on itself its own negation by setting itself in motion; it thereby also brings about its own fulfillment. This drama of the self-dismembering and remembering of the forms of the Notion is played out in the transformation of Vorstellung into its display, *Darstellung*.

As we have seen, one of the problems we immediately face as English-speaking readers of Hegel is that both of these terms, Vorstellung and Darstellung, often are translated without distinction as "representation." While these terms *should* be connected as moments of the same general process, which could provisionally be called representation, they must nevertheless be distinguished as *particular* moments.[2] What complicates this problem is that both terms also appear under a variety of other translations even when translated by the same person. For example, Vorstellung appears as representation, conception, view, figurate conception, image-loving thought, picture-thought, and idea. (Its translation as "idea," of course, causes problems when the term *Idee* also appears as "Idea," even when the latter is capitalized, if for no other reason than that Hegel goes to great lengths to distinguish between his terms, and uses them in quite specific and sometimes idiosyncratic ways, playing one off the other in ways anticipating the linguistic and etymological play of Martin Heidegger and Jacques Derrida.) In turn, Darstellung appears as exposition, exhibition, expression, setting forth, depiction, definitive description, and so on. The beauty of words, Hegel claims, or their superiority over hieroglyphs, is their naming function: "The name is the simple sign for the exact Vorstellung, . . . and has for its sole function to signify and represent sensibly [*sinnlich vorzustellen*] the simple idea as such," while with the hieroglyph, "the relations of concrete mental ideas to one another must necessarily be tangled and perplexed. . . . [T]he analysis of these . . . appears to be possible in the most various and divergent ways" (E §459; 217). Such is also the case in translation, as the above illustrates: either one English word, such as "representation," obliterates the distinctions obvious in the German text or several English words take the place of the single German one, as in the case of Vorstellung. The irony of the situation is that since we often have to relearn even familiar words in Hegel's writings because of his deliberate defamiliarization of them, readers would be better served by learning and making our own the German terms and their functions in Hegel's exposition.

This commentary on translation should not be viewed as beside the point; for what is at stake in this discussion is the question of presentation itself in Hegel. Translation is, after all, a question of presentation and therefore serves here as a preliminary immersion into the issues of propriety and property in the cultural formation of representation, of the spiritual or mindful dialectic of linguistic transformation.

The context of Hegel's discussions of Vorstellung and Darstellung is crucial, which is his search for a method and mode of thought capable of presenting the insights of speculative philosophy, the philosophy in which Mind or Spirit recognizes itself in the products of its own activity, the point at which the Subject recognizes itself as the self-movement of its own determinations. Hegel needs a method of presentation that raises itself from ordinary consciousness (which depends heavily on Vorstellung) to the level of Science (which can only be brought about by a dialectical Darstellung).[3] The difference is that between a dwelling in things and the journey of becoming, between a setting before and a setting in motion. This question of setting forth or placement comes from the root of both terms, which is *Stellung* or presentation, placement, setting, which Hegel relates to his crucial concept of *setzen*, the positioning, positing, or placing act of the Subject through which it sets itself in motion. This is the movement that Fichte, Edmund Husserl, and Julia Kristeva refer to as the Thetic, the basic act of consciousness, and that has become canonized in usual discussions of Hegel as the Thesis, the first moment of the dialectical triad. The dialectic is thus a movement of positionings, positings, or placements. Vorstellung holds out the image or pictorial sense of the unitary moment while Darstellung displays the movement, the system, the dialectical whole that is nothing other than the movement of its moments. If the various Vorstellungen are the products of the collective Subject, Darstellung stages the productive process itself and brings about the recognition that our products are not static external objects but rather the externalization of our own activity. Darstellung is thus a response to and revelation of the reification of the products of consciousness—the fetishism of the commodities of collective thought.[4]

In both English and German, a certain etymological thread puts this question of positioning into play with several of Hegel's key concepts, such as positioning [*stellen*] and positing [*setzen*], position [*Stellung*] and proposition [*Satz*], presupposition [*Voraussetzung*] and exposition [*Darstellung*]. Vorstellung places an object before us and is thus related to the proposition (in ways I will soon examine); Darstellung stages the unfolding of the proposition and is thus an exposition, a projecting forward and an exposing of the positing process. While Darstellung is an exhibition, a staging of the act of display, Vorstellung is an inhibition, an internalization of the presupposed object. Darstellung enacts a drama; Vorstellung presents a picture. But this drama is that of the self-negation of the Vorstellungen themselves, just as an exhibition or display in a gallery stages the dissolution of each individual painting or image into the movement of comprehending the ensemble as a whole; the individual image's status as individual passes into its negation, the display as a whole; but simultaneously, the whole exists only as the movement from one image to the next. Science is for Hegel the recognition and display of this dialectical drama of the collective Subject's self-negation and self-fulfillment [Erfüllung].

Before discussing Vorstellung as a mode of philosophical presentation, it is helpful to first look at Hegel's detailed exposition of Vorstellung as a psychological process in the *Encyclopedia*, where it appears not simply as a textual process but a rudimentary operation of the mind. The distance between this psychological mode of Vorstellung, which every thinking human shares, and philosophical Vorstellung is enormous, but since Hegel's critique of Formalism draws on important connections between the two modes, I need to expose their relationship. And while the relationship between form and content will become increasingly self-conscious in philosophical discourse, this basic "economy of intelligence" outlined in the *Encyclopedia* will continue to unfold throughout Hegel's system.[5]

What is at work psychologically is the development of cognition to the point where Mind or Spirit recognizes its productions—intuitions, images, and signs—as its own and thereby fulfills itself as the passage through necessity (Nature) to freedom (Spirit whose Idea has come back to itself). It is only as a result of this development, Hegel claims, that thinking (free cognition) as such can be said to exist and operate. This means that not all processes of the mind can be called thinking. Like Kant before him, Hegel explores the relationships between intuition, imagination, understanding, and reason; yet unlike Kant, Hegel rejects the formal separation of these faculties—even for purely schematic purposes—because such a schematic formalism merely articulates this process through the separating act of understanding rather than through the unifying act of reason. The faculties are not to be presented as independent and coexistent actors but as moments of a dialectical process in which the first is negated by the second, sublated by the third, and so on.

Keeping in mind that for Hegel each moment, though necessarily negated and sublated in the further determinations of the system, is itself necessary and therefore locally valid (it has important and specific work to do; the truth of this moment—to be realized in its negation—cannot come about without this moment, precisely because truth will have been the truth of *this* moment), we must then look for the necessity of Vorstellung, for it is only through the work of Vorstellung that Darstellung can come about, this movement of Darstellung being nothing other than the staging and the playing out of the self-dissolution (*Auflösung*) of these images, these Vorstellungen. This necessity is to be found in the transformations of the Imagination. Imagination (*Einbildungskraft*: the power of forming [*Bildung*] unified images [*Bilden*]) lies quite literally at the center of Hegel's economy of intelligence, "Theoretical Spirit" (whose job it is to free knowledge from its presupposedness—to show that what appears as pre-posited before cognition has actually been posited *by* cognition) being divided into three faculties: Intuition [*Anschauung*], Representation [*Vorstellung*], and Thinking [*Das Denken*]. Vorstellung, then, plays the role of the transformer, the mediator between the sensible (distinct from the sensuous consciousness of the *Phenomenology*) and the intelligible, the appropriator of the seemingly alien object that is actually one's own. Vorstellung is the recollection or inwardization [*Erinnerung*] of the intuition, the middle stage between the immediate passivity of intuition and the free self-determination of thought—the point of Spirit's self-transformation from necessity to freedom. (In Marx's terms, this movement is the economy of the transformation of commodity fetishism into the reappropriation of Value—and the concomitant recognition of the necessity of the commodity form for this reappropriation.)

Vorstellung in general is the universalizing synthesis of the contents of intuition into a unity (image, symbol, sign) capable of serving as a vehicle for intelligence. Hegel divides Vorstellung up into three distinct moments: Recollection [*Erinnerung*], Imagination, and Memory [*Gedächtnis*]. Recollection interiorizes the intuition (which posits its product as something external) and stores these inwardized intuitions in an unconscious pit or mine shaft. The immediate and particular intuition (the positing of a particular external object) is transformed into a universal image [*Bild*] that can be retrieved from the unconscious pit [*bewußtlos schact*] when intelligence confronts another such object; this retrieved image classifies the intuition by assigning the latter a universal form by which intelligence can identify the object. In this way, the particular is represented as universal: "This 'synthesis' of the internal image with the recollected existence [*erinnerten Dasein*] is *representation* proper [*eigentliche Vorstellung*]; by this synthesis, the internal now has the qualification [*Bestimmung*] of being able to be *presented* [*gestellt*] before intelligence and to have existence [*Dasein*] in it" (ε §454, 205). The existence of the intuited object is posited as Dasein, Being-there, external. Through Erinnerung, this object— now an image—has its Dasein or field-of-existence within intelligence, presented [gestellt] and made present before intelligence by a stand-in, an actor, a representative image. The power behind this synthesis is "the *reproductive imagination* [*reproduktive Einbildungskraft*], where the images issue forth from the inward world belonging to the ego" (ε §455, 206). This reproduced image, through the work of the imagination, then gives rise to the general Vorstellung—"the Vorstellung in the strict [eigentlichen] sense of the word"—which connects individual images according to what is common to them, raising them to universality by dissolving the empirical manifold of intuitive determinations. The second moment of Imagination, according to the *Zuzatz* (supplement) for §455, is thus association, the active work of intelligence. Nevertheless, Imagination is not just reproductive or associative but also creative imagination or *Phantasie*. *Phantasie* provides the general Vorstellung with an independent existence: though its material is still derived from intuition, the Vorstellung, thanks to *Phantasie*, can be called up at will, freely, without the aid or instigation of an external object. The phantastic representation is distinct from the phenomenon in that though both are modes of showing (as their common etymological basis implies), the phantastic is a product of the free activity of intelligence: "Thus are these Vorstellungen each self-determined and their interiorized contents imagistically unified [*einbildend*] through *Phantasie*—the symbolic, allegoric, and poetical imagination" (*E* §456, 209; my translation).

This freely produced phantasy-image is nonetheless internal, subjective, and lacks the side of existence [*Existenz*]; it needs to be externalized in order *to be*, and in order to be *re*cognized as one's own. So the work of Phantasie is not yet done: it must next unite—though still subjectively—the general Vorstellung (the inward side that lacks figuration) and the image (the outward side that lacks universality) into a single compound now both universal and figurative: the concrete auto-intuition or *the sign*. The sign is the subjectively produced and universalized intuition, which means that the external object now posited before intelligence is clearly one of its own creations. Signs are not all that Phantasie produces, however, in its authentication [*Bewärung*] or objectification of the general Vorstellung and the difference between signs and this other product—*the symbol*—will prove to be crucial for grasping Hegel's later comments on Vorstellung's relationship to philosophical practice. The Symbolic [*symbolisierende*] Phantasie isolates the quality or qualities of some external object that best coincides with the general Vorstellung to be represented. Since eagles are thought to be strong, Hegel explains, they come to symbolize the strength of Jupiter. The production of this symbolic eagle displays the intellect's freedom in relation to the passive intuition of a specific living eagle, and in this process the general Vorstellung is subjectively authenticated; but since this symbol still refers to the material qualities [*Stoffe*] of the image of the eagle, it is less free than the objective authentication provided by the sign, which no longer depends on any quality specific to the image. The image as sign is now completely arbitrary in its relation to the general Vorstellung it represents, which means that the general Vorstellung now has an immediate relationship to itself in its image. "The sign is some immediate intuition, representing a totally different import from what naturally belongs to it; it is the pyramid into which a foreign soul has been conveyed, and where it is conserved" (E §458, 213). In this way, Hegel illustrates the necessity of dialectical movement in its totality for the realization of the unity of subject and object that Schelling sought in his Intellectual Intuition. The mind is capable of such intuition, Hegel confirms, but only after the strenuous and patient labor of the dialectic.

John McCumber points to the inherently social nature of this moment of externalization: "An utterance's unique form of existence is thus to be perceived, heard and understood, by others. But when someone gives utterance to an idea, those who hear it change and appropriate it—just as the master, earlier in the *Phenomenology*, appropriated the products of the bondsman. Taken up and interpreted by my community in ways that cannot be exactly what I intended, my words acquire a new significance, more universal because shared."[6] There are two key issues here that relate this position of Hegel's to Lacan. First is Lacan's notion of communication: successful communication has occurred when I receive my words back to me in their true—inverted—form. The *truth* of my statement is its appropriation by the community—an appropriation that often is at odds with my original intention. The second point is that, as McCumber indicates, this moment in the universalization of the word functions as an intersubjective bond in the way that the Thing functions in the Master-Slave relationship. Hegel describes that relationship as follows: "The lord puts himself into relation with both of these moments, to a thing as such, the object of desire, and to the consciousness for which thinghood is the essential characteristic. And since he is (a) qua the Notion of self-consciousness an immediate relation of being-for-self, but (b) is now at the same time mediation, or a being-for-self which is for itself only through another, he is related (a) immediately to both, and (b) mediately to each through the other" (s §190, 115). "What differentiates human society from animal society," Lacan writes in response to the Master-Slave dialectic in Hegel, " . . . is that the former cannot be grounded upon any objectifiable bond. An intersubjective dimension as such must come into it."[7] The Thing of Desire thus constitutes intersubjectivity as such.[8]

Vorstellung has yet a third moment to develop before playing itself out into thought, and that is the internalization of this new intuition. The name for this Erinnerung of the sign is Memory or Gedächtnis. "The name as the combination of the intellectually-produced intuition and its signification [Bedeutung] is above all a single transitory product, and the combination of the Vorstellung (as the internal) with intuition (as the external) is itself external. The Erinnerung of this externality is Gedächtnis" (ε §460, 218; my translation). When we confront a sign as an intuition, as the name for some Vorstellung, we confront an empty external word unless we can interiorize the signification of that name and connect it to a Vorstellung. "Of primary importance here, therefore, is the retention of the meaning of names, of our ability to remember [errinern] the Vorstellungen objectively linked to linguistic signs" (ε §461, 219). And like the Erinnerung with which Hegel began this discussion of representation, this Gedächtnis must both retain and reproduce its intuitions, now in the form of names. "Given the name lion, we need neither the actual vision of the animal, nor its image even: the name alone, if we *understand* it, is the unimaged simple representation [*die bildlose einfache Vorstellung*]. We *think* in names" (ε §462, 220). We now have the Vorstellung that has been liberated from the image. The mere name is an empty, indeterminate externality; the sound of the name vanishes in time and is thus a merely abstract negativity, which means that the sign must go elsewhere to attain its true negation and passage into Dasein or determinate existence. "The true, concrete negativity of the linguistic sign is *intelligence*, since by this the sign is changed from something outward to something inward and is thus transformed and preserved. Words thus attain an existence [Dasein] animated by thought" (ε §462, *Zuzatz*, 221). Through this extreme interiorization of the Vorstellung by Gedächtnis into Thought (*Gedanke*) the dialectical movement of representation at the same time achieves its extreme self-externalization [*Entäusserung*] as a "consummated appropriation" of both inward (meaning/signified) and outward (name/signifier) that abolishes the distinction between them. "Gedächtnis is in this manner the passage into the function of thought, which no longer has a meaning [Bedeutung], i.e. its objectivity is no longer severed from the subjective, and its inwardness does not need to go outside for its existence [*seiend*]" (ε §464, 223). From this unity of existence [*Existenz*] as Thought, which is Reason's active form, "it follows that Reason only exists in a Subject, and as the function of that Subject" (ε §464, 223). It is in exercising this function that the Spirit as Subject realizes its freedom by reappropriating its own. The path through Vorstellung is a necessary one for the realization of this communism of the Spirit.

ŽIŽEK AND THE PERFORMATIVE

A crucial link between Hegel's theory of Gedächtnis and the speculative proposition lies in the question of the name as exteriorization (Entäusserung). The key point that Hegel has developed so far in his theory of Vorstellung and language is the increasing independence of the thought from any sensuous content, such as image and sound; but such independence is only possible retroactively, after having passed through the stuff of Vorstellung. The name, as we have seen, externalizes the internal Vorstellung as a new intuition—this time a purely intellectual one rather than the sensuous intuition with which this process began. Through Gedächtnis, this intellectually produced intuition is reinteriorized as the unity of sign and signified. With the word, Žižek claims, humans have arrived "at an external, arbitrary sign whose link with its meaning is wholly arbitrary. It is only this abasement of sign to a pure indifferent externality that enables meaning to free itself of sensible intuition, and thus to purify itself into true universality" (*ME* 44).

As usual, Hegel breaks the topic of Gedächtnis down into three parts: retentive memory, reproductive memory, and mechanical memory. In retentive memory, the name comes first and we come to attach a meaning to it until this attachment becomes automatic; when we come across the word, we retain the connection between name and meaning. Once we can produce the name for a meaning we wish to express, we have passed to reproductive memory. Hegel uses the example of learning a foreign language, in which we normally come across the foreign word first and then learn to attach a meaning to it through experience (retentive memory); once we can come up with the word to express a meaning we wish to convey, we have passed to reproductive memory, the ability to reproduce the word in a new context. At this point, however, we are still operating within the limits of Vorstellung: the relationship between word and meaning is still posed in terms of an external, finite representation and a transcendent, external content. As Žižek suggests, "What is missing here is a word that would not merely represent its external content but would also constitute it, bring it forth—a word through which this signified content would become what it is—in short, a 'performative'" (*ME* 45). The answer to this dilemma is not to purge the meaning of its merely external sign—a thinking without words—but rather the evacuation of meaning itself from the words: but this means, Hegel writes, "that intelligence thereby takes on the nature of a *thing* and to such a degree that subjectivity, in its distinction from the thing, becomes quite empty, a mindless container of words, that is, a mechanical memory" (*E* §462, *Zuzatz*, 221). In this way, intelligence externalizes itself to the extreme and thereby renders itself as "mere *being*, the universal space of names as such, i.e. of meaningless words" (*E* §463; 222). Mechanical memory, rote mnemonic learning, separates the word from its content, presenting it as simply the pure and empty word *as such.* The memorization of lists of words, for example, opens up the word to the empty, meaningless negative activity of subjectivity itself—subjectivity as nothing but this succession of meaningless things.

This externalization of subjectivity as the meaningless thing is the primary obsession of Žižek's reading of Hegel, and marks the relationship between representation brought to its extreme and the speculative proposition. The word as fixed universal—posited as the one true and timeless representation of its particular content—is set in motion, its seemingly eternal fixity sundered and opened up to the play of pure becoming. In the list of memorized terms, "the meaning of a name can reside only in the fact that it follows on and/or triggers other such names. *It is only here that the true, concrete negativity of the linguistic sign emerges*: for this negativity to emerge, it is not sufficient for the word to be reduced to the pure flux of self-obliteration—its Beyond itself, meaning, has to be 'flattened,' it has to lose all its positive content, so that the only thing which remains is the empty negativity that 'is' the subject" (*ME* 45).

It is through this reduction of universality to empty negativity (subjectivity) that the performative dimension beyond the simply representative dimension of the word opens up. To illustrate how this works, Žižek recounts Hegel's example of the question "What is this?" The naming function is not simply representational: when I say that an elephant is a four-footed mammal with a trunk, I have grouped a series of properties into a unifying marker and have produced a representation, a term that immediately abbreviates this series of properties into a unifying term, marker, or sign that maintains an external relationship to its signified (the signified is thought of as existing in itself apart from the representational name that abbreviates it). But when I say "This is an elephant," I have carried out a dialectical reversal of representational constative to a performative. Now the word "elephant" brings its object into being by adding a symbolic unifying feature to its other properties listed in the representational sentence "An elephant is . . . " and thereby converts this bundle of properties into a symbolic totality. As Žižek puts it:

> The paradox of symbolization resides in the fact that the object is constituted as One through a feature that is radically external to the object itself, to its reality; through a name that bears no resemblance to the object. The object becomes One through the appendage of some completely null, self-

obliterating Being, *le peu de réalité* of a couple of sounds—the fly that makes the elephant—as with the Monarch, this imbecile contingent body of an individual that does not merely "represent" the State *qua* rational totality but constitutes it, renders it effective. This performative dimension, by means of which the signifier is inscribed into the signified content itself as its constituent (or, as Lacan puts it, by means of which the signifier "falls into the signified"), is what is lacking in the representational name. (*ME* 47)

The ideological dimensions of this performative name become clearer when we talk not of elephants but of Jews, Communists, homosexuals, Republicans. The statement "This is a Jew" confers an identity onto the individual so named through the addition of the mere marker "Jew," the "little piece of the real" that comes to function as the individual's hidden ground. The unifying feature of the thing is simply the name we add to it, thereby retroactively constituting it *as this thing*. The name brings the thing into being by adding the surplus element that is more thinglike than the thing itself, "in you more than you," the *this* that constitutes the thing as such. In the *Science of Logic*, Hegel writes:

> The individual, which in the sphere of reflection exists as a *this*, does not have the exclusive relation to another one which belongs to qualitative being-for-self. *This*, as the one reflected into itself, is for itself and without repulsion, or repulsion in this reflection is one with abstraction and is the reflecting *mediation* which attaches to the this in such wise that the this is a *posited* immediacy *pointed out* by someone external to it. The *this is*; it is *immediate*; but it is only this insofar as it is pointed out. The "pointing out" is the reflecting movement which collects itself inwardly and posits immediacy, but as a self-external immediacy. Now the individual is certainly a this, as the immediate restored out of mediation; but it does not have the mediation outside it—it is itself a repelling separation, *posited abstraction*, yet in its very act of separating, it is a positive relation. (*SL* 622)

It is at this point of the self-externalization and repelling separation that I turn to the question of the proposition as judgment.

THE INFINITE JUDGMENT

In *The Sublime Object of Ideology*, Žižek writes: "Herein lies the 'last secret' of dialectical speculation: not in the dialectical mediation-sublimation of all contingent content, empirical reality, not in the deduction of all reality from the mediating movement of absolute negativity, but in the fact that this very nega-tivity, to attain its 'being-for-itself,' must embody itself again in some miserable, radically contingent corporeal leftover" (*soi* 207). He makes this claim in his discussion of the speculative proposition from Hegel's *Phenomenology* that "the Spirit is a bone"; and like Rose, Žižek emphasizes the way such a proposition "provokes in us a sentiment of radical, unbearable contradiction; it offers an image of grotesque discord, of an extremely negative relationship" (207). It is precisely this discord, this failure at the level of the understanding, that pro-duces the speculative truth of the proposition.[9] In the terms I have been de-veloping above, the speculative proposition passes beyond the level of represen-tation or Vorstellung and occupies instead a level of *presence*. We should thus take the English word "presentation" quite literally: presentation is the placing of an object that, merely because of its inert presence, fills out the void of the failed representation of the first reading of the speculative proposition. In Žižek's words, this object "embodies, literally 'gives body' to, the ultimate failure of the signifying representation of the subject," for the subject is "*noth-ing but* the impossibility of its own signifying representation" (208). The spec-ulative proposition presents a leftover that escapes the circuit of representation and thereby enacts the negative movement, the impossibility, that is the subject.

Propositions such as "The spirit is a bone," Žižek contends, are examples of what Hegel refers to as infinite judgments. In the third book of the *Science of Logic*, Hegel notes that the judgment "is the *determinateness* of the Notion *posited* in the Notion itself" (*sl* 623). As we have seen, for Hegel we can know the Absolute only through its determinations, not through some Schellingian abstract indeterminacy: "The judgment can therefore be called the proximate *realization* [*Realizierung*] of the Notion, inasmuch as reality [*Realität*] denotes in general entry into *existence* [Dasein] as a *determinate being*" (ibid.). It is only through the judgment that the subject and predicate of the proposition, being indeterminate in themselves, become determined. Prior to their determination through the judgment, subject and predicate are no more than mere names linked to one another through the copula; the copula itself, however, sublates this mere externality of subject and predicate by indicating that, according to Hegel, "the predicate belongs to the *being* of the subject and is not merely externally combined with it" (626). Such externality is valid in a merely gram-matical relationship, but grammar does not immediately equal judgment, which requires that the relationship between the subject and predicate be that of a universal to a particular or individual. The external connection of the indeterminate subject and predicate is merely a determination of Vorstellung. The judgment, on the other hand, posits a determination of the Notion: "The news that my friend N. has died," Hegel writes, "is a proposition; and it would be a judgment only if there were a question whether he was really dead or only in a state of catalepsy" (626).

The judgment (*Urteil*) is an originary division (*Ur-Teilung*), the self-diremption [Entzweiung] of the Notion as it passes from the inert unity of the Vorstellung through the judgment as proposition (in which subject and predicate are at one and the same time held as separate and united) to the syllogism (*der Schluß*), "the restoration of the *Notion* in the *judgment*," as Hegel states (664). The judgment stages the self-imposed drama of the split identity of the Notion: in the passages through judgment, one begins with the split between the subject and predicate and ends up with the split between the Notion and itself. Table 1 provides a summary of Hegel's analysis of this dialectical transformation of the relationship between the subject and predicate in the judgment:

Table 1. Outline of Hegel's Theory of Judgment

TYPE	EXAMPLE	SUBJECT-PREDICATE RELATIONSHIP
Judgment		The judgment originally divides the Notion (N) into S and P.
I. Existence		
a. positive	The rose is red (U).	The determinatedness of an individual is externalized; the P is some abstract, universal property acquired by the S.
b. negative	The rose is not red (P).	The determinatedness of the P that was initially posited as an abstract universal is now specified as something particular.
c. infinite		

TYPE	EXAMPLE	SUBJECT-PREDICATE RELATIONSHIP
i. negative	The rose is not an elephant (I).	Negates not only some (particular) P but the universal domain itself that was present in the negation of the particular P.
ii. positive	The rose is a rose.	Tautology: because S and P are completely external, no P can adequately determine the S but the S itself.
iii. affirmative	The rose is an elephant.	Absolute contradiction: the S is none other than the nonidentity-with-itself of the P.
II. Reflection		J of R transposes the center of gravity from S to P as substantial moment.
a. singular	This man is mortal (I).	
b. particular	Many men are mortal (P).	
c. universal	All men are mortal (U).	
III. Necessity		J of Necessity: mere formal shift from "all" to "universality," the necessary determination of the Notion as such (immanent self-determination of X as such).
a. categorical	Woman is human.	The categorical relationship between S and P is posited as the relationship between a species and its genus. (Problem: more than one species per genus.)
b. hypothetical	Where there are women, there are also men.	Posits a particular content (species) of the genus in its necessary relationship with another species.
c. disjunctive	A human is either a man or woman.	Particular content is explicitly posited as self-articulation (specification) of universal N.

TYPE	EXAMPLE	SUBJECT-PREDICATE RELATIONSHIP
IV. Notion		The content of the P in the J of N is the very relationship of S to its N. (Truth = the adequacy of the object to its own N)
a. assertoric	This house is good.	Problem: not every house is good; contingent circumstances.
b. problematic	Whether a house is good or not depends on what kind of house it is.	Problematizes precisely these contingent circumstances.
c. apodictic	Such and such a construction of a house is good.	Displays in positive form conditions of "truth" of the S.
V. Syllogism	Such and such a construction of a house is good.	
	This house is built in such a way.	
	This house is good.	

This table of judgments must be kept in mind when one reads Žižek's claim that it is only the affirmative form of the infinite judgment ("The spirit is a bone") that "fully expresses the speculative 'lack of identity' by means of affirming the impossible identity of two mutually exclusive moments" (FTK 119). It may be true that such propositions "embody" the speculative lack of identity in some "contingent, corporeal leftover," but a few questions should arise at this point: If only the infinite judgment provides the full expression of dialectical identity as the lack, as the split subject, as the immanent bifurcation of the Notion itself, then why does Hegel go on to identify nine other propositional forms of the judgment before passing on to the syllogism? Why not end with the third form, the infinite judgment? Doesn't this form become sublated as the dialectic of the *Science of Logic* continues? And furthermore, how can we accept this claim for the infinite judgment when Hegel himself writes that, in their utter nonsense and absurdity, these judgments "are *not judgments at all*" (SL 642)?

To take the last question first, for Hegel the judgment expresses a relationship between subject and predicate. Judgment is a process the Notion must pass through in order to be actualized; the Notion splits up into subject and predicate, and through the dialectical process of the twelve forms of judgment achieves greater and greater self-determination until, in the judgment of the Notion, the Notion takes itself as its own determinate content. In the infinite judgment, not only is the particular sphere of the predicate negated by the form of the judgment itself but so is its universal sphere. In the negative infinite judgment, such as "The rose is not an elephant," the possibility of the identity of subject and predicate, individual and universal, is denied by the simple "not." In the positive infinite judgment, "The rose is a rose," the subject finds as its predicate not some determinate content but itself as the mere repetition of the empty name and thus the undoing of the relationship of identity that the propositional form itself asserts. Finally, in what Žižek refers to as the affirmative form of the infinite judgment, "The rose is an elephant," there is the enactment of the impossibility of identity between subject and predicate. Since the purpose of the judgment is to express the degree of identity between subject and predicate, and since the infinite judgment negates such an identity, the infinite judgment cannot properly be called a judgment: this is Hegel's point when he makes this claim above.

So what is the role of this judgment that is not a judgment? How can it be said to be the ultimate expression of speculative identity? It should come as no surprise that this impossibility that is embodied by the speculative proposition or the infinite judgment is for Hegel an enabling one; the impossibility of this particular judgment sets in motion the reflection on the form of the judgment itself and ends with the impossibility of the judgment *as such* as it passes on to the syllogism. The infinite judgment is necessary in order to bring about the speculative reversal that distinguishes speculation as such from the propositions of the understanding. Žižek writes that "it is not enough to say that there is a 'lack of identity' between Substance and Subject—if we do only that, we still presuppose Substance and Subject as two (positive, identical) entities between which there is no identity; the point is rather that *one of the two moments (Subject) is none other than the non-identity-with-itself of the other moment (Substance)*. 'The spirit is a bone' *means that* bone itself can never achieve complete identity with itself, and 'Spirit' is none other than that 'force of negativity' which prevents bone from fully 'becoming itself' " (FTK 119). As such, the speculative proposition is the *presentation* of this impossible identity in which the relationship between subject and predicate is nothing but the staging of the negative self-relationship of the Notion *as negativity itself*.

GOD IS A PROPOSITION

To return yet again to the passage from the *Phenomenology* quoted earlier in this chapter: "The need to represent [vorzustellen] the Absolute as *Subject* has found expression in the propositions: God is the eternal, the moral world-order, love, and so on." Hegel significantly identifies Vorstellung here as a need [*Das Bedürfnis*]; in fact, he goes so far in his preface to the second edition of the *Logic* to say that "there is no human desiring or willing without Vorstellung" (*SL* 33). We are no longer dealing simply with a nonreflective psychological activity that can be discarded as we progress intellectually but with *a need for figuration as such*. When dealing with the Absolute as Subject, we require and desire a Vorstellung, an imaginative identification of the two. And this need takes the form of or finds expression in the proposition. The proposition, as we have seen, operates at the level of Vorstellung, which adds an interesting twist to the development of the image into the word in the *Encyclopedia*. This serves as a reminder that language is not the simple progression out of Vorstellung; in fact, Hegel places the development of the sign within the larger development of Vorstellung, which means that the image and sign operate along a very similar economy of intelligence. And if Sätze, which can be translated both as "propositions" and "sentences," operate as a species of Vorstellung, this means that the difficulty of the image is not just the merely external substitutive (or vertical) relationship of image to imaged but also the contiguous (or horizontal) one of sign to sign, as Hegel points out in the *Encyclopedia*: "In this way several isolated simple predicates are strung together: but in spite of the link supplied by their subject, the predicates never get beyond mere contiguity. In this point Vorstellung coincides with Understanding: the only distinction being that the latter introduces relations of universal and particular, of cause and effect, etc., and in this way supplies the necessary connection to the isolated ideas of Vorstellung, connected only by a bare 'and' " (*E* vol. I, §20, 30–31). The sentence reproduces the problems inherent in the image (the illusion of immediacy in the relationship between the subject and predicate) while at the same time forcing the bifurcation of that immediacy. Even though the sentence might posit the immediate relationship between God and the Absolute—"God is the Absolute"—the form of the sentence itself makes any such immediacy impossible. The proposition posits immediacy, but the sentence *is* mediation; it sets itself in motion by formally negating the identity posited by its own terms.

"In such propositions," Hegel continues in the *Phenomenology* passage, "the True is only posited [gezetzt] *immediately* as Subject, but is not presented [dargestellt] as the movement of reflecting itself into itself." As we have seen, for Hegel the subject is nothing but the negativity of this reflexive movement, so a mode of presentation true to the True must exhibit this negation in its own form, must make the sentence itself the negative self-movement of the Subject that God is supposed to be. But in "a proposition of this kind one begins with the word 'God.' This by itself is a senseless sound, a mere name; it is only the predicate that says *what God is*, gives Him content and meaning. Only in the end of the proposition does the empty beginning become actual knowledge." The predicate ends up taking on the responsibility of presenting the subjectivity of God as Absolute, while the subject remains a null and inert nothing. "This being so, it is not clear why one does not speak merely of the eternal, of the moral world-order, and so on, or, as the ancients did, of pure notions like 'being,' 'the One,' and so on, in short, of that which gives the meaning without adding the *senseless* sound as well."

It should be noted that what we have here is the presentation, through the failure of the proposition itself, of the word as the null, empty embodiment of the Subject as such. A word such as "being" or "the One" cannot present the subjectivity implied in its name precisely because subjectivity is nothing but the place of this failure of the word in its immediacy to present the negativity of the Subject. The attempt to picture [vorzustellen] God as immediate is denied by the Darstellung of the proposition. Only the single word—which does not enter into the mediating movement of the sentence—can display this immediacy, but this immediacy is meaningless precisely because it is not yet mediated; if the word is meaningful—such as the words "Absolute," "Being," and so forth—that is only because it is the result of prior propositional chains—in short, because it is the result of prior determinations. Hegel goes on to say that "it is just this [type of] word that indicates that what is posited is not a being, or essence, or a universal in general, but rather something that is reflected into itself, a Subject. But at the same time this is only anticipated." The proposition can only gesture toward the self-reflective movement that defines the Subject; on a first reading, its Subject-Copula-Predicate structure does not move as the Subject but an inner negation nevertheless sets the proposition in motion out of itself. In other words, in the proposition "God is the Absolute," one finds the declaration of identity between the subject of the sentence (God) and its predicate (the Absolute). The subject is an abstract and general immediacy; the predicate's job is to qualify this abstract universal, to determine it, to assign it determining and defining qualities that are supposedly identical to it. But this work of the proposition as such undermines this particular proposition by determining and mediating that which is supposed to be indeterminate and immediate. If one wants, along with Fichte and Schelling, to conceive of God as that which is beyond mediation, one is confronted with the contradiction of this claim set to work by the propositional form itself. God is the Absolute, Hegel also claims, but not by remaining static and immediate, and therefore before or beyond conceptualization; God only becomes Absolute through the work of the negative set in motion by the proposition. The proposition—an attempt to picture or figure the Absolute in a single Vorstellung—by its own failure to do so embodies the Subject as a contingent Thing and sets in motion the chain of further determinations and propositions necessary to carry out the absolute impossibility of this equation of identity. In terms of the Understanding, Hegel argues, the

> Subject is assumed as a fixed point to which, as their support, the predicates are affixed by a movement belonging to the knower of this Subject, and which is not regarded as belonging to the fixed point itself; yet it is only through this movement that the content [Inhalt] could be presented [darge-stellt] as Subject. The way in which this movement has been brought about is such that it cannot belong to the fixed point; yet, after this point has been presupposed [Voraussetzung], the nature of the movement cannot really be other than what it is, it can only be external. Hence, the mere anticipation that the Absolute is Subject is not only *not* the actuality of this Notion, but it even makes the actuality impossible; for the anticipation posits the subject as an inert point, whereas the actuality is self-movement.

In terms of the Understanding there are thus two Subjects: the Subject who posits and predicates (the knower as the source of this predicative movement), and the fixed and motionless Subject thereby posited as the supposed ground of these predicates. The two are separate, external, alien, depending on the predicates to fulfill the empty fixed point; but this movement of positing between the two Subjects is the true locus of the Subject (at once positing and posited, the movement of reflection into self). The actuality of the Notion—its self-movement and self-positing—depends on the proposition whose two halves exhibit [*darstellen*] the identity in difference of the subject and predicate as a self-predication that is not merely presupposed but consciously and willfully enacted. With this demand, Hegel passes from the mere proposition (in the form of picture thinking, Vorstellung) to the exhibition of the system as a whole. Such articulation, in other words, must project the necessity of the movement of the whole *Phenomenology of Spirit*, and beyond that, the *Logic* and the *Encyclopedia*, which can only be carried out and represented [dargestellt] by speculative philosophy. "The difference between Vorstellung and Thought [Gedanken] is of special importance: because philosophy may be said to do nothing but transform Vorstellungen into thoughts—though it works the further transformation of a mere thought into a Notion" (*E* vol. I, §20; 30–31). Only through the drama of this speculative Darstellung can the process of Vorstellung be staged as the self-dissolution and self-negating of the static externality of the empty name of God in its transformation into the movement of the system of Geist.

"THE ACTUAL IS THE RATIONAL" REVISITED

So in the context of all that has been argued to this point, I can now return to my initial question: Is Rose right? Is Hegel's statement about the rational and the actual true to the movement of the *Philosophy of Right*? Rose's claim, basically, can be put in Žižekian terms as follows: When Hegel writes in his study of the state that the actual is the rational, he wants this statement to be read speculatively, as a speculative proposition, or more specifically, as what Žižek has called an affirmative infinite judgment. But does such a "speculative" reading of this statement make sense in the context of the preface to Hegel's book on political science? Again, if Hegel wanted to assert that the modern state is in its current form neither actual nor rational, why didn't he just say so? As I hope will be clear by now, just saying so, presenting the truth in the simple form of the proposition, is hardly adequate for the presentation of speculative truth. The truth about the state, Hegel claims, needs to be *comprehended, begreifen,* thought in terms of its Begriff or Notion. In other words, truth must be understood speculatively, comprehended "so that the content which is already rational in itself may also gain a rational form and thereby appear justified to free thinking" (*PR* 10).

As in the preface to the *Phenomenology*, Hegel is concerned in the preface to the *Philosophy of Right* with modes of presentation. The statements that in terms of the Understanding posit a merely external relationship between the subject and predicate must be broken up from within through the work of judgment. As Žižek contends, the affirmative infinite judgment is the absolute form of this presentation of internal contradiction in its staging of the incommensurability of the subject and predicate: "It is only this judgment that fully expresses the speculative 'lack of identity' by means of affirming the impossible identity of two mutually exclusive moments: this judgment is—if we read it immediately—experienced as patently absurd, the discrepancy between the moments is absolute; however, the 'Spirit' as power of absolute negativity is none other than this absolute discrepancy" (FTK 119). So how are we to take Hegel's claim concerning the actual and the rational?

Hegel's main point in the preface to the *Philosophy of Right* is that philosophy must rise above the state it has fallen into, or at the least, reveal how it already rises above the charges imputed against it—that it presents the truth in abstract, arbitrary, relativistic, and essentially counterproductive or contradictory ways. Hegel's own problem with typical philosophical presentation is that it either depends too much on the abstract, external relationships posited by the Understanding (that is, failing to reveal the *notional* connection between content and presentation) or it depends on mere "enthusiasm" and impressionistic intuitivism at the expense of thought itself (making it a quite *anti*philosophical approach). A properly speculative, scientific approach to philosophical presentation will be true in its mode of presentation to the matter at hand, even if—or perhaps even especially when—that mode proves confusing to the unsuspecting reader. Since the philosophical question of right concerns right's relationship to its own Notion, then the question of actuality is the supreme issue to have settled.

Thus, we must take seriously the problems that arise when readers of Hegel (in this case, the editor of a recent translation of the *Philosophy of Right*) make claims such as the following:

> Hegelian ethics is founded on *freedom*. Hegel regards the state as the "actuality of the ethical idea" (PR §257) only because the state is "the actuality of concrete freedom" (PR §260). Hegel often makes his meaning obscure, but these statements are uncharacteristically lucid; their meaning is quite plain. Nevertheless, we tend to react to them either with puzzlement or outrage. His association of the state with freedom sounds absurd to us because we simply cannot get it through our heads that anyone could hold the view they express. We can interpret it only as an obscure philosopher's paradox, or else

as some sort of preposterous Orwellian lie devised by a demented totalitarian who seeks to subvert our common sense.[10]

According to a speculative reading, however, this puzzlement and outrage against common sense are precisely the point. Let me take an example from the *Philosophy of Right*: Hegel starts out with the assertion that the question of right is ultimately one of *will*; it will only be actualized when it recognizes itself as its own source of determination, when will becomes true to its Notion as pure self-willing. But since the particular wills of isolated persons come into conflict with one another, the state is necessary as the ultimate expression of *the will of a people* in which the particular person's will is recognized and, to the extent that it is consistent with the rational whole, actualized, brought to its full potential. The freedom of each person is dependent on the freedom of the whole. Yet in order for this state to be fully actualized in its rationality, its will must be represented in the figure of the monarch, for it is only through this embodiment of will that each individual achieves a distance from the substance of the state and becomes a subject: "subjectivity attains its truth only as a *subject*, and personality only as a *person*, and in a constitution which has progressed to real [*reellen*] rationality, each of the three distinctive moments of the concept has its distinctive shape which is *actual for itself*. This absolutely decisive moment of the whole, therefore, is not individuality in general, but one individual, the *monarch*" (PR §279; 317), the point of the "I will" of the fully rational state.

Is this not some Orwellian joke? Hegel recognizes this effect and admits that the "concept of the monarch is therefore extremely difficult for rationation—i.e., the reflective approach of the understanding—to grasp, because its rationation stops short at isolated determinations, and consequently knows only grounds, finite viewpoints, and deduction from such grounds" (ibid., 318). The understanding presents the right of the monarch as derivative rather than "entirely self-originating"—originating, that is, from the self of the state, the Spirit [Geist] of the people as it is articulated through the rational whole of the modern state with its division of powers. Hence, the affirmative infinite judgment "The actual is the rational" achieves its greatest concrete expression in the *Philosophy of Right* in the form of another such infinite judgment, "The state is the monarch." Any prior articulation of the whole through the figure of the monarch, such as through the Vorstellung of divine right, remains approximate but not yet actualized.

It should be noted, moreover, that the arrival at the infinite judgment of state equals monarch comes only after the Notion of will has played itself out and achieved its form of *apodeictic judgment*, the highest form of the judgment of the Notion. As we recall from the previous discussion, apodeictic judgment is precisely a judgment of actualization. To what extent is a given example true to its Notion? Is a given state true to the rational Notion of the state as such? Recognizing that actualization and the full articulation of rationality are subject to contingency—a given thing may arrive at its truth only by way of a constant unfolding of non-as-yet-true moments—Hegel explains that any particular state will fall short of such "truth": "In this judgment the Notion is laid down as the basis, and since it is in relation to the object, it is an ought-to-be to which the reality may or may not be adequate" (SL 657). The question of right concerns the questions of freedom and will, of free will: "The state is the actuality of the substantial *will*, an actuality which it possesses in the particular *self-consciousness* when this has been raised to its universality; as such it is the *rational* in and for itself. . . . The state in and for itself is the ethical whole, the actualization of freedom, and it is the absolute end of reason that freedom should be actual" (PR §258, Addition, 279). Yet Hegel cautions that in "considering the Idea of the state, we must not have any particular states or particular institutions in mind; instead, we should consider the Idea, this actual God, for itself. . . . The state is not a work of art; it exists in the world, and hence in the sphere of arbitrariness, contingency, and error, and bad behavior may disfigure it in man respects. But the ugliest man, the criminal, the invalid, or the cripple is still a living human being; the affirmative aspect—life—survives in spite of such deficiencies, and it is with this affirmative aspect that we are here concerned" (258). The "ugliest" state does not negate the Notion of the state as such but simply emphasizes the relationship of contingency to actualization.

So how exactly is the actual rational? One point I have omitted thus far in my discussion is that Hegel's proposition is twofold, that he also stresses that the rational is actual. If we are to avoid the indeterminate and therefore utterly null positing reflection of the Fichtean I = I, as well as the null and empty Ought, then we must ground our determination of rationality in actuality. Reason is as reason does. That is, any discussion of the actuality of reason and vice versa must ground itself in the present: "To recognize reason as the rose in the cross of the present and thereby to delight in the present—this rational insight is the *reconciliation* with actuality that philosophy grants those who have received the inner call *to comprehend*, to preserve their subjective freedom in the realm of the substantial, and at the same time to stand with their subjective freedom not in a particular and contingent situation, but in what has being in and for itself" (PR 22).[11] The particular is the Prussian state, but the Idea of freedom as contingent on the (always imperfectly realized) constitutional embodiment of the rational will is here, now, before as the critique of the present made possible by the present's own immanent negation. It is foolish and useless to try to transcend one's time and imagine (in light of Vorstellung) that one can build a world "as it ought to be" (PR 22) without taking into account that any present ought is made possible by the present actuality. Our "delight in the present" is far from mere acceptance of the status quo, but rather the setting into motion— through the speculative act that retroactively grounds itself in the historical conditions of its own possibility—of the negativity proper to the present, as the *Philosophy of Right* itself attempts to do despite Hegel's recognition that no particular state has ever lived up to such a model. This does not keep us from *thinking the state as such.*

The speculative proposition is no mere wordplay; it is to be taken literally in all its contradiction and seeming idiocy as the embodiment of the idiocy at the heart of actual rationality—as in the idiocy of the king's stupid body that represents [*vertreten* rather than vorstellen] the subject as such—the power of absolute negativity, the hole in the social-symbolic fabric—at the center of the rational whole. Speculative language is not some foreign word from above that captures in itself the import it means to convey, for as we have seen, Hegel's theory of language denies any such immediacy. The sign must be emptied out, become some stupid, contingent, and meaningless thing devoid of any associations with a particular image or intuition (Vorstellung), and through the radical negativity of its stupidity embody the point of articulation of the subject. Speculative language is ordinary language, only more so: "Our 'ordinary' language is more than sufficient" to provide us with an adequate presentation of the drama of the speculative—"all we have to do is, so to speak, to take it more literally than it takes itself; to become aware of how even the most crude judgments succeed *by means of their very failure*" (FTK 139 n. 19).

As Rose argues in the concluding chapter of her *Hegel Contra Sociology,* Hegel's speculative propositions present through their very failure the inadequacy at the heart of contemporary actuality. In a society determined by bourgeois law and property relations, we cannot escape the dichotomies inherent to rationation, the mode of thought of the Understanding; the best we can do in our own presentation, without seeking to transcend the "cross in the rose of the present," is to stage this schism between universal and particular, Notion and

Intuition, Begriff and Vorstellung. If the culture of art relies too heavily on the image or intuition, and the culture of religion relies too heavily on the abstract Notion, the culture of philosophy that Hegel announces can only stage the negative unity of the two through the negativity of the speculative proposition: "The law which is both universal and individual has never existed. Thus it can only be thought in the *Logic*" (HCS 206), lying as it does outside the purview of the *Philosophy of Right*, which simply attempts to provide a phenomenology of Right rather than issue "*instructions on how the world ought to be*" (PR 23).

The mealy-mouthed babblers of German vulgar economy fell foul of the style of my book.—Karl Marx, on the reception of *Capital*

Althusser's ultimate claim in *Reading Capital* is that the whole question of Marx's theoretical "break" with Hegelian dialectics "can be entirely summed up in the concept of 'Darstellung,' the key epistemological concept of the whole Marxist theory of value, the concept whose object is precisely to designate the mode of presence of the structure in its effects, and therefore to designate structural causality itself" (RC 188). This means that Marx's decisive break concerns a question of the relationship between presentation and knowledge. It is a question of a concept capable of designating structural causality "itself." But the problem for Althusser is that this concept of structural causality remains unspoken, unwritten, in the Marxist text. Althusser's job, then, is to argue for the preeminence of a concept that Marx himself never seems to have articulated, and yet this concept is indispensable for the understanding of Marx's dialectical method itself. Indeed, as Althusser acknowledges, Marx himself never seemed to know that he had produced such a concept, but through a "symptomatic reading" of Marx's texts and through a painstaking analysis of Marx's own practice we can produce the concept that is the answer to a question Marx had never asked: How is it possible to define the concept of a structural causality?

What is at stake, ultimately, is our ability to define the relationship between economic phenomena and the whole of the capitalist structure. What is at stake is our ability to operate as *Marxists*, to carry out the type of economic analysis appropriate to Marxist science, whose object differs from that of bourgeois political economy. If we are to analyze economic or social or ideological phenomena in terms of the mode of production within which they operate, then we must construct a concept capable of conveying the type of causality at work in the whole. The representations or Vorstellungen at work in earlier attempts to convey the concept of causality have proven inadequate to the task of Marxist presentation or Darstellung.

As with Kant and Hegel, what one finds in Althusser is a treatise on the distinction between Vorstellung and Darstellung. Marxist science, in fact, depends on the strict opposition of these terms. And yet the two remain confused to a certain degree even in Marx's work itself. The task facing readers of Marx, Althusser implies, is to purify the Marxist text of its prescientific metaphors, its figures, its Vorstellungen, its dependence on representation. The key is to produce a Marxist language that no longer depends on the vehicle of representation but goes directly to the production of the concept—a concept freed of its ties to the extraneous material of the figure, the stand-in, the proxy term that inevitably distances us from the presentness of the presentation. The problem with Marx, Althusser tells us, is that he continued to flirt with Hegelian terminology, with figures from an ideological problematic, when his job should have been to purge himself of his Hegelian parentage, to rid himself of the messy stuff of the afterbirth, to have emerged full-blown from the head of Jupiter *not* trailing clouds of Hegelian glory. But Marx did not do this. And this leads to a dramatic problem: "I call it a *dramatic* theoretical problem because although Marx *'produced' this problem he did not pose it as a problem*, but set out to solve it practically in the absence of its concept, with extraordinary ingenuity, but without completely avoiding a relapse into earlier schemata which were necessarily inadequate to pose and solve this problem" (RC 187).

To put this in Kantian terms, what bothers Althusser is the necessity of Versinnlichung. For Kant, we will remember, no representation, no Vorstellung, can ever be adequate for the presentation or Darstellung of the concept. And yet conversely, no concept can ever be presented without the fleshing out made possible by the representation, without the move toward sensibility (Versinnlichung) that the representation accomplishes. There will always be a gap, a chasm, separating the concept from its representation—but the gap is better

than nothing: the space of inadequacy separating the concept from its representation is nevertheless the only space of possibility available. No thought can
occur without this sublime expanse of impossibility. Figuration is at once our
curse and our blessing. But Althusser wishes for a grasping of the concept that
has outgrown and shed its representational cocoon:

> We have seen Marx *practicing* this concept in the use he makes of the "*Dar-
> stellung*," and trying to pinpoint it in the images of changes in the illumina-
> tion or in the specific weight of objects by the ether in which they are
> immersed, and it is expressed in a novel but extremely precise language: a
> language of metaphors which are nevertheless already *almost perfect con-
> cepts*, and which are perhaps only incomplete insofar as they have not yet
> been *grasped*, i.e., retained and elaborated as concepts. This is the case each
> time Marx presents the capitalist system as a mechanism, a machinery, a
> machine, a construction . . . ; or as the complexity of a "social metabolism."
> (RC 192)

"Each time Marx *presents* the capitalist system as . . . ": the goal of *Capital* is
just such a presentation or scientific Darstellung of the capitalist system, yet
because of his own historical limitations, because of the retroactive nature of
scientific development (remember Hegel's owl of Minerva), Marx is not able to
find the mode of presentation adequate to its goal.

What should be noted is that there are three different, though related senses
of Darstellung operating here at once:

— the Kantian sense of Versinnlichung, with its emphasis on the fleshing out of
   the concept, and that is a transcendental function occurring more or less
   unconsciously and automatically;

— the Hegelian sense of scientific method, the mode of exposition adequate to
   the nature of the dialectic, and that must be thoroughly conscious of its
   concept in order to be successful; and

— a sense that I have yet to explore and that Althusser points to above, the
   Marxist sense of the presentation of value in commodity production that, as
   we shall see, has a relationship to but cannot be reduced to consciousness,
   which must rather be seen as an objective, historical, *structural* effect.

Althusser's call for the grasping (begreifen) of the concept (Begriff) beyond
the language of metaphors involves all three of these senses of Darstellung.

STRUCTURAL CAUSALITY

As we have seen above, the importance of Darstellung for Althusser lies in its prefigurative relationship to the concept of structural causality. The turn to Darstellung is Marx's "least metaphorical" way of attempting to flesh out the concept he could not yet speak or write but that he nevertheless produced in his practice. But before exploring the relationship between Darstellung and structural causality, I need to outline in detail what Althusser means by "structural causality."[1]

The question of structural causality is first of all, of course, one of causality: What is the relationship between the whole and the elements that make up the whole? Nothing could be more fundamental for Marxism than this question of totality and determination. The problem, however, lies in the way we conceptualize that relationship. As is well known, Althusser sees in *Capital* an effort to think through to a new conception of causality that can do justice to its object of study: the relationship between the commodity form and the rest of the social formation as manifested in the capitalist mode of production. A social formation based on the production of commodities will be determined throughout, to a greater or lesser degree, by the commodity form. But how do we think this determination? What metaphors best present the nature of the causal relations in question? The two predominant models of causality prior to Marx's, Althusser suggests, were transitive causality and expressive causality.

The concept of transitive causality is based on the model of Cartesian space, according to which linear and mechanical relations dominate. This is the so-called billiard ball model: one element affects another when it comes into contact with the latter, each element otherwise existing as independent and discrete items. It is in terms of this model that the classical "vulgar Marxist" version of the base-superstructure relationship operates: change the base, and the elements of the superstructure follow suit "more or less rapidly," like bowling pins on impact with the bowling ball. The key problem with this metaphor, according to Althusser, is that "it could not be made to think the effectivity of a whole on its elements, except at the cost of extraordinary distortions" (RC 186). And since it is precisely this effectivity of the whole that concerns Marx in *Capital*, the transitive metaphor, while useful under some circumstances, was inadequate for Marxist science.[2] The problem is the externality of the terms in their relationship to one another—that is, the inadequacy of this relationship for a dialectical analysis of the social whole.

Expressive causality, on the other hand, is capable of thinking the effectivity of the whole on each of its elements, "but on the absolute condition that the whole [is] not a structure" (RC 187). The relationship between terms now appears to be immanent rather than external, although the elements that make up the whole now operate as the expression of its inner essence.[3] If the commodity form is seen as the essence of the capitalist mode of production (and Marx himself at times refers to it as such), then the "superstructural" elements will be seen as expressing this same relationship, of carrying this commodity relation within itself as the universal hidden essence of its own form. Various historical forms of religion, for example, will be seen as the expression of the particular dominant form of the relations of production, with the hierarchical organization of the Roman Catholic Church, for example, functioning as the expression of feudal class relations. But such a conception of expressive causality, which Althusser attributes to Hegel, is incapable of thinking the concepts of overdetermination and relative autonomy that lie at the heart of the concept of structural causality.

One of Althusser's more interesting moves is to discuss expressive causality in terms of "empiricism." For Althusser, the empiricist problematic—its structure of questions and assumptions that frames its approach to problem solving, which defines the limits and functions of the terms within which it operates—includes not only the traditional empiricists but Kant and Hegel as well. What they have in common is the "empiricist conception of knowledge," which sees knowledge as a process taking place between a given object and a given subject: subject and object exist as external, independent, and preexisting entities. Knowledge is obtained when the subject conducts a process of abstraction, "an extraction of the essence from the real which contains it, a separation of the essence from the real which contains it and keeps it in hiding" (RC 36). This model privileges the images of inside/outside, kernel/husk, invisible essence/visible phenomenon, veil/transparency—all of which attempt to convey the distinction between the essential and inessential. The real is conceived of as being structured "as a dross of earth containing inside it a grain of pure gold," containing within itself "two distinct real parts, the essence and the inessential." The whole function of knowledge is to separate the essential from the inessential, as in Michelangelo's "aesthetic of artistic production based not on the production of the essential form out of the marble material, but on the *destruction* of the non-form which enveloped the form to be *disengaged* even before the first chip is cut" (RC 37 n. 16).

From this empiricist conception of knowledge comes a particular conception of reading, what Althusser refers to as the "religious myth of reading" that seeks the immediate reading of essence in existence according to the ancient religious fantasies of "epiphany and parousia, and the fascinating myth of the Scriptures, in which the body of truth, dressed in its words, is the Book: the Bible" (RC 16). The conception of expressive causality involves this religious myth of reading, for if causality actually functions according to the expression of an essential core of truth in the phenomenal elements of the totality, then our job is to uncover that essence, to extract it from the dross of its various express forms. As Althusser would have it, Hegel presented us with exactly this sort of approach to truth, reading, and method, and the measure of the distance between Marx and Hegel is the distance Marx has traveled from this religious myth of expressive causality. But what do we do, then, with all of those passages in Marx where he seems to be referring to precisely this particular model of essence and appearance? This is exactly the issue at stake in Althusser's attempt to read in the absences of Marx's own texts the signs of the concept of structural causality. For Marx himself was once a prisoner of the religious myth:

> The Young Marx of the *1844 Manuscripts* read the human essence at sight, immediately, in the transparency of its alienation. *Capital*, on the contrary, exactly measures a distance and an internal dislocation (*décalage*) in the real, inscribed in its structure, a distance and a dislocation such as to make their own effects themselves illegible, and the illusion of an immediate reading the ultimate apex of their effects: *fetishism*. (RC 17)

The distance we have to travel, then, in order to read Marx's rupture with expressive causality and his production of the conception of structural causality is the distance between alienation and fetishism. And the key is the concept of Darstellung.

Now to Althusser's characterization of structural causality. As we can see in the reference to the religious myth of reading, this question of causality is essentially an epistemological problem. Althusser poses this problem as follows:

> By means of what concept is it possible to think the new type of determination which has just been identified as the determination of the phenomena of a given region by the structure of that region? More generally, by means of what concept, or what set of concepts, is it possible to think the determination of the

elements of a structure, and the structural relations between those elements,
and all the effects of those relations, by the effectivity of the structure? And a
fortiori, *by means of what concept or what set of concepts is it possible to think*
the determination of a subordinate structure by a dominant structure; In other
words, how is it possible to define the concept of a structural causality? (RC 186)

Structural causality refers to the effectivity of the structure. What this means
is that effectivity cannot be seen as the transitive relationship between discrete
and unrelated objects nor as the expressive relationship between the essence of
the structure and its elements, precisely because a structure is a whole (not an
aggregate of discrete elements) and a structure (a differential rather than a
spiritual whole). Determination within the structure takes place as a result of
the structure itself as an objective structure of relationships. If we remember
that we are talking here about a mode of production—that is, about a social
whole consisting of nothing but social relationships (which include the socially
produced relationships not just between people themselves but also between
people and things)—then the specificity of this problem should become clear.[4]
The question at stake here is an epistemological one concerning our ability to
read the structural determinations of the value relation—a relation that appears
in a mystified form in a society based on commodity production. The key is to
see this mystification, however, not as a problem of our ability to see, of our
consciousness, of our ideological shortcomings, of our failure to see what lies
before us and is simply hidden beneath a mystifying exterior (a problem that
would leave us at the level of the empiricist reference to the religious myth of
reading) but to see this mystification instead as a structural effect, an effect of
the very structure of commodity production itself. Fetishism is an objective
effect of the structure of the value relation in commodity production, not a
subjective illusion or shortcoming. We cannot correct this problem, then, by
learning to see what is there, before us, but hidden from our view; we must
instead learn to read the absences existing in the very fullness of our vision.
"The fact," Althusser writes, "that it only exists in its effects does not mean that
it can be grasped completely in any one of its determinate effects: for that it
would have to be *completely present* in that effect, whereas it is only present
there, as a structure, in its *determinate* absence. It is only present in the totality,
in the total movement of its effects" (RC 180–81).

Althusser emphasizes the importance of this determinate absence through
his conception of the cause behind structural causality as *an absent cause*:

> The structure is not an essence *outside* the economic phenomena which comes and alters their aspect, forms and relations and which is effective on them as an absent cause, *absent because it is outside them. The absence of the cause in the structure's "metonymic causality" on its effects is not the fault of the exteriority of the structure with respect to the economic phenomena; on the contrary, it is the very form of the interiority of the structure, as a structure, in its effects.* This implies that the effects are not outside the structure, are not a pre-existing object, element or space in which the structure arrives to *imprint its mark*: on the contrary, it implies that the structure is immanent in its effects, a cause immanent in its effects in the Spinozist sense of the term, that *the whole existence of the structure consists of its effects*, in short, that the structure, which is merely a specific combination of its peculiar elements, is nothing outside its effects. (RC 188–89)

The structure is nothing outside its effects. The question of inside/outside, we will remember, belongs to the empiricist problematic, in which the structure and its effects exist as discrete elements that, precisely because they are separable and discrete in the operation of extraction, can only enter into an external relationship to one another. Even the immanentism implied by the expressive model—the essence by definition existing in an internal relationship to its elements—is at base operating according to an external logic in the sense that essence and appearance are considered as two separate elements of the totality. As we have seen in chapter 2, Hegel is well aware of this problem, and Althusser's characterization of Hegelian dialectics in these terms cannot be upheld; in fact, Althusser's formulation of this problem follows Hegel's own in the "Doctrine of Essence" of the *Logic*.[5] But I will postpone further discussion of this confrontation for the moment. Suffice it to say at present that for Althusser, this absent cause is the antiessentialist response that he sees Marx posing to Hegel's "spiritual effectivity." What we have is the tautological recognition that the effects are determined by the structure, but that the structure itself is determined by its effects.

ALTHUSSER ON DARSTELLUNG

So what, then, is the relationship between Althusser's concept of structural causality and Marx's (pre)concept of Darstellung? What does a conception of presentation have to do with this meditation on absence? What, for that matter, does Althusser mean by Darstellung or presentation? The closest Althusser comes to defining this "key" term is to discuss it as a theatrical metaphor:

> We find a different image, a new quasi-concept, definitely freed from the empiricist antinomies of phenomenal subjectivity and essential interiority; we find an objective system governed in its most concrete determinations by the laws of its *erection* (*montage*) and *machinery*, by the specifications of its concept. Now we can recall that highly symptomatic term "*Darstellung*," compare it with this "machinery" and take it literally, as the very existence of this machinery in its effects: the mode of existence of the stage direction (*mise en scène*) of the theater which is simultaneously its own stage, its own script, its own actors, the theater whose spectators can, on occasion, be spectators only because they are first of all forced to be its actors, caught by the constraints of a script and parts whose authors they cannot be, since it is in essence *an authorless theater*. (RC 193)

For a passage that functions as one of Althusser's few significant attempts to convey the meaning of Darstellung, this certainly remains all too suggestive and dense. It can be broken down as follows:

1. Marx presents a series of images (Vorstellungen) (the capitalist system equals a mechanism, a machinery, a construction, a social metabolism) that have not yet achieved the status of a concept.

2. These particular images are freed from the empiricist obsession with visibility or phenomenality and its essentialist ground.

3 They seek to present a concept of an objective system (not a subjective illusion or misperception).

4 This objective system's "most concrete determinations" are governed by the laws of its erection and machinery; the elements of the structure, in other words, are governed by structural causality.

5 Darstellung refers precisely to this very existence of the machinery (commodity production) in its effects (it is not the machine's/commodity's material existence but its social operation that determines the production of value).

6 This machinery existence is just like the mode of existence of the stage direction of the theater, which is simultaneously its own "concrete determinations":

    a. its own stage;

    b. its own script;

    c. its own actors;

    d. its own spectators (who are forced to be its actors); and

    e. its authorless essence.

But what kind of theater is this? In offering an analogy that should help clarify the nature of this quasi-concept, Darstellung, Althusser makes use of yet another image or representation (Vorstellung), the existence of the stage direction in its effects—yet this image is just as puzzling as the quasi-concept he is seeking to flesh out.[6] Where is this "authorless" theater to which he compares the mode of presence of the structure in its effects?

Michael Sprinker has pointed out that in the 1965 edition of *Reading Capital*, Althusser expanded on this metaphor in a passage that he subsequently dropped from the 1968 edition (on which the English translation is based).[7] That passage, translated by Sprinker, reads as follows:

> "Darstellung" signifies in German, among other things, *theatrical representation*, but the figure of theatrical representation adheres immediately to the sense conveyed by the word that signifies "presentation," "exhibition," and, in its most profound root, "position of presence," presence offered and visible. In order to express its specific nuance, it may be instructive to oppose "Darstellung" to "Vorstellung." In Vorstellung, one certainly has to do with a position, but one which is kept *behind* this pre-position, something which is represented by that which is kept out front, [represented] by its emissary: the *Vorstellung. In Darstellung on the contrary, there is nothing behind*: the very thing is there, "*da*," presented [*offerte*] in the position of presence. The entire text of the play is thus there, presented [*offert*] in the presence of the representation (the Darstellung). But the presence of the entire play is not exhausted in the immediacy of the deeds or the words of the character: we "know" that it is the presence of a completed whole which lives in each moment and in each character, and in all the relations among the characters given in their personal presence. [It is] only to be grasped, however, as the presence of the whole, as the latent structure of the whole, *in the whole*, and only intuited [*pressentie*] in each element and in each role. (LC 170)

First of all, as I have done up to this point, I would stress the problem with translating both Vorstellung and Darstellung, especially in this context, as "representation." Again, while both terms are used in this sense in German, in the present context it is important to distinguish between representation and pre-sentation. Vorstellung, as we have seen and as Althusser emphasizes in this passage, operates according to the inside/outside opposition of empiricism—a position operating in a space distinct from that which is re-presented there by its proxy. As Althusser has argued above, the cause is an *absent* cause, but absent not because it stands outside the structure but because it exists nowhere but in the metonymic relationship of the elements of the structure itself. The question of representation, then, does not apply to the quasi-concept of Darstellung. The phrase "theatrical representation," then, is a misnomer here since the "script" to be "represented" or "reproduced" in the action of the drama exists nowhere outside (or in another position behind) that action itself. "*In Darstellung on the contrary, there is nothing behind*: the very thing is there, '*da*,' offered in the position of presence." Yet what is the nature of this thing? What is the nature of this position of presence? Where exactly do we locate this "there"? The thing is the absent cause; its position is in the space of failure, the space of inadequacy opened up between the actors and their roles; and the "there" is the latent structure of the whole in its effects. These actors are the concepts Marx "flirts" with in his attempt to produce the concept of structural causality; their role is this very concept to which they can never be adequate, but that they present through their very failure. It is in the space of inadequacy of the Vorstellung that the Darstellung is called into being:

> Perhaps therefore it is not impermissible to think that if Marx does "play" so much with Hegelian formulae in certain passages, the game is not just raf-fishness or sarcasm, but *the action of a real drama*, in which old concepts desperately play the part of something absent *which is nameless*, in order to call it onto the stage in person—whereas they only "produce" its presence in their failures, in the dislocation between the characters and their roles. (RC 29)

This passage doesn't talk about Darstellung itself as dramatic but the use of the "quasi-concept" of Darstellung and its avatars as players in this drama of the production of the concept—Darstellung is itself one of the stand-ins, the actors, in this drama, calling forth the absent actor through its very failure to present the concept as such. At the same time, it is we who are the actors who can never be adequate to the roles assigned us by the structure of the commodity form.[8] Yet once again, this is an objective inadequacy, an overdetermined failure, a misrecognition made possible by the very process of the presentation of value in its appearance form, the commodity.

Althusser tells us that this key epistemological concept of Darstellung, which prefigures the concept of structural causality, plays a role in Marx's theory of value, but what exactly does the value question have to do with all of this?

MARX ON DARSTELLUNG

I have several reasons for exploring the issue of Darstellung in Marx's works. First of all is the question of Marx's relationship to the approaches to Darstellung I examined in chapters 1 and 2. What if anything does Marx's approach to this problem of presentation have in common with these two critical thinkers who preceded him and, as Žižek has argued, helped prepare the ground for the development of the materialist approach to the question of ideology? The relationship between Marx and these two predecessors on this issue will become clear in my discussion below of the problem of fetishism. And second, as has been made clear in this chapter already, I will seek to clarify Althusser's relationship to Marx on the question of Darstellung. Does Marx use the term in the way Althusser describes? Is this term, this quasi-concept, really an avatar of the undeveloped concept of structural causality? This latter question will bear the burden of this exposition.

Marx and Darstellung as Scientific Method

As we have seen in chapters 1 and 2, Kant's elaboration of the problem of Darstellung in his critique of the faculty of judgment prepared the way for Hegel's transformation of what appeared to be a question about transcendental operations and turned it into one of dialectical scientific method. For it is the problem of a dialectical method based on historical and materialist presuppositions, as opposed to the historical though idealist ones that Marx imputed to Hegel, that concern most of Marx's meditations on presentation. One of Marx's earliest discussions of Darstellung in this context takes place in his *Critique of Hegel's Philosophy of Right*.[9] Here we find the rhetorical form that will characterize Marx's critique of Hegel throughout his life—a form that he refers to as the inversion or the turning right side up of what Hegel had placed on its head, as in this passage from the afterword to the second German edition of *Capital* (Althusser's whole career, I should note here, could be seen as an attempt to distinguish the later Marx's approach to scientific method from this earlier emphasis on the simple inversion of idealist dialectics): "The mystification which dialectic suffers in Hegel's hands, by no means prevents him from being the first to present [dargestellt] its general form of working in a comprehensive and conscious manner. With him it is standing on its head. It must be turned right side up again, if you would discover the rational kernel within the mystical shell" (CI 20). The rhetorical form at work here is the chiasmus: *A does not determine B, but B determines A*. The relationship between subject and predicate is reversed in a chiasmic exchange of properties. In his *Critique of Hegel's Philosophy of Right*, for example, Marx writes, "The concern of philosophy is not the logic of the subject-matter but the subject-matter of logic. Logic does not provide a proof of the state but the state provides a proof of logic" (CHPR 73).

Marx identifies four major problems with Hegel's mode of presentation: Hegel makes subjects out of abstract logical categories (that is, he makes subjects out of substance); he reverses the order of subject and predicate; he turns the true starting point into the final predicate of dialectical movement; and he turns the concrete into the formal and the formal into the concrete. These problems result from the fact that "Hegel's true interest is not the philosophy of right but logic" (ibid). Concrete determinations, rather than being viewed as the historical sources of abstract categories such as "will" and "spirit," become predicates of abstractions turned into subjects: Will and Spirit. The point is that a scientific mode of presentation must reverse the poles of Hegel's method and begin with the true beginnings, the concrete, the "real [*wirkliche*] life" of real people.

Marx's interest in this chiasmic reversal recurs in his discussion of method in *The German Ideology*. There one reads that "life is not determined by consciousness, but consciousness by life" (GI 1, 155). His target is again the Hegelian dialectic, which "descends from heaven to earth," while Marx ascends "from earth to heaven" (154):

> Where speculation ends—in real [wirkliche] life—there real, positive science begins: the Darstellung of the practical activity, of the practical process of the development of men. Empty talk about consciousness ceases, and real knowledge has to take its place. Philosophy's independence loses its medium of existence with the Darstellung of reality. At best its place can only be taken by a summing-up of the most general results, abstractions which arise from the observation of the historical development of men. Viewed apart from

real history, these abstractions have in themselves no value whatsoever. They can only serve to facilitate the arrangement of historical material, to indicate the sequence of its separate strata. But they by no means afford a recipe or schema, as does philosophy, for neatly trimming the epochs of history. On the contrary, our difficulties begin only when we set about the observation and arrangement—the real Darstellung—of our historical material, whether of a past epoch or of the present. The removal of these difficulties is governed by presuppositions [Voraussetzungen] which it is quite impossible to state here, but which only the study of the actual life-process and the activity of individuals of each epoch will make evident. (155)

As with Hegel in the preface to the *Phenomenology*, with Marx "true science" begins with the question of Darstellung. And for both Hegel and Marx, that Darstellung must be the presentation of dialectical movement itself. The difference, according to Marx, is where each locates the *origin* of that dialectical movement. Not in ideas or representations [Vorstellungen], says Marx, but in human practical activity, in "real" or "actual" history. But what is this real history, and how do we have access to it? As Marx suggests above, this is where the true difficulties begin: which presuppositions are to govern our presentation?

The first presupposition has to be that people "must be in a position to live in order to 'make history'" (155–56). The first "historical act," then, is the production of the means of subsistence, "the production of material life itself"—an act that though historically "original," must be repeated every day. This historical act includes the production of new needs, the reproduction of humans through propagation, and the inauguration of the social—the mode of cooperation necessary for maintaining a mode of production. "Only now," Marx writes, "do we find that man also possesses 'consciousness,'" which is "from the beginning a social product" (158). This is maintained in contradistinction to the German ideologists, on the other hand, for whom the social is a product of consciousness. Marx claims that this social mode of cooperative consciousness-production, through the contradictions of historical development, ultimately gives rise to civil or bourgeois society (*bürgerliche Gesellschaft*), which "is the true source and theater [*Schauplatz*] of all history" (163), the stage on which the dramas of consciousness are played out.

It is in light of this conception of history that Marx's approach to Darstellung as scientific presentation takes on its significance:

This conception of history depends on our ability to expound [*zu ent-wickeln*] the real process of production, starting from the material produc-tion of life itself, and to comprehend the form of intercourse connected with this and created by this mode of production (i.e., civil society in its various stages), as the basis of all history; and to present [*darzustellen*] it in its action as State, to explain all the different theoretical products and forms of con-sciousness, religion, philosophy, ethics, etc., etc., and trace their origins and growth from that basis; by which means, of course, the thing can be pre-sented in its totality [*die Sache in ihrer Totalität . . . dargestellt werden kann*] (and therefore, too, the reciprocal action [*die Weckselwirkung*] of these vari-ous sides of one another). It has not, like the idealistic view of history, in every period to look for a category, but remains constantly on the real *ground* of history; it does not explain practice from the idea but explains the forma-tion of ideas from material practice. (164)

In the afterword to the second German edition of *Capital*, Marx distin-guishes between Darstellung and *Forschung*, presentation and inquiry: "The latter has to appropriate the material in detail, to analyze its different forms of development, to trace out their inner connection. Only after this work is done, can the actual movement be adequately presented [dargestellt]. If this is done successfully, if the life of the subject-matter is ideally reflected as in a mirror, then it may appear as if we had before us a mere a priori construction" (*C1* 19). This mode of presentation proves scandalous to the bourgeoisie because

it includes in its comprehension an affirmative recognition of the existing state of things, at the same time also, the recognition of the negation of that state, of its eventual breaking up; because it regards every historically de-veloped social form as in fluid movement, and therefore takes into account its transient nature not less than its momentary existence; because it lets nothing impose upon it, and is in its essence critical and revolutionary.

The contradictions inherent in the movement of capitalist society im-press themselves upon the practical bourgeois most strikingly in the changes of the periodic cycle, through which modern industry runs, and whose crowning point is the universal crisis. That crisis is once again approaching, although as yet but in its preliminary stage; and by the universality of its theater and the intensity of its action it will drum dialectics even into the heads of the mushroom-upstarts of the new, holy Prusso-German empire. (*C1* 20)

GRUNDRISSE

The key discussion of Darstellung as scientific method for Althusser, however, is in the 1857 introduction to the *Grundrisse*.[10] It is from this discussion that Althusser gets the justification, in Marxist terms, for his concepts of theoretical practice, overdetermination, and structural causality. In his concern with the question of scientific method, Marx challenges the usual method of political economy, which begins with a seemingly concrete category, such as population, and develops its argument into increasingly abstract ones. Like Hegel before him, Marx's point is that the "concrete" that the political economists start with is in fact an abstraction from the concrete dialectical whole, and as such, remains at the level of representation. Intuition (Anschauung) and representation (Vorstellung) must indeed begin with the merely concrete, but scientific presentation *ends* with the concrete—the concrete worked up by the productivity of the theoretical process or thought (*Denken*). Here again is the distinction Marx makes in *Capital* between Forschung and Darstellung. The problem for Darstellung is that if we begin with the concrete, it can only be the simple concrete of a "chaotic representation," a representation that has not been transformed through the productive activity of thought into a concept (Begriff).

Thought as the transformation of intuitions and representations into concepts: this surely sounds like Hegel. In anticipating this response, Marx points out that while he and Hegel share the view that scientific Darstellung must follow such a process, the problem with Hegel is that he identifies this concept with the real. What is interesting is that this is no longer the language of the reversal, of the chiasmus that characterizes Marx's usual reproach to Hegel's dialectical method. Rather than a reversal, Marx here insists on a separation and clarification. It is true, Marx claims, that thought produces its object; but it must be kept in mind that this object cannot be confused or identified with the real object. Thought does not produce the real; it appropriates it:

> The concrete totality is a thought-totality [*Gedankentotalität*], a thought-concrete [*Gedankenkonkretum*], in fact a product of thinking and comprehending; but not in any way a product of the concept which thinks and generates itself outside or above intuition and representation; a product, rather, of the working-up [*Verarbeitung*] of intuition and representation into concepts. The totality as it appears in the head, as a totality of thoughts, is a product of a thinking head, which appropriates the world in the only way it

can, a way different from the artistic, religious, practico-mental appropriation of this world. The real subject retains its autonomous existence outside
the head just as before; namely as long as the head's conduct is merely
speculative, merely theoretical. Hence, in the theoretical method, too, the
subject, society, must always be kept in mind as the presupposition of the
representation [*als Voraussetzung stets der Vorstellung vorschweben*]. (G 01–2)

The real object functions as the presupposition of the representation, but it remains a mere chaotic representation if we fail to distinguish between the real object and the conceptual object and take this representation as our object of
knowledge. The process of the appropriation of the real must pass through the representation to the abstract concept; at this point only can scientific presentation
then do its work, beginning with the concept and working it up into the thought-
concrete.[11] Marx calls this a process of Verarbeitung, of working-up, a process
Althusser will refer to at one point (as we shall see) as Generality II. Writes Marx:

> [The method, whereby I work retroactively from the simplest determina-
> tions to more concrete concepts such as "population,"] is obviously the
> scientifically correct method. The concrete is the concrete because it is the
> concentration of many determinations, hence the unity of the diverse. It
> appears in the process of thinking, therefore, as a process of concentration,
> as a result, not as a point of departure, even though it is the point of depar-
> ture for intuition [Anschauung] and representation [Vorstellung]. Along the
> first path [that of seventeenth-century economists] the full representation
> was evaporated to yield an abstract determination; along the second, the
> abstract determination leads towards a reproduction [*zur Reproduktion*] of
> the concrete by way of thought. In this way Hegel fell into the illusion of
> conceiving the real as the product of thought concentrating itself, probing its
> own depths, and unfolding itself out of itself, by itself, whereas the method of
> rising from the abstract to the concrete is the only way in which thought
> appropriates [*anzueignen*] the concrete, reproduces it as a mental concrete
> [*als ein geistige Konkretes*]. But this is by no means the process by which the
> concrete itself comes into being. (G 101)

In the last sentence above, Marx maintains the point that scientific presentation works retroactively. We must not confuse the sequence of historical
development, Marx insists, with that of theoretical development. Labor, he
claims, has existed throughout human history in many different forms. But to

understand *labor as such* we cannot go back to some prehistorical beginning and trace the development of labor through time. Rather, the scientific presentation of history must operate archaeologically, working backward from the present state of things. So long as people's identities were defined by particular forms of labor, labor as such could not rise to consciousness as a category. It took the development of capitalist society, in which the relationship between the individual and a particular type of labor remains largely contingent and mobile, for labor to appear as *abstractable*, as an object for conceptual appropriation and working up. The same is true for the concept of capital: capital has existed in various forms through many widely differing historical social formations, but it was not until the full development of capitalism that capital *as such* could become an object of investigation and presentation: "The simplest abstraction, then, which modern economics places at the head of its discussions, and which expresses an immeasurably ancient relation valid in all forms of society, nevertheless achieves practical truth as an abstraction only as a category of the most modern society" (105). "Human anatomy contains a key to the anatomy of the ape. . . . The bourgeois economy thus supplies the key to the ancient, etc."

Capital *and Darstellung as the Presentation of Value*

Now we must turn to *Capital* itself to see if Althusser's *Reading Capital* is really about reading *Capital*. First, let's recall Althusser's claim cited at the beginning of this chapter about the importance of the concept of Darstellung for understanding *Capital*: The problem of structural causality or overdetermination "can be entirely summed up in the concept of 'Darstellung,' the key epistemological concept of the whole Marxist theory of value, the concept whose object is precisely to designate the mode of presence of the structure in its effects, and therefore to designate structural causality itself." Darstellung is said to be key for understanding the epistemological presuppositions of Marx's theory of value. But in what way is Marx's theory of value implicated in the question of overdetermination? Althusser implies here, as we have seen, that the presentation involved is "the mode of presence of the structure in its effects." So if we turn to *Capital* and explore the role of the concept of Darstellung in Marx's theory of value, we should see this question of structural causality in its as yet unstated form—in the form of a provisional, semi-metaphorical quasi-concept of presentation.

Althusser, as we have seen, connects the problem of fetishism with the question of Darstellung. His statement above, then, could be fleshed out as follows: "The concept whose object is precisely to designate the mode of presence of the structure [commodity-form] in its effects [fetishism]." Then the appearance-form of the equivalent in its relation to the relative form would be at the base of this *epistemological* question. But does Marx's discussion uphold such a view? Or even if it doesn't, does it anticipate such a view and give credence to Althusser's claims for symptomatic reading? The key section of *Capital* for this question is chapter 1, "The Commodity."

I am interested in the role of the metaphors Marx uses to characterize the nature of this presentation of value, for this is where the problem Althusser poses lies. To what extent are his tropes, his Vorstellungen, adequate to the quasi-concept of presentation that according to Althusser prefigures the concept of structural causality? To put this in more Althusserian terms, to what extent do Marx's tropes participate in the empiricist problematic of the essential/inessential opposition that inheres in all of the metaphors referring to veils, illusions, and false sightings? To what extent, if any, do they gesture beyond this problematic and provide in their very presence the absence of the question to which they pose the unasked-for answer: With what concept are we to think the determination of either an element or a structure by a structure—a structure whose whole existence consists of its effects?

The question of Darstellung in chapter 1 of *Capital*, volume 1, is a problem because Marx seems to use this key term primarily in two distinct ways. I will introduce these two uses by way of discussing a third, more idiosyncratic use of the term that will prepare us for the issues involved in the primary two to follow. "Socially necessary labor-time," Marx writes, "is the labour-time required to produce [darzustellen] any use-value under the conditions of production normal for a given society and with the average degree of skill and intensity of labor prevalent in that society" (*c1* 129). This use of Darstellung as "production" (*pro-ducere*, to lead forth), while not immediately connected to the sense of Darstellung as representation or presentation, is interesting in this context in that Althusser is arguing for a reading of *Capital* in which Darstellung is intimately related to the problem of the production of a concept (structural causality). He quotes Friedrich Engels in this context: "Priestly and Scheele had *produced* [dargestellt] oxygen *without knowing* what they had laid their hands on" (*rc* 150).[12] Engels is referring to the eighteenth-century quasi-concept of phlogiston, an absolute combustible existing in air that separates from a burning object. But in 1774, Joseph Priestley "produced" a pure form of air that he called "dephlogisticated air," and that later became known as oxygen after the development of phlogiston theory by Antoine-Laurent Lavoisier. Engel's point was that "Marx stands in the same relation to his predecessors in the theory of surplus-value as Lavoisier stood to Priestley and Scheele" (c2 16). Marx's predecessors had discovered the characteristic of value that Marx labeled as surplus-value. Yet in order "to understand what surplus-value was, Marx had to find out what value was," and in this investigation discovered the substance of value to be not exactly labor, as David Ricardo has assumed, but labor-power—a discovery that was to revolutionize value theory. What Engels is discussing here is the *production* of a concept made possible by a shift in problematics.

I cite this usage of Darstellung for several reasons, not least of which is to indicate the circular relationship established here between the production of the *content* of a given concept—structural causality or overdetermination—and the *mechanics* of that very concept at work in its own production: through a process of structural causality (the structural determination of the possibility of the very ability to conceive of a given concept), the concept of structural causality itself was produced. The concept refers to its own conditions of possibility. That is, the development of the concept of structural causality had to wait for the development of commodity production under capitalism, which itself operates according to structural causality. Structural causality makes certain concepts possible; the concept of structural causality is itself structurally caused. While the general use of Darstellung in the sense of production is in no way necessarily related to its use as representation or presentation, it is the production of the concept of presentation (the Darstellung of the concept of Darstellung) that makes Marx's work so valuable for Althusser.

Another reason for beginning with the "productive" use of Darstellung is that the above sentence joins together the production of use-values with the concept of labor-time and thus leads into the other senses of Darstellung: value as the Darstellung of labor and exchange-value as the appearance form of the Darstellung of value.

VALUE AS THE DARSTELLUNG OF LABOR

Marx begins *Capital*, as is well known, by focusing on the commodity as the elementary form of the capitalist mode of production. He first distinguishes between two forms of value "embodied" in the commodity: use-value and exchange-value. This initial distinction is somewhat misleading, however, since his introduction of exchange-value really serves to raise the question of value itself, which then will be followed by the analysis of exchange-value proper. The question of the value/Darstellung relation will be quite different from that of the exchange-value/Darstellung relation, as we will see.

Marx first refers to the commodity's use-value, its "substance [*Substanz*]," (its commodity-body [*Warenkörper*] "independent of the labor required to appropriate its useful qualities"), and second, to what he refers to as exchange-value, its magnitude ("the quantitative relation, the proportion, in which use-values of one kind exchange for use-values of another kind") (*c1* 126). In order to arrive at the common element that makes commodities with a wide variety of use-values exchangeable, one must subtract from all of them the qualities extraneous to this process of equalization. Exchange-value, then, "cannot be anything other than the mode of expression [*die Ausdrucksweise*], the 'appearance-form,' of a content distinguishable from it" (127). Exchange-value as an appearance-form will be the subject of Marx's second major reference to Darstellung. At this point, however, he must find this "content" distinguishable from it.

"Let us now take two commodities," Marx begins, "for example corn and iron. Whatever their exchange relation may be, it can always be represented [*darstellbar*] by an equation in which a given quantity of corn is equated to some quantity of iron, for instance 1 quarter of corn = x cwt of iron" (ibid.). This equation functions as the sign of the common element that exists in these two different things—this element being *a third thing*: "Both are therefore equal to a third thing [*Ding*], which in itself is neither the one nor the other" (ibid.). Yet since commodities differ in terms of their "natural bodies," in the physical materials of which they are made, this common entity cannot be a qualitative material but a quantitative magnitude that is totally independent of their use-value—for how could we profitably compare the use values of corn and iron? This third thing, this common factor, "which presents itself in the exchange relation or in the exchange-value of the commodity, is therefore its value" (128).

But what exactly is value? One of Marx's definitions early in *Capital* is that value is the embodiment or objectification of labor. Each commodity is a product of labor and can therefore be reduced to its value-substance: labor. Commodities now present themselves in the same "phantom-like objectivity," appearing merely as "congealed [*Gallerte*] quantities of homogeneous human labor," as "crystals of the same social substance," as values (ibid.). And just as commodities differ in terms of physical qualities and use-values, the various types and degrees of labor also differ in their physical nature and must also be reduced to a third common element: human labor in the abstract, labor as such. The only element these various manifestations of labor have in common is time, and so value is measured in terms of labor-time.

I should note the tropes at work here: the images of congelation and crystallization. "A use-value, or useful article, therefore, has value only because abstract human labor is objectified [*vergegenständlicht*] or materialized [*materialisiert*] in it" (129). In the commodity, abstract human labor is materialized, congealed, objectified, crystallized in the form of value. Darstellung, then, is the presentation in the form of value—by way of the value-form—of abstract human labor as it is materialized in the body of the commodity. And this tropological move gives rise to a series of questions: If Marx argues that abstract human labor-time is objectified in the value of the commodity, isn't this a case of Darstellung as *representation* rather than *presentation*? That is, doesn't value function as the stand-in, the proxy for labor? Isn't the value/labor relationship an external one, in which a given quantity of labor enacted in the past is objectified in the present commodity's value? And isn't the above operation whereby I distinguished labor as the common content of all commodities a process of abstraction in Althusser's sense of an empiricist search for the essence? And isn't Marx's claim that exchange-value is "nothing other than *a mode of expression*" an example of expressive causality? The argument so far seems to imply that labor-value, the content common to all commodities, finds its expression in exchange-value. How can we think such a content without thinking of it as the essence of commodities? And doesn't the concept of an appearance-form install us on the terrain of empiricism and its essential extraction? This is the problem Althusser faces: Marx seems incapable of grasping fully the breakthrough Althusser imputes to him and must consequently think in borrowed terms, parade his new concepts in borrowed clothing: Althusser writes that

> the whole history of the beginnings of sciences or of great philosophies shows . . . that the exact set of new concepts do not march out on parade in single file; on the contrary, some are long delayed, or march in borrowed clothes before acquiring their proper uniforms—for as long as history fails to provide the tailor and the cloth. In the meantime, the concept is certainly present in its works, but in a different form from that of a concept—in a form which is looking for itself inside a form "*borrowed*" from other custodians of formulated and disposable, or fascinating concepts. (RC 51)

In the end, it all comes down to how we characterize the content common to all commodities. But before discussing all commodities, I need to return to the exchange relationship of the simple form, which takes place between two commodities.

To give a preliminary answer, yes, as Marx has outlined the determination of value up to this point, there is no reason to suspect that anything other than a process of representation is operating here. If this is the case, then we have an equation as follows:

LABOR representation VALUE

The implication behind this metaphorics is that a certain stable and identifiable unit (labor-time) is objectified in the commodity as the latter's value. But this language of objectification carries with it the implication that the value of a given commodity that was created in x number of hours will maintain the same value as it embodied at its production. If the labor-time necessary for the production of identical commodities decreases, however, then the value of the original commodity also decreases, even though the labor "objectified" in it remains the same. "Socially necessary labor-time," we will remember,

> is the labor-time required to produce [darzustellen] any use-value under the conditions of production normal for a given society and with the average degree of skill and intensity of labor prevalent in that society. The introduction of power-looms into England, for example, probably reduced by one half the labor required to convert a given quantity of yarn into woven fabric. In order to do this, the English hand-loom weaver in fact needed the same amount of labor-time as before; but the product of his individual hour of labor now only represented [stellte . . . dar] half an hour of social labor, and consequently fell to one half its former value. (c1 129)

The difficulty with the trope of representation to play in the value-represents-labor series is that we remain at the level of the single commodity and its relation to an originary moment of labor-time. The concept of value at this level overrides the temporal disjunction between the labor-production of commodities and the circulation of commodities in exchange, and posits the labor-power moment as the precondition for exchange. But in the turn to the dialectic of the value form (from simple to extended to general), Marx reveals (to anticipate) that our ability to "embody" the commodity in this first way depends on a retroactive projection made possible by the structure of the commodity as it functions within capitalist exchange. For the definition of "commodity," we should remember, is an object of utility produced in order to be exchanged. It is the system of exchange itself that predetermines labor as value. And it is in the dialectic of the value-form that value itself is *presented*, that the system of commodities presents itself as value.

DARSTELLUNG AND THE DIALECTIC OF THE VALUE FORM

After his initial distinction between use-value and exchange-value, Marx goes on in chapter 1 of *Capital* to outline the dialectical transformation of the value-form. I began with value as the Darstellung of labor; now I move to the equivalent-form as the Darstellung of value. In order for value to present labor, it must itself first be presented. The presentation of value begins with the simple form, develops into the expanded form, and passes over into the general form of the general equivalent and, ultimately, the money form.

The Simple Form

In order for commodities to be exchanged, they must in some way be equivalent. This demand is what led Marx, as we have seen, to distinguish exchange-value from use-value, in order to see what corn and iron, for example, have in common that allows them to function as equivalent units of exchange. Central to Marx's development of the value question is his concept of the appearance-form (*Erscheinungsform*). This is where the question of presentation comes in: in what various forms does value present itself? The active reflexive determination here of value's self-presentation (*sich darstellt* could as well be translated in the passive form as "is presented") is crucial if we are to adhere to the notion that what Marx is describing in *Capital* is an objective structure of this mode of appearance rather than a subjective one. The appearance-form is a structural effect of the commodity form itself.

The purpose of the discussion of the simple form is to characterize the simplest relationship behind commodity exchange. But even in this simple form, it has already advanced beyond the value-represents-labor series in posing the problem of value as a question of relationship—here, a relationship between two commodities. If we think of a commodity as the embodiment of a certain magnitude of value (coagulated labor), then it seems appropriate to expect to see that value by looking closely at the commodity. Nevertheless, what Marx reveals in his exploration of the simple form of value is that value appears not in the com-

modity but in the relationship between commodities (such is the basis, we will
see, for Marx's theory of fetishism). For example, in production human labor
has accumulated in a coat. "From this point of view," Marx writes, "the coat is
a 'bearer of value' ['*Träger von Wert*'], although this property never shows
through, even when the coat is at its most threadbare" (*c1* 143). The search for
the value of a particular commodity in that commodity itself involves us in a
tautology, a kind of Hegelian infinite judgment that sets the dialectic of the
value-form in motion. For if we simply look to a coat for its own value, all we can
ever arrive at is **1 coat = 1 coat**. We know no more than we began with; nothing
new has presented itself. The value of one commodity can only present itself in
the body of a second commodity: **20 yards of linen = 1 coat**. In this case, the linen
and the coat play completely different roles: the linen is in the position of what
Marx calls the relative form of value, while the coat is in what he calls the
equivalent form. "Since a commodity cannot be related to itself as equivalent,
and therefore cannot make its own natural shape into the expression of its own
value, it must be related to another commodity as equivalent, and therefore must
make the natural shape of another commodity into its own value-form" (148). A
crucial distinction is being made here then between value as such (which is determined by labor-time) and the value-form through which value must appear
(147). Value as such remains invisible (no matter how thinly worn the coat) and
thus depends on the appearance-form which is exchange-value. Exchange-value
is the value-form, the appearance-form, the mode of presentation of value as
such; and this value-form itself is made up of the relative and equivalent forms.

Here we see the extent to which value is a relationship between rather than a
property specific to particular commodities. In order to discover the value of
linen, we must compare it to some other commodity, a coat. The value of the
first commodity, then, can only be presented relatively. "It is not the latter
commodity whose value is being expressed. It only provides the material [*das
Material*] in which the value of the first commodity is expressed" (140). The
first commodity's value cannot be equal to itself, and thus can only be presented
as relative to the value of another (hence the term "relative value") that is its
equivalent. While the coat and the linen can change positions, the coat now
being the relative and the linen the equivalent form of value, they now express a
different relationship: now the value of the coat is what is being presented by
the body of the linen. The equivalent, still in the form of a use-value, becomes
the value-body (*Wertkörper*) for the relative form, the mirror of the relative
form in which the latter's value appears. But the same commodity cannot

simultaneously appear in both forms in the same value-expression.

> The body [*Körper*] of the commodity, which serves as the equivalent, always counts as the embodiment [*Verkörperung*] of abstract human labor and is always the product of some specific useful and concrete labor. This concrete labor therefore becomes the expression [*Ausdruck*] of abstract human labor. If the coat is merely abstract human labor's realization [*Verwirklichung*], the tailoring actually realized in it is merely abstract human labor's realization-form [*Verwirklichungsform*]. In the expression of value of the linen, the use-fulness of tailoring consists, not in making clothes, and thus also people, but in making a body [Körper] which we at once recognize as value, as a congelation [Gallerte] of labor, therefore, which is absolutely indistinguishable from the labor objectified [vergegenständlichten] in the value of the linen. In order to act as such a mirror of value [*Wertspiegel*], tailoring itself must reflect [*widerspiegeln*] nothing apart from its own abstract quality of being human labor. (150)

The coat thus functions as the "existence-form of value [*Existenzform von Wert*], as the Value-Thing [*als Wertding*], for only as such is it the same as the linen. On the other hand, the linen's own value-being [*Wertsein*] comes into view or receives an independent expression, for it is only as value that it can be related to the coat as being of equal value to it, or exchangeable with it" (141).

As I suggested earlier, the attempt to "uncover" a commodity's value simply by looking deeply or intently at that commodity grows out of a tautological assumption: **1 coat = 1 coat**. But this form is no different from Fichte's equation of identity, **I = I**. And for the same reasons as discussed in chapter 2, such an attempt to present equivalence in the form of a proposition or mathematical equation falls in on itself and reveals its own impossibility, for either we are presented with the claim **subject = subject**, which tells us nothing at all apart from the utter nullity of the subject in question, or we have **subject = predicate**, which in its very terms and spacing contradicts the identity it attempts to present. Notice, however, that the **subject = predicate** equation is in fact the form in question here in Marx's text: **relative form = equivalent form**. The equivalent, in its position as predicate of the equation, fleshes out the impossibility of the relative form in the subject position. The relative form is nothing but the impossible identity of value to itself, the void of its own inadequation. Value must become something other, it must become the value-thing that exists apart from its own value-being (Wertsein). The equivalent thing thereby fleshes out the very impossibility of the full presence-in-presentation, the impossible presence-to-itself of value as such. Yet without this impossible gesture toward presentation we are left with nothing but the nullity of the use value, the inert, abstract thing of no value. Substance must become Subject, it must be set in motion by the impossible movement of equivalence inaugurated by the production of commodities. "The product of labor," Marx observes, "is an object of utility in all states of society; but it is only a historically specific epoch of development which presents the labor expended in the production of a useful article as an 'objective' property of that article, i.e. as its value" (153–54).

The simple value form at first appears as a relationship of simple unity: **x commodity A = y commodity B**. But as we examine the determinations of the simple form of value further, what we get is the identity of the two polar opposites that we saw constituting the commodity: (exchange) value and use-value. The value of linen can only be expressed through its presentation in the form of the use-value of another commodity, the coat, whose own value remains unexpressed. In order to find the value of the coat, on the other hand, we must reverse the poles and now view the linen as a use-value that embodies the value of the coat. The simple form of value thus provides a relationship of difference: commodities are identical in terms of value and nonidentical in terms of use-value, yet in the value-form (exchange-value) both of these forms, which are fundamentally exclusive of one another in terms of the function of the single commodity, are necessarily combined in their opposition in order to present value. "The internal opposition between use-value and value," Marx explains, "hidden within the commodity, is therefore presented on the surface by an external opposition, i.e. by a relation between two commodities such that the one commodity, *whose own* value is supposed to be expressed, counts directly only as a use-value, whereas the other commodity, *in which* that value is to be expressed, counts directly only as exchange-value" (153). The merely abstract and immanent opposition of value and use-value in the single commodity with which Marx began his investigation has now been dialectically transformed into the *external* abstract opposition of these two forms, each of which is manifested in a different commodity.

The Expanded Form

Once the differential relationship of nonadequation between the two commodities is revealed, the arbitrary nature of their combination is also revealed. As members of a social system of commodities, these two can enter into a relationship with any other commodity. The presentation of the value of commodity A is thus extended out onto the whole world of commodities as an endless series of equivalents: **z commodity A = u commodity B or = v commodity C or = w commodity D or = x commodity E or so on**. What this extension of equivalents reveals is that the particular nature of the use-value functioning as the equivalent in its presentation of value is now completely "a matter of indifference" (155). The presentation of value can take place in any available commodity-body; there is no necessary relationship between the two commodities. In this way, the nature of the labor determining value becomes more concrete (in the dialectical sense) in that since any commodity will do as the presentation of value, then any mode of labor-power is as good as any other in the production value. "It is thus that this value first shows [*erscheint*] itself as being, in reality, a congealed quantity of undifferentiated human labor. For the labor which creates it is now explicitly presented as labor which counts as the equal of every other sort of human labor, whatever form it may possess, hence whether it is objectified in a coat, in corn, in iron, or in gold" (ibid.).

As with the development of the simple form, the expanded form also comes up against its dialectical limit. The major problem is that "the series of presentations never comes to an end" (156). This is the problem Hegel referred to as "bad infinity." Value as such cannot be presented in its concrete form because while the entire world of commodities is implied in the expanded form, the relative form of value of each one can only be expressed one commodity at a time, and the relative form of each commodity will differ from the relative form of the others. Nevertheless, we have progressed beyond the limited nature of the presentation implicit in the simple form: whereas the simple form was simple yet isolated, the expanded form is now infinite and particular. The general form of value, subsequently, will be simple and common or general. Through this dialectical transformation, then, the simple form of presentation has returned as universal; the presentation of value now takes place throughout the entire system of commodity relations at once, this presentation-relation having itself become embodied in the general equivalent. As such, the general equivalent becomes the presentation of *presentation itself*.

The General Form

In this way, the general form of value is the reflective moment of the dialectical development of the forms of presentation. This means that the infinite and "motley" series of presentations (*Darstellungsreihe*) in the expanded form has been reversed and thereby embodied in the general equivalent. The expanded relationship between the relative form and the infinite series of equivalent forms could be expressed as follows:

20 yards of linen = 1 coat
20 yards of linen = 10 pounds of tea
20 yards of linen = 40 pounds of coffee
20 yards of linen = 1 quarter of corn
20 yards of linen = 2 ounces of gold, and so forth

Since the relative and equivalent poles can always be reversed, one ends up with the following relationship:

1 coat
10 pounds of tea
40 pounds of coffee   **= 20 yards of linen**
1 quarter of corn
2 ounces of gold, and so forth

The linen, now in the equivalent form, presents the value of all other commodities and is therefore the general equivalent.

The consequences of this dialectic can now be drawn out. The problem that initiated this dialectical articulation of the value-form was the proposition that I began with: **value (re)presents labor**. The problem was that the commodity, when looked at in isolation from the whole system of commodity relations, stands as an inert contradiction: that of the immanent opposition of exchange-value and use-value. Value as such cannot present itself in this opposition precisely because it is not a property specific to the single commodity but a social relationship articulated through the whole commodity structure of which the single commodity is only one part. The development of the value-form, the appearance-form of value as exchange-value, depends on the presentation of the social character of exchange-value and, thus, of value itself. Use-value, which functions in the equivalent form, must be isolated not only from the single commodity in order for that commodity's value to come into view; it must also drop out of the equation of the differential system of commodities as a whole. But this cannot happen simply by eliminating use-value from the equation, for then all that is left is value itself in its disembodied and therefore nonarticulated state, its abstract immediacy. Such would bring us back to the merely tautologous equation of **value = value** or **value (re)presents value**. This was exactly the problem with the initial deduction of value through the reduction of all extraneous qualities to the one common element, labor-time. Such a reduction only produces a negative presentation of value through the process of abstraction (Althusser's essential extraction). The dialectic of the value-form, on the other hand, employs a positive presentation of value as the effect of the social structure of the commodity system as a whole: "The general value-form, in which all the products of labor are presented as mere congealed quantities of undifferentiated human labor, shows by its very structure that it is the social expression of the world of commodities" (c1 160).

Here we have arrived at Marx's description of structural causality through the concept of presentation. Value is the effect of structure in that the structure presents itself, through the elaboration of the value-form, as the articulation of homogeneous human labor-power. But what has happened to the use-value that has functioned as the embodiment of value, as the vehicle of presentation itself? Marx has not simply tossed use-value aside but has instead revealed the paradoxical point that use-value as such is inadequate as the presentation of value, yet a particular use-value is necessary as the embodiment of the whole social structure of value for value to be presented in its differential, social nature. In the simple form of value, the value of linen is presented by the use-value coat. Value can only appear in the form of another use-value. But the necessary separation of exchange-value and use-value has not yet come into view (has not yet been presented) since the two terms can easily be reversed, in which case the linen's own use-value now comes back into view while its value drops out of sight. In the expanded form, the linen's value stands out more clearly in contrast to its use-value because now it is related as the relative form to all other commodities as use-values (equivalents). This provides a series of use-values, but not a structure of values. The general form of value reverses this expanded relationship: now one use-value is singled out as the equivalent use-value embodying the value of all other commodities. The social structure of value can only be presented by excluding one particular commodity from that structure and having that commodity function only as the equivalent use-value, but never as its own value. The totalized network of values as value can only be presented by the exceptional One excluded from this circuit.

The Money Form

I now arrive at the object of Marx's critique of political economy: their conception of the derivation of money. While they recognize certain things that Marx emphasizes, such as that labor-time is the source of value, they cannot come to terms with money as a social relationship growing out of the dialectic of the value-form. Once that dialectic has reached the point of the general equivalent, it has at the same time arrived at the derivation of the money form. The money form is nothing but the general equivalent once it has become the socially accepted medium of exchange—that is, once a particular use-value has been excluded from the circuit of value and left as the embodiment of value as such. Linen can embody the money form if linen is singled out as the socially accepted general equivalent. But the historically determined use-value chosen for this function has in fact been gold. "Gold confronts the other commodities as money only because it previously confronted them as a commodity" (*c1* 162).

Žižek has argued that the money form is in fact different from the general form that precedes it. In drawing a parallel between Marx's dialectic of the value-form and Lacan's dialectic of the subject, Žižek offers the following outline of the development of these forms (substituting the terms "signifier" and "subject" for, respectively, "commodity" and "value"):

1. The simple form: "for *a* signifier, *another* signifier represents the subject" (i.e. "*a* signifier represents the subject for *another* signifier");

2. The expanded form: "for *a* signifier, *any* of the other signifiers can represent the subject";

3. The general form: "*a* (*one*) signifier represents the subject for *all the other* signifiers";

4. The money form: "*a* (*one*) signifier *for which all the other* signifiers represent the subject." (*FTK* 24, 26)

In explaining the significance of this elaboration of the money form out of the general form, Žižek argues that

> the signifier which, with the emergence of the "general form," is posited as the "general equivalent" representing the subject for "all the others" is *not* the finally found "proper" signifier, a representation which is not a misrepresentation: it does not represent the subject at the same level, within the same logical space, as the others (the "any of the others" from form 2). This signifier is, on the contrary, a "reflective" one: in it, the very failure, the very impossibility of the signifier's representation is reflected into this representation itself. In other words, this paradoxical signifier represents (gives body

to) the very impossibility of the subject's signifying representation—to resort to the worn-out Lacanian formula, it functions as the "signifier of the lack of the signifier," as the place of the reflective inversion of the lacking signifier into the signifier of the lack . . . [and thereby] "totalizes" the battery of "all others." (ibid., 24–25)

As we have seen in Marx, the general form reverses the relationship between the relative form and its equivalents as posited in the expanded form; that is, from the expanded form that proclaims that any of the other commodities can represent the value of the relative commodity (the "can represent" is precisely the problem of this bad infinity—the presentation of value is purely contingent), we next arrive at the general form that states that one commodity represents all of the other commodities. The contingent, infinite series of equivalents has been transformed from "any" to "all" once they are reversed into occupying the relative position; they have been totalized as a structure of value by the exclusion of the *one* that now presents value as such. As Žižek suggests, this one now embodies the impossibility of representation that existed in the expanded form once it is excluded from the circuit of value and gives body to the space of this inadequation in its very body, its thingness, its use-value.

The shift from the general form to the money form, in Žižek's posing of this relationship, reverses the poles yet again, but this time maintaining the totality of the "all" that was restricted to the chaotic series of the "any" of the expanded form: " 'all' represent for the One the subject, whereas the One represents for 'all' the very impossibility of representation" (27).

There appear to be two problems with Žižek's formulation here, as suggestive and useful as it is: as I have argued throughout this chapter, the term "represent" should be replaced by "present," a point I will elaborate on below; and if we reverse the general form, the One now functions as the relative form and the "all" function as the equivalent. Žižek supports this reversal by noting that it has a historical foundation: initially the commodity with the most use-value was singled out as the general equivalent, since this commodity was the one for which most would want to exchange their own commodities. Through time, however, the commodity with the least use-value, gold, becomes the general equivalent. Marx discusses this process in the *Grundrisse*:

> It is the particular usefulness of the commodity, whether as a particular object of consumption (hides), or as a direct instrument in production (slaves), which stamps it as money in these cases. In the course of further

development precisely the opposite will occur, i.e. that commodity which has the least utility as an object of consumption or instrument of production will best serve the needs of *exchange as such*. In the former case, the commodity becomes money because of its particular use value; in the latter case it acquires its particular use value from its serviceability as money. . . . The *precious* metals then split off from the remainder by virtue of being inoxidizable, of standard quality etc., and they correspond better, then, to the higher stage, in that their direct utility for consumption and production recedes while, because of their rarity, they better represent value purely based on exchange. From the outset they represent superfluity, the form in which wealth originates. (*G* 166)

Presumably it is because of its lack of use-value that Žižek sees gold as the embodiment of the failure of representation, this failure evidently conceived of by Žižek as the inadequation of exchange-value and use-value. Marx certainly maintains such an impossibility due to the antagonistic nature of the value-form. But hasn't Žižek, in his transformation of the general equivalent into the money form, imported use-value back into the equation of the dialectic of the value-form, when it was precisely Marx's argument that through this dialectic use-value drops out of the circuit of value and simply functions as the inert material use-value (gold) that embodies value as such? The shift that Žižek describes places the entire world of commodities into the position of the equivalent and thus installs on this whole network of commodities their determination as use-values that now as a whole rather than as a series, present the value of money itself. In the *Grundrisse*, Marx does suggest that "all" represent value as such for the One: "Money is originally the representative of all values; in practice this situation is inverted, and all real products and labors become the representatives of money" (*G* 149). But doesn't Marx's derivation of the value-form demand that the general equivalent by its very function *as equivalent* must forego the presentation of its relative value? Otherwise, Marx claims, we would have either the tautologous relationship of **gold (relative form) = gold (equivalent)** or the reversion to the expanded form: "The commodity that figures [*figuiert*] as universal equivalent is . . . excluded from the uniform and therefore universal relative form of value . . . ; its value [could only be] expressed relatively in the infinite series of all other physical commodities" (*c1* 161). Marx argues in chapter 1 of *Capital* that the transition from the general equivalent to the money form is simply the point at which "the form of direct and universal exchangeability, in other words the universal equivalent form, has now by social custom finally become entwined with the specific natural form of the commodity gold" (ibid., 162). The money form is simply the stabilization of the general equivalent to one universally accepted commodity body. Yet according to Žižek, this is not simply a reversion to the expanded form, for that form has itself been transformed by way of the general equivalent from the infinite "any" to the totalized "all," as we have seen.

Can Žižek's claim be squared within the terms of *Capital*? Yes. The key lies in the fact that money plays a transitional role: as the final moment of the commodity-form, money simply takes the form of a commodity singled out by social custom as the general equivalent. But money at this point also leads into the dialectical transformation of the commodity-form into the money-form, and the money-form into the capital-form. The immanent antagonisms of these forms, while having developed out of the initial antagonism of the commodity-form—use value versus value—now take on new forms: "The further development of the commodity does not abolish these contradictions, but rather provides the form within which they have room to move" (198). Precisely because of the totalization of the system of commodities through the development of the general equivalent, commodities now enter into relations with one another as part of a "social metabolism" (*Stoffwechsel*), the process of exchange. "Exchange," Marx writes in volume 1 of *Capital*, " . . . produces a differentiation of the commodity into two elements, commodity and money, an external opposition which presents the opposition between use-value and value which is inherent in it" (199). Presentation has thus become externalized as a unity-of-differences, the exchange process itself. Through exchange, the commodity undergoes a formal metamorphosis which Marx plots as follows:

Commodity—Money—Commodity

or

C—M—C

This process is actually made up of two different transactions that are opposite in form: **C—M**, which is the moment of the sale (the exchange of a commodity for money), and **M—C**, the moment of the purchase (the exchange of the newly acquired money for a different commodity). In the exchange, then, value presents itself through the metamorphosis of one commodity into money and then into another commodity. Marx's comment on this metamorphosis supports Žižek's claim above:

This unity of differences presents itself at two opposite poles, and in each pole in an opposite way. This is the alternating relation between the two poles: the commodity is in reality a use-value; its value-being [Wertsein] appears [erscheint] only ideally, in its price, through which it is related to the real embodiment of its value [als ihre reelle Wertgestalt], the gold which confronts it as its opposite. Inversely, the material of gold ranks only as the materialization of value [als Wertmateriatur], as money. It is therefore in reality exchange-value. Its use-value within appears only ideally in the series of expressions of relative value within which it confronts all the other commodities as the totality of real embodiments of its utility [als den Umkreis seiner reellen Gebrauchsgestalten]. (199)

The relative value of money itself is presented by "all the other commodities" as the totality of use-value equivalents. This reversal occurs in the second metamorphosis of the appearance-form of value in exchange, the purchase. It is here that money's relative value comes into view as presented in the totality of all commodities up for sale: **M—C**. And this characteristic of the money-form which Žižek emphasizes reached its dialectical heights in the transformation of the money-form into the capital-form, when the circuit **C—M—C** is reversed as **M—C—M**. Now the process begins with a purchase (**M—C**), although the purpose of this exchange is no longer the exchange of commodities in order to consume the second commodity's use-value but to increase the initial money's value through circulation. That is, money is spent on a commodity in order to sell that commodity at a higher price. The final moment, then, is the sale (**C—M**). The circuit of capital, if successful, is no longer simply **M—C—M** but **M—C—M'** (in which **M'** = **M** + the excess over its original value). Now the whole system of commodities appears as nothing but the mode of expression of value of the money, only through this process that value is increased through its presentation and ends up presenting not only value but also surplus-value. Value thus appears as its own superadequation, and in this way the subject of capital, labor-power, presents itself as its own superadequation.[13]

FETISHISM AND STRUCTURAL CAUSALITY

Fetishism arises from the commodity-form itself. The commodity form is itself made up of three forms that transform particular aspects of labor into the aspects of the products of labor: the material (sachliche) form, in which equal human labor is objectified into equal products of labor as values; the value-magnitude form, in which the measure of expenditure of human labor power is transferred to the measure of value of the products of labor; and the social-relation form, in which the social relation between producers is manifested as a social relation between the products of labor. In all three aspects, the social nature of the labor of producers is objectified as a social relation between the products of that labor. Exchange-value is the mode of presentation of value in capitalist commodity production and it is only through exchange that the agents of production come into contact with one another through the products of their labor. As Marx writes in *Capital*, volume 1:

> The mysterious character of the commodity-form consists therefore simply in the fact that the commodity reflects [*zurückspiegelt*] the social characteristics of men's own labor as objective characteristics of the products themselves, as the socio-natural properties [*gesellschaftliche Natureigenschaften*] of these things [Dinge]. Hence it also reflects the social relation of the producers to the sum total of labor as a social relation between objects, a relation which exists apart from and outside the producers. Through this substitution, the products of labor become commodities, sensible supersensible or social things. (164)

This objectification of labor is the structural effect of the commodity form itself as it is manifested through its appearance-form, exchange-value.

"Fetishism" is Marx's name for this necessary appearance of the commodity-form, as he sees this process as analogous to the transformation in religion of products of the human mind into "autonomous figures endowed with a life of their own" (165). Fetishism is thus "inseparable" from the mode of presentation of the commodity form.

For Marx, this is an unconscious yet inescapable effect of the appearance-form of commodities, of the presentation of value. Fetishism, then, is an effect of structural causality. This transformation of every product of labor into a "social hieroglyphic," therefore, does not go away simply by our becoming aware of its effect, for we still live within a society based on commodity production. Like Hegel's owl of Minerva, we will only become fully aware of the effectivity of the value-structure after the production of commodities has been fully developed. "The determination of the magnitude of value by labor-time is therefore a secret hidden under the apparent movements [*erscheinenden Bewegungen*] in the relative values of commodities. Its discovery destroys the semblance [*Schein*] of the merely accidental determination of magnitude of the value of the products of labor, but by no means abolishes that determination's material [sachliche] form" (168).

This mystified appearance-form is not a necessary form of products of labor as such but is itself the historical development of the transformation of products of labor into commodities. In the relations of production of medieval Europe, for example, "there is no need for labor and its products to assume a fantastic [*phantastiche*] form different from their reality [Realität]. . . . The natural form [*Naturalform*] of labor, its particularity—and not, as in a society based on commodity production, its universality—is here its immediate social form" (170). And in a society based on a communist mode of production, "an association of free men, working with the means of production held in common, and expending their many different forms of labor-power in full self-awareness as one single social labor force" (171), the social relations between workers and their products will present themselves as transparent and rational.

BEYOND REPRESENTATION?

Now to return to the question I have posed for *Capital*: Does the Darstellung of Marx's study of the value-form function as representation or presentation? In the initial discussion that takes place in terms of the series *value-Darstellung-labor*, there is indeed a relationship of representation: in the void of the value position within the commodity, labor appears as the essential residue remaining after the process of reduction and abstraction from all inessential qualities. The expression of value here can only be the result of an expressive causality. But it is precisely this inadequation inherent in this value-form that moves Marx to elaborate the dialectical value-form. It is in this move that the nature of Darstellung as presentation is fleshed out.

This is not a process of representation, of the positioning of one thing in the place of another thing that preexists its representative, for value does not preexist, it does not exist, it is nothing but the retroactive process of this presentation of abstract human labor in the value-form. For this reason, the metaphor of expression is misleading to the extent that the term "expression" implies a preexisting thing that is to be presented in its new phenomenal form. Value, however, is nothing but its own expression in its various appearance-forms. It is the appearance brought about by the demands of the commodity-form itself, as the basis of the capitalist mode of production, that produces the transformation of human labor into value. It is the production of commodities—use-values produced in order to be exchanged—that demands the reduction of labor to socially necessary abstract human labor and the reduction of use-values to values. Value is never present before its elaboration of the value-form; rather, it is a product of this elaboration itself. Thus what was never present before the elaboration of the commodity-form itself cannot be *re*-presented by that form.

But what is the nature of this presence that is presented by the value-form? We are not dealing here with a metaphysical presence of any sort but of a social relationship that appears only through the structural effectivity of the whole system of commodity production and its transformation of labor into value. In precapitalist societies labor had no need to appear as value, for its relationships were immediate and particular, Marx explains, not structurally mediated and universal. Hence, as Althusser has argued, Marx's concept of presentation in his theory of value is nothing but a quasi-concept for structural causality itself.

The implications of this are immense, for discussions of Marx's theory of value have traditionally posed this problem as one of representation, and the English translations of *Capital* support this tradition by translating Darstellung oftentimes as "representation."[14] The representation model depends on an anthropologism that constructs human labor as the essence of the value form that is the former's expression. But it is in the move from the theory of alienation to that of fetishism, and its concomitant move from representation to presentation, that Marx leaves behind the empirico-anthropological problematic of his youth.

This distinction between presentation and representation could go a long way in addressing the kind of issue Spivak is concerned with in her critique of the conflation of Darstellung and Vertretung.[15] Such a conflation, as illustrated in the works of Foucault and Deleuze, has the effect of erasing the questions of ideology (and thus class interest) as well as constitutive contradiction from view. The result, Spivak contends, is not some liberation from the "subject" but rather a reduction of the subject to the transparent subject of Western intellectual desire. In Marx's works, Vertretung refers to political representation, in the sense of the representation of class interest. Spivak's example is Marx's discussion of the "Name" of Napoleon as the point of subjective condensation, the figure that gives shape to the otherwise amorphous "mass." What Spivak wants to emphasize is the contrast between these terms that "Foucault and Deleuze slide over, the contrast, say, between a proxy and a portrait. There is, of course, a relationship between them, one that has received political and ideological exacerbation in the European tradition at least since the poet and the sophist, the actor and the orator, have both been seen as harmful. In the guise of a post-Marxist description of the scene of power, we thus encounter a much older debate: between representation or rhetoric as tropology and as persuasion."[16] What is required is an elaboration of the relationship between Darstellung (as "presentation" in the sense of the value-form) and Vertretung as the function of the general equivalent. The effect of this alliance will become clear in my discussion of Althusser's theory of interpellation below.[17]

As we saw, Žižek follows the usual practice of translating Darstellung as "representation." Yet it should now be apparent that when he discusses the dialectic of the value-form in relation to the subject of the signifier, the signifier does not represent the subject but *presents* it, for the subject is nothing but the point of negativity immanent in this function of the signifier. This is key, then, to rewriting the language of Lacan's discussion of the Master Signifier as a question of representing the subject: the one signifier is not *represented* (either in the sense of Darstellung, Vorstellung, Vertretung, or Repräsentierung) but *presented* by all others, the void of its absence (which is the subject) fleshed out by the chain of all other signifiers. As the language of "fleshing out" suggests, what we have here is a dialectical development of Kant's conception of presentation as Versinnlichung. The concept, the subject, value: all are presented, fleshed out, through the dialectical process of the movement from the simple form through the expanded form to the general form of presentation itself.

ALTHUSSER REDUX: THE UNITY OF
THE FORMS OF DARSTELLUNG

One of the continuing benefits of the Althusserian legacy is his attempt to produce a theory that would unite in practice (materialist and dialectical) the questions of theory and practice, and the distinctions between thought and the object of thought.[18] As we have seen, in Marx's works the term Darstellung refers to two different problems: the problem of scientific practice and that of presentation in value theory. What Althusser has done is provide a model for bringing the questions of method and subject matter together in one of the most successful ways, ironically enough, since Hegel's own attempts to define the relationship between thought and its objects.

I am not exactly calling for a "return to Althusser" (which Althusser?) but for an elaboration of the issues he has raised in his effort to think through the problem of Darstellung and structural causality. Althusser's attempts here could only go so far. This is particularly so because of his sustained polemic against "Hegel." He was right to attack the elements of what he referred to as empiricism, humanism, and expressive causality, all of which he embodied in the figure of a certain Hegel, but as the works of Jameson and Žižek attest, the question of our relationship to Hegel is hardly put to rest. It has more appropriately passed over to the quite different question, "Which Hegel?"

Žižek's elaboration of Hegel and Marx through a renewed reading of Lacan has proven especially helpful in reconfiguring the issues at stake here in these decidedly post-Hegelian and post-Marxist times. But in terms of the argument I have developed to this point in this chapter, Žižek's most intriguing move is his foregrounding of the Hegelian Thing that, as we have seen, fleshes itself out in Marx's turn to the general equivalent. And here I come to the element missing from Althusser's conception of structural causality. Marx does indeed, through the quasi-concept of Darstellung, arrive at a conception of structural causality. But this structural causality can only operate because of the exceptional One, the commodity excluded from the structure of values. The existence of the structure can only be presented by an element excluded from that structure, excluded as that structure's excluded One. Althusser's language approaches this issue:

> The same connection that defines the visible also defines the invisible as its shadowy obverse. It is the field of the problematic that defines and structures the invisible as the defined excluded, *excluded* from the field of visibility and *defined* as excluded by the existence and peculiar structure of the field of the problematic; as what forbids and represses the reflection of the field on its object, i.e., the necessary and immanent inter-relationship of the problematic and one of its objects. This is the case with oxygen in the phlogistic theory of chemistry, or with surplus-value and the definition of the "value of labor" in classical economics. (RC 25–26)

Althusser is correct to point to the excluded object, the object excluded from visibility within the field, as this field's excluded. But what he does not do is follow Marx's very Hegelian move of defining this excluded as the general equivalent. It is the general equivalent as excluded from the field-circuit of value that allows value to present itself *as such*. It is through the devaluation of the general equivalent that the valorization of the other objects within its circuit can take effect. Althusser does approach this realization in his theory of interpellation, according to which "the interpellation of individuals as subjects presupposes the 'existence' of a Unique and central Other Subject, in whose Name the religious ideology interpellates all individuals as subjects" (LP 178).[19] Still, what remains missing is the relationship between this subjectivation through the Subject and the circuit of structural causality in which this subjectivation takes place as the effect of structure. Through the representative (vertretend) function of the Subject of the Name, the presentation (Darstellung) of value as the effect of structure takes place.

THE "SUBJECT" OF STRUCTURAL CAUSALITY

The impoverished view of the subject-effect of structural causality as presented in *Reading Capital* can be illustrated by the following passage:

> The structure of the relations of production determines the *places* and *functions* occupied and adopted by the agents of production, who are never anything more than the occupants of these places, insofar as they are the "supports" [*Träger*] of these functions. The true "subjects" (in the sense of constitutive subjects of the process) are therefore not these occupants or functionaries, are not, despite all appearances, the "obviousnesses" of the "given" of naïve anthropology, "concrete individuals," "real men"—but *the definition and distribution of these places and functions. The true "subjects" are these definers and distributors: the relations of production* (and political and ideological social relations). But since these are "relations," they cannot be thought within the category *subject*. (RC 180)

Again, what is missing in this elaboration of the bearers (*Träger*) of capital is the reduction of the "new subjects" of capital to the void of absolute negativity of the structure-in-process. While Althusser is right in posing this subject as "irreducible to any anthropological inter-subjectivity," he overlooks the function of the Name that he later turns to in his theory of interpellation.[20] And it is in this light that Althusser's identification of history as a process without a subject must be read.

Because of the importance of this question, I present here a lengthy but suggestive passage in which Althusser outlines his theory of the "subject" of structural causality and its relationship to those "subjects" who are to engage in the symptomatic reading he envisions as precisely the form of practice in which all of the different modes of Darstellung I have been discussing here will be played in concert:

> To see this invisible, to see these "oversights," to identify the lacunae in the fullness of this discourse, the blanks in the crowded text, we need something quite different from an acute or attentive gaze [*regard*]; we need an *informed* gaze, a new gaze, itself produced by a reflection of the "change of terrain" on the exercise of vision, in which Marx pictures the transformation of the problematic. Here I take this transformation for a fact, without any claim to analyze the mechanism that unleashed it and completed it. The fact that this *"change of terrain"* which produces as its effect this metamorphosis in the gaze, was itself only produced in very specific, complex and often dramatic conditions; that it is absolutely irreducible to the idealist myth of a mental decision to change "view-points"; that it brings into play a whole process that the subject's sighting, far from producing, merely reflects in its own place; that in this process of real transformation of the means of production of knowledge, the claims of a "constitutive subject" are as vain as are the claims of the subject of vision in the production of the visible; that the whole process takes place in the dialectical crisis of mutation of a theoretical structure in which the "subject" plays, not the part it believes it is playing, but the part which is assigned to it by the mechanism of the process—all these are questions that cannot be studied here. It is enough to remember that the subject must have occupied its new place in the new terrain, in other words that the subject must already, even partly unwittingly, have been installed in this new terrain, for it to be possible to apply to the old invisible the informed gaze that will make that invisible visible. Marx can see what escaped [Adam] Smith's gaze because he has already occupied this new terrain which, in what new answers it had produced, had nevertheless been produced, though unwittingly, by the old problematic. (RC 27)

Unfortunately, it is precisely this analysis of the mechanism that unleashed and completed the transformation of the problematic that we need and that Althusser refused to elaborate on here. Part of the difficulty lies in the metaphor of terrain as a trope for structure, as Althusser himself noted: "I retain the spatial metaphor. But the change of terrain takes place *on the spot*: in all strictness, we should speak of the mutation of the *mode* of theoretical production and of the change of function of the subject induced by this change of mode" (ibid., n. 9).[21] Such a trope leaves us with the challenge of "mapping" the new terrain and its newly produced objects with our own newly produced gaze. This is precisely what is behind Jameson's trope of "cognitive mapping." In chapter 5, I examine Jameson's use of this trope in his concept of figuration and the political unconscious in its relation to the Real. As we will see, this turn to Darstellung, the move to presentation beyond representation, that I have outlined here does not free us from the problems of representation. Jameson's major point throughout his work is that while the old apparatus of representation no longer suits us in these postmodern, postexpressive days, the effects of structural causality and presentation themselves go through historical mutations. As Kant showed, representation is both a blessing and a curse, but it is the only curse we have. Presentation is an effect of structure retroactively installed like the owl of Minerva. Cognitive mapping is a trope that functions as a call to grow new perceptual organs at a moment of historical development when the current structures and their effects have not yet matured sufficiently to present us with Minerva's owl.

The matter of Darstellung will also afford some final insight into the status of "totality,"
of which we have said both that the concept, in some sense its body serf, reproduces its
untruth and its form of domination, and that it is itself somehow unthinkable and
unrepresentable, very specifically in our present sense of the word.—Fredric Jameson,
Late Marxism

One of the most intriguing and least discussed motifs of Jameson's *The Political
Unconscious* is the picture developed there of some collective unity of consciousness.[1] At one point Jameson claims, for example, that "only a collective
unity—whether that of a particular class, the proletariat, or of its 'organ of
consciousness,' the revolutionary party—can achieve" the transparency required for the subject—here a collective, social, political subject—to be fully
conscious of its determination by class and "be able to square the circle of
ideological conditioning by sheer lucidity and the taking of thought" (*PU* 283).
As the title of his book suggests, however, *The Political Unconscious* is not so
much concerned with the conditions of possibility of such lucidity—a lucidity
possible only for some future, as yet unimaginable collectivity—but rather with
the mechanisms whereby we attempt to "square the circle" of ideological limitation by projecting a world, as the phenomenologists would say, in which our
actions and values would attain a seemingly timeless and natural legitimacy, a
process of wish-fulfillment that Jameson models on Freud's development of

that concept in *The Interpretation of Dreams*. What I am interested in here is this process of wish-fulfillment—of worlding, projection, construction, production, or what you will—a process that Jameson refers to, but never explicitly, coherently, or completely outlines, as *figuration*.[2]

Jameson refers to figuration throughout his writings. It is the process at work in the political unconscious, and as such it demands to be articulated. How does such a process work? Is this process to be seen as a topic for some properly Marxist psychology (assuming there could be such a thing)? How does such a concept extend our understanding of the individual internalization of a socially produced ideology? That is, is figuration to be seen as necessary for some version of Althusser's theory of interpellation or does it offer an alternative account of how the individual answers to the call to identity? Further, what is the relationship between Jameson's conception of this figural process and a more obviously idealistic account of figuration in Kant and Hegel? And, finally, what does such a concept make possible for contemporary Marxist cultural studies? These are the questions that underlie this book.

FIGURATION

While it is correct on one level to refer to figuration as a process, I must make it clear at the outset that such a process is not psychological; that is, it is not something that happens within the individual consciousness and then gets recorded in the various cultural texts we might study at the university. Figuration is a collective process of the text itself. What this means is that texts are collective, objective social forms that operate in culturally specific ways, emitting culturally specific messages that shape the way the text's putative content is received. In this way, Jameson follows the lead of Lacan and Althusser by insisting that *the unconscious is outside*, in the field of signification itself.[3] Here is one place, to anticipate, where Jameson's figuration is radically different from Kant's (although its relationship to Hegelian "idealism" remains to be drawn out): figuration is precisely *not* a subjective process; rather, the subject is itself the result of an objective figurative process of textualization or—assuming for the moment that the two are equivalent—narrativization. The Kantian schema—the relationship between imagination and understanding in the synchronization of images and concepts—must be externalized and objectified, as though turning Kant inside out like a glove (which might be as good a description of Hegelianism as one might hope for). For Jameson, individual consciousness is shaped by historically contingent and socially produced narrative forms.

In his discussion of the film *Dog Day Afternoon*, Jameson refers to figuration as a *requirement*: If we are to "become aware of class, the classes [must] already be in some sense perceptible as such" (*sv* 37). But this requirement can be fulfilled only when the social conditions of our daily lives "have developed to the point at which [their] underlying class structure becomes *representable* in tangible form" (ibid.). What we have here is a kind of social Versinnlichung (as Kant referred to it; see my chapter 2), a rendering in terms of sense what cannot be represented in literal language. Presumably, then, in the early stages of a particular mode of production or a significant internal development of a mode of production, such as the shift from monopoly capitalism to late or multinational capitalism, the new configuration of class relationships has not yet reached a point of visibility or—a term that is synonymous with figuration— representability (*cm* 348; *gpa* 4). Class consciousness as such is not yet possible because this condition of figurability does not yet exist; reality has not successfully "striven towards thought." Herein lies the basic claim of Jameson's concept of the political unconscious (that which makes all ideological productions a symbolic meditation on the destiny of community [*pu* 70]): through a dialectical process, social reality works its way into what cannot yet be called consciousness—consciousness itself being dependent on the prior process of figuration, the fleshing out or concretization of class relations into representable figures (what Hegel refers to as Vorstellungen). The point is that at particular historical moments, class consciousness is not fully possible because that historical culture has not achieved figurability; such is the case in the present period, the postmodern. "The relationship between class consciousness and figurability, in other words, demands something more basic than abstract knowledge, and implies a mode of experience that is more visceral and existential than the abstract certainties of economics and Marxian social science" (*sv* 37).

This "visceral and existential" mode of experience is the domain of culture, where the classes have to take on the function of characters. In other words, at the most basic level class consciousness is always allegorical, each class achieving figurability to the extent to which we can represent it—unconsciously through art, narrative, and other ideological productions—as a character with its own particular qualities and "personality." Figuration, then, is essentially a mode of allegorical personification.

ALLEGORY

Psychoanalysis and Marxism, two theoretical systems crucial in Jameson's elaboration of his conception of the political unconscious (the marriage of the two existing in the phrase "political unconscious" itself), are profoundly allegorical. Such a reliance on these two great master narratives might prove unsettling in its insistence on "imposing" its own terms on otherwise unrelated material were it not true, according to Jameson, that all thought is fundamentally allegorical. This assertion accounts for the slippage, common to most of Jameson's terms related to figuration, between the figural or allegorical operations of the political unconscious itself and interpretive method. All interpretation is at base allegorical (PU 58), various interpretive models functioning not so much as theories per se but rather as "unconscious structures and so many afterimages and secondary effects" of a given historical mode of figuration (PM 417). Allegory, then, is both unconscious (thought in general) and conscious (say, dialectical thought in particular), just as cognitive mapping is something we always do—so why not, to whatever extent possible at a given historical moment, do so consciously and critically?

Because all interpretation is allegorical, Jameson turns to those methods that are deliberately allegorical, such as psychoanalysis, whose major interpretive trope is not so much sexuality as wish-fulfillment. But to the degree that psychoanalysis proper remains bound to categories of individual (un)consciousness, Jameson prefers a different interpretive model that also takes its key concept to be wish-fulfillment and desire: the four-level allegorical system of Northrop Frye.

Since Frye's system is an elaboration on the earlier patristic hermeneutic model of four allegorical levels—and since religion as a meditation on community lies at the heart of each (art being a later mode of religious representation for Frye)—I will begin with Jameson's discussion of the medieval system in *The Political Unconscious*. All allegorical methods are (unconscious) attempts to articulate a system for representing History. For the patristic hermeneuticists, history itself is "God's book," its particular historical happenings now read as so many figures in this divine narrative—a narrative laden with hidden meanings that unfold on four different allegorical levels. This is not to suggest, however, that the acts of the Old Testament were to be seen as "merely figurative," in the sense of phantom objects or imaginary terms standing in for *the real thing* (Christ). As Eric Auerbach has argued, for the patristic hermeneuticists, all four levels were equally real, equally concrete, but simply coexisted on different historical or spiritual planes. *Figura*, Auerbach tells us, "is something real and historical which announces something else that is also real and historical. The relation between the two events is revealed by an accord or similarity."[4] We should read the relationship between figure and fulfillment, then, in much the same way as Kant reads the symbol: as a coincidence according to the rule, not according to the content. The content of each is equally concrete; we simply abstract from each the like rule.

Jameson charts the four levels as follows (*PU* 31):

Literal	historical or textual reference
Allegorical	allegorical key or interpretive code (life of Christ)
Moral	psychological reading (individual subject) (individual soul's need for redemption)
Anagogic	political reading (collective "meaning" of history) (destiny of the human race)

THE LITERAL: At this level, the Old Testament is taken as the initial historical reference. The job of allegory is to translate this pre-Christian history into three different allegorical levels listed above in order to identify a systematic unity of divine intent underlying disparate and seemingly contradictory histories (the Old and New Testaments).

THE ALLEGORICAL: Here, Old Testament history is read as the prefiguration of the life of Christ, the New Testament serving as the fulfillment of hidden Old Testament prophecies; "a familiar, even hackneyed, illustration is the rewriting of the bondage of the people of Israel in Egypt as the descent of Christ into hell after his death on the cross" (*PU* 30). In this way, one God can coherently serve two different religions.

THE MORAL: At this level, the story of the Israelites in Egypt is rewritten as the thralldom of the pre-believer to sin and interest in the worldly matters of the flesh. The literal level is rewritten, then, in terms of the condition of the individual's soul and his or her need for redemption. The occurrences of the Old Testament are lessons for moral behavior once we develop the ability to read "God's book" in this light.

THE ANAGOGIC: At this fourth level, "the text undergoes its ultimate rewriting in terms of the destiny of the human race as a whole, Egypt then coming to prefigure that long purgatorial suffering of earthly history from which the second coming of Christ and the Last Judgment come as the final release" (*PU* 31).

As has been already suggested above, the importance of this theological apparatus for Jameson is its function as a meditation on the destiny of the human collectivity. What can be seen here in this allegorical process is the production of what Jameson refers to as a libidinal apparatus: a particular narrative structure, in this case the Old Testament, is emptied of its original content while its form is objectified and alienated, making it available for new forms of *ideological investment*. The reduction of the two histories—of the people of Israel and the life story of Jesus (the movement from the Literal to the Allegorical)—to the analogical rule common to both at first sight seems to lack any promise for a more collective figuration of History proper to Marxism. But this process itself articulates the structure of this history in such a way that, having been opened to the vicissitudes of one individual's story, it can then be expanded at the Moral level as a paradigm for *every* individual's story. Here, however, we are still dealing with individuals as individuals, whereas in the move from the Moral to the Anagogic level we enter into the story of universal human destiny. While the Literal continues to be seen as literal, the structure of the Literal history of the people of Israel has now been liberated (objectified and alienated) for reinvestment as a universal history of humanity as such, "precisely the functional and ideological transformation which the system of four levels was designed to achieve in the first place" (*PU* 31).

Frye's own allegorical system follows this four-tiered structure. In fact, it could be said that the patristic hermeneutic has itself been transformed into a libidinal apparatus that Frye can then reinvest with a different content to serve a quite different ideological impulse. Frye's system of literary interpretation also begins with the Literal level, to be followed by the Formal, the Mythical or Archetypal, and finally the Anagogical.

Formal	the work as symbolic structure or symbolic world
Mythical	archetypal universal symbols of desire (poetry as human society's self-developed form)
Literal	verbal organization or the order of language
Anagogical	the all-englobing body of infinite human being as the imaginative limit of desire

The key for Jameson is that whereas the patristic hermeneutic system ultimately opened up the individual level to the more universal one of community, Frye seems to invert this process: the phase that Frye refers to as the Mythical operates on the same plane as the patristic Anagogical level (the social); Frye's final phase, *his* Anagogical, on the other hand, operates on the patristic level of the universal individual. The process of figuration is here reversed in that the social (Archetypal) becomes a figure for the infinite individual rather than the other way around. In the process, the social is recontained within individualistic terms even though *this* individual is made up by us all. Rather than standing in as the figuration of the social, the libidinal body instead becomes the "imaginative limit of human desire." The political unconscious, it should be remembered, is ultimately the process of a figurative meditation on the destiny of community.[5]

Jameson's own "social hermeneutic," then, like its patristic forerunner, will attempt to draw out this figurative meditation on social destiny (*PU* 74) within Marxist terms. The first thing to note in Jameson's own libidinal transformation of the allegorical apparatus is his reduction of the four-level system to a three-level one. Each level is to be seen as a particular horizon within a larger concentric mechanism, each horizon opening out onto a more universal and globalizing plane. In keeping with the charts above, Jameson's system appears as follows:

Historical	the ideology of form as a matrix of symbolic messages related to different coexisting modes of production
Social	the ideologeme as a unit in class discourse
Political	individual cultural object as a symbolic act

Keeping in mind that Jameson describes his system as one of concentric circles, it should be thought of in a schematic sense as seen in figure 1.

POLITICAL: In this horizon, the text or cultural object itself is examined as a symbolic act, much as Claude Lévi-Strauss viewed primitive art as a symbolic resolution to an unthinkable social contradiction (a point to be discussed further below). As we can see, this horizon functions as a symptom, as a figure for social contradiction that otherwise manifests itself as an intellectual aporia, an irresolvable binary opposition.

SOCIETY: At this second level or horizon, Jameson inserts the text-as-symbolic-act generated in the first horizon into the broader, extratextual

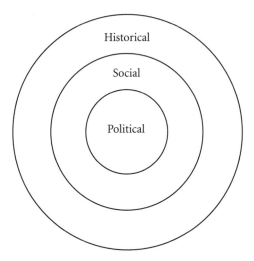

Figure 1

horizon of class discourse. The text is now seen as one utterance in this dialogic structure and will function as an ideologeme, "the smallest intelligible unit of the essentially antagonistic collective discourses of social classes" (*PU* 76).

HISTORY: At the third and final horizon, the level of human history as a whole seen as the long and antagonistic process of cultural revolution (*PU* 95), Jameson shifts his focus to the text as a sedimented form that carries the traces and anticipatory signs of different modes of production. The text is now seen as participating in an ideology of form, which provides the all-embracing unity of a single code, a cultural dominant specific to a given mode of production that provides the terms in which each text will achieve its intelligibility (as with postmodernism, the cultural dominant of late capitalism, which overdetermines the functions and relationships of other cultural modes [*PU* 89; *PM* 4]). At this point, "History itself becomes the ultimate ground as well as the untranscendable limit of our understanding in general and our textual interpretations in particular" (*PU* 100).

It is here that Jameson's conception of figuration receives its force. If "History" were some positive content available from the start, then there would be no need for figuration; figuration is necessary because the process of cultural revolution is not a positive, empirically available event but rather a structural limitation on how we perceive ourselves and our relationship to the larger social totality that determines us: "History can be apprehended only through its effects, and never as some reified force" (*PU* 102). The three figurative levels of the text that Jameson outlines provide a "way of seeing" this process called History, this absent cause that we experience in the form of Necessity in terms of tangible figures or stand-ins that flesh out the limits to praxis that the contradictions of History pose for us. This search for ways of seeing, whether conscious or unconscious, is the process of cognitive mapping by way of which we obtain the figures necessary for locating ourselves in History.

Allegorical criticism does not so much *interpret* a given subject matter through the terms of another, master narrative—where interpretation is seen as the unearthing of some deeper meaning below the surface—as *rewrite* that subject matter in terms of a different code. Allegory is a process of *diversion and reinvestment*: the initial terms are diverted from their "surface" function into "the service of other, ideological functions, and reinvested by what we have called the political unconscious" (*PU* 142). The interpretive desire proper to the function of the symbol (from romanticism through certain variants of modernism) has, for historically objective reasons, been superseded generally by the allegorical desire that, having waned in the early nineteenth century after a half millennium or so of favor (that is, of ideological effectivity), has reappeared in the postmodern age of late capitalism—an age for which the one-to-one correlations of essence and appearance underlying the symbolic mode no longer work for a simultaneously more fragmented and totalized world system. Such an approach, conscious as well as unconscious, cannot but be the case if we accept Jameson's fundamental hypothesis that "all thinking today is *also*, whatever else it is, an attempt to think the world system as such" (*GPA* 4). In today's postnational period, the older national allegories that allowed us to plot our relationship to the (national) systems that defined us necessarily give way to an array of "random, minute, or isolated landscapes" that now "function as a figurative machinery in which questions about the system and its control over the local ceaselessly rise and fall, with a fluidity" nowhere possible in the older libidinal apparatus of national allegory (*GPA* 5). And for what used to be called the subject, allegory now provides "a host of partial subjects, fragmentary or schizoid constellations, [which] can often now stand in allegorically for trends and forces in the world system, in a transitional situation in which genuinely transnational classes, such as a new international proletariat and a new density of global management, have not yet anywhere clearly emerged" (ibid.).

In other words, allegory allows the part to stand in for the whole and for the whole to achieve its figuration in a constellation of parts; what distinguishes this from an older, more stereotypically Hegelian (symbolic) dialectic of part and whole, though, is the provisionality and replaceability of these contingent constellations. Dialectical thought is allegorical in the sense that the immediate local surface meaning of a text or concept is "*at one and the same time* taken as the *figure* for Utopia in general, and for the systemic revolutionary transformation of society as a whole" (*IT2* 73) and thus involves a constant duality of focus. Key to understanding this dialectical stereoscopy is the awareness that the urge and ability to "impose" these two levels of meaning on a given narrative is not a casual and arbitrary "choice" on the part of the critic but is to be seen at once as immanent to the structure of the work itself and made possible as a choice only by objective social conditions. Both the text and critical approach will share this fundamental characteristic: each

> will from the dialectical point of view be found to conceal its own contradictions and repress its own historicity by strategically framing its perspective so as to omit the negative, absence, contradiction, repression, the *non-dit*, or the *impensé*. To restore the latter requires that abrupt and paradoxical dialectical restructuration of the basic problematic which has often seemed to be the most characteristic gesture and style of dialectical method in general, keeping the terms but standing the problem on its head. . . . The dialectical critique of these [options] is, however, not a merely negative and destructive one; it leads, as we shall see, to their fulfillment and completion, albeit in a very different spirit from the one they initially pose. (*PU* 109–10)

Such a dialectical approach is necessary since "any doctrine of figurality must necessarily be ambiguous: a symbolic expression of a truth is also, at the same time, a distorted and disguised expression, and a theory of figural expression is also a theory of mystification or false consciousness" (*PU* 70).[6]

COGNITIVE MAPPING

The term Jameson developed during the 1980s for extending his conception of figuration was "cognitive mapping." As a response to the problems of figuration posed by late capitalism and evident in the dominant (postmodern) works of this latest transfiguration of the capitalist system, cognitive mapping provided a new way of figuring the figuration process itself. Since our dominant aesthetic is a spatial one, according to Jameson's analysis of contemporary culture in his now famous essay, "Postmodernism, or, the Cultural Logic of Late Capitalism," the figure of cognitive mapping was posed as a spatial response to our incapacity to locate ourselves in this new, unrepresentable space of late capitalism. Drawing at once on the work of Kevin Lynch's analysis of consciousness in the city—cognitive mapping here working as the individual's ability to locate himself or herself in terms of the city as a whole according to identifiable monuments, buildings, and other positioning markers, an ability exasperated in the modern generic grid city—and Althusser's definition of ideology as "the representation of the subject's *Imaginary* relationship to his or her Real conditions of existence," Jameson calls for an aesthetic of cognitive mapping that would help individuals integrate their immediate existential experience with a knowledge of the larger social whole that provides objective limits to that individual experience. According to the Althusserian formula, individual experience and knowledge of the whole are never coterminus and require ideology to span this gap, as "a way of articulating those two distinct dimensions with each other" (*PM* 53).[7] Here again, we are at the heart of the question of figuration as the symbolic meditation on the nature and destiny of community, as a question of the representational dialectic of codes and symbolic systems.

Jameson's call for such an aesthetic is worth quoting at length:

> An aesthetic of cognitive mapping—a pedagogical political culture which seeks to endow the individual subject with some new heightened sense of its place in the global system—will necessarily have to respect this now enormously complex representational dialectic and invent radically new forms in order to do it justice. This is not then, clearly, a call for a return to some older kind of machinery, some older and more transparent national space, or some more traditional and reassuring perspectival or mimetic enclave: the new political art (if it is possible at all) will have to hold to the truth of postmodernism, that is to say, to its fundamental object—the world space of multinational capital—at the same time at which it achieves a breakthrough to some as yet unimaginable new mode of representing this last, in which we may again begin to grasp our positioning as individual and collective subjects and regain a capacity to act and struggle which is at present neutralized by our spatial as well as our social confusion. (ibid., 54)

Social space was not always organized in this way, however, not even in the relatively short history of capitalism itself. Drawing on Ernest Mandel's *Late Capitalism*, Jameson, throughout his work of the last fifteen years, describes capitalism as made up of three identifiable stages, each with its own kind of "space" (an experiential horizon or field, determined by the dominant mode of production, which allows (or not) for our individual positioning within that social space itself). The first stage is classical or market capitalism, the second the stage of monopoly capitalism or imperialism, and the third multinational or late capitalism. Each stage is marked by its own kind of social space and figurational condition as seen in table 2:

Table 2

STAGES	MARKET	MONOPOLY	MULTINATIONAL
Space:	grid	absence-presence	suppressed distance
Subject:	standardization	monadic relativism	schizophrenic de-centering
Network:	commodity	absent colonial world	de-centered global capital
Experience:	infinite equivalence	global relativity	radical discontinuity
Technology:	steam	internal combustion	computer
Art Value:	mimesis	irony	pastiche, paranoia
Mode:	realism	modernism	postmodernism

Jameson claims that the first stage, market capitalism, does not conjure any acute problem for figuration. Giving rise to Enlightenment ideology, market capitalism led to the de-figuration of feudal ideology based on religion and prescientific views of the cosmos. The great revolutionary job of this early stage of capitalism was to rid consciousness of its reliance on all forms of superstition and irrational thought and, as such, was a process of decoding and desacralization rather than a figurative recoding and reinvestment. The space particular to this stage is marked by what Jameson refers to as the "logic of the grid": "a reorganization of some older sacred and heterogeneous space into geometrical and Cartesian homogeneity, a space of infinite equivalence and extension" (410). The "world-space" is thus homogenized while the subject is standardized and universalized.

The second stage, on the other hand, that of monopoly capitalism, inaugurates the difficulties for cognitive mapping that are dialectically complicated as we later pass on to the third stage. The second stage, based as it is on imperialism and the figure of the nation-state, brings about a "growing contradiction between lived experience and structure" (410). Now the "truth" of the daily individual experience of the Londoner lies across the seas in the colonies, "yet these structural coordinates are often not even conceptualizable to immediate lived experience" (411); accordingly, the new subjective experiential space of this stage of capitalism becomes that of absence and presence as the subject confronts the difficulties of representing the absent cause of this space, the imperialist system. Nevertheless, at this point figuration is still possible, as in the cases of national allegories (Jameson's definitive analysis of this figural process being *Fables of Aggression*) and the individual consciousness—the alienated subject of many modernisms—closed to any "authentic" relationship to the outside world, this inside-outside opposition being another form of the essence-appearance form that dominates this space of monadic relativism.

The third stage of capitalism, the multinational, does not offer even this space of inside-outside, for such a dilemma at least affords a sense of spatial distance (and with it a temporal sense of historical relationship). For the postmodern subject, however, this space has been collapsed, imploded, as it were, into the subject to the point where the postmodern body is "now exposed to a perceptual barrage of immediacy from which all sheltering layers and intervening mediations have been removed" (412–13). Figuration, it seems, demands a certain spatial distance as well as a sense of relationship or connectedness. We can't, as the old cliché goes, see the forest for the trees. The gap separating the individual subject from some way of imagining this global totality is now, in a sense, internal to the system itself, much like a demonic form of Hegel's transition from the essence logic of the *Science of Logic*, marked as above by a sense of inside-outside or essence-appearance, to a notional logic according to which the gap between essence and appearance is internal to appearance itself, the "mirage" of some spatial differentiation required by an essence logic now giving way to the dialectical unity of the two: according to this notional logic, essence and appearance were never really separate to begin with but simply the projection of external reflection. We postmoderns cannot be so happy as Hegel, though, since to us the elaboration of the notion has turned out to be nothing but a figure for the elaboration of capital itself as it works its way into every last nook and cranny of social and individual space, colonizing the last vestiges of nature, the globe, and the unconscious. The figure of cognitive mapping itself fails to capture this saturation, as Jameson himself points out, since the map still implies a space external to the subject open to mapping in the first place: "Cognitive mapping, which was meant to have a kind of oxymoronic value and to transcend the limits of mapping altogether, is, as a concept, drawn back by the force of gravity of the black hole of the map itself (one of the most powerful of all human conceptual instruments) and therein cancels out its own impossible originality" (416). Yet this does not relieve us, however, of the responsibility of developing some conceptual instrument on the order of mapping, but more appropriate to this imploded postmodern space; still, the objective conditions for such an instrument have yet to avail us of such a possibility. We must, according to one of Jameson's most visual figures, develop new sensory organs that can enlarge our imaginative capacity for taking in the sublime—unrepresentable—space of late capitalism.

SYMBOLIC ACTS AND CHARACTER SYSTEMS

Figuration, in addition to its other functions I have been outlining here, is a mode of collective storytelling. Jameson's version of this figurative process depends on an elaboration of, among other things, Lévi-Strauss's analysis of mythical thought. Lévi-Strauss, Jameson writes, views myth as "a narrative process whereby tribal society seeks an imaginary solution, a resolution by way of figural thinking, to a real social contradiction between infrastructure and superstructure" (*IT2* 77). For Jameson, however, this narrative process is found not only in tribal societies but in all societies. Here Jameson explictly connects his theory of "narrative" as a socially symbolic act, or the political unconscious, and the process of figuration.[8] Jameson writes that "in the absence of any genuine historical and social self-consciousness, what has been conceptually unformulizable becomes the raw material and the occasion for a very different type of mental operation, namely what must be called the work of figuration" (ibid., 93). We can rarely if ever form a concept of our own social contradiction; we can only think this contradiction as a conceptual antinomy or binary opposition. That is, the social appears as simply the illogical, the historically contingent problem of social relations appearing as an eternally necessary problem of thought. Lévi-Strauss, for example, argues that the social contradiction between, as Jameson puts it, "the tribal infrastructure of the kinship system, and the religious or cosmological systems" of that same culture seem irreconcilable with one another (77–78), and only achieve symbolic resolution once posed in terms of the Oedipus myth. Oedipus, then, becomes the figure who reconciles on a purely symbolic level the contradiction here between kinship and religious systems. "Myth" for Lévi-Strauss is precisely this resolution-through-figuration. If it can't be thought, it must be figured.

When a culture does not offer a social resolution to its contradictions—

when, to elaborate further on Lévi-Strauss's example, I cannot reconcile or mediate my social relationships as both a capitalist (infrastructural relationship) and a Christian (superstructural relationship)—then that resolution must come about figurally, through art and narrative. But as suggested earlier, this process is not internal to me as an individual but is made possible by the objective figural apparatuses available to me. In this way the text draws "the Real" into its own texture as its immanent "subtext," not as something external or extrinsic to the text but as Jameson notes, "something borne within and vehiculated by the text itself, interiorized in its very fabric in order to provide the stuff and the raw material on which the textual operation must work" (81). This is not to suggest, however, that "the Real" does not exist outside the text but rather that it only becomes available to thought through the figurative process of working it up into the text. Jameson describes this process as follows in *The Political Unconscious*: "The literary work or cultural object, as though for the first time, brings into being that very situation to which it is also, at one and the same time a reaction. It articulates its own situation and textualizes it, thereby encouraging and perpetuating the illusion that the situation itself did not exist before it, that there is nothing but a text" (82). He then elaborates on this point:

> It seems useful, therefore, to distinguish, from this ultimate subtext which is the place of social *contradiction*, a secondary one, which is more properly the place of ideology, and which takes the form of the *aporia* or the *antinomy*: What can in the former be resolved only through the intervention of praxis here comes before the purely contemplative mind as logical scandal or double bind, the unthinkable and the conceptually paradoxical, that which cannot be unknotted by the operation of pure thought, and which must therefore generate a whole more properly narrative apparatus—the text itself—to square its circles and to dispel, through narrative movement, its intolerable closure. (82–83)

Figuration, then, is an operation of "squaring circles." What this means is that the binary opposition of the two antinomic terms produces an intolerable closure, a vicious circularity of moving from one term to the other, treating each in its turn as the privileged term in the opposition. This back-and-forth movement gestures toward a resolution to this aporia by suggesting that one or the other of the terms can finally achieve some privileged status, but this resolution only occurs through the mediation of a third term. Figuration pro-

Figure 2

vides such a resolution by projecting this third term that, in good Hegelian fashion, at once preserves, cancels, and sublates the two initial terms. It is this third term that squares the circle. For Jameson, this process of figuration lies at the base of the political unconscious.

So far this conception of the figurative process remains at the simple triadic level of Lévi-Strauss's mythical thought. But what interests Jameson is the way in which A. J. Greimas's semiotic rectangle fleshes out this triad into a full-blown semiotic system exhausting all of the logically possible permutations of the initial binary terms. If the first of the two terms is referred to as **S**, then its opposite would be **-S**, with the third term figuring as their resolution (figure 2).

The fleshing out of all the logical permutations resulting from, and the ways out of the "interminable closure" of this initial opposition would then be represented as shown in figure 3.

The relationship between **S** and **-S**, as we have seen, is that of opposition between two positive yet irreconcilable terms. The relationship between **S** and $\overline{\textbf{S}}$, on the other hand, is that of negation: $\overline{\textbf{S}}$ is simply **not-S**. The same is true as well of the relationship between **-S** and **-$\overline{\textbf{S}}$**. And finally, the relationship between **-$\overline{\textbf{S}}$** and $\overline{\textbf{S}}$ is again simple opposition, this time between the semiotic system's two negative points. Greimas refers to what I call position **C**, the resolution of the initial contraries, as the complex position, while what I refer to as position **N** is the neutral position, the emptying out or neutralization of the value of the initial binary. As we shall see, the complex resolution is the process that Lévi-Strauss refers to as myth, while the neutral position is the process that Louis Marin refers to as Utopic discourse.

One place where Jameson illustrates the relationships between these terms is in his discussion of Honoré de Balzac's *La Vieille Fille*. Pointing out that Balzac's tale is a sexual farce, Jameson goes on to say that such a narrative centers on a sexual secret and, consequently, initiates the search for this secret information. By initiating this activity through which the secret slowly unfolds, through which the unknown manifest content translates into the known, the sexual farce also sets itself up to be read as allegory, another structure demanding

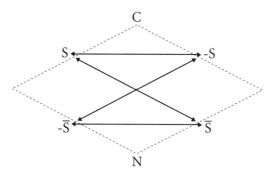

Figure 3

decoding. Once the transcoding structure is set in motion, in other words, it does not simply end at the level of sheer content but rather projects this mystery-structure outward. What is significant here, then, is that the allegorical transcoding or hermeneutical activity of the reader doesn't end once the sexual mystery is solved; as Jameson puts it, "The function of the sexual comedy is to direct our reading attention toward the relationship between sexual potency and class affiliation" (*PU* 163). Once this happens, the story then revolves around the struggle for power over France as figured by Mademoiselle Cormon's hand in marriage. Having identified the dominant binary opposition structuring Balzac's political allegory to be the *Ancien Régime* versus *Napoleonic Energy*, Jameson expands on the initial binary terms in figure 4.

In this way Jameson is able to chart out what he refers to as Balzac's "character system"; each synthesis is embodied in the narrative by a particular character who displays the particular traits of that synthesis. The Count de Troisville, for example, embodies the *contrary* (positive yet opposing) relationship between the characteristics of both the Ancien Régime (standing for organic society and legitimacy) and Napoleonic Energy. So the Count de Troisville—the ideal yet unattainable (because married) husband prospect for Mademoiselle Cormon, the novel's center—embodies the *complex* resolution of these two positive poles. Further, the Ancien Régime is also in a *contradictory* relationship with the Bourgeoisie (not-organic, not-legitimate); and Energy in turn is in a contradictory relationship with Culture (not-activity, or passivity). The character who embodies the synthesis of Energy and the Bourgeoisie, we can see, is Du Bosquier, while the Chevalier synthesizes the traits of legitimacy and passivity. Finally, the *neutral* resolution is embodied by Athanase, the passive and powerless romantic poet. The figurative contradiction to the Count, then, is

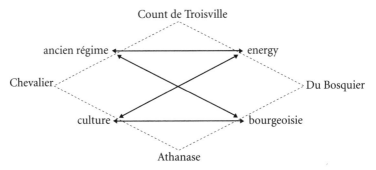

Figure 4

romanticism, which here functions as the neutralization or emptying out of the positive values embodied by the Count.

One form figuration takes, then, is the elaboration of a character system such as the above. The key point is that faced with the contradiction between tradition and dynamism that marks early bourgeois society in post-Napoleonic France, Balzac writes a farce that serves as an apparatus for playing out the fantasmatic manifestations of his social desire. This apparatus—the sexual farce—is not somehow unique to Balzac, as though it expresses his personal psychic dynamics. Rather, it is a social form from the start that offers Balzac a certain figurative response to the social contradiction he faces—the coexistence of late feudal and early capitalist social relations.

LIBIDINAL APPARATUS

Confronted with the intolerable aporia of binary logic, the political uncon-scious, as illustrated in the above example from Balzac, thus projects a system of symbolic resolutions to this aporia. Jameson refers to this system as a "libidinal apparatus," which can be seen operating in *La Vieille Fille*:

> [*La Vieille Fille* is informed by the] binary opposition between aristocratic elegance and Napoleonic energy, which the political imagination seeks des-perately to transcend, generating the contradictories of each of these terms, mechanically generating all the syntheses logically available to it, while remaining locked into the terms of the original double bind. Such a vision is not to be taken as the logical articulation of all the political positions or ideo-logical possibilities objectively present in the situation of the Restoration, but

rather as the structure of a particular political fantasy, as the mapping of that particular "libidinal apparatus" in which Balzac's political thinking becomes invested—it being understood that we are not here distinguishing between fantasy and some objective reality onto which it would be projected, but rather, with Deleuze or with J. F. [Jean-François] Lyotard, asserting such fantasy or protonarrative structure as the vehicle for our experience of the real. (*PU* 48)

The libidinal apparatus, as Jameson uses the term, is a vehicle for ideological investment. But this point should be taken in its broadest application, in such a way that the "ideological" does not figure as false consciousness, as a mode of thinking that can be avoided, any more than the unconscious can be avoided. We all "experience the real," as Jameson puts it, by means of these libidinal apparatuses. There is no outside of ideology in this sense; in fact, this very metaphor of ideology as a space or terrain that could be thought in terms of inside and outside is misleading to the degree that it keeps us from seeing ideology, like the Lacanian unconscious, not as something internal to individual consciousness as such but as external, as the effect of certain social practices that are displayed by, staged by, condensed in libidinal apparatuses.

Jameson develops this term most extensively in his discussion of Wyndham Lewis in *Fables of Aggression: Wyndham Lewis, the Modernist as Fascist*. There he discusses what he calls the transition from national allegory to libidinal apparatus. Jameson claims that in Lewis's work, "national allegory" does not simply operate through the representative national figure—the "German" or the "Italian," whose traits we know ahead of time precisely because they are *essential* to German-ness or Italian-ness as such. Lewis's allegorical system is not essential and predictable but relational and contingent; unpredictable momentary alliances crop up between normally antagonistic national figures. For Jameson, such a state of affairs produces a dialectically new and more complicated allegorical system. "Under these circumstances, allegory ceases to be that static decipherment of one-to-one correspondences with which it is still so often identified and opens up that specific and uniquely allegorical space between signifier and signified" (*FA* 90–91). What we get, then, in Lewis's work is a new allegory that figures "the ultimate conflictual 'truth' of the sheer, mobile, shifting relationality of national types and of the older nation-states which are their content," as Jameson puts it (91). To understand the transition from such a national allegorical system to the libidinal apparatus, one passage from *Fables of*

Aggression in particular is worth quoting at length, especially so because of its presentation of the different elements involved in this figurational process of the libidinal apparatus:

> We have not done with national allegory . . . when we have specified the conditions for its emergence as a narrative system. Once in place, such a system has a kind of objectivity about it, and wins a semiautonomy as a cultural structure which can then know an unforeseeable history in its own right, as an object cut adrift from its originating situation and "freed" for the alienation of a host of quite different signifying functions and uses, whose content rushes in to invest it. This is the point, then, at which we mark the transformation of national allegory into what J. F. Lyotard has called a *libidinal apparatus*, an empty form or structural matrix in which a charge of free-floating and inchoate fantasy—both ideological and psychoanalytic—can suddenly crystallize, and find the articulated figuration essential for its social actuality and psychic effectivity.
>
> In the case of Tarr, we will suggest that the empty matrix of national allegory is then immediately seized on by hitherto unformulable impulses which invest its structural positions and, transforming the whole narrative system into a virtual allegory of the fragmented psyche itself, now reach back to overdetermine the resonance of this now increasingly layered text. (95)

If the various elements are separated out from this rather dense passage, three major stages in this transformation from narrative allegorical structure to libidinal apparatus can be isolated: objectification, alienation, and investment. These stages themselves can be elaborated as a series of seven steps in this process of figural transformation:

— emergence of allegory as narrative system;

— objectification of system;

— semiautonomization as cultural structure;

— alienation by cutting adrift;

— crystallization;

— investment; and

— overdetermination.

As we have seen, the first stage is the production of the allegorical narrative system—in this case, the national allegory. That allegorical system itself becomes objectified, seen no longer as a peculiar historical event but as a transitory structure that in stage three, achieves the semiautonomous status that can then cause it to be cut adrift, isolated from its historical context to operate according to new, alien demands. Once alienated, emptied out, and crystallized as a free-floating structure, the national allegory has become a libidinal apparatus, available for investments of foreign content—a content that then retroactively reinvests and overdetermines the national characters that had set such a structure in motion to begin with. In Lewis's *Tarr*, the empty structure of the national allegory—composed by the figures of Tarr and Kreisler—is invested with the content of the psyche, Tarr figuring as the ego and Kreisler as the id. The transition from national allegory to libidinal apparatus in this case, then, occurs in the shift from the equation *character A = stock national type B* to *stock national type B = psychic mechanism C*. The extended equation would then be *Kreisler = German = id*. Germanness no longer points strictly to its initial content (national characteristic) but has become an objective and alienated structure now invested with new content (psychic mechanism).

We can also see this process at work in Jameson's discussion of Freud's development of allegorical models:

> The history of Freud's own work may be invoked as testimony for such a process of figuration and reinvestment or overdetermination: not only are the Freudian models allegories, they can also be shown to depend for their figural expression on elaborate and preexisting representations of the topography of the city and the dynamics of the political state. This urban and civil "apparatus"—often loosely referred to as a Freudian "metaphor"— is the objective precondition for Freud's representation of the psyche, and is thus at one with the very "discovery" of the unconscious itself, which may now be seen to have presupposed the objective development—the industrialization, the social stratification and class polarization, the complex division of labor—of the late Victorian city. Nor is the post-War transformation of this properly Freudian "libidinal apparatus" into the "energy model" of the rivalry of Eros and Thanatos without striking similarities to the "break" in Lewis' work which is contemporaneous with it. (*FA* 95)

Jameson examines Freud's "sexual apparatus" in terms conforming to the stages I have just isolated. Freud's turn to the sexual as the allegory through which he could write the dynamics of nonsexual psychic experience depended on "a process of isolation, autonomization, specialization, developed into an independent sign system or symbolic dimension in its own right; as long as sexuality remains as integrated into social life in general as, say, eating, its possibilities of symbolic extension are to that degree limited, and the sexual retains its status as a banal inner-worldly event and bodily function. Its symbolic possibilities are dependent on its preliminary exclusion from the social field" (PU 64). This exclusion from the social field conforms to the stage referred to above as the emergence of a narrative system, just as, say, according to Walter Benjamin, art's exclusion from the social realm of religious ritual prepared the way for its alienation and reinvestment in both aestheticist and avant-garde terms. After this initial exclusion and objectification of sex as an independent system with its own significatory operations, this sexual system can then be *alienated*; that is, the sexual system is emptied of its content (sexual drive and activity) and becomes an "empty matrix," as Jameson puts it, an empty form that can be invested with new "nonsexual" content (namely, the structure and operations of conscious and unconscious life). This reinvestment of the empty form is the point of figuration in Jameson's system. Nevertheless, one should remember that figuration is an operation of the *political* unconscious, which means that all allegory is at a fundamental level political allegory, which for Jameson is another way of saying that figuration is a process of libidinal investment that produces and sets in motion "a sometimes repressed ur-narrative or master fantasy about the interaction of collective subjects" (PU 80). It is precisely the externalization and objectification of the narrative system as a product and process of the body politic that makes such wish-fulfilling investment possible. Jameson's job, then, is thus to identify the apparatuses at work in the material he studies and to map out the system of ideological closure such apparatuses play out.

UTOPIA

One of the key places where Jameson discusses his use of the concept "figuration" is in his little-discussed essay, "Of Islands and Trenches: Neutralization and the Production of Utopian Discourse," which appears in *Syntax of History*, volume 2 of his *Ideologies of Theory*. Again we are dealing with Greimas's semiotic rectangle, only this time without emphasizing its function as an apparatus for symbolic resolution—the process occurring in the *complex* synthesis of the two positive poles of the initial binary—but now with the *neuter* synthesis. The latter is the neutralizing synthesis of the two negative or subpoles that stand in contradictory relation to the two positive poles. As such, Utopian discourse is not so much a process of constructing or representing some fantasy space but instead a process of neutralizing the Real. Jameson's purpose is to

> understand the Utopian text as a determinate type of *praxis*, rather than as a specific mode of representation, a praxis that has less to do with the construction and perfection of someone's "idea" of a "perfect society" than it does with a concrete set of mental operations to be performed on a determinate type of raw material given in advance, which is contemporary society itself—or, what amounts to the same thing, on those collective representations of contemporary society that inform our ideologies just as they order our daily experience. (*IT2* 81)

To further distinguish this utopian operation from the "mythic," to use Lévi-Strauss's term once more, I return to the example of Balzac's *La Vieille Fille*. Balzac's narrative drives the text on to the production of the Count, the positive synthesis of legitimacy and energy, the two countervailing values presented by the narrative. This figurative operation is therefore mythic. But had the narrative driven on toward the neutralization rather than the synthesis of these two values, it would then have been a utopian operation, and would have posed Athanase, the romantic poet, as the key figure of the text. The purpose of this figurative movement would have been to empty out the dominant cultural values of legitimacy and energy available at the time and would then have functioned as a utopian critique rather than a symbolic resolution of Restoration values. The utopian way out of the intolerable closure of the binary opposition is the neutralization of that opposition itself.

Drawing on the work of Louis Marin, Jameson shows this utopian process at work in Sir Thomas More's *Utopia*. As Marin points out in his book *Utopics*, More's England is confronted with both the dissolution of the feudal manor system and the development of the capitalist market system. Rather than synthesize two positive values, More's text neutralizes two negative values related to the feudal/capitalism split: pride and money. So the detailed descriptions at work in *Utopia* function not so much to offer a view of this no-place (*ou-topos*) but to cancel out the vices of More's own society. I will return to this opposition of vices in a moment.

First, however, I need to plot out the spatial opposition that seems a more

likely candidate for cancellation by this utopian text. Utopias as a genre function as a critique of contemporary society, and often in a transparent way. Thus
we have the detailed accounts in utopian scholarship that line up textual elements with subtextual references. For example, as Jameson notes, we might
look at the fifty-four city-states of Utopia as a thinly veiled reference to the fifty-
three counties (plus London) of More's England. Utopia as a spatial neutralization, then, would be some version of not-England. The text itself provides these
possibilities: the New World and Asia, for which England functions as the
complex synthesis and Utopia as the neutralization. Yet the values at stake in
Utopia do not correspond to America and Asia (whatever such values might be:
innovation versus stagnation, opportunity versus stasis?). As the very name
Utopia suggests, what is at stake is not to be identified as a question of place,
which is another way of indicating that the detailed work of representation in
utopian texts is a smokescreen or diversion from the real work to be done,
which is, as we have seen, not representation but neutralization. Again following Marin, Jameson contends that on the level of representation *Utopia* reveals
itself to be a contradictory work. Descriptions of dwellings, for example, do not
logically correspond to accounts of population. The egalitarian economic
structure contradicts the hierarchical political structure. An island of identical
cities has a privileged capital city at its center. These contradictions at the level
of representation reveal a more fundamental contradiction at work in the text
that this exhaustive attempt at representation should have covered up.

A clue to that contradiction lies not in the description of Utopia itself but in
the frame narrative of Hythloday's debate with the courtiers regarding capital
punishment and, finally, with his condemnation in the conclusion of two vices,
pride and money. The debate on capital punishment points to a fundamental
contradiction at the social level. The debate centers on the question of pun-
ishing the rapidly increasing number of thieves in the English countryside.
Hythloday's condemnation of capital punishment focuses on his belief that
thievery is not so much a moral issue as an economic one: with the dissolution
of the feudal manors—the displacement of mercenaries and petty bureaucrats
in the attempt to streamline the manorial system—and with the turning out of
farmers and peasants due to the enclosure movement, thousands of people
were driven into poverty and, consequently, thievery. It is not Utopia as another
place but rather Utopia as an alternative set of values and practices based on
an alternative mode of production—agrarian communism—that appeals to
More's political imagination. Feudalism has outlived itself as a legitimate sys-

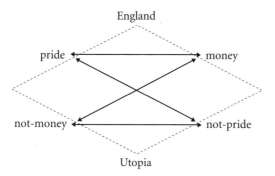

Figure 5

tem and nascent capitalism is already proving itself no better in terms of providing for a just society: both systems cause the widespread poverty and crime that England in the early sixteenth century is experiencing. A chart of *Utopia* as a libidinal apparatus is depicted in figure 5.

Another way of posing this distinction between representation and neutralization is to look at the object in question in each operation: the Real. Here is where Jameson's insistence on the political unconscious as a figurative rather than a literal mode of representation comes into play. The England of *Utopia* (or the England of any narrative, for that matter) cannot be thought of as some objective, empirically perceptible world known by the name of England to which More's narrative critically responds and that can be described negatively through the positive description of Utopia. "England" is itself an ideological construct, and it is this construct that is neutralized in More's text. The Real—in this case, "England"—is therefore a construct. Jameson elaborates on this process of construction:

> If . . . we try to accustom ourselves to thinking of the narrative text as a
> process whereby something is done to the Real, whereby operations are
> performed on it and it is in one way or another "managed" . . . or indeed
> "neutralized," or under other circumstances articulated and brought to
> heightened consciousness, then clearly we will have to begin to think of the
> Real, not as something outside the work, of which the latter stands as an
> image or makes a representation, but rather as something borne within and
> vehiculated by the text itself, interiorized in its very fabric in order to provide
> the stuff and the raw material on which the textual operation must work.
> (*IT2* 81)

We have now arrived at the pivotal point of Jameson's entire project: the relationship between representation and the Real, between figuration and History. In order to sort out the details of this relationship, one must first understand what exactly Jameson means by "the Real."

THE SUBLIME LOGIC OF THE REAL

I would suggest that Jameson's whole theory of the political unconscious stands or falls with his use of the concept of History as the Real. One way of getting a handle on how exactly Jameson uses the concept of the Real is to see how he presents Lacan's use of the term. The primary source here is, of course, Jameson's essay "Imaginary and Symbolic in Lacan" (*IT1* 75–113). An additional motivation for looking at this essay is to see not only how Jameson understands Lacan but more to the point, how he incorporates this understanding into his own conception of figuration and the political unconscious. The question is then not so much one of adequacy—is Jameson true to Lacan?—but strategy: What function does this reading of Lacan play in Jameson's development of his own theory?[9] The key lies in Jameson's somewhat offhand statement that "it is not terribly difficult to say what is meant by the Real in Lacan. It is simply History itself" (*IT1* 104), for it is with this equation that Jameson seeks to stage a confrontation, if not so much a synthesis, between Marxism and psychoanalysis, the two operable "materialisms" left in this critical climate that, Jameson contends, overemphasizes the Symbolic to the exclusion of the Real (a point to be elaborated below). But this equation doesn't help terribly much if the sense of this term "History" is equally unclear. So in addition to wondering what Jameson means by the Real, one also has to ask what he means by History.

JAMESON'S LACAN

But first to the question of Lacan and the Real. The Lacan essay is perhaps the only place where Jameson supplies anything like a phylogenetics of the political unconscious—that is, a sense of how we have developed into the figuring beings we are. The key is in Jameson's attention to the Kleinian elements of Lacan's concept of the Imaginary, for Jameson's concept of ideology in large part depends on this way of understanding the Imaginary. The Imaginary is the result of what Lacan refers to as the mirror stage—the point, necessary for the development of primary narcissism, at which the child "first demonstrably 'recognizes' his or her own image in the mirror, thus tangibly making the connection between inner motricity and the specular movements stirring before him" (*ITI* 84). This stage, having produced "a fundamental gap between the subject and its own self or imago that can never be bridged" (ibid., 85), installs us into a kind of existential space peculiar to the Imaginary—a space operating according to a binary logic of inside-outside, us-versus-them, that characterizes ideology as such. Jameson's depiction of this space is worth quoting:

> A description of the Imaginary will therefore on the one hand require us to come to terms with a uniquely determinate configuration of space—one that is not yet organized around the individuation of my own personal body, or differentiated hierarchically according to the perspectives of my own central point of view, but nonetheless swarms with bodies and forms intuited in a different way, whose fundamental property is, it would seem, to be visible without their visibility being the result of the act of any particular observer, to be, as it were, always-already seen, to carry their specularity upon themselves like a color they wear or the texture of their surface. (85–86)

This specular swarming of bodily identifications in turn gives rise to the two axes of the Imaginary, transitivism and aggressivity. Transitivism refers to psychic identification, such as in the famous Freudian story of "a child is being beaten." Our psychic identity in this Imaginary space is transitive, making it possible for us to identify with the situation of another to the extreme of being incapable of separating ourselves from others. Love could be seen as an element of this transitivism; hate, on the other hand, is the result of Imaginary aggressivity. In the psychic space of the Imaginary there are only two positions: ours and theirs. In order to protect what is ours, we repel or attack what is theirs. This, Jameson claims, is the source not only of the binary logic of ideology but the binary logic of ethical thought as well with its dependence, as Nietzsche showed, on the opposing poles of good and evil.

More important for Jameson's interest in Lacan, however, is the way this transitivism, dependent on the Imaginary transposition of one object for another, gives rise to the ability to form symbols (these Kleinian "symbols" referring more properly to the Imaginary than to Lacan's own Symbolic, which depends not on binary logic but on the differential logic of language itself). This Imaginary transposition is marked by the affective or libidinal valorization of protean objects, a process whereby we gain the ability to invest a whole host of objects with libidinal charge—the objects themselves functioning merely as inert and transferable markers of libidinal charge as such. This is what Melanie Klein refers to as symbolization, the fluctuating substitution of and reinvestment in a variety of external objects, particularly, for the young child, the breast and feces. This psychic investment, inaugurated by the loss of the maternal object, is the root of Klein's symbol formation or Jameson's figuration, the latter, as we have seen, being a process of libidinal-ideological investment in contingent objects and structures or apparatuses. The object world offers a storehouse of substitute objects for the lost breast; symbolization, the inauguration of the metonymy of desire itself (the constant pursuit of the unattainable object), compensates for the irreducible gap marking our psychic identifications that can never be bridged. This process, Jameson remarks, "may be said to be figural in its very essence, figuration being that property of language that allows the same word to be used in several senses" (94). Once we are talking about language, however, we have already moved on to talking about the Symbolic as distinct from the Imaginary. While Imaginary substitution prepares us for the use of language as such, it is only through our accession to the Symbolic that the Imaginary ever operates to its full extent. Without the Symbolic—marked by the displacement of one signifier by another as they move along the signifying chain—the Imaginary never adequately develops, as can be witnessed in the language of the schizophrenic, which functions "something like a zero degree in the so-called animal languages, which constitute the very prototype of the code proper to the Imaginary, involving no demands on the Other, but simply a fixed one-to-one relationship between signifier and signified, between signal and place, from which the more properly human phenomenon of figuration is absent," according to Jameson (94–95). Figuration gets its start, then, in the Imaginary substitution and reinvestment of objects, and then comes into its own in the semiotic, psychic dispersal of the Symbolic, which produces yet another alienating split in what can only now be called the subject. Figuration is then at once our curse and our blessing, our mark of alienation and our compensation.

At this point we have the Lacanian split subject. The acquisition of language functions as a kind of primary repression, a repression of the Imaginary logic of identification, which constitutes the subject as divided, mediated by language (the subject can never coincide with the signifier that represents it). The binary logic of the Imaginary is broken up by the introduction of this mediating third—the Other, the unconscious, language itself. This is the point of Lacan's translation of the concept of the Oedipus complex into linguistic terms: the mediation of language (the Name-of-the-Father) prohibits our (impossible)

Imaginary union with the Mother; that is, the mediation of language prohibits Imaginary identification by dispersing us along the signifying chain. As a result of this splitting or *Spaltung*, we are forever separate not only from images of the maternal other (what will be referred to as the *petit objet a* [*autre*], the small *a* to be distinguished from the Big *A* of the Symbolic Other [the Big *Autre*]) but separate as well from the Big Other and the sign that represents us. The unconscious, "the discourse of the Other," is the result of this primary split that constitutes the subject of language.

This impossibility of Symbolic coincidence, then, marks our relationship to the Real. We can never fully grasp through language the referent itself, that which, according to Jameson, persists "behind our representations, . . . that indestructible nucleus of what Lacan calls the Real, of which we have already said above that it was simply History itself" (106). While we can never produce a coincidence of representation and referent, however, Jameson nevertheless wants to distance himself from the structuralist "ideology" that claims that the referent itself doesn't exist. What Jameson wants to do is to distinguish between knowledge and truth: truth, the adequation of representation and referent, is impossible since the Real is, as Lacan has said, "that which resists symbolization absolutely." But this does not mean that we cannot have a knowledge of the Real, however inadequate. As Jameson maintains,

> A materialistic philosophy of language reserves a status for scientific language of this [psychoanalytic or Marxian] kind, which designates the Real without claiming to coincide with it. . . . A materialistic philosophy of language is not a semanticism, naive or otherwise, because its fundamental tenet is a rigorous distinction between the signified—the realm of semantics proper, of interpretation, of the study of the text's ostensible meaning—and the referent. The study of the referent, however, is the study, not of the meaning of the text, but of the limits of its meanings and of their historical preconditions, and of what is and must remain incommensurable to objective knowledge (in other words, to what is of such a different order of magnitude and organization from the individual subject that it can never be adequately "represented" within the latter's lived experience save as a term limit) is conceivable only for a thought able to do justice to radical discontinuities, not only of the Lacanian "orders," but within language itself, between its various types of propositions as they entertain wholly different structural relations with the subject. (108)

The Real and the subject exist on incommensurable planes and thus always bypass one another, maintaining at best an asymptotic relationship. Yet this term limit of the Real nevertheless functions as an "absent cause" (107): we cannot represent the Real (this is precisely what sets figuration in motion), but the Real can and does limit our representations. In fact, the Real can only be known *as* this limitation to representation, as that which frustrates any attempt at coincidence, commensurability, or adequation. The Real emerges from the split that constitutes the subject *as such*.

HISTORY AND THE POLITICAL UNCONSCIOUS

In *The Political Unconscious*, Jameson tells us that his goal is to conceive of "History as a ground and as an absent cause" (101). "History" cannot serve as simply another allegorical key allowing us to thematize a work's content according to some "Marxist" version of History as a "prior" content (according to which the text would simply reflect the class relations and class consciousness available in a particular mode of production such as feudalism, capitalism, and so on). This is not to say that the text will not have a determinate relationship to History as such but that that relationship will not be one of simple correspondence between content and historical ground. History, in Jameson's view, *is* the ground and subtext of the text, but everything depends on what exactly we mean when we make such a claim. The key is the conception of History, the Real, as an absent cause. This is what is meant by saying that History is a "term limit" to representation that itself lies beyond representation. History is known only through its effects, through the objective limitations that the inexorable form of necessity sets for our actions and our thoughts. "History," Jameson explains, "is what hurts, it is what refuses desire and sets inexorable limits to individual as well as collective praxis," and though we may try to ignore its effects, "we can be sure that its alienating necessities will not forget us" (*PU* 102). This "absent cause," a term borrowed from Althusser and that Jameson equates with Lacan's concept of the Real (ibid., 82), is nothing but an effect of structure: "Nowhere empirically present as an element, it is not a part of the whole or one of its levels, but rather the entire system of relationships among those levels" (36). History is "not a text, not a narrative, master or otherwise, but . . . , as an absent cause, it is inaccessible to us except in textual form, and . . . our approach to it and to the Real itself necessarily passes through its prior textualization, its narrativization in the political unconscious" (35).

Jameson elaborates on this relationship between History and textuality in the following passage:

> Still, we need to say a little more about the status of this external reality, of which it will otherwise be thought that it is little more than the traditional notion of "context" familiar in older social or historical criticism. The type of interpretation here proposed is more satisfactorily grasped as the rewriting of the literary text in such a way that the latter may itself be seen as the rewriting or restructuration of a prior historical or ideological *subtext*, it being always understood that that "subtext" is not immediately present as such, not some common-sense external reality, not even the conventional narratives of history manuals, but rather must itself always be (re)constructed after the fact. The literary or aesthetic act therefore always entertains some active relationship with the Real; yet in order to do so, it cannot simply allow "reality" to persevere inertly in its own being, outside the text and at a distance. It must rather draw the Real into its own texture, and the ultimate paradoxes and false problems of linguistics, and most notably of semantics, are to be traced back to this process, whereby language manages to carry the Real within itself as its own intrinsic or immanent subtext. Insofar, in other words, as symbolic action . . . is a way of doing something to the world, to that degree what we are calling "world" must inhere within it, as the content it has to take up into itself in order to submit it to the transformations of form. The symbolic act therefore begins by generating and producing its own context in the same moment of emergence in which it steps back from it, taking its measure with a view toward its own projects of transformation. The whole paradox of what we have here called the subtext may be summed up in this, that the literary work or cultural object, as though for the first time, brings into being that very situation to which it is also, at one and the same time, a reaction. It articulates its own situation and textualizes it, thereby encouraging and perpetuating the illusion that the situation itself did not exist before it, that there is nothing but a text, that there never was any extra- or con-textual reality before the text itself generated it in the form of a mirage. One does not have to argue the reality of history: necessity, like Dr. Johnson's stone, does that for us. That history—Althusser's "absent cause," Lacan's "Real"—is *not* a text, for it is fundamentally non-narrative and nonrepresentational; what can be added, however, is the proviso that history is inaccessible to us except in textual form, or

in other words, that it can be approached only by way of prior (re)textual-
ization. (81–82)

Unraveling this extremely dense passage should take us far in my attempt to
sort out the issues involved in this question of the Real. In order to do so, I will
examine this passage one unit at a time.

1. "Context." The passage occurs in a discussion of the first phase of Jameson's allegorical hermeneutic, in which he sees literary and cultural texts as
"symbolic acts" that resolve determinate social contradictions (see my discussion above on figuration). What is in question, then, is how exactly these social
contradictions make their way into the textual process of the symbolic act.
What is the relationship, in other words, between the text and History? He asks
this question in order to go beyond the limitations he sees in Kenneth Burke's
own use of the concept of symbolic act, which ambiguously functions, first,
positively in the sense that literature is itself *an act*, yet, second, negatively in
that this act is *purely imaginary* and as such does not affect the "real world,"
the point of origin, we must assume, of the social contradiction on which the text
operates. Consequently:

2. "Still, we need to say a little more about the status of this external reality, of
which it will otherwise be thought that it is little more than the traditional
notion of 'context' familiar in older social or historical criticism." Obviously,
the contradiction at work in the text cannot be reduced to some inert and
external "reality." Its *status* must be defined otherwise.

3. "The type of interpretation here proposed is more satisfactorily grasped as
the rewriting of the literary text." This interpretive method must be distinguished from the earlier models of "older social or historical criticism" that do
not see the interpretive act as a rewriting of the text but as an objective, reflective view of an objective, reflective text that points to external reality yet does
not affect it in any sense. Like texts themselves, interpretation must be seen as a
transformative process.

4. "As the rewriting of the literary text in such a way that the latter may itself
be seen as the rewriting or restructuration of a prior historical or ideological
subtext," . . . interpretation rewrites the text in such a way that the text itself is
seen as a process of rewriting. The text does not merely reflect a *con*text but
rewrites a *sub*text.

5. "It being always understood that that 'subtext' is not immediately present

as such, not some common-sense external reality, not even the conventional narratives of history manuals, but rather must itself always be (re)constructed after the fact." The symbolic act is a retroactive (re)construction of the historical subtext that in some way did not exist as such prior to its own textualization. If this is so, however, then what is one to make of the "(re)" in "(re)construction"? First, the subtext, it seems, was already a construction, not some pregiven externality. The text rewrites what was in some sense already available only in textual form. This sounds awfully close to the (post)structuralist credo that History is always already a text (a claim Jameson adheres to) because it is nothing but a text (a claim Jameson distances himself from and that he refers to as the key motif of structuralist ideology).

6. "The literary or aesthetic act therefore always entertains some active relationship with the Real; yet in order to do so, it cannot simply allow 'reality' to persevere inertly in its own being, outside the text and at a distance." There are two points here: the distinction between "reality" and the Real, and the active relationship between the symbolic act and the Real. One place where Lacan develops the reality-Real distinction is in seminar 11, *The Four Fundamental Concepts of Psychoanalysis*. His point is that our everyday distinction between dream and reality ignores the fact that it is in the dream where we come closer to confronting the Real, whereas in our awakenness we exist in a fantasy-construct, which we call reality, that functions as a buffer between our psyche and the Real. Jameson's point is similar: our objective accounts of external reality are just as subject to the Real as are our aesthetic constructs. This is not to say, nevertheless, that fiction is "more real" than reality but that fiction stages more clearly its "fictive," constructed status. The points at which we crash upon the reef of the Real are often more obvious in symbolic or aesthetic texts than in "historical" ones. This is because of the second point at issue here: that the symbolic act, as the word "act" suggests, has an active relationship to the Real.

7. "Insofar, in other words, as symbolic action . . . is a way of doing something to the world, to that degree what we are calling 'world' must inhere within it, as the content it has to take up into itself in order to submit it to the transformations of form. The symbolic act therefore begins by generating and producing its own context in the same moment of emergence in which it steps back from it, taking its measure with a view toward its own projects of transformation." The world indicated by the text can only be a world presented, pro-

duced, vehiculated by the textual apparatus—the text can't give us anything but text. The relationship between the text and its world takes place within the text, its putative context being in fact its self-generated *subtext*:

8. "The whole paradox of what we have here called the subtext may be summed up in this, that the literary work or cultural object, as though for the first time, brings into being that very situation to which it is also, at one and the same time, a reaction." Here is the paradox of structural causality mentioned above. It is in terms of the concept of structural causality that one can speak of the Real as an absent cause, as Althusser does in the following passage from *Reading Capital*, in which he discusses the relationship between economic phenomena and the mode of production as a whole:

> The structure is not an essence *outside* the economic phenomena which comes and alters their aspect, forms and relations and which is effective on them as an absent cause, *absent because it is outside them. The absence of the cause in the structure's "metonymic causality" on its effects is not the fault of the exteriority of the structure with respect to the economic phenomena; on the contrary, it is the very form of the interiority of the structure, as a structure, in its effects*. This implies that the effects are not outside the structure, are not a pre-existing object, element or space in which the structure arrives to *imprint its mark*: on the contrary, it implies that the structure is immanent in its effects, a cause immanent in its effects in the Spinozist sense of the term, that *the whole existence of the structure consists of its effects*, in short, that the structure, which is merely a specific combination of its peculiar elements, is nothing outside its effects. (RC 188–89)

To put this in the terms I have been dealing with, "the Real" should be substituted for "the structure" and "the text" for "the effects." In other words, the text is an effect of the Real; the Real, eo ipso, is the cause of the text. Yet this should not be taken, as Jameson has insisted, in the sense that the Real is a cause existing outside and prior to the text. The Real, in Althusser's language, is immanent in its effects; the whole existence of the Real consists of the text. Or at least this seems to be what is implied thus far in the Jameson passage I have been annotating. But he goes on:

9. "It articulates its own situation and textualizes it, thereby encouraging and perpetuating the illusion that the situation itself did not exist before it, that there is nothing but a text, that there never was any extra- or con-textual reality before the text itself generated it in the form of a mirage. One does not have to

argue the reality of history: necessity, like Dr. Johnson's stone, does that for us. That history—Althusser's 'absent cause,' Lacan's 'Real'—is *not* a text, for it is fundamentally non-narrative and nonrepresentational; what can be added, however, is the proviso that history is inaccessible to us except in textual form, or in other words, that it can be approached only by way of prior (re)textualization." This is a paradox indeed. What are we to make of this seeming reversal, the claim that the Real *does* exist prior to the text, like Johnson's stone, following the elaborate argument for reading the Real as a product of the text? In what way, if any, does the subsequent claim that the Real, though not a text, is accessible only in textual form get out of this antinomy? The problem is that neither claim—Real-as-outside or Real-as-inside—can be held in isolation. Both must somehow be maintained simultaneously. If we claim simply that the Real is only a product of the text, then we are guilty, in Jameson's eyes, of structuralist ideology. If on the other hand, we claim only that the Real preexists the text, as any rock against the head will "prove," then we are guilty of naive semanticism. The first (structuralist) position is one holding to Lacan's Symbolic at the expense of the Imaginary; the second (realist) position holds to the Imaginary at the expense of the Symbolic. The aim, however, for a dialectician is to find the point at which both positions are maintained and superseded. To state things baldly before elaborating in more detail, the key is to conceive of the Real *not* as a positive condition that precedes textuality—a position forcing us into the structuralist-realist conundrum—but to conceive of the Real in negative terms—a negativity that manifests itself according to varying social conditions. History is the experience of limitations to freedom; History is the experience of the impossibility of coincidence; History is the absence cause that manifests itself only through its negative effects, through the contradictions into which it leads any narrative or other symbolic act; History is the experience of the fissure forever separating knowledge from truth, not because knowledge is not yet complete but because knowledge, being the knowledge of the split subject, is constitutively contradictory, fissured, incommensurable. But for all this, we cannot then say that it does not exist. We can only say that as the immanent limit to representation itself, it is necessarily unrepresentable—which is not to say, though, that it is not figurable, for it is the experience of this constitutive gap or contradiction itself that sets the machinery of figuration in motion.

I have now come to my major question for Jameson and his entire project: Is the Real sublime? And if so, is this sublime Kantian or Hegelian?

THE LOGIC OF THE KANTIAN SUBLIME

As we have just seen, the Real for Jameson is manifest in the negative experience of Necessity. When we come up against the limits of representation, what we have is the presentation of the inexorable limits of History. As we saw in chapter 2, this is the condition that Kant refers to as negative Darstellung. For Kant, what is presented, what is thus dargestellt, is the Idea, mathematical or dynamic, of an infinite power, of an infinite beyond, the beyond of representation. Through the painful breakdown of the representational apparatus, we achieve the negative presentation of that infinite totality that only a god, in its divine intuition, could perceive. The experience of the sublime, for Kant, leads us to the rational proposition of the Beyond (although we can have no determinate knowledge of this beyond). In its very failure, at its extreme limit, representation passes beyond itself. The question is, Does Jameson conceive of the Real as such a Beyond?

One way of sorting out the issues involved here is to examine them in light of Hegel's concept of "positing the presuppositions." We are dealing with a causal relationship here—the relationship of determination that underlies, among other things, such binaries as inside/outside, essence/phenomena, ground/conditions, cause/effects, and subject/predicates. This is the question Hegel examines in "The Doctrine of Essence" in his *Science of Logic*. In Hegelian terms, Jameson's symbolic act posits its own presuppositions: it retroactively presents as given the very presuppositions that are supposed to render it valid and possible in the first place. In other words, faced with its own immanent limitations to understanding (as in the case with Lévi-Strauss's primitive thought), the political unconscious, through the symbolic act, projects its own conditions of comprehensibility. When we are in the thick of things, we always operate within a certain gap between knowledge and experience (what Hegel refers to as consciousness in-itself or positing reflection). Having become aware of our perceptual shortcomings, we then tend to posit the incommensurability between reality and consciousness as the cause of our limitations (Hegel's consciousness for-itself or external reflection)—we see reality as the essence behind our limited perceptions, as the true substratum beyond our comprehension. Appearances are deceiving, we say, suggesting that behind these appearances lies the truth that could explain all if only we had the capacity to perceive it. As we have seen, however, the point here is that the Real is *not* some essence existing behind appearances, invisible only because we have not yet developed the organs with which to record or represent it (although Jameson's language often implies such a relationship); the point is that the truth of appearance lies within appearance itself, or, to continue with Jameson's terminology, the Real does not preexist the symbolic act but is rather born at the moment the structural limitations of a given ideology come up against the contradictions of History; the Real is the effect of the split internal to appearance itself that because contradictory, imposes on us the necessary illusion of a coherent, noncontradictory truth that would explain or illuminate matters—and that thus sets into motion the machinery of figuration, promising (or rather, substituting for) immanence or the commensurability of thought and experience: "What this impossibility of immanence means in practice is that the dialectical reversal [from individual to collective consciousness] must always involve a painful 'decentering' of the consciousness of the individual subject, whom it confronts with a determination (whether of the Freudian or the political unconscious) that must necessarily be felt as extrinsic or external to conscious experience" (*PU* 283–84). The suggestion here is that individuals, as such, are always condemned to a certain degree of external reflection, of the mirage of truth behind the appearances, but that a future collective subject might achieve the lucidity promised by the quest for immanence.

To return to the question of Kant: his theory of the sublime can be read as such a form of external reflection. The Kantian sublime is the paradoxical experience of the negative presentation of an idea through the breakdown of our representative faculty, the imagination. The point is that ideas of reason, unlike concepts of the understanding, are incapable of presentation (Darstellung). That is, the only accord between intuition and concepts (imagination and the understanding) is an empirical one, that which makes possible the production of sensible objects of knowledge. Ideas, however, because they by definition refer to *super*sensible "objects," are incapable of being fused with a sensible intuition. Nevertheless, reason is interested in ideas having "objective reality. That is to say, it is of interest to reason that nature should show a trace or give a hint that it contains in itself some ground or other for assuming a uniform accordance of its products with our wholly disinterested delight" merely in the judgment of pure form, the forms of the beautiful in nature and the forms of practical maxims (*CJ* §42, 159). Reason can posit this accord, however, only by analogy, through the presumed kinship between taste (aesthetic judgment) and moral feeling (intellectual judgment). Our feeling in response to the sense of purposiveness without purpose in the beautiful object in nature becomes associated here with our feeling in response to the only other object in nature to which we can ascribe this free purposiveness—ourselves. In this way, then, reason can only find its objective reality through analogy (the topic of the second half of the *Critique of Judgment*, teleology). If we were to posit an *empirical* relationship between objective purposiveness (that which we attribute—but only as an analogy—to organic forms in nature) and our own subjective purposiveness, then we would be operating at the level of what Hegel refers to as positing reflection. That is, if we took the feeling we experience in judging the beautiful as *evidence* of a purposive supersensible substrate common to both nature and ourselves, then we would be guilty of what Kant refers to as a transcendent (mis)use of reason, of attempting to give an idea the status of an empirical (that is, sensibly presentable) object. Only as such could we posit a positive relationship between the imagination and reason, but Kant's entire critical project is to deny the validity of any such positive—or, rather, metaphysical—relationship. To return to Jameson for a moment before moving on to Kant's concept of the sublime, the equivalent of positing this "metaphysical" relationship between imagination and reason would be the positing of an immediate relationship between our everyday experiences and some larger sense of history as the process that in just such a positive way, gives structure and coherence to those experiences. But such immediate access to "History" is precisely what Jameson's concept of the political unconscious denies. At this point in my argument, then, Jameson's History should be seen as a Kantian idea that by definition, cannot be represented.

Like the Kantian sublime, though, History can be negatively presented. For Kant, the experience of the sublime is made up of two different steps: the painful failure of representation (the breakdown of the Imagination) and then the pleasant experience of respect (in response to the negative presentation of the powers of reason). Through the confrontation with the sublime, the imagination, whose job it is to provide a sensible intuition as the presentation of a concept (the fundamental schematic relationship), cannot provide such an intuition, for the phenomenon in question outstrips the imagination's ability to comprehend it as a totality. That is, the phenomenon is too vast to take in in one image or too powerful to understand in terms of human power. In both cases (mathematical and dynamic sublime respectively) the imagination is overwhelmed and pained at the failure to follow through with its defining task: the production of a comprehensible, unified image. The accord between the imagination and the understanding, which is reassured in the experience of the beautiful, is broken in the experience of the sublime. But this very failure of representation in the phenomenal realm opens up the space for the (negative) presentation of the beyond of the noumenal realm. And with this split between the phenomenal and the noumenal, appearance and essence, we pass from positing to external reflection.

> We have no reason to fear that the feeling of the sublime will suffer from an abstract mode of presentation like this, which is altogether negative as to what is sensuous. For though the imagination, no doubt, finds nothing beyond the sensible world to which it can lay hold, still this thrusting aside of the sensible barriers gives a feeling of being unbounded; and that removal is thus a presentation of the infinite. As such it can never be anything more than a negative presentation—but still it expands the soul [*die Seele*]. Perhaps there is no more sublime passage in the Jewish Law than the commandment: Thou shalt not make unto thee any graven image, or any likeness of any thing that is in heaven or on earth, or under the earth, &c. (*CJ* General Remark, 127)

ŽIŽEK ON HEGELIAN REFLECTION

While the question of reflection might appear to be purely epistemological— "To what degree is our mode of reflection true to the reality which it reflects?"— for Žižek the question is ultimately practical: How do we ground our actions, our choices, after we have already acted and chosen? Reflection, that is, refers to the problem of causality: "We acted this way because. . . ." And herein lies the ultimate value of the question of the Real for Jameson as well. What relationship does History have to our actions? To what degree are we historically determined? What are the consequences for humans as effective actors on the stage of history if the ultimate cause of history itself is inaccessible to us, if History appears only in sublime (unrepresentable) moments? At what point or to what extent can we characterize the subject as free, and how can we characterize the nature of this freedom itself? For Žižek, the way to elaborate on these questions is primarily by way of Hegel as he responds to Kant and anticipates Lacan. The act, for Žižek, can never be separated from a discussion of ideology for the act is always a retroactive act of symbolization, *a symbolic act*.

Reflection itself is an act: this must be understood from the start in order to grasp the twist Žižek gives in discussing our relationship to the Real. For

Hegel, the reflective act involves the orchestration of essence and appearance, noumena and phenomena according to various causal narratives or presuppositions. The elementary act of reflection is what Hegel refers to as positing reflection, which is inverted through external reflection, after which the relationship between these two forms of reflection is itself inverted by determining reflection. To anticipate my reason for this foray into Hegelian reflection, the question here is where to locate the concept of the Real: Is such a concept an example of external reflection or determining reflection? Is there a difference in terms of these modes of reflection between the way Kant, Hegel, Lacan, and Jameson figure the space of the Real? Žižek's meditations on the status of the Real and its relationship to the act of reflection provide a way of sorting out these issues.

The distinction between the above three moments of reflection depends on three different ways of positing or figuring the relationship between essence and appearance. In order to illustrate the motivation behind these reflective moments, Žižek begins by constructing a context in which these moments operate or to which they are a response—that context being the retroactive assumption of responsibility for what has already happened to us. The initial activity of positing reflection is the positing of its presuppositions. When, for example, despite our best-laid plans, we find ourselves in an unexpected situation, we next tend to "reflect" back on the particular events leading to the current situation in order to "sort out" how we got where we are now. What we in fact do at this point is (re)construct retroactively the causal sequence of events or influences that shaped us. In so doing, we rescue the situation from the contingencies of existence and restructure it according to some previously "hidden" causality or necessity, a cause to which we were (necessarily) blind while in the thick of things. This is the moment Hegel refers to when he writes that "it is only when actuality has reached maturity that the ideal appears opposite the real and reconstructs this real world, which it has grasped in its substance, in the shape of an intellectual realm" (PR preface, 23). That is, it is only after the fact that we can look back and see what "actually" took place by reconstructing it in "the shape of an intellectual realm," or, to speak in Lacanian terms, to effect retroactively this symbolization of the Real. The owl of Minerva "begins its flight only with the onset of dusk" (ibid., 23).

"What actually happened": this is the essence which we could not see, that only appears after the fact. We retroactively "posit the presuppositions" that later make sense of history. Such is the relationship between essence and appearance for positing reflection, which posits appearance as "mere appearance" in contrast to the essence, what really took place. The problem with positing reflection, in terms of the act of positing the presuppositions, is that the key presupposition must of necessity remain "unposited," and that is the presupposition of positing itself, of positing appearance as appearance (it didn't appear as mere appearance until we posited it as such). What the positing cannot account for is its own positing act: the presupposition of ourselves as positing beings and of appearance as mere appearance remains *external to* this purely negative act of the essence that opposes itself to the appearance. Positing reflection presupposes the positive world of appearance as the realm upon which it sets to work in its negative unmasking of mere appearance as the appearance of the essence that lies beyond this reflective movement. Without this presupposition of the realm of appearance, positing reflection could not unmask the appearance covering up the true essence beyond the flux of events and shaping them behind the scenes; the essence needs appearance in order for the essence to appear.

This externality of the presupposition of the positive, objective world of appearance—appearing in its otherness to us, appearing as our other—is not enough to move us on to external reflection quite yet, for the externality of this presupposition is still a moment of positing the presuppositions, a presupposition posited as external to positing, but posited nonetheless. We pass over to external reflection when the reflection becomes reflexive, when the essence reflects on itself. At this moment essence posits *itself* as its own other. There are two posited moments of otherness, then, in the work of positing the presuppositions: the positing of the objective phenomenal world as the other of essence; and the positing of essence itself as its own other. This latter moment—the moment of alienation, of seeing one's own activity as the activity of some other entity beyond the movement of negativity—is the moment proper to external reflection. Remembering that for positing reflection, essence is posited at first as the pure movement of negativity (the power of the understanding to dissolve mere appearance into its essential nature, the unmasking of appearance and the revealing of essence), we can now see the ideological function of positing some entity (God, the Absolute, etc.) as existing beyond or external to this negative power: subjectivity, which is nothing but this pure negative movement, never becomes *subjectivized* or subjectivity as such until it posits itself as external to its own negative movement, until it reflects itself as existing beyond its own deconstructive movement in the figure of the Absolute. The essence posits itself as some pure, indeterminate X, some transphenomenal hard kernel of being beyond predication. To put it in terms I have been using above, reflection cannot reflect on itself until it reflects itself as an external entity beyond its own reflective movement. This means that reflection as such is always already internally split; without this split, this gap internal to reflection or essence, appearance could not appear. It is this immanent fracture of essence that opens up the space for the appearance of appearance.

If the essence proper to external reflection is by definition external *to* reflection, then it cannot be reflected, it cannot be represented, it cannot be known as such. Here we have the characterization of the Real proper to external reflection: the Real by definition is external to representation, it cannot be positively presented, it exists in the beyond of representation, it exists for us only as *the failure of representation*. The Real can only be presented negatively; that is, this external reflection of the Real operates according to the logic of the Kantian sublime, the formal conversion of the impossibility of representation into the (negative) presentation of impossibility. But what does a logic of the sublime look like in terms of determining reflection? According to Žižek, this is what is at stake in Hegel's passage from external to determining reflection; this Hegelian sublime is an example of what Žižek refers to as "redoubled" reflection.

According to external reflection, as we have seen, God, the Absolute, exists in the beyond of reflection, protected from the negative power of reflection itself. For Kant, this gap separating the noumenal Absolute, the Thing-in-Itself, from the phenomenal world can never be traversed in any positive sense; it can only be negatively presented by revealing through the breakdown of reflection the power of reason in its ability to think (but not to reflect) the noumenal beyond. While reflective judgment plays a crucial role in providing us with glimpses, however negative (sublime) or analogical (teleology), of the beyond of the phenomenal world, reflective judgment can never determine the noumenal. Only determining judgment can operate on phenomena. It is important to recognize, however, that Hegel's passage from (Kantian) external reflection to (Hegelian) determining reflection (the sublation of determining and reflective judgment) is not a relapse to pre-Kantian metaphysics. And this can best be illustrated in the passage from the Kantian to the Hegelian sublime.

The problem for Hegel with the Kantian sublime as the negative presentation of that which surpasses representation is that Kant remains bound to the logic of representation (Vorstellung). As in my discussion above of the necessity for positing reflection to presuppose the existence of appearance as the world upon which it works in order to exercise its transformative, negative power, so Kant must presuppose the world of appearance in order to conceive of the sublime as the limit of representation. "Precisely when we determine the Thing as a transcendent surplus beyond what can be represented," Žižek writes, "we determine it on the basis of the field of representation, starting from it, within its horizon, as its negative limit: the (Jewish) notion of God as radical Otherness, as unrepresentable, still remains the extreme point of the logic of representation" (*SOI* 205). Žižek goes on to argue that "Hegel's position is, in contrast, that there is *nothing* beyond phenomenality, beyond the field of representation. The experience of radical negativity, of the radical inadequacy of all phenomena to the Idea, the experience of the radical fissure between the two— this experience is already *Idea itself as 'pure,' radical negativity*" (ibid.). The beyond of the sublime is thus not some positive (alienated) Thing existing beyond representation; the beyond is nothing but the experience of this radical negativity itself. The difference between the sublime object for Kant and that for Hegel, then, is crucial: the sublime object for Kant is simply the phenomenal object that stretches our representative faculties beyond their limit, while the sublime object for Hegel is the obscene *embodiment* of the Nothing beyond representation—the embodiment of radical negativity. We experience the sublime when we come in contact with the miserable object that through its very wretchedness, embodies this negativity.

One of Žižek's favorite examples of this sublime object (which he gets from Hegel) is Christ. The figure of the sublime Christ is contrasted with the eighteenth-century view of the sublime God of Judaism, the entity beyond representation, the God who prohibits all graven images or attempts at representation. God can only be negatively presented as the limit to mere human understanding; as such, this God functions within the logic of external reflection. But with Christianity, the divine is represented by the broken body of Christ in such a way that what at first sight appears as defeat—Christ's crucifixion—is then seen as a victory. The point for Žižek is that the negativity of the divine, which is prohibited for "Jewish" external reflection, is embodied as such in Christian determining reflection: through the very incommensurability between the death of the broken body of Christ and the nature of God, the negativity proper to the "beyond" of reflection is reflected back into itself. The opposition human-divine is sublated not by some reconciliation, some positive synthesis, but by the projection of the miserable human figure into the heart of essence itself. One human among all others is excluded from the normal circuit of human nature and functions as the subject in the heart of the divine substance. Here is how substance becomes subject: by projecting the qualities of subjectivity into the heart of substance in order to ground the subjectivity of the rest of us. Without this exceptional Subject, the rest of us cannot function as subjects, for to do so requires the split of essence (subjectivity) that opens up the space for our own subjective identity. We are only fully subjectivized when we see (reflect) the essence of our subjectivity in the heart of the substance opposing us. The purely negative, unrepresentable God of external reflection remains pure substance, alien, impenetrable, beyond.

In determinate reflection, then, essence *redoubles* itself—that is, it "reflects itself in itself, not only in appearance" (*SOI* 228). Reflection, as we have seen above, takes place on two levels: essence as the power of absolute negativity that makes every positive immediacy into "mere appearance" and thus sets up the essence-appearance opposition; and essence as it is reflected in itself "in the form of its own presupposition, of a given-immediate substance. Reflection of the essence into itself is an immediacy which is not 'mere appearance' but an inverse-alienated image of the very essence" (ibid.). Reflection is thus redoubled in the sense of reflecting outward in the essence-appearance distinction and then reflecting inward in the alienation of itself as its own other projected into the heart of substance. The religious subjects can realize themselves only by means of redoubling themselves as an alien embodiment of the divine through the One who is the point of exception that totalizes, subjectivizes, the community of subjects. As Žižek puts it, "And now, finally, we can also give a precise formulation to the passage from external to determinate reflection: the condition of our subjective freedom, of our 'positing,' is that it must be reflected in advance into the substance itself, as its own 'reflexive determination'" (230).

So how does the question of the Real relate to that of determining reflection? If the Real of external reflection follows the logic of the Kantian sublime, in which the Real figures as the Thing beyond representation, the Real of the Hegelian sublime must be redoubled in the sense outlined above: the sublime Thing of determining reflection must be the exceptional One projected into the heart of substance, functioning as the guarantee of our own freedom as it embodies the radical negativity of freedom itself. To resort to another Hegelian example common in Žižek's writing, absolute democracy in Hegel's thought is absolute negativity, the pure self-consuming void of negativity as exemplified by the Jacobin Terror: if this flight from every content or determination "remains purely theoretical, it becomes in the religious realm the Hindu fanaticism of pure contemplation; but if it turns to actuality, it becomes in the realm of both politics and religion the fanaticism of destruction, demolishing the whole existing social order, eliminating all individuals regarded as suspect by a given order, and annihilating any organization which attempts to rise up anew. Only in destroying something does this negative will have a feeling of its own existence [*Dasein*]" (PR 38). This purely negative freedom cannot be represented, and any attempt to embody the space of this negativity will be taken as treason to the idea of freedom itself; yet for Hegel, the political subject can become effectively free through determining reflection, through the projection of itself as its own other into the heart of substance (the state in its opposition to human will). For Hegel, this can only come about when a representative of the people also represents the radical negativity of freedom itself through the embodiment of incommensurability, through the absolute divorce between symbolic mandate (the king as embodiment of the state) and objective content (the contingencies of any actual biological individual who happens to fill this symbolic space). By emphasizing the radical incommensurability between these two positions through the inherently irrational process of identifying the monarch according to birthright—by projecting the most irrational element of biological facticity into the heart of the rational state—the impossibility of any true representation becomes embodied, symbolized, gentrified, and made manageable. We can only become *effectively* free when all pretense to effective representation of freedom itself in the body of any individual is presented in its utter absurdity and negativity. In this sense, Ronald Reagan was the perfect American president in that the effective work could go on while the symbolic functions of representation, the redoubling of reflection, worked themselves out through the absurd embodiment of the sublime Thing, the president-actor as embodiment of radical negativity.

THE JAMESONIAN SUBLIME

So once again, the question: Does Jameson's conception of History as the Real operate according to a Kantian, external reflection or a Hegelian, determining reflection? Now I am in a position to answer this question. In order to do so, I will return to the lengthy Jameson passage quoted and broken down above in order to reread segments of it in light of my intervening discussion of sublime and reflection.

The Jameson passage opens with a denial of the standpoint of positing reflection, which regards "this external reality" as "little more than the traditional notion of 'context' familiar in older social or historical criticism" (*PU* 81). Such a position posits the external world as a positive fact that is ready to hand for the negative work of reflection, ready for its transformation from "external reality" into "mere appearance." But Jameson qualifies that claim, as we have seen, by asserting the following: The literary text "may itself be seen as the rewriting or restructuration of a prior historical or ideological *subtext*, it being always understood that that 'subtext' is not immediately present as such, not some common-sense external reality, not even the conventional narratives of history manuals, but rather must itself always be (re)constructed after the fact" (ibid.). What is the status of this subtext? If it were thought of as a form of causality outside the text, not as "some common-sense external reality" but rather as an absent cause "inaccessible to us except in textual form" (82), then wouldn't this be an example of external reflection, of the proposition that the real "reality," essence, the Real exists in some inaccessible beyond of the text? Such certainly seems to be the case when Jameson turns to the question of Dr. Johnson's stone. And certainly the description of History as the term limit to representation sounds like the Kantian experience of the breakdown of representation when confronted with the (Kantian) sublime, the experience by which the imagination experiences its utmost limitation as the negative presentation of that which lies beyond the limit, yet is only known through the limit as such. But how does this claim of external reflection jibe with the claim that the symbolic act "begins by generating and producing its own context in the same moment of emergence in which it steps back from it, taking its measure with a view toward its own projects of transformation" (ibid.)? This certainly sounds like a claim made from the point of view of determining reflection according to which the relationship between positing and external reflection is precisely that of reflection itself in its own redoubling, from its positing of its own presuppositions, to its projection of its own negative activity into the beyond of the split between essence and appearance, to its recognition that this split, internal to itself, is precisely its own negativity as it opens up the space for appearance and its beyond.

I would suggest, however, that a crucial moment or mechanism of determining reflection is missing from this account, and that without such a moment this account remains trapped in the vicious circle of positing and presupposing, in which ground and determination continuously pass through one another without ceasing—the vicious circle Hegel refers to as absolute negativity. What is missing is the moment in which this radical negativity is embodied by the sublime object, the object that embodies the space opened up between essence and appearance as the space of negativity itself. Without this moment, according to Hegel, we remain powerless before the negativity of pure substance; it is only through the projection of reflection itself in the form of the sublime object existing in the heart of this substance that substance becomes Subject and the rest of us become subjects. Does such an embodiment exist in Jamesonian theory, or are we continuously passing from alienation to immersion, from the modernist conception of substance as the world in its opposition to us, to the postmodernist conception of substance as that which sucks us into its own center, subsuming all phenomenological experience under the sticky, palpable substance of the "hysterical sublime" of postmodernity?

A look at the transformations brought about through Jameson's elaboration on the definition of "History" in the final pages of chapter 1 of *The Political Unconscious* should help provide an answer. In explicating the way in which the object of study for the Marxist literary critic, the "text," is transformed as we pass between the three interpretive horizons that Jameson lays out in his book—the political, the ideological, and the historical—Jameson asserts that we pass from the text as symbolic act (which has been the focus of my book to this point), to the text as an utterance in class discourse, to the text as the sedimented content of form. The unifying point for all three of these levels is *contradiction*, which is registered ("reflected") in different forms at each level. At the first level, as we have seen, the text functions as a symbolic act that seeks a figural resolution to some unthinkable social contradiction; at the second level, the text functions as an ideologeme, an utterance in the larger dialogue between contradictory class discourses; and at the third level, the text functions as the ideological sedimentation at the level of form or genre itself of the larger process of "cultural revolution," the ongoing contradictory process in which historical classes vie for hegemony. The point behind this last is to distinguish between a naive categorization according to the mode of production—"This text is the formal reflection of the processes at work in capitalism or feudalism or what have you," each taken singly—to a more dialectical awareness that the text's form will register not just one class interest or one productive structure but the ongoing conflict between dominant, residual, and anticipatory modes of production that all assert themselves to varying degrees at a given moment.

In light of these distinctions, we can now say what History is: "With this final horizon," states Jameson in *The Political Unconscious*, "we emerge into a space in which History itself becomes the ultimate ground as well as the untranscendable limit of our understanding in general and our textual interpretations in particular" (100). This ultimate ground and untranscendable limit takes "the form of Necessity: why what happened (at first received as 'empirical' fact) had to happen the way it did. From this perspective, then, causality is only one of the possible tropes by which this formal restructuration can be achieved, although it has obviously been a privileged and historically significant one" (101). This ultimate ground is a purely negative one: "Necessity is here represented in the form of the inexorable logic involved in the determinate failure of all the revolutions that have taken place in human history" and is grasped as "the operation of objective limits" (102). This last note marks the point at which the negative cannot be perceived as some structural constant affecting us all alike regardless of space or time. What we brush up against are "objective" limitations, which are only experienced as such according to the historically contingent confluence of circumstances. The whole Marxian apparatus is erected in the space opened up by this objective negation of people's activities and intentions—an apparatus whose function is to remind us that subjectivity is a reactive formation of reflection as it reflects on its own failure and impossibility: "This is indeed the ultimate sense in which History as ground and untranscendable horizon needs no particular theoretical justification: we may be sure that its alienating necessities will not forget us, however much we might prefer to ignore them" (ibid.).

The relationship between Hegel's theory of reflection and Jameson's theory of the political unconscious can be fleshed out by examining the details of Jameson's argument in his Balzac chapter in *The Political Unconscious*. This chapter, along with his *Fables of Aggression*, is one of the few places in which Jameson argues at length the Lacanian underpinnings of his own theory of the political unconscious (and if we follow Žižek in reading Lacan and Hegel as operating according to similar logics through different vocabularies, we can, for our purposes here, take this Lacan-Hegel homology for granted). The chapter's opening sentence sets the tone for my study: "The novel is the end of genre in the [following] sense . . . : a narrative ideologeme whose outer form, secreted like a shell or exoskeleton, continues to emit its ideological message long after the extinction of its host" (151). It is at this point that my exploration of figuration and ideological apparatuses can be brought together with the present examination of Hegelian reflection and the Real.

Jameson opens with the question of the novel per se in order to show from the start the historical role the novel played in the long, ongoing process of bourgeois cultural revolution in which, through the "systematic undermining and demystification, the secular 'decoding,' of those preexisting inherited traditional or sacred narrative paradigms" (152), the cultural productions of a dying mode of production are reprogrammed for their new functions in the reproduction of the means of (re)production of the new world of capitalism. Here, we have another paradoxical passage working out the same logic as the above passage on the relationship between the text and the Real:

> The "objective" function of the novel is thereby also implied: to its subjective and critical, analytic, corrosive mission must now be added the task of producing as thought for the first time that very life world, that very "referent"—the newly quantifiable space of extension and market equivalence, the new rhythms of measurable time, the new secular and "disenchanted" object world of the commodity system, with its post-traditional daily life and its bewilderingly empirical, "meaningless," and contingent *Umwelt*—of which this new narrative discourse will then claim to be the "realistic" reflection. (ibid.)

Again, this is a question of the text as that which calls into being the very world to which it "refers." The point, in Hegelian terms, is that the text must posit its own presuppositions, the text ultimately functioning as the condition of possibility of its own conditions of possibility. Jameson clarifies this logic in his discussion of "the relationship between desire, ideology, and the possibility for certain types of narrative apparatus to lay claim to a social and historical 'realism'" (179). Jameson provides a schema according to which the relationships between these three elements can be plotted as shown in figure 6.

THE SOCIAL: The point of origin here is the social, presented as class allegory. This is the point at which we can explore the question of the political "referent" in more detail and try to decipher its relationship to the Real. The interesting thing here is that for Jameson the political is never present as such in the sense of a set of historical, empirical facts that carry their own objective and preideological value, for we only encounter these "facts" in allegorical terms— terms according to which the facts take on different values in different narrative contexts or registers. It is in this sense that the already-allegorical political and social "reality" "reflected" in the text is not the Real that by definition eludes such factual representation. One of the motivating forces behind Jameson's

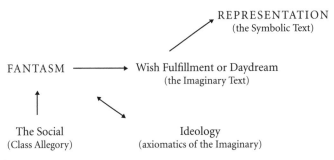

Figure 6

elaboration of the question of class allegory is his wish to distinguish this relationship between class and allegory from Lukács's theory of typification, which can be said "to be incomplete on two counts: on the one hand, it fails to identify the typifying of characters as an essentially allegorical phenomenon, and thus does not furnish any adequate account of the process whereby a narrative becomes endowed with allegorical meanings or levels. On the other, it implies an essentially one-to-one relationship between individual characters and their social or historical reference, so that the possibility of something like a system of characters remains unexplored" (162). We cannot simply identify such-and-such character as the bourgeois, another as the lumpen proletariat, and so on, and then feel we have explained the force of the narrative process. Lukács's theory of typification should in this context be seen as a primary example of positing reflection, according to which our task is simply to line up appearances with their underlying realities, which themselves are presumably clear from the point of view of the proletarian subject of history (or at least from the perspective of the proletariat's representative—the party intellectual). Such a position treats class identification as an inert given lying intact outside the text, whereas Jameson's task is to show the textual reflection as constitutive of the value of this outside, as an allegorical process that produces alternatives to empirical history by emptying them of their finality and reorchestrating them in terms of some master fantasy structure of *fantasm*.

FANTASM: The fantasm is to be seen as the allegorical recoding of the above social contradiction in terms of a manipulable and repeatable core narrative structure, and that functions as a mediating structure between a collectivity and the given social contradiction. Jameson distinguishes the term "fantasm" from "fantasy." The latter refers to daydreaming and wish fulfillment, which are more properly identified as processes characteristic of the Imaginary text discussed in the following subsection, "Wish Fulfillment." "Fantasm," on the other hand, refers to the unconscious master narrative, which according to Jameson, is "an unstable or contradictory structure, whose persistent actantial functions and events (which are in life restaged again and again with different actors and on different levels) demand repetition, permutation, and the ceaseless generation of various structural 'resolutions' which are never satisfactory, and whose initial, unreworked form is that of the Imaginary, or, in other words, of . . . waking fantasies, daydreams, and wish-fulfillments" (180). In his reading of Balzac, Jameson sees the latter's constant referral to some primal antagonistic family relationship as just such a master narrative at work behind his novels. Being "unconscious," however, this master narrative is nowhere present as such, but must be retroactively posited by the critic in order to flesh out the "fantasmatic subtext" to which the various works of the author are different, yet equally unsuccessful attempts at rewriting and resolving.

WISH-FULFILLMENT: This textual register operates according to the logic of the Imaginary. In his reading of the works of Balzac, Jameson singles out two, *La Vieille Fille* and *La Rabouilleuse*, as operating within this register. "These Imaginary or wish-fulfilling texts are then the first stage or moment in the process whereby the original fantasm seeks an (impossible) resolution" (181). Here, we return to the question of libidinal investment that I explored in my discussion of the libidinal apparatus, only now in much more detail. This investment at the Imaginary level is not that of an apparatus or empty schema made available for reinvestment but rather the condensation of this process in the libidinalization of an object in the text as an object of desire. In fact, it is at this point that one can recognize the now conspicuous lack of the question of desire in this study of the unconscious thus far. As Jameson remarks, a narrative element normally comes to be seen as an object of desire when someone desires it; the element becomes desirable when it occupies the position of the desirable object set up by the narrative. The peculiarity of the Imaginary Balzacian object, however, is that it reverses the order of this process: an object must be positioned as desirable in itself, prior to any subjective determination, in order to set the narrative apparatus and its subjective development to work. Through this libidinalization of the anonymous object of desire—an object not referable to any particular subject's desire but to desire as if in some pure, presubjective state—this object becomes "allegorical of all desire in general and of Desire as such" (156). This Utopian object of collective desire establishes the ultimately Imaginary status of this narrative apparatus, with its refusal to limit desiring identity to any one subject position but instead to throw "biographical subject, Implied Author, reader, and characters" (157) all into the same soup, as a transsubjective identification that refuses individuation. The object in question here, the house of the Cormon family, gives body to the Utopian, Imaginary fantasy apparatus of the text:

> A peace released from the competitive dynamism of Paris and of metro-politan business struggles, yet still imaginable in some existent backwater of concrete social history; a well-nigh Benjaminian preservation of the store-house of the past, and of its quintessential experience, within the narrative present; a "chaste" diminution of the libidinal to its mildest and least afflic-tive murmur; a Utopia of the household, in whose courtyards, hallways, and garden paths the immemorial routines of daily life, of husbandry and do-mestic economy, are traced in advance, projecting the eternal cycle of meals and walks, marketing and high tea, the game of whist, the preparation of the daily menu and the commerce of faithful servants and with habitual visi-tors—this mesmerizing image is the "still point" around which the disorder and urgency of a properly novelistic time will turn. (ibid.)

This tangible image of the Cormon house functions as the symbolic resolu-tion to the "twin 'semes' of bourgeois commercial activity and aristocratic tradition, the social and ideological contradiction around which the novel will turn" (ibid.).

Such fantasy or wish-fulfillment, though, flies in the face of the Real. As a result, other textual registers need to be constructed that will keep this fantasy construct in its place and, in the face of the demands of the Real as that which resists desire, make a space for such fantasies within the economy of the textual apparatus, a benign and protected space that gives value to the other textual registers while remaining bound by them. It is the function of the axiomatic, as Jameson calls it, to provide such a space for fantasy to play itself out.

IDEOLOGY/AXIOMATICS: Here is where Jameson works out his own ver-sion of Hegel's concept of positing the presuppositions. "Axiomatic" refers to "those conceptual conditions of possibility or narrative presuppositions which one must 'believe,' those empirical preconditions which must have been se-cured, in order for the subject successfully to tell itself this particular daydream" (182). Here again we have the logic of the formal conversion of figure into ground: "The production of the fantasy-text knows a peculiar 'unconscious' reflexivity, as, in the process of generating itself, it must simultaneously secure its own ideological preconditions" (ibid.). The point of positing the presup-positions is thus the point of access into the workings of ideology in relation to figuration and representation. In order to produce the wish-fulfilling text, we must first produce the ideology that will serve as its narrative condition of possibility. Althusser's definition of ideology as "the imaginary representation of the subject's relationship to his or her real conditions of existence" (LP 162) is hereby refined by this distinction between fantasy or imaginary representation and its axiomatic. Ideology is thus the positing of the presuppositions that makes a particular fantasy possible.

REPRESENTATION: Not only must the Imaginary text depend on its ideo-logical preconditions as above, it must also submit itself to a peculiar dialectic "in which the desiring subject is forced to enumerate the objections to his or her Imaginary gratification in order to realize the latter even on the level of a daydream." Such enumeration takes form in the Symbolic text: "One which is not to be satisfied by the easy solutions of an 'unrealistic' omnipotence or the immediacy of a gratification that then needs no narrative trajectory in the first place, but which on the contrary seeks to endow itself with the utmost repre-sentable density and to posit the most elaborate and systematic difficulties and obstacles, in order the more securely to overcome them, just as the philosopher imagines in advance the objections his triumphant argumentation will be sum-moned up to confute" (PU 183). The irony here is that the Symbolic text is in the service of the Imaginary. The Symbolic is not just some maturity gained by taking the reality-principle into account (although it is that); this maturity itself functions to provide a space for Imaginary fulfillment in the face of the obsta-cles thrown in its way by "reality." The more "real" the description of the conditions that get in the way of libidinal gratification, the more luxurious that gratification feels once achieved or, perhaps better yet, held out as always-to-be-achieved just over the horizon. But the limitations of "reality" may be drawn so well that they summon up the untranscendable limit of the Real. As Jameson notes in *The Political Unconscious*:

> This is the sense in which Lukács is right about Balzac, but for the wrong reasons: not Balzac's deeper sense of political and historical realities, but rather his incorrigible fantasy demands ultimately raise History itself over against him, as absent cause, as that on which desire must come to grief. The Real is thus—virtually by definition in the fallen world of capitalism—that which resists desire, that bedrock against which the desiring subject knows

the breakup of hope and can finally measure everything that refuses its fulfillment. Yet it also follows that this real—this absent cause, which is fundamentally unrepresentable and non-narrative, and detectable only in its effects—can be disclosed only by Desire itself, whose wish-fulfilling mechanisms are the instruments through which this resistant surface must be scanned. (184)

The Real's position in the above schema, then, as it maps out the relationships between these various textual registers I have been examining here—the Social, the fantasm, the Imaginary, the axiomatic, the Symbolic—is in the blank space outside the Symbolic text of representation. While the double-pointed arrow connecting the Imaginary with the axiomatic refers to the reciprocality of the relationship between fantasy and ideology, the arrow connecting the fantasy to representation goes only one way, for the limit of representation cannot return in any positive form. The Real has a space in the above schema only in the sense of the negative space opened up by the negative movement of desire (negative in the sense of denying the limitations on itself) until desire breaks down on upon reaching its term limit beyond which it can no longer go—the space of the breakdown as such that opens up as a space to be filled by the various apparatuses that operate in the projecting moments schematized above. It is in this sense that the negation of the negation of desire, in Jameson's words, "may be said to be a kind of modernizing formula in which the object to be fantasized is magically evoked by way of its very renunciation" (183).

External reflection? If Jameson had drawn a curved arrow joining the Symbolic text back to the Social or class allegory, and had thereby turned the whole schema into the vicious circle of positing and presupposing, then we would have a case of external reflection as the negative presentation of the Thing-in-itself lying beyond representation yet asserting its power positively as an idea shaping our circle of desire. But the real as posed here is nothing more than the limit immanent to desire, the limit that constitutes desire as such and imposes on us the endless process of figuration. I had asked earlier where the embodiment of the sublime, the sublime object, might lie in Jameson. The answer lies in the figure itself. The process of figuration is the embodiment of the radical negativity of reflection in the figure drawn to life by the symbolic act: each text produces the figure that will embody the point of contradiction and, through this embodiment, temporarily domesticate the immanent limits of desire; the series of failed figures gives body successively to the contradiction that makes perpetually impossible the realization of the fantasm; the semic logic of the text as it gives rise to a character system projects from out of the various points of possible identification the One, the master signifier, the signifier without signified that for however brief a moment embodies the negativity of the Real as the breakdown of all ideologies and yet through this subjectivation of substance provides the moment of possibility of subjectivity in all its ideological splendor.

Therefore this will also apply to the maker of tragedy, if he is an imitator; he is naturally third from a king and the truth, as are all the other imitators.—Socrates, *The Republic*

At this point in my study of the problem of representation as it has been displayed from Kant up through certain Marxist theories of postmodernism, I want to weave the various threads that have been at play throughout this book together through a common metaphor or figure, a figure that has as its "literal" meaning the figural as such. That figure is the theater, by which I mean both the theater in its usual sense as a dramatic art of the stage as well as its figurative sense as a stage for the performance of various modes of subjectivity, various calls or interpellations that transform the spectator into an actor. Performativity, then, will be used in its dramatic sense as well as its Hegelian, Lacanian, and Analytical senses. Performativity, then, is a tropic-concept that attempts to represent the process of presentation itself. That is, "performativity" functions as a representation or Vorstellung that stages the elaboration of presentation or Darstellung.

Such a trope, I will show, offers a way of extending the seemingly innocent questions proper to philosophical discourse into certain political questions. The way we conceive of the social or political space in which we stage the ideological performances proper to certain political questions will influence the ways we conceive of those political questions themselves. I will examine the effectiveness and limitations, then, of a set of tropes that equate social space with the stage. As in the earlier chapters of this book, the analysis of this space will depend on the dynamics of the vicious circle and the stupid thing elaborated on in chapter 1. And it is this drama that will stage the turn from questions of epistemology to those of hegemony in my closing chapter on the politics of cultural representation.

ALTHUSSER'S THEATER

As we saw in chapter 4, Althusser, in the closing pages of his contribution to *Reading Capital*, turns to an analogy between Darstellung and theater. The context for this dramatic trope at this point in the argument is the distinction in Marx's language between images and concepts. In order to present the concept of presentation, Marx drew upon "a language of metaphors which are nevertheless already *almost perfect concepts*, and which are perhaps only incomplete insofar as they have not yet been *grasped*, i.e., retained and elaborated as concepts" (RC 192). Althusser is referring, of course, to the passage in the *Grundrisse* in which Marx describes what Althusser will refer to as the structure-in-dominance as it is governed by structural causality: "In all forms of society," Marx writes, "there is one specific kind of production which predominates over the rest, whose relations thus assign rank and influence to the others. It is a general illumination which bathes all the other colors and modifies their particularity. It is a particular ether which determines the specific gravity of every being which has materialized within it" (G 106–7). These images or metaphors for structural causality—"general illumination," "particular ether"—would be "perfect concepts" if only they could be "grasped." Such grasping requires retaining and elaborating as concepts. To what extent, one might then ask, does Althusser's own image of dramatic presentation attain to this conceptual perfection? To what degree does the theatrical trope help to retain and elaborate it as a concept? What Althusser is asking for is an image that can in itself function as a concept.

What makes these images of illumination and ether closer to perfection than Marx's images of the camera obscura or the standing-on-head of his opponents? Althusser's answer is that the preceding images are new "quasi-concepts" in that they are freed from the "empiricist antinomies of phenomenal subjectivity and essential interiority." Althusser continues:

> We find an objective system governed in its most concrete determinations by the laws of its *erection* (*montage*) and *machinery*, by the specifications of its concept. Now we can recall that highly symptomatic term "Darstellung," compare it with this "machinery" and take it literally, as the very existence of this machinery in its effects: the mode of existence of the stage direction (mise en scène) of the theater which is simultaneously its own stage, its own script, its own actors, the theater whose spectators can, on occasion, be spectators only because they are first of all forced to be its actors, caught by the constraints of a script and parts whose authors they cannot be, since it is in essence *an authorless theater*. (RC 193)

In a curious reversal, we are asked to take the image of machinery literally, which means to see this machinery-image in terms of another image, the mode of existence of the staging of the theater. This grand deus ex machina comes swooping onto the stage as the embodiment of presentation itself. The presentation presents itself and exists only as its own self-presentation. In this way, Althusser attempts to lift us out of the problematic of representation by installing us at the level of the self-producing and self-reproducing machinery. The subject of representation is simply an effect of the self-staging of the machinery of capital as it presents value and surplus-value as its own mode of existence. And we grasp this point by retaining and elaborating the machinery-trope through its reincarnation as the theater-trope. But this is not just any theater, and this is not just any trope.

Althusser provides an aesthetic parallel to this machinery-drama in his discussion of theatrical presentation in "The 'Piccolo Teatro': Bertolazzi and Brecht."[1] Althusser is drawn to the works of these two authors (we are not yet, strictly speaking, concerned here with "authorless theater") because of their remarkable internal dissociation, their "latent assymetrical-critical structure, the dialectic-in-the wings structure" (FM 142). These plays are marked by "an unresolved alterity" built into their temporal structure; that is, they present the spectators with a drama operating on two different temporal planes—planes that never ground themselves in each other in any kind of mutual integration. For example, in Bertolazzi's *El Nost Milan*, a stationary time is confronted by a "dramatic" one. The stationary time is an empty time, in which nothing happens, that functions as a chronicle; the dramatic time, on the other hand, is a full time, in which history takes place, and that functions as a tragedy (melodrama). The historical dramatic tragic time "abolishes the other time and the structure of its spatial representation" (ibid., 137). Yet what we are presented with is not the valorization of this full historical dramatic temporality and the devalorization of the stationary chronicle temporality. Rather, the reverse is true: this historical drama is played out in the wings of the stage, in the margins of the society represented throughout most of each act; the melodramatic consciousness can only exist in such isolation from the ebb and flow of daily existence. It bursts as a lightning flash to distinguish itself in its bourgeois glory from the emptiness of common life, as a "very exact image for the quasi-null relation of a false consciousness to a real situation" (140). One consciousness cannot step beyond itself within its own terms. Its "dialectic" can only be revealed in its nondialecticity when its structure is ruptured by a foreign temporality. Yet such a temporal rupture must be experienced not by the characters but by the spectators. Althusser describes this process in terms similar to those above describing the machinery-drama trope:

> The structure is nowhere exposed, nowhere does it constitute the object of a speech or a dialogue. Nowhere can it be perceived directly in the play as can the visible characters or the course of the action. But it is there, in the tacit relation between the people's time and the time of the tragedy, in their mutual imbalance, in their incessant "interference" and finally in their true and delusive criticism. It is this revealing latent relation, this apparently insignificant and yet decisive tension that [Giorgio] Strehler's production enables the audience to perceive without their being able to translate this presence directly into clearly conscious terms. Yes, the audience applauded in the play something that was beyond them, which may have been beyond its author, but which Strehler provided him: a meaning buried deeper than words or gestures, deeper than the immediate fate of the characters who live this fate without ever being able to reflect on it. Even [the character] Nina, who is for us the rupture and the beginning, and the promise of another world and another consciousness, does not know what she is doing. Here we can truly say that consciousness is delayed [as in Hegel's Owl of Minerva]— for even if it is still blind, it is a consciousness aiming at last at a real world. (141–42)

As in the machinery-drama discussion, the perception of structural causality depends on the symptomatic reading by a certain spectatorial consciousness. Althusser wants to develop a sense of spectatorial consciousness that outstrips the limitations of the two dominant models in Western culture: critical distance and identification. The problem with the "critical distance" model is that it assumes a self-contained independent consciousness that views the drama unscathed. Conversely, the problem with the identification model is that it is based on a psychological concept (projection) that cannot by itself account for the social, cultural-aesthetic, and ideological dimensions of this identification. The spectator is sociologically and ideologically predisposed to identify (or not) with the drama: "Before becoming the occasion for an identification (an identification with self in the species of another), the performance is, fundamentally, the occasion for a cultural and ideological recognition" (149). Althusser's third model depends on the notion that the "play itself is the spectator's consciousness—for the essential reason that the spectator has no other consciousness than the content which unites him to the play in advance, and the development of this content in the play itself: the new result which the play produces from the self-recognition whose image and presence it is. . . . [T]he play is really the production of a new spectator, an actor who starts where the performance ends, who only starts so as to complete it, but in life" (150–51). Althusser places himself in this spectatorial position: he is neither the distant critic who would have known all ahead of time nor the identifying member who merges as a consciousness with the "consciousness" of the hero (as if a character could be described as a consciousness); Althusser himself has been shaped, produced as a spectatorial consciousness by the play, and his own essay on Bertolazzi and Bertolt Brecht is itself a moment in the elaboration of that consciousness:

> I look back, and I am suddenly and irresistibly assailed by *the* question:[2] are not these few pages, in their maladroit and groping way, simply that unfamiliar play *El Nost Milan*, performed on a June evening, pursuing in me its incomplete meaning, searching in me, despite myself, now that all the actors and sets have been cleared away, for the *advent* of its silent discourse?" (*FM* 151)

Here is an unexpected elaboration on the motif of symptomatic reading: the symptom produces *its own reading, its own readers*. In just the way that *El Nost Milan* outstrips its author, producers, actors, script, etc., Marx's *Capital* outstrips its author, producers, actors: "We even owe it to him that we can see his weaknesses, his lacunae, his omissions: they concur with his greatness, for, in returning to them we are only returning to the beginnings of a discourse interrupted by death. The reader will know how Volume Three ends. A title:

Classes. Forty lines, then silence (RC 193)." The actors go home, the books get put on the shelves, the authors disappear beyond the pale of death, and we are left as the site for elaboration cleared out of an interrupted discourse in the space of a certain silence. This is how we the spectators "on occasion" become the drama's actors. This is how even a play or a book *with an author* presents itself as an authorless theater. The latent structure of the drama produces its own spectators who in turn (in turning, in twisting by way of the trope, the drama's self-presentation as its own tropic circulation) embody the groping and grasping necessary for the elaboration of the concept.

To clarify this relationship between the spectator-actors and the authorless text, I turn to Michael Sprinker's reading of this trope in the final chapter of his *Imaginary Relations.* For Sprinker, the theatrical metaphor fails to do justice to the "epistemological complexity" of Althusser's discussion of Darstellung.

> The metaphor [of an authorless theater] glosses Althusser's old assertion that human beings are, from the point of view of historical science, bearers of structures that determine the limits of their power to act as agents of history. So construed, the text or script of history (the absent structure which never ceases to act upon the human agents whose roles it determines) is, as it were, already written in advance and is, per definition, imposed upon the actors from outside the theater. No matter that no one (God, the World Spirit, Reason, the iron laws of the economy) can be said to have written the script down; its existence prior to the performance is the necessary presupposition of the dramatic metaphor. The actors will not be allowed to improvise their parts. One sees why voluntarists like Edward Thompson and Norman Geras would find this scenario offensive. (IR 290–91)

If this were what Althusser were suggesting by using the theatrical metaphor for structural causality, then Sprinker would be correct here. Such notions as "written in advance," "imposed . . . from outside," and "existence prior to" make no sense in terms of Althusser's emphasis on metonymic causality, according to which there is no advance, outside, or priority that is not already the structure's own advance, outside, and priority. The absent cause is precisely not outside the structure but is, rather, immanent in that structure's effects. Yet the notion of a script prior to the action is also precisely *not* what Althusser suggests in his metaphor of an authorless theater. True, there is a script one can point to prior to the action, a script entitled *El Nost Milan* or *Mother Courage*; but this is not the script Althusser identifies in his dramatic trope. The authorless script is that latent structure that having been set in motion by a particular authored script (in the traditional sense), produces the spectator-actors whose function it is to elaborate the drama beyond its limitations as a particular authored script. It is thus not true that the actors are not allowed to improvise their parts; such improvisation, after the "actors" have gone home and the sets have been taken down, is exactly what makes this absent script an authorless one: this script is dependent on the contingencies of the spectatorial consciousness that this script itself sets in motion for its own elaboration. Some spectators were moved to denounce Strehler's production of *El Nost Milan*, while others—such as Althusser—were impelled to improvise their parts by writing, precisely, an essay on Bertolazzi and Brecht, and through such "action" to elaborate on the script latent in Strehler's production. The script in no way exists prior to Althusser's or any other spectator's response; it exists nowhere else but in and as Althusser's writing in response to the production on stage. The Darstellung of this theatrical presentation must be staged beyond the limits of the stage. The alternative interpretations of the agency inherent in this metaphor, then, cannot be limited in advance to those of voluntarism and Stalinism.

Of particular value in Sprinker's presentation, nevertheless, is his translation of a passage from the 1965 French version of *Reading Capital* that contains a section omitted from the 1968 edition and thus the English translation. As we saw in chapter 4, this passage is important in that it offers a further elaboration of the Vorstellung-Darstellung opposition as well as an elaboration of the drama-trope. Sprinker's translation reads as follows:

> "Darstellung" signifies in German, among other things, *theatrical representation*, but the figure of theatrical representation adheres immediately to the sense conveyed by the word that signifies "presentation," "exhibition," and, in its most profound root, "position of presence," presence offered and visible. In order to express its specific nuance, it may be instructive to oppose "Darstellung" to "Vorstellung." In Vorstellung, one certainly has to do with a position, but one which is kept *behind* this pre-position, something which is represented by that which is kept out front, [represented] by its emissary: the Vorstellung. *In* Darstellung *on the contrary, there is nothing behind*: the very thing is there, "*da*," presented [*offerte*] in the position of presence. The entire text of the play is thus there, presented [*offert*] in the presence of the representation (the Darstellung). But the presence of the entire play is not ex-

hausted in the immediacy of the deeds or the words of the character: we "know" that it is the presence of a completed whole which lives in each moment and in each character, and in all the relations among the characters given in their personal presence. [It is] only to be grasped, however, as the presence of the whole, as the latent structure of the whole, *in the whole*, and only intuited [*pressentie*] in each element and in each role. (*LC* 170; *IR* 291)

This is a peculiar presence—a presence that is present only in its absence: the whole is nowhere present in any of its elements, nor is it present elsewhere, in some beyond of the elements. Like the Kantian sublime, this presentation presents what can only ever be absent since it exists nowhere other than in its presenting elements and thus can only be presented negatively, as that which is present only in its absence. Yet unlike the Kantian sublime, we are not thus led to the Idea of the Infinite or the Almighty as that intuitive intellect that out-strips our puny human discursive understanding. For this reason, Sprinker's translation of pressentie as "intuition" involves us in a terminological confu-sion if we are to elaborate on Althusser's trope in Kantian terms (as Sprinker goes on to do): the point is that the whole can never be intuited, it can only be inferred. That which can only be presented negatively can never be an object of intuition in the strict sense, although we can posit its existence through "reflec-tive judgment" in the way that Kant comes to posit an objective purposiveness in the operations of nature. But such a positing is an example of teleological rather than aesthetic judgment, the latter operating strictly in subjective terms that can never lead to objective conclusions.[3]

Before returning to the excised Althusser passage above, then, it would prove instructive to follow this Kantian connection that Sprinker seeks in Althusser's trope. As Sprinker describes it:

> Kant proposed as the distinctive manner of making aesthetic judgments their subsumption of the particular under the universal when only the particular is given and the universal is that which must be discovered. Putting aside the dubious uses to which Kant himself put this principle in his own conception of how empirical science must proceed, we can nonetheless recognize how Althusser supposes just this sort of reflective judgment in grounding his epistemology in the apprehension of the structure in its immanence. (*IR* 292)

First, such a problem does not apply to aesthetic judgment, which simply concerns our feelings of pleasure or pain when confronted with the representation of purposiveness or nonpurposiveness respectively. Second, Kant's conception of reflective judgment cannot be reduced to a purely inductive (abductive?) model of reasoning, according to which the particular is subsumed under the universal "when only the particular is given and the universal is that which must be discovered." To be sure, Kant does make a statement that could imply, if taken alone, that such a relationship between particular and universal was in fact what Kant had in mind by laying out the grounds of reflective judgment: "The reflective judgment which is compelled to ascend from the particular in nature to the universal, stands, therefore, in need of a principle" (*CJ* §4: 18). What is key here in terms of reflective judgment is not simply the relationship between particular and universal but the need for a principle according to which such a relationship can then be posited. This principle—purposiveness—can only be transcendental, not empirical, and can thus only be posited by reflective judgment itself and not derived "from any other quarter (as it would then be a determinant judgment)" (ibid., 19). Whereas the universal laws of nature have their ground in our (discursive) understanding, those particular empirical laws that fall outside of our understanding must be regarded as the products of some other understanding that "had supplied them for the benefit of our cognitive faculties, so as to render possible a system of experience according to particular natural laws!" (ibid.) (The question of aesthetic judgment would only apply to the pleasure we feel when the otherwise contingent accord between subjective and objective purposiveness appears as presented to us by some other understanding.) But this posited archetypal understanding is itself simply the result of an analogy. The principle of purposiveness that is to "ground" reflective judgment on those natural phenomena that fall outside the laws of our own understanding is itself the product of a tropic extension (as we saw in chapter 2)—in light of which Kant then properly poses the following problem: "The only question is whether such a representation of purposiveness exists at all" (*CJ* §7, 30).

Apart from the difficulties of Sprinker's use of "Kantian" principles, the question of Althusser's relationship to Kantian reflective judgment is nevertheless an intriguing one, as is the question of the relationship between Althusser's comments on aesthetics and his quest for the concept (of structural causality). I would like to deploy a preemptive strike at this moment, however, by drawing attention to Althusser's claim above that the spectator's consciousness is the play itself. Rather than an exploration of the transcendental principles underlying tropic displays of concepts, Althusser provides a more Pascalian apparatus in the sense that the key to our actions must be looked for not internally but externally, in our practices themselves. With this in mind, one can begin to see in the "Piccolo Teatro" essay the glimmer of the staging these questions would undergo in the ISA essay. In *Lenin and Philosophy*, Althusser reminds us of "[Blaise] Pascal's defensive 'dialectic' for the wonderful formula which will enable us to invert the order of the notional schema of ideology. Pascal says more or less: 'Kneel down, move your lips in prayer, and you will believe'" (168). The theater, like any other ideological apparatus, defines the rituals governing the practices that inscribe the "Ideas" emerging from it; yet the theater, as art, functions differently, according to Althusser, in that it allows us to "see" and "feel" this ideology from the inside as it constructs us as its own spectator consciousness. Althusser continues, "It therefore appears that the subject acts insofar as he is acted by" the material system of ideological interpellation (170). It is because we are always already subjects, prior to our entering the theater, prior even to our birth, that we are capable of being spectators.[4]

Thus one could argue that Althusser's theater-trope functions aesthetically in two ways: that the ideology which we "feel" and "see" in the production is akin to the representation in response to which we feel pleasure. But the feeling that Kant has in mind is, again, purely subjective: it is in response only to the accord established between our subjective representational faculties. One would have to argue that we respond in a purely subjective-aesthetic way to the ideology we feel in art, but this is not how Althusser describes this effect: "What art makes us *see*, and therefore gives to us in the form of '*seeing*,' '*perceiving*,' and '*feeling*' (which is not the form of knowing), is the *ideology* from which it is born, in which it bathes, from which it detaches itself as art, to which it *alludes*" (LP 222). Allusion implies interest, whereas for Kant aesthetic judgment must remain completely disinterested. Yes, Kant also distinguishes feeling from knowledge in speaking about the aesthetic, but in order to continue the analogy we would have to be able to equate purposiveness with ideology (in the case of "A Letter on Art") or with structural causality (in the case of the "Piccolo Teatro" essay) (which in turn raises the question of the relationship between ideology and structural causality). The implication is, on the one hand, that what we feel in the work of art, because of its internal distantiation from the ideology it presupposes, is the process of interpellation itself. On the other hand, the implication is that we "feel" the structural causality that rises into its absent presence through the ruptures and slippages within the structure of the work. What comes to the fore here, as it does throughout *Reading Capital*, is the question of a crucial ambiguity in all of Althusser's writings: Is the object to which we are responding a function of knowledge (Science) or the social formation about which we are trying to gain a certain knowledge? In other words, are we confronted with the map or the terrain? Are we talking about a problematic or what that problematic allows us to see as its visible and invisible? One reason for elaborating on the now safely interred corpse of Althusser is that this ambiguity is also at play in Jameson's conception of cognitive mapping: Is the emphasis on the subjective function of mapping or objective structure to be mapped?

This brings us to the question of the relationship between art and science for Althusser. Again, it is useful to distinguish the argument developing here from Sprinker's. Another problem with Sprinker's commentary on Althusser's theatrical metaphor for structural causality is Sprinker's determination of the place of aesthetics in Althusser's project overall. "It is the domain of the aesthetic as a general epistemological category," Sprinker argues, "which, as Kant was perhaps the first to recognize, offers to bridge the gap between the precepts of practical being and the principles of rational understanding. That Althusser should appeal to just such a problematic at this point in his argument can scarcely have been fortuitous" (*IR* 290). One possible application of this reference to the bridging function of the aesthetic for Kant here implies that Althusser, in his response to the theory/practice distinction, inserts the aesthetic in just such a way; that is, the aesthetic is presumed to play a bridging role in Althusser's development of the concept of theoretical practice. One response to Sprinker's assumption would have to be that for Althusser the concept of theoretical practice already bridges any such gap in and of itself, which is precisely its function within Althusser's argument. In terms of his own argument, Althusser does not need the aesthetic moment in order to pull off such a union. In fact, unlike the development of Kant's critical philosophy, the development of Althusserian "Science" must subordinate the aesthetic moment to the theoretico-practical one. Such was the crux of Althusser's rejection of Marx's figural language in *Capital* in favor of the "quasi-concept" of Darstellung as the stand-in for structural causality (as we have seen in chapter 3). Only a problematic that provides for the production of the *concept* of structural causality can be considered scientific. "The real difference between art and science," Althusser writes, "lies in the *specific form* in which they give us the same object in quite different ways: art in the form of 'seeing' and 'perceiving' or 'feeling,' science in the form of *knowledge* (in the strict sense, by concepts)" (*LP* 223). As we have seen, the work of art, operating within a given ideology, may produce a distance within itself from that constitutive ideology (an "internal distantiation") that allows us to "see" that ideology and "feel" what it is like to live it; but it cannot provide us with a knowledge of that ideology. In order to arrive at such a knowledge, we must first have developed a knowledge of art itself: "Like all knowledge, the knowledge of art presupposes a preliminary *rupture* with the language of *ideological spontaneity* and the constitution of a body of scientific concepts to replace it" (*LP* 226).[5] Kant's concept of aesthetic judgment cannot be anything but such a language of spontaneity.

Another sense in which Althusser's turn to aesthetics could be seen as an attempt at bridging is to see art as the bridge between ideology and science rather than theory and practice, and this is more likely what Sprinker has in mind. The difficulty here, however (and this problem is particularly apparent in Althusser's "A Letter on Art"), is that such a schema treats these three "practices"—the ideological, the aesthetic, and the scientific—as distinct levels or realms or, to return to Althusser's trope in *Reading Capital*, territories. Borrowing the bridging metaphor from Kant only heightens this distinction. But the beauty of an essay such as "Piccolo Teatro" is that we see ideology not as some distinct realm or set of illusions or ideas but as a mode of subjectivization. In this sense, we feel an ideology not as some preexisting body but as a structure into which we are inserted or, more appropriately, out of which we are produced.[6] We don't feel what it is like to *be* a certain type of ideological subject (versus the critical observer we presumably remain throughout the performance); we feel what it is like to *become* one because such a subject (or more accurately, subject-position) exists only through such experiences. The difficulty, though, is that the language of seeing and feeling implies a subject-object distinction that is precisely the object of attack in Althusser's work, in that it unwittingly returns us to the "empiricist problematic" that poses the problem of knowledge in epistemological rather than practical or productivist terms. The Kantian conception of the aesthetic itself falls under such an "empiricist problematic" and could not serve, except by contrast, as a key to Althusser's questions about art. For him to turn to the Kantian problematic at this or any other point would be fortuitous indeed.[7]

ALTHUSSER'S TROPIC-CONCEPTS

For the third time, I will present the excised passage on structural causality as theatrical Darstellung:

"*Darstellung*" signifies in German, among other things, *theatrical representa-*
tion, but the figure of theatrical representation adheres immediately to the
sense conveyed by the word that signifies "presentation," "exhibition," and,
in its most profound root, "position of presence," presence offered and
visible. In order to express its specific nuance, it may be instructive to oppose
"Darstellung" to "Vorstellung." In *Vorstellung*, one certainly has to do with a
position, but one which is kept *behind* this pre-position, something which is
represented by that which is kept out front, [represented] by its emissary: the
Vorstellung. In Darstellung on the contrary, there is nothing behind: the very
thing is there, "*da*," presented [*offerte*] in the position of presence. The entire
text of the play is thus there, presented [*offert*] in the presence of the representation (the Darstellung). But the presence of the entire play is not exhausted in the immediacy of the deeds or the words of the character: we
"know" that it is the presence of a completed whole which lives in each
moment and in each character, and in all the relations among the characters
given in their personal presence. [It is] only to be grasped, however, as the
presence of the whole, as the latent structure of the whole, *in the whole*, and
only intuited [*pressentie*] in each element and in each role. (*LC* 170; *IR* 291)

As we saw with Kant and Hegel in the earlier chapters of this book, the
distinction between Vorstellung and Darstellung is here called up in order to
clarify a question concerning the problem of representation. In this passage,
Vorstellung clearly operates within what Althusser has referred to as the empiricist problematic. The re-presentation functions as a proxy, as a stand-in for that
which stands behind the scene. One problem with metaphor, then, is that it
makes use of an image in the place where there should be a concept. The image
(mis)leads us in that it carries us out of the given field of inquiry into some
other unrelated field. The image opens up a gap between the word before us
and the concept to be grasped. And as we have seen, Althusser's reading of
Capital is motivated in part by the need to rescue Marx from the tropic tangents
that his language sets in motion in the very places where he should be pinning
things down, making things clear, grasping things by the root. Representation,
then, opens up a gap that must be closed by the elaboration of the trope. The
problem, however, is that this version of metaphor and representation reduplicates the empiricist problematic in the very place where it is to be expelled once
and for all. This version makes all the more problematic the turn to Darstellung
as the mode of presentation that finally, after the long labor of tropic circula-

tion, brings the concept here, "presented in the position of presence." Such an immediacy looks suspiciously like the post-Kantian reaction in light of which (or in the lack of light of which) all cows are black. The very proposition "The concept is here," as Hegel has shown, falls in on itself through the negativity of the copula that transforms the here into a there (an ambiguity already "present" in the German "da" itself: Dasein as being-there, determinate negation, externality, ex-sistence). Darstellung cannot save us from the incommensurability of Vorstellung if we conceive of the former as simply the closing up of the gap inaugurated by the work of the latter. A presentation beyond representation cannot be posed as the simple return to the self-presence of the concept that presumably was set adrift by the tropic circulation of the image.

This problem is especially ironic since as critical as Althusser is about the use of images as pseudo-concepts, he himself depends on images at the most crucial points in his project. Why, in the closing paragraphs of his contribution to *Reading Capital*, should Althusser turn to the trope of the theater to present us with the workings of the "quasi-concept," Darstellung, which itself is a stand-in for structural causality? And what is the term "structural causality" itself if not an effaced trope (the comparison of the effectivity of a social totality to a structure)? Plato, it will be remembered, concluded *The Republic* with the Myth of Er. This dependence on tropes is what bothers Terry Eagleton about both Althusser's and Pierre Macherey's discussions of aesthetics: "Althusser and Macherey appear to want to rescue and redeem the text from the shame of the sheerly ideological; yet in these passages they can do so only by resorting to a nebulously figurative language ('allude,' 'see,' 'retreat') which lends a merely rhetorical quality to the distinction between 'internal distantiation' and received notions of art's 'transcendence' of ideology" (CI 84).

But I would argue, following Thomas E. Lewis, that this version of metaphor—metaphor as correspondence or resemblance—is not the one that Althusser, however inconsistently, develops. In "Reference and Dissemination: Althusser after Derrida," Lewis argues that Althusser develops a theory of metaphor in which metaphor is reduced to metonymy.[8] What Lewis is suggesting is that like Umberto Eco, Althusser sees the metaphorical relationship not in terms of figure and ground, signifier and signified, image and referent, or any other binary opposition that presents the metaphorical operation as the movement between two separate levels (the figural and the literal). Such a position merely reduplicates the "empirical problematic" that Althusser challenges.

Metaphor is instead to be seen as the horizontal or metonymic sliding on the same level from figure to figure. Lewis summarizes Eco's point:

> Eco considers metaphor in fact to be an effect of metonymy: "each metaphor can be traced back to a subjacent chain of metonymic connections which constitute the framework of the code and upon which is based the constitution of any semantic field" [*The Role of the Reader* (Bloomington: Indiana University Press, 1979), 68]. Rather than resulting from a process of substitution, therefore, metaphor, when analyzed semiotically, is said to result from a process of displacement. Between the terms that are installed in any "metaphorical" sign function, for example, other interpretants necessarily intervene; it is the discursive elision of an unaccustomed number of such interpretants that accounts for the appearance of metaphor as a process of substitution. Yet the ascription of meaning(s) to a metaphor depends precisely on the conscious or unconscious ability to grasp—or invent—an underlying chain of interpretants that is capable of correlating a content or content nebula to the "metaphorical" expression. In Eco's view, the effect of metaphor thus is produced by manifestly "short circuiting," or "bypassing," a series of interpretants that either are available as contiguous elements within a code or that are available as operators of code switches: "a metaphor can be invented because language, in its process of unlimited semiosis, constitutes a multidimensional network of metonymies, each of which is explained by a cultural convention rather than by an original resemblance" [*Role*, 78]. (RD 44–45)

This version of metaphor as elided metonymy goes a long way toward seeing Althusser's view of metaphor as more congenial to his view of metonymic causality than it at first appears. In Althusser's own conception of metaphor, Lewis contends, he "generally considers not only that concepts are metaphors in and for theory but also that concepts are to be understood as operating metonymically so as to move the users of concepts along specific interpretantial chains in order that they may arrive at a specific place and perform a specific act" (ibid., 49). In this way, according to Lewis, Althusser has developed "an understanding of concepts as 'tropic-concepts,' that is, as discursive operations that provisionally enable one to accomplish specific tasks by activating various series of metonymical chains in and for specific circumstances" (50). Thus, when Althusser refers to Marx's tropes of "general illumination" and "particular ether" as "a language of metaphors which are nevertheless already *almost perfect con-*

cepts, and which are perhaps only incomplete insofar as they have not yet been *grasped*, i.e., retained and elaborated as concepts," we can now see this process of retention and elaboration as the metonymic displacement of interpretants that Lewis discusses above. Althusser outlines a chain of discursive displacements of tropes in Marx's elaboration of the concept that never achieved its final condition as grasped until Althusser, moved by the drama of the absent cause or latent structure negatively presented in Marx's texts, pursuing in him its incomplete meaning, searching in him, despite himself, for the advent of its silent discourse interrupted by death. These almost perfect concepts are not simply posed over against the concept as such but are enlisted (retained [*erinnert*?], elaborated, sublated?) in a chain of substituting tropic-concepts.[9]

I wish to explore further the ramifications of Althusser's tropic-concepts in *Reading Capital* and elsewhere in two distinct ways. The first is an elaboration of the concept of metonymic causality as written across Kafka as well as Laclau and Mouffe; the second is an elaboration of the spectator consciousness as written across Nietzsche and Žižek-Lacan.

ALTHUSSER METONYMY CHINA WALL

Kafka's "The Great Wall of China" opens with an enclosure, a definition of a political space:

> "The Great Wall of China," the narrator explains, "was finished off at its northernmost corner. From the southeast and the southwest it came up in two sections that finally converged there. This principle of piecemeal construction was applied also on a smaller scale by both of the two great armies of labor, the eastern and the western. It was done in this way: gangs of some twenty workers were formed who had to accomplish a length, say, of five hundred yards of wall, while a similar gang built another stretch of the same length to meet the first. But after the junction had been made the construction of the wall was not carried on from this point, let us say, where this thousand yards ended; instead the two groups of workers were transferred to begin building again in quite different neighborhoods. Naturally in this way many great gaps were left, which were only filled in gradually and bit by bit, some, indeed, not till after the official announcement that the wall was finished. In fact it is said that there are gaps which have never been filled in at all, an assertion, however, that is probably merely one of the many legends to which the building of the wall

gave rise, and which cannot be verified, at least by any single man with his own eyes and judgment, on account of the extent of the structure. (cs 235)

I want to explore a certain resemblance between Althusser's description of ideological and social terrain in *Reading Capital* and Kafka's description of the production of a political terrain in "The Great Wall of China." While I propose to engage one text in dialogue with the other, to situate them on the same discursive plane, I do not mean to imply some necessary relationship or influence between the two. In other words, I am not proposing to unearth a set of preexistent connections that makes Kafka somehow Althusserian or vice versa but to stage those connections as an examination of the ideological value of the horizontal or metonymic enclosure of a certain terrain and the related question of a vertical or metaphoric transcendence. While both writers demystify the gesture toward transcendence in much the same way Marx had in his discussion of religion as an opiate, their explanations differ as to the exact relationship between the constructions of horizon and transcendence. They differ as well, I might add, in their depiction of the possibility or even desirability of plucking the illusory flower from the chain of oppression as Marx had demanded.

But I first want to look at the familiar distinction between metaphor and metonymy.[10] Metaphor can be seen as a transcendent movement; through metaphor we translate the terms from one field into the terms of another, the relationship or positioning between these terms seen as vertical, a substitution from above to below, inside to outside. Metaphor assumes a certain equivalence, a reduction of differences, between the two terms in order for this substitution to be possible. Political representation is thus a form of such substitution and mediation. Metonymy, on the other hand, works laterally, establishing relationships of contiguity through pairings and displacements. This shift from metaphor to metonymy moves us from transcendence to immanence. As both Althusser and Kafka suggest, metaphor is inherently theological in its structuring of mediation itself as a relationship to something outside or above the structure or terrain, and by its positioning of the mediator as one who inhabits a space or opening between us and some external power. Metaphor, despite its initial reduction to some presupposed equivalence, creates the possibility of hierarchy, while metonymy creates a nonhierarchical contiguous space of equality-in-difference. It is this denial of metaphor that drives Althusser's desire to rid Marxism of its Leibnizian or Hegelian theology of expression and leads him to isolate Darstellung as the key epistemological concept in

Marx's theory of value. What particularly interests Althusser, as we have seen, is that this concept of Darstellung, only one of the concepts that Marx uses in *Capital* in order to think the effectivity of the structure, is "both the least metaphorical and, at the same time, the closest to the concept Marx is aiming at when he wants to designate at once both absence and presence, i.e., *the existence of the structure in its effects*" (RC 188).

As I pointed out in chapter 4, Althusser thus seeks a mode of representation appropriate for thinking the metonymic causality of the structure, a way of mapping the social terrain that forces us to think differently the very notion of terrain itself. Althusser seeks to mark out, in the least metaphorical way possible, the structure, the boundaries, the absences or necessary blind spots of a given problematic, but to do so in such a way that the question of sight and blindness, visible and invisible, cannot simply be appropriated into a model of false consciousness, with the necessary implication of an available true consciousness. The whole problem of oversight must be represented, in other words, on a terrain that does not lead to the binaries of inside/outside, essence/phenomena, true/false, visible/invisible—all of which offer the possibility of transcendence as that which somewhere, somehow lies outside the present terrain, the field of vision. The symptomatic reading that Althusser proposes, then—the reading of the absent questions of a text that provides new answers to questions it never asked, indeed cannot ask within its given terrain— must operate metonymically rather than transcendentally. "It is impossible to leave a closed space," Althusser insists, "simply by taking up a position *outside it*, either in its exterior or its profundity. [It still belongs] to *that* circle, to *that* closed space, as its repetition in *its* other-than-itself. Not the repetition but the non-repetition is the way out of this circle" (ibid.).

Right now I want to suggest that Kafka's concerns are quite similar, that he will interrogate a structure much like Althusser's metonymic totality, and that such inquiry will lead to a meditation on the presence and absence of the high command who order the building of the wall. His tale itself—if it can be called that—must also be seen as a metonymic structure, a series of answers that reveal more urgent questions than the previous ones, a continuous displacement of frames and strategies of closure—such as historical narratives, childhood reminiscences, secret maxims, and parables—that like the Imperial Messenger, never reach their intended end but continue the lines of flight Deleuze and Guattari identify as the crucial political gesture of Kafka's texts.[11]

The building of the wall presents an enigma: Why would the high command, in their intention to safeguard us from the fierce nomads of the north, plan this piecemeal method of construction that leaves gaps and lacunae in the protective structure? The answer to this leads to more enigmas. The high command, in their infinite wisdom, really intended to produce the side effects of the wall-building process—the sense of purpose, the unity, the cooperation, the willful, even enthusiastic submission to the dictates of the high command—rather than the wall itself. Or as one scholar explains, the high command really wanted to build a foundation for a tower that would complete the abandoned project of the Tower of Babel. But how can a quarter-circle structure with extensive gaps provide such a base? Hence the conclusion that the tower must be meant spiritually, metaphorically. Which raises the next question: Why then build the wall itself if the tower is only a metaphor? The narrator's answer, which comes later in the tale and with no explicit connection, is that the tower is a metaphor for the "superficial culture mounting sky-high around a few precepts that have been drilled into people's minds for centuries, precepts which, though they have lost nothing of their eternal truth, remain entirely invisible in this fog of confusion" (cs 242). The building of the wall, the enclosure of a political and an ideological space, somehow provides a base for the installations of the high command itself in the tower, elevating them above the people like the myste-rious and absent gods they appear to be to the common people. The building of the wall, in other words, maintains and constantly reproduces the conditions of hierarchy that make possible in the first place the high command, the imperial sun itself, in its metaphoric transcendence beyond the world of the village. "But it is precisely this question of empire," the narrator tells us, "which in my opinion the common people should seek to answer, since they after all are the empire's final support" (ibid.). The support of the tower, then, is not the wall at all but the people in their process of building it as an enclosure.

The tower is the answer, but no one besides the narrator seems to recognize the question itself, the question of empire. The people, in building the wall, thus provide an answer to a question they are unable to ask. In his discussion of symptomatic reading, Althusser asks: "Why is political economy necessarily blind to what it produces and to its work of production? Because its eyes are fixed on *the old question*, and it continues to relate its new answer to its old question; because it is still concentrating on the old '*horizon*' within which the new problem '*is not visible*'" (rc 24). So long as the people in Kafka's tale look to the wall, thought to exist in its totality as the empire's horizon, rather than to the production that makes the wall and indeed the tower possible—in short, so long as the people take the old terrain as a given—they will not be able to provide themselves with the terrain that will make the question of empire visible. As Althusser explains, "It is the field of the problematic that defines and structures the invisible as the defined excluded" (ibid., 25–26). The questions of surplus value or of empire "are rejected in principle, repressed from the field of the visible: and that is why their fleeting presence in the field when it does occur (in very peculiar and symptomatic circumstances) *goes unperceived*, and becomes literally an undivulged absence—since the whole function of the field is not to see them, to forbid any sighting of them" (26).

Kafka's narrator claims that we may be certain that in the office of the high command, forever absent from view, "through the window the reflected splendors of divine worlds fell on the hands of the leaders as they traced their plans" (CS 240). But the question remains, as we have seen: How could this command, tracing the plans of the divine, deliberately command something so inexpedient as the piecemeal construction of the wall? In answer, the narrator relates an ancient maxim: "Try with all your might to comprehend the decrees of the high command, but only up to a certain point; then avoid further meditation" (ibid.). This interdiction seems to imply that there is some danger in going beyond that certain point; but it implies as well that it is possible to do so. We might be able to travel out to the margins of the empire and see for ourselves the condition of the wall; we might be able to follow the Imperial Messenger home and discover the location of the high command. Yet perhaps the danger lies not in what we might find in the borderlands or in the tower but in the recognition that we will never know, no matter how hard we search, even where the center or the margins are, not because we did not look long or far enough but precisely because it is impossible to reach those points: "The limits that my capacity for thought imposes on me are narrow enough," the narrator explains, "but the province to be traversed here is infinite" (241).

> Thus the parable of the Imperial Messenger: The Emperor, so [the parable] runs, has sent a message to you, the humble subject, the insignificant shadow cowering in the remotest distance before the imperial sun; the Emperor from his deathbed has sent a message to you alone. . . . The messenger immediately sets out on his journey; a powerful, an indefatigable; now pushing with his right arm, now with his left, he cleaves a way for himself through the throng; if he encounters resistance he points to his breast, where the symbol of the sun glitters; the way is made easier for him than it would be for any other

man. But the multitudes are so vast; their numbers have no end. If he could reach the open fields how fast he would fly, and soon doubtless you would hear the welcome hammering of his fists on your door. But instead how vainly does he wear out his strength; still he is only making his way through the chambers of the innermost palace; never will he get to the end of them; and if he succeeded in that nothing would be gained; the courts would still have to be crossed; and after the courts the second outer palace; and once more stairs and courts; and once more another palace; and so on for thousands of years; and if at last he should burst through the outermost gate—but never, never can that happen—the imperial capital would lie before him, the center of the world, crammed to bursting with its own sediment. Nobody could fight his way through here even with a message from a dead man. But you sit at your window when evening falls and dream it to yourself. (244)

When we set out toward the horizon, no matter how long we travel a horizon lies just as far before us. We can never reach the horizon, never willfully step outside the field, simply because the horizon is an effect of the field itself. This horizon-value—the ideological illusion of an elsewhere, an outside, a traversable limit or boundary beyond which lies the truth or the real or the divine—threatens, Althusser warns, "to induce a false idea of the nature of this field, if we think this field literally according to the spatial metaphor as a space limited by another space outside it. This other space is also in the first space which contains it as its own denegation; this other space is the first space in person, which is only defined by the denegation of what it excludes from its own limits" (RC 26–27).

As Derrida has commented,

> That "horizon"-value, that pure infinite opening for the presentation of the present and the experience of meaning, suddenly becomes framed. Suddenly it is a part. And just as suddenly apart. Thrown back into play. And into question. Its de-formations are no longer even negatively regulated by any *form*, which is another name for presence. The transformations of meaning no longer hinge on any enrichment of "history" and "language" but only on a certain squaring of the text, on the obligatory passage through an open surface, on the detour through an empty square, around the column of fire.

It is precisely this pure infinite opening that Kafka describes in the parable of the Imperial Messenger—infinite in the sense that it lies forever before us, keeps us from making any progress toward our destination simply because there is no beyond proper to the empire where we now stand, amid all its dense populace and sedimentation. The empire's horizon is not the demarcation of a field outside our own but the internal effect of our own, its presence forever at a distance as the horizon-value of our own dream work as we sit at the window at nightfall when the horizon will fade into darkness. Nevertheless, this very illusion, "this very weakness [is] one of the most unifying influences among our people," so says Kafka's narrator; "indeed, if one may dare to use the expression, the very ground on which we live" (CS 247). And it is for this reason that the narrator decides to follow the ancient secret maxim and refuses to disillusion the people: "To set about establishing a fundamental defect here would mean undermining not only our consciences, but, what is far worse, our feet. And for that reason I shall not proceed any further with my inquiry into these questions" (247–48).

Kafka, on the other hand, did proceed further in that inquiry by writing "The Great Wall of China." But what are we to make of this politically? Is the narrator's refusal to disillusion his people necessarily a retrograde action? Is Kafka's ungrounding or de-territorialization of his reader necessarily a revolutionary one? Apart from the political charge of these gestures, can we even think of them as possible, as effective in the first place? What is the meaning of agency in a territory such as Kafka's or Althusser's where the plane continually falls away as the surface of the globe or falls in on itself as the inescapable interiority of the Imperial Capital? The implication in both Kafka and Althusser is that this ungrounding is a necessary antidote to mystification and transcendence. What is needed, Althusser claims, is a change of terrain, the discovery of a new continent not out beyond the horizon but right here, on the spot, as an articulation of the possibilities manifested within the absences or lapses or black holes of the first continent. But can one change terrain at will? Can Althusser or Kafka succeed where the Imperial Messenger failed? In other words, can they carry their message from the new terrain to the inhabitants of the old? Althusser himself points out that we can't ignore that

> this *"change of terrain"* which produces as its effect this metamorphosis in the gaze [the production of an informed or demystified gaze] was itself only produced in very specific, complex and often dramatic conditions; that it is absolutely irreducible to the idealist myth of a mental decision to change "view-points"; that it brings into play a whole process that the subject's

> sighting, far from producing, merely reflects in its own place; that in this process of real transformation of the means of production of knowledge, the claims of a "constitutive subject" are as vain as are the claims of the subject of vision in the production of the visible; that the whole process takes place in the dialectical crisis of the mutation of a theoretical structure in which the "subject" plays, not the part it believes it is playing, but the part which is assigned to it by the mechanism of the process. (RC 27)

Here again we have the subjectivization of the subject through the staging of "subject" as the extension of the play.

This metaphor of the dramatic mechanism highlights the difficulty of characterizing the social and the ideological in terms of a single monolithic terrain or field. While this topography escapes an "empiricist" conception of the inside/outside terrain implied by the term "false consciousness," it nevertheless reduces the social to an enclosed, sutured totality, and reduces agency purely to the effect of a position within this unilinear terrain. But politics depends by definition on the possibility that the production of subject-positions is not restricted so totally to assigned points in a structure. While the palimpsestic image of the superimposed terrains complicates and appears to open up the univocity of this model, Althusser's insistence on the mechanical processes nevertheless restricts us at a given point to only one of the two terrains. But there is no reason to restrict ourselves to this singular model. We could instead point to the co-existence of multiple open-ended terrains that merge and repulse and cancel each other out in various ways according to specific local conditions. The margins of these various ideological fields would thus function as the sites of articulation and contestation, the local instances of struggle made possible and limited no longer by the closure of a single field but precisely by the contiguity of these multiple ones. Such would be the poststructuralist, postmarxist response to the closure of the Althusserian figure.

Laclau and Mouffe, for example, in *Hegemony and Socialist Strategy*, see the terrains proposed by Althusser and Kafka quite differently. (I elaborate on Laclau and Mouffe's argument in chapter 7 below.) A first crucial distinction is that between moments and elements: moments are differential positions that are articulated into a discourse or ideological field; elements, conversely, are those differential positions that are not articulated, that function within a discursive field as floating signifiers. A second distinction is between a logic of equivalence and a logic of difference. Like metaphor, *equivalence* works as a point of condensation where the differences between moments are dissolved to the point that the social breaks down into two opposing camps; the identities of these two camps are established through a relation of negativity, the one defined simply as the negation of the other, as with colonizer versus colonized, black versus white, or male versus female. Like metonymy, on the other hand, *difference* works as contiguity and displacement, and a moment's identity derives from its differential position in a given field. Neither logic is ever complete unto itself, however, for then there could be no floating elements and thus no space for articulation, rupture, and change. What becomes crucial here is to recognize the proliferation of nonarticulated spaces, interstitial spaces of no-man's-land at the limits of the established fields. These sites provide the potential for local struggles as nodal points of articulation that can subvert the established fields at their margins.

Althusser's terrain, both social and ideological, resembles that governed by Laclau and Mouffe's logic of difference. The pure interiority that Althusser posits assigns to each moment its necessary position and function within this seamless space of the totality. While Althusser's emphatic rejection of external causation has been instrumental in leading a whole tendency within theoretical Marxism to reject the essentialism of earlier tendencies based on either Cartesian or Hegelian models, his reduction of the social to this single space of difference closes off any possibility of hegemonic politics. To be sure, he tried to reinsert the political into his later work by positing the reproduction of the conditions of production by Ideological State Apparatuses, and even later in his insistence on the essential role of class struggle in the functioning and construction of these ISAs, but these after-the-fact additions still failed to explain how class struggle could ever operate within what remains a sutured model of the totality. Thus a certain exteriority is necessary for political change. This of course cannot be a positive exteriority demarcating a different terrain outside the present one but instead a negative exteriority that exists simply as the limit of the social and the impossibility of its complete closure: "It is in this terrain," Laclau and Mouffe explain, "where neither a total interiority nor a total exteriority is possible, that the social is constituted. . . . Thus, neither absolute fixity nor absolute nonfixity is possible. . . . A system only exists as a partial limitation of a 'surplus of meaning' which subverts it. . . . *The practice of articulation, therefore, consists in the construction of nodal points which partially fix meaning; and the partial character of this fixation proceeds from the openness of the social, a* result, *in its turn, of the constant overflowing of every discourse by the infinitude of the field of discursivity*" (HSS 113).

Interestingly, it is Kafka's "China Wall" rather than Althusser's *Reading Capital* that shows this hegemonic process at work in the production of a Chinese imaginary. The Great Wall, after all, has to be built; it does not already lie there as the border between the Chinese people and fierce nomads of the north. And its construction is by no means guaranteed; the Chinese are prepared, molded, scripted from infancy to recognize their roles within the social structure. The performative dimension of their interpellation as wall-building "subjects" can be seen in their education when the teacher makes them build miniature models of the wall, and then smashes the tiny walls as a lesson in the need to build the wall ever better. The building of the wall is in fact the constant structuring and articulation—in Laclau and Mouffe's terminology—of the free-floating Chinese elements into moments of the totality. By structuring the equivalence of all Chinese as the negation of the nomads from the north—who have never actually been seen, I might add, but have simply been "represented" in the legends about them—the dominant powers construct and maintain the metaphoric transcendence of the tower. The conclusion Kafka seems to imply is that once the wall ceases to exist, only then will the tower cease. The nonclosure of the horizon—which denies the reduction to equivalence necessary for transcendence—is precisely that which the wall serves to contain. It is this no-man's-land of a negative exteriority that makes antagonism and articulation—and therefore political action—possible. While Althusser's conception of the social terrain subverts the metaphorical move outside the structure, it nevertheless denies these antagonistic nodal points of negative exteriority that reveal the limits and impossibility of the social. Althusser attempts to produce a pure metonymy within a single enclosed terrain, without recognizing, it seems, that it is enclosure itself that makes the gesture toward metaphor so tempting. Kafka, on the other hand, points to horizon building, the attempt to limit or redirect the displacements and combinations of metonymy, as the necessary condition for hegemony.

NIETZSCHE AND TRAGIC FIGURATION

As I indicated in chapter 4, a key element missing from Althusser's conception of the subject of structural causality is the Thing, the excluded figure that precisely as the excluded from the circle of representation, embodies the point of radical negativity at the heart of this structural circulation. Again, Althusser does identify this Thing in his conception of the Subject to which the subject is subject, by means of which the subjects become subjectivized. What I want to suggest here is that Nietzsche provided a model for just such a figure in his meditation on the tragic process of figuration in *The Birth of Tragedy*. It is in Nietzsche's early work that this moment missing from Althusser's theorization is prefigured in the relationship between Dionysus and Apollo. To anticipate, I will further state that Dionysus figures for the radical negativity of the reveling throng while Apollo embodies the purely figural Thing, the shining illusion or Schein, which rises up in the midst of the throng and thereby subjectivizes the reveling mass. But through this Apollonian dream image, it is not Apollo himself who is fleshed out but Dionysus. Through the Apollonian figural process, the throng projects its own radical negativity onto the figure of the god who rises up in their midst.

Yet what is the nature of this figuration or Schein? In order to understand the function of figuration in Nietzsche's theory of tragedy, we must first understand his conception of the metaphysical need for art. Nietzsche opens his discussion by distinguishing between the concept and the figure. "The terms Dionysian and Apollonian we borrow from the Greeks, who disclose to the discerning mind the profound mysteries of their art-intuitions [*Kunstanschauung*], not, to be sure, in concepts, but in the intensely clear figures [*Gestalten*] of their gods" (*BT* 33). These two gods are the figures for two distinct art drives—drives that give rise to "the separate art worlds of *dreams* and *intoxication*" (ibid.). The poets give witness to the necessity of this dreamworld of artistic figuration and the philosophers give witness to the reality of existence as marked by the reality-appearance (*Wirklichkeit-Schein*) distinction. That reality is summed up by the comments of the wise Silenus: "Oh, wretched ephemeral race, children of chance and misery, why do you compel me to tell you what it would be most expedient for you not to hear? What is best of all is utterly beyond your reach: not to be born, not to *be*, to be *nothing*. But the second best for you is—to die soon" (42). To which Nietzsche responds: "The Greek knew the terror and horror of existence [Dasein]. That he might endure this terror at all, he had to interpose between himself and life the radiant dream-birth of the Olympians" (ibid.). In order to live, in order to endure existence—the traumatic experience of the radical negativity of the utter dissolution in Da-sein—the Greeks produced a "transfiguring mirror [*verklärenden Spiegel*]" in the light of which existence is desirable in itself: "Thus do the gods justify the life of man: they themselves live it—the only satisfactory theodicy" (43).

Verklärung: transfiguration through radiance, effulgence, illumination, ecstasy in the light of the god of dreams, Phoebus Apollo, the shining one, the god of the sun who reverses the wisdom of Silenus—the Nietzschean response to the *Aufklärung* of the Enlightenment. Apollo is the shining god of Schein. In *Crossings: Nietzsche and the Space of Tragedy*, John Sallis explains the range of associations that must be kept in mind when reading the word Schein in Nietzsche:

> Here as well as throughout *The Birth of Tragedy* the word Schein will need to be read in its full range of senses: shine, look, appearance, semblance, illusion. Or, rather, more precisely, it will need to be read in its full spread of sense, since clearly it is not here a matter of simple polysemy. Even the very briefest sketch of a phenomenological analysis could indicate that it is a matter of senses so interlinked and mutually dependent that they form a field or spread rather than a series of distinct senses: in order for something to have a certain look, it must show itself, it must shine forth; only insofar as it shines so as to have a look can it then become an appearance, for instance, an appearance *of* something else that perhaps does not shine forth; and only insofar as something has a certain look can it look *like* something else that it is not, hence become a semblance; finally, both appearance and semblance can develop into various modes of illusion, for instance, something can look so much like something else that it gives itself out as that other thing. Heidegger's analysis of phenomenon remains the paradigm of such analyses.[12]

Referring to Schein as "illusion" or "mere appearance," then, as Walter Kaufmann does in his translation of *The Birth of Tragedy*, does not capture this full range of associations that must be thought simultaneously if we are to get a fuller appreciation of the Apollonian function in Nietzsche's thought. What this multifunctionality of the image of the god of dreams does is provide Nietzsche with a way of posing art in terms that move beyond the simple figure/concept or appearance/reality dichotomy in the same way that Althusser's metonymic flattening of the empirical problematic does by taking up the tropic-concept. The appearance/reality split in Nietzsche is more Lacanian than Platonic: reality or actuality is nothing but the traumatic substratum underlying existence to which appearance as Schein is a redemptive gesture, not an epistemological one.[13] Schein reconciles us to existence not by providing a truth-as-adequation or a truth-as-resemblance but, again as with Althusser's model, a truth-as-production: this truth is Schein itself, the necessary illusion that allows us to fool ourselves into believing that life is worth living. Truth, for Nietzsche, is nothing but the shining forth of this redemptive illusion:

> For the more clearly I perceive in nature those omnipotent art drives [*Kunst-triebe*], and in them an ardent longing for Schein, for redemption through Schein, the more I feel myself impelled to the metaphysical assumption that the truly existent primal unity [*Ur-Eine*], eternally suffering and contradictory, also needs the rapturous vision, the pleasurable Schein, for its continuous redemption. And we, completely wrapped up in this Schein and composed of it, are compelled under this Schein as the truly nonexistent [*das Wahrhaft-Nichtseiende*]—i.e., as a perpetual becoming in time, space, and causality—in other words, as empirical reality. If, for the moment, we do not consider the question of our own "reality," if we conceive of our empirical existence [Dasein], and of that of the world in general, as a continuously manifested Vorstellung of the primal unity, we shall then have to look upon the dream as a Schein of Schein, hence as a still higher appeasement of the primordial desire [*Urbegierde*] for Schein. (BT 44–45)

Kant's empirical reality of time, space, and causality; Plato's dismissal of artistic representation as the mere image of an image, illusion of an illusion, Schein of Schein: both are not so much inverted as crossed. That is, the dichotomous terms (visible/intelligible), through the production of the tragic process, become written or staged or presented on the same side of the divide; on the other side are those primal forces that threaten to swallow us up. Through music the Dionysian artist, identifying with the pain and contradiction of the primal unity or trauma of the Real, repeats and recasts this Real, producing a copy of it in the "inchoate, intangible reflection" that music provides. This music compels the lyric poet to "figurative speech. Language can never adequately render the cosmic symbolism of music, because music stands in symbolic relation to the primordial contradiction and primordial pain in the heart of the primal unity, and therefore symbolizes a sphere which is beyond and prior to all phenomena" (ibid., 55). The lyric poet, at once musician and imagist, Dionysian and Apollonian, produces a "symbolic dream image," a second mirror that shows the poet his or her identity with the Real. The Real, through this double mirroring, is redeemed, and the poet becomes a subject through this identification with and projection onto the "I" of the frenzied dream state of the lyric, the lyric poet functioning, "as it were, as the medium through which the one and only truly existent subject celebrates his release in appearance" (52). The artistic genius is "at once subject and object, at once poet, actor, and spectator" (ibid.), like Althusser's spectator-became-actor (keeping in mind, of course, Althusser's Spinozan insistence on history as a process without a subject, which is precisely my point of distinction here).

The lyric poet nevertheless remains too fused with this inchoate Dionysian identity and, having gained knowledge of the essence of things, remains, like Hamlet, too nauseous to act. The beauty of Greek tragedy for Nietzsche, then, is the space it opens up between the Dionysian and Apollinian, the space of tragedy as such. The answer comes with the development of the satyr chorus, the tragic source of "metaphysical comfort." The public of the Greek tragic theater, Dionysian in its origin, sees itself represented (repräsentieren) by the satyrs, and the satyrs see themselves represented by the figure of the god who rises up before them on the scene. The satyr chorus, like the lyric poem, thus offers a double mirroring for the Dionysian spectator-participant: "The satyr chorus is, first of all, a vision of the Dionysian mass of spectators, just as the world of the stage, in turn, is a vision of this satyr chorus" (63). In this way, the reveling throng of chorus-spectators are transformed into genuine poets themselves: "For a genuine poet, metaphor is not a rhetorical figure but a vicarious image that he actually beholds in place of a concept" (ibid.). The place of the concept is literally embodied by the figure of the god who makes himself visible through the Apollinian dream image to the Dionysian throng. The nature of the tragic process, this urphenomenon of all drama, is that of a certain seeing— a seeing of oneself magically transformed "before one's own eyes and to begin to act as if one had actually entered into another body, another character" (ibid.). Rhapsodists and painters do not become fused (verschmiltzt) with their images (Bildern); they see these images outside themselves as objects of contemplation. The seeing proper to the rhapsodist and the painter is marked by this externality of subject and image as a Vorstellung. But with the tragic chorus, on the other hand, "we have a surrender of individuality by way of entering into [Einkehr] a foreign nature [fremde Natur]. And this phenomenon is encountered epidemically: a whole throng experiences this magic transformation [verzaubert]" (64). The seers become one with the image before them; they see themselves, there, over yonder in there being-there, beyond the position of subjective distance necessary for representation. The subjectivity of the tragic throng is manifested in the opening of the space of tragedy—the space that splits the subject in the moment of spectatorial vision and installs that subjectivity in the image made possible by the shining god of the sun. In fact, this splitting is redoubled in the tropic turn of the tragic, in the Schein of Schein: "In this magic transformation the Dionysian reveler [*Schwärmer*] sees himself as a satyr, and as a satyr, in turn, he beholds a god, which means that in his metamorphosis [*Verzauberung*] he beholds another vision outside himself, as the Apollonian complement of his own state. With this new vision the drama is complete" (ibid.). The throng, in the ceaseless circulation of its subjective negativity (like Hegel's French Revolution), is subjectivized by this externalization or discharge of this negativity into the figure of the god. This dialectic between the place of the chorus and the place of the scene (in which shines the envisioned god) opens up the space of tragedy as such.

> In several successive discharges [*Entladungen*] this primal ground of tragedy radiates this vision of the drama which is by all means a dream apparition [*Traumerscheinung*] and to that extent epic in nature; but on the other hand, being the objectification [*Objektivation*] of a Dionysian state, it presents [*darstellt*] not Apollonian redemption through *Schein* but, on the contrary, the shattering of the individual and his fusion with primal being [*Ursein*]. Thus the drama is the Apollonian embodiment [*Versinnlichung*] of insights and effects and thereby separated, as by a tremendous chasm, from the epic. (65)

Who better than the sun god could bring about this embodiment, this decidedly non-Kantian Versinnlichung? For the sun itself embodies this redoubled splitting of the tropic-concept, as Derrida has argued: "Heliotropic metaphors are always imperfect metaphors. They provide us with too little knowledge, because one of the terms directly or indirectly implied in the substitution (the sensory sun) cannot be known in what is proper to it. . . . Thus, metaphor means heliotrope, both a movement turned toward the sun and the turning movement of the sun."[14] Thus the Schein of Schein, the master signifier, the redoubling of representation beyond itself in the space of tragedy.

This tragic space of ideological articulation is precisely what is missing from Althusser's tropic-concept of dramatic Darstellung. It is not enough to say that the whole is present in the parts; the redoubled turn of the tropic-concept—if it is to be grasped, elaborated on, and retained—must manifest itself in the Part that particularizes these parts, the Subject that subjectivizes the subjects, the Thing that embodies the radical negativity of the social and, through such embodiment, totalizes the social. The immanence of the absent cause must be externalized in the symbolic function of the exceptional One who looms up into sight before the satyr chorus.[15]

> The disclosure achieved in tragedy leads one back in an overcoming that leaves one comforted. . . . [T]ragedy alone knows how to turn these disgusting thoughts about the horror of existence into representations with which one can live: the *sublime* as the artistic taming of the horrible. Let it be said, then, that tragedy exposes one to the abyss, disclosing the abyss by way of a double mimesis; *and yet*, that tragedy, in its very disclosure of the abyss, protects, saves, even heals one from the destructive consequences that such exposure can have. Tragedy leads one back, leaves one finally comforted, by letting the horrible turn into the sublime. Exposing one mimetically to the abyss, tragedy at the same time lets the abyss be displaced, lets it be replaced with the sublime. As a mimetic supplement, tragedy is a *disclosing of the abyss as sublime.* Let it not go unremarked that such disclosure, precisely because it is abysmal, cannot but recoil upon the *is*, crossing it out even if letting it remain legible. As tragedy, too, crosses out what it discloses, letting it nonetheless remain: displaced and replaced.[16]

This abysmal dis-closure is the tragic form of Heidegger's αληθεια. This recoil of the disclosure on the *is* of being opens up the space of displacement-as-replacement, Schein as representation. For Heidegger, the poet is the one who ventures into the abyss, the ungrounded, and thereby discloses "the Open" in the place of the abyss: "The Open is the great whole of all that is unbounded. It lets the beings ventured into the pure draft draw as they are drawn, so that they variously draw on one another and draw together without encountering any bounds. Drawing as so drawn, they fuse with the boundless, the infinite. They do not dissolve into void nothingness, but they redeem themselves into the whole of the Open."[17] Darstellung therefore consists in the presentation of the nature of that which is drawn into the pull toward the center as consisting *in the way it is thus drawn* toward the center. The poets, the ones more venturesome than the technologists (for whom language is instrumentally bound to metaphysical duality), are the ones who dare the venture with language, who dare to venture the saying:

> Their saying concerns the inner recalling conversion of consciousness which turns our unshieldedness into the invisible of the world's inner space. Their

saying, because it concerns the conversion, speaks not only for both realms but from the oneness of the two, insofar as that oneness has already come to be as the saving unification. Therefore, where the whole of all beings is thought of as the Open of the pure draft, the inner recalling conversion must be a saying which says what it has to say to a being who is already secure in the whole of all beings, because he has already accomplished the transmutation of the represented [*vorgestellten*] visible into the courageous invisible. This being is drawn into the pure draft by one side and the other of the globe of Being. This being [*Wesen*], for whom borderlines and differences between drawings hardly exist any longer, is the being who governs the unheard-of center of the widest orbit and causes it to appear [*erscheinen*]. This being, in Rilke's *Duino Elegies*, is the Angel.[18]

Tragic figuration for Nietzsche is a way of organizing the radical negativity of the throng, the revelers (Schwärmer). It is worth pausing for a moment to recall Kant's own reference to this *Schwärmerei* in the *Critique of Judgment*. There, Kant discusses the process of negative presentation characteristic of the sublime. One might fear, Kant surmises, that this negative presentation might lead to "a cold and lifeless approbation" completely devoid of emotion (*CJ* General Remark, 127). But Kant points out just the opposite: once the experience of the sublime has presented the Idea of morality, the danger lies precisely in that Idea's nonconnection to any sensible image. Without the grounding in the image, the presentation of the Idea could lead to wild and unbounded imaginative "enthusiasm." Enthusiasm of this sort, however, is itself a sublime phenomenon, and as such must be distinguished from its dangerous counterpart, fanaticism (Schwärmerei). Fanaticism engages in the "delusion that would will some VISION beyond all the bounds of sensibility" (ibid., 128). The very negative character of the presentation of the sublime (its complete lack of a sensible image that could project the fanatic into the beyond) prevents it from falling prey to the dangers of fanaticism.

Žižek comments on the connection between the fanaticism Kant fears above and that associated with radical democracy:

> The structural homology between Kantian formalism and formal democracy is a classical topos: in both cases, the starting point, the founding gesture, consists of an act of radical emptying, evacuation. With Kant, what is evacuated and left empty is the locus of the Supreme Good: every positive object destined to occupy this place is by definition "pathological," marked

by empirical contingency, which is why the moral Law must be reduced to the pure Form bestowing on our acts the character of universality. Likewise, the elementary operation of democracy is the evacuation of the locus of Power: every pretender to this place is by definition a "pathological" usurper; "nobody can rule innocently," to quote Saint-Just. And the crucial point is that "nationalism" as a specifically modern, post-Kantian phenomenon designates the moment when the Nation, the national Thing, usurps, fills out, the empty place of the Thing opened up by Kant's "formalism," by his reduction of every "pathological" content. The Kantian term for this filling-out of the void, of course, is the fanaticism of *Schwärmerei*: does not "nationalism" epitomize fanaticism in politics? (*TWN* 221)

For the same reason, Nietzsche distinguishes between his Dionysian revelers mediated-subjectivized by the Apollonian vision and the Dionysian barbarians.[19] It is here that we can see that Nietzsche has his own Other that must be excluded from the circle of revelers, his own version of irrational fundamentalism. The barbarians take the Dionysian injunction literally, whereas the goal of tragedy is to submit this injunction to the Apollonian transformation of the vision of the god. The figure in the midst of the revelers subjectivizes the throng and lifts it out of the vicious circle of the radical negativity of the barbarian Schwärmerei. The key is to approach this figure through fetishistic disavowal: I know very well that this figure who subjectivizes the throng is nothing but a collective illusion, yet I will act nonetheless as though it were real. This is a necessary illusion if we are to forego the wisdom of Silenus, if we are to affirm life and, by affirming, transfigure it. Tragic figuration is thus, for Nietzsche, the ideological grounding that prevents the self-destruction of the negativity of the throng.

SOCRATIC SHINING

Let us now imagine the one great Cyclops eye of Socrates fixed on tragedy, an eye in which the fair frenzy of artistic enthusiasm has never glowed. To this eye was denied the pleasure of gazing into the Dionysian abysses.—Friedrich Nietzsche, *The Birth of Tragedy*

It must nevertheless be remembered at this point that *The Birth of Tragedy* also records the *death* of tragedy. The redoubling of tragic space demands a certain stereoscopic vision that the one-eyed Socrates could never attain. Socrates, like the tragedians, also sought to deliver us from the wisdom of Silenus, but his problem was taking his illusions seriously, misrecognizing the performative dimension of the Socratic method.[20] The dialectic will drive Dionysus out of the abyss, all the while blind to its own Apollonian shine. Nietzsche's Schein of Schein bears more than a family resemblance to Plato's imitation of imitation in *The Republic*. It functions quite consciously as the inversion of Socratism, of "theoretical man," in its contra-Socratic vindication of the simulacrum. "Consider," Nietzsche asks us, "the consequences of the Socratic maxims: 'Virtue is knowledge; man sins only from ignorance; he who is virtuous is happy.' In these three basic forms of optimism lies the death of tragedy" (BT 91).

Now this Nietzschean reversal of Socratism might be perceived as a simple reversal of priority in the basic metaphysical couple, visible/intelligible or phenomenal/noumenal. One problem with this formulation is that for Nietzsche, the reality behind this appearance is no more intelligible than it is visible; it is a Lacanian Real, not a Platonic ideal.[21] A second problem with conceiving of Nietzsche's position as simply a reversal is that Nietzsche sees his own position as the end result of Socratism, the point at which Socratism turns in on itself after its almost twenty-five-hundred-year span. And a third problem with this image of a reversal is that this Socratic distinction itself is not so much one of a binary opposition but rather extension or degree.

Let me begin with the third problem first (the first problem, that of the Nietzschean Real, has been developed above). Platonic truth as αληθεια must be read in its Heideggerian sense as an unconcealment rather than a transport to an other "ideal" realm.[22] What is involved, then, is not the reconciliation of two distinct levels (truth as resemblance) but two different ways in which those "ideal forms" or ειδη show themselves, shine forth in such a way as to present themselves to a seeing. John Sallis, in *Being and Logos*, presents this sense of the ειδη as follows:

> Socrates uses the word "ειδος"; later he uses, more or less synonymously, the word "ιδεα." The word "ειδος" is derived from the verb "ειδω," meaning "*see*." Thus, its root meaning is: that which is seen, the seen, that which presents itself to a seeing, that which shows itself (which makes itself manifest) to a seeing. Likewise, "ιδεα" is derived (by way of "ιδειν") from "ειδω" and refers even more pointedly to the look of something, to its way of showing itself to a seeing. The reference of these words to a seeing, to something's showing itself to a seeing, is of utmost importance. If they are thoughtlessly

translated as "form" or "idea" and regarded as meaning something like "concept," then the issue to which these words are addressed in the dialogues will simply be left untouched. (*BL* 383)[23]

This conception of the ειδη is important in sorting out the issues involved in Plato's attack on mimesis in Book 10 of *The Republic*. The painter is the "artisan" who is able to "make" everything in existence simply by holding up a mirror and carrying it around everywhere. In this way, the artist can make all things "so that they look like they *are*; however, they surely *are* not in truth" (*R* 596d). The distinction here is between *being* and *not-being*: the image is not, but merely appears to be. The image is a "dim thing" when compared to the truth (ibid., 597a). That which is true, on the other hand, is not dim but shines forth in its truth. Painting is directed not toward the being as it is but its looking as it looks (το φαινομενον, ως φαινεται): "Therefore, imitation is surely far from the truth; and, as it seems, it is due to this that it produces everything— because it lays hold of a certain small part of each thing, and that part itself is only a phantom [ειδωλον]" (598b). And herein lies the danger of art: its capacity to deceive "children and foolish human beings" (ibid.) into taking an image for truth.

Imitation thus provides a partial view of the ειδος—that part being the phantom or ειδωλον. The distinction between image and truth, then, is that between part and whole, as Plato suggests in book 5 of *The Republic*, the point at which Plato provides for the philosophical grounding of his assertion concerning mimesis in book 10. The philosopher is the lover of the sight of the truth, which means that truth is on the side of the visible; the visible/intelligible distinction is consequently not one of opposition but of degree of coincidence. For instance, the beautiful and the ugly, though each is in itself one, show up as the many: "The same argument also applies then to justice and injustice, good and bad, and all the forms [ειδων]; each is itself one, but, by showing themselves everywhere in a community with actions, bodies, and one another, each is an apparitional many" (476a). The philosopher's thought is knowledge because he or she is able to catch sight both of the beautiful itself and what participates in it, whereas the uncritical lover of sights sees the beautiful in what participates in it yet is incapable of distinguishing between the two and thus denies the independent oneness of the beautiful itself.[24] This person's thought is not knowledge but opinion, the point of seeing between knowledge (light) and ignorance (darkness), between the one and nothingness, between being and not-being. The one who opines rather than knows sees only the opinable, the "wanderer between" (R 479d).

We thus have two modes of showing for the same εἶδος: the beautiful can show itself as the one (the knowable) or the many (the opinable), in the company of actions, bodies, and the other εἴδη. Sallis characterizes this distinction between the two modes of showing as follows:

> What does this say about the character of the distinction between the knowable and the opinable? It indicates that the difference between the knowable and the opinable is just the difference between the two modes of showing. This means, in turn, that the distinction between the knowable and the opinable is not fundamentally a distinction between two kinds of things, between which some relation would subsist, but rather a distinction between two ways in which an *eidos* can show itself. It is a distinction between a showing in which an *eidos* shows itself as it itself is (as one) *and* a showing in which an *eidos* shows itself as it is not (as many). In both cases *what shows itself is the same thing* (the *eidos*)—which is to say that the knowable and the opinable are not parallel regions of things. A beautiful thing is just that which stands forth in a showing in which the beautiful itself shows itself as it is not (i.e., in the second mode of showing); this—and *only* this!—is the proper sense in which a beautiful thing is an *image* of the beautiful itself. (BL 394)

The distinction between the image and the εἶδος itself, then, cannot be thought of as a boundary between two distinct terrains but rather in a continuum of participation, of shining forth, of phenomenal presentation. Hence, Nietzsche's reversal of Socratism cannot be seen as the simple reversal of a binary opposition. It is at this point where the third problem of this Nietzschean reversal suggested above passes over into the second: the view according to which this reversal is not an alternative or an opposition but an extension, a folding back upon itself of the limits of Socratic representation itself.

> But science, spurred by its powerful illusion [*Wahne*], speeds irresistibly toward its limits where its optimism, concealed in the essence of logic, suffers shipwreck. For the periphery of the circle of science has an infinite number of points; and while there is no telling how this circle could ever be surveyed completely, noble and gifted men nevertheless reach, e'er half their time and inevitably, such boundary points on the periphery from which one gazes

into what defies illumination. When they see to their horror how logic coils up at these boundaries and finally bites its own tail—suddenly the new form of insight [*Erkenntnis*] breaks through, tragic insight which, merely to be endured, needs art as a protection and remedy. (*BT* 98)

Despite his attack on mimesis, Plato needs art "as a protection and remedy." We have gone from abyss to periphery, which gives us an inversion of the landscape of Kafka's China, the negative space of the abyss turned inside out like a glove, like the twist along the Möbius strip where the negative becomes positivized, projected outward and upward as the tower.

THE BONAVENTURE HOTEL AND THE HYSTERICAL SUBLIME

What would we have if we could somehow combine Kafka's Chinese wall and the tower? A dome. In such a dome, the space-in-dispersal of Kafka's China, the perpetually receding empire whose boundaries and center can never be reached by the Imperial Messenger, would now be enclosed. And yet such an enclosure would remain beyond our perceptual capacities for taking it in in one intuition. Kant experienced a version of such a sublime enclosure, in response to which he was moved to attempt to "account for the bewilderment, or sort of perplexity, which, as is said, seizes the visitor on first entering St. Peter's in Rome. For here a feeling comes home to him of the inadequacy of his imagination for presenting the idea of a whole within which that imagination attains its maximum, and, in its fruitless efforts to extend this limit, recoils upon itself, but in so doing succumbs to an emotional delight" (*CJ* §26, 100). The dome is in one sense the inverse of the abyss—we are now safely if confusingly *inside the abyss*. Such an experience, nevertheless, cannot properly be called sublime since as an obvious construct of the human mind and thus a form developed according to a given interest, this object, however colossal ("almost too great for presentation"), remains determined by a concept and is therefore "tainted" by a judgment of understanding or reason. This dome is not quite an inverted abyss, though; while such a dome is enclosed, our response to it is still determined by its spatial expanse. As such, it is simply an upside-down abyss. The truly inverted abyss would be one in which the expansiveness of empty space is also inverted, turned from its outward emptiness-in-dispersal to an internal saturation. Such is the experience of what Jameson refers to as "hyperspace." This properly postmodern inversion gives rise to the "hysterical sublime."

So I come finally to my principle point here, that this latest mutation in space—postmodern hyperspace—has finally succeeded in transforming the capacities of the individual human body to locate itself, to organize its immediate surroundings perceptually, and cognitively to map its position in a mappable external world. It may now be suggested that this alarming disjunction point between the body and its built environment—which is to the initial bewilderment of the older modernism as the velocities of spacecraft to those of the automobile—can itself stand as the symbol and analogon of that even sharper dilemma which is the incapacity of our minds, at least at present, to map the great global multinational and decentered communicational network in which we find ourselves caught as individual subjects. (PM 44)

The theater that Jameson chooses for the staging of this hyperspace is the Westin Bonaventure Hotel in Los Angeles, designed by John Portman.[25] Again, the problem of theater is the problem of the actor-spectator's relationship to this theatrical space, to this stage. Each theater-space puts into play its own variant of an apparatus of subjectivization as the actor-spectator negotiates the coordinates and spatial relationships of a given structure. It is through this itinerary that the radical negativity of the subject is quilted, materialized, performed, and, thus, positivized. For each itinerary is a narrativization. And each subject, upon acting out a role made possible by this narrative, not only gives body to itself through this performativity but to the social network itself. In this way, the social depends on—is nothing but—the performance of its subjects. What we encounter in the Jamesonian version of hyperspace, however, is the actor who does not know what or how to perform. The distance required for such performance has been saturated and thus nullified, like some return of the repressed of a Freudian Primary Narcissism, which is also marked by a saturated space in which the boundaries determining the not-yet-a-subject's motility are constantly in flux or so pressed against the skin that the distinction between self and other is just so nullified. The space necessary for representation is too thick, sticky, stuffy—saturated with enjoyment. Such is the space of postmodern paranoia. And this mutation of social space in late capitalism presents itself, Jameson claims, as a demand to grow new organs.

The Bonaventure Hotel appears to be a Utopian space, an island cut off from the mainland of Los Angeles, itself simply a metonym for late capitalism as such as it stretches across the globe in one great total network, one great worldwide web. And yet the spatio-social relations of the postmodern hotel do not neutralize the space of late capitalism but reproduce it in concentrated and minia-ture form. What the Hotel does attempt to neutralize is Los Angeles itself, the older built space of the city that contextualizes and complicates the narrative of the Hotel space. As such, we have the paradox of this pseudo-Utopian hyper-space: the Hotel can only become the metonym for the world system by cutting itself off from the "world itself"—Los Angeles, in this case, or Atlanta, To-ronto, . . .—in the sense of some space that bears the sedimented traces of historical moments gone by, moments that still insist their way into our post-contemporary lives despite our most heroic attempts at neutralization through pastiche. The instantaneity of hyperspace must eclipse any earlier category of time as such. The problem of the Kantian sublime was a problem of time: one can only take in so much intuitional inscription at a time; as one continues to scan a given surface or space, the earlier intuited portions of that object recede from the space of representational memory. In this hyperspace, on the other hand, no moment of time, however brief, is adequate. The problem isn't simply one of synthesizing a train of intuitions into one representation but of achiev-ing any recognizable intuition at all. The mechanism of Darstellung has broken down.

One is reminded, in reading Jameson's description of the hyperstroll leading up to and through the Bonaventure, of K.'s approach to the castle and his wanderings through the passageways of the courts. The Bonaventure is the tower from the outside and the empire from within. Upon approaching the Hotel, the Jamesonian hyperflaneur is repulsed by the building's very surface, its "great reflective glass skin" that "achieves a peculiar and placeless dissocia-tion of the Bonaventure from its neighborhood: it is not even an exterior, inasmuch as when you seek to look at the hotel's outer walls you cannot see the hotel itself but only the distorted images of everything that surrounds it" (PM 42). The hyperflaneur gains access nevertheless through one of the nondescript and somewhat displaced entranceways.

The inside is another story. We have the same cramped and stuffy atmo-sphere as Kafka's courts, but ironically the stuffiness of hyperspace results from its diffusion and unremarkability rather than from some literally claustro-phobic space. One significant element of this space is that the modern stroller is replaced by the postmodern "passenger," so to speak. The lobby is filled with people movers—that is, grand escalators and elevators that add much to the drama of the lobby space. What these machines do is guide us through bodily narratives, "our physical trajectories through such buildings [now functioning] as virtual narratives or stories, as dynamic paths and narrative paradigms which we as visitors are asked to fulfill and complete with our own bodies and movements" (ibid.). But what does this narrative tell us? What story are we enacting as we offer our bodies up to this controlled space? Our movement in this way becomes the allegorical signifier for the older displaced promenade and for movement as such. Our bodily relationship to space and time, in other words, is now reified and enacted for us as we are moved along these narrative trajectories. This narrative disorients our modernist urban sense of space and movement and thus prepares us for the experience of the totality of this space as such. As Jameson comments,

> I am more at a loss when it comes to conveying the thing itself, the experience of space you undergo when you step off such allegorical devices into the lobby or atrium, with its great central column surrounded by a miniature lake, the whole positioned between the four symmetrical residential towers with their elevators, and surrounded by rising balconies capped by a kind of greenhouse roof at the sixth level. I am tempted to say that such space makes it impossible for us to use the language of volume or volumes any longer, since these are impossible to seize. Hanging streamers indeed suffuse this empty space in such a way as to distract systematically and deliberately from whatever form it might be supposed to have, while a constant busyness gives the feeling that emptiness is here absolutely packed, that it is an element within which you yourself are immersed, without any of that distance that formerly enabled the perception of perspective or volume. You are in this hyperspace up to your eyes and your body; and if it seemed before that that suppression of depth I spoke of in postmodern painting or literature would necessarily be difficult to achieve in architecture itself, perhaps this bewildering immersion may now serve as the formal equivalent in the new medium. (42–43)

The central column functions as the tower-center of this inapprehensible space, yet its function is merely visual and structural, the center thus sitting in its inhuman and inert stupidity, the panopticon effect thus neutralized by the nonreflective nature of the column. This is not to say that the panopticon-function has disappeared; for above this amorphous space of the central atrium is the turning top floor housing the lounge:

> [We] may suggest that the glorious movement of the elevator gondola is . . . a dialectical compensation for this filled space of the atrium—it gives us the

chance at a radically different, but complementary, spatial experience: that of rapidly shooting up through the ceiling and outside, along one of the four symmetrical towers, with the referent, Los Angeles itself, spread out breathtakingly and even alarmingly before us. But even this vertical movement is contained: the elevator lifts you to one of those revolving cocktail lounges, in which, seated, you are again passively rotated about and offered a contemplative spectacle of the city itself, now transformed into its own images by the glass windows through which you view it. (43)

As I have suggested above, I would qualify Jameson's description of the rotating lounge-window view of Los Angeles: the transformation of Los Angeles into its own images is not simply a contemplative spectacle but also a panoptic one. That is, the transformation of Los Angeles into its own images serves to contain and to neutralize the conflicting and contradictory forces that make up Los Angeles "itself." Downtown, Hollywood, UCLA, Venice Beach, Compton, East LA, Anaheim, Pasadena, all contained like an island itself by the Pacific and the mountains—all are seemingly homogenized and neutralized by the Utopian transformation of this conflictual space into one great revolving image. The experience here is in a sense a radical transformation of the panopticon, with the subject now no longer the viewed but the viewer. Just as the atrium provides the experience of being inside the abyss, the lounge provides the experience of being inside the panopticon—an experience of temporarily inhabiting the space of figural power, the space in which the contradictions of the social are transformed into images of themselves. Yet this position of the surveyor is itself a figural position, one more element of the narrative of the hotel space in which we are transported and transformed, much like at Disneyland. But Jameson insists that this is not Disneyland: "I am anxious that Portman's space not be perceived as something either exceptional or seemingly marginalized and leisure-specialized on the order of Disneyland" (44). The point is not that the Bonaventure experience is not equally constructed and scripted but that it is missing the obviousness of the fantasy space of Disneyland as marginal, as something other from what we experience in our daily lives. For Jameson, the Bonaventure adventure, on the other hand, is a figure for our daily lives, despite its leisurely pace and appearance, in that it functions as figural shorthand for the experience of the postmodern space of late capitalism. I would argue, nevertheless, that the Bonaventure enters into a structural relationship with Disneyland in the sense that it completes and competes with the narrative established by the layout of Disneyland itself as Louis Marin has described it in *Utopics*.[26]

> Disneyland is the representation realized in a geographical space of the imaginary relationship that the dominant groups of American society maintain with their real conditions of existence, with the *real* history of the United States, and with the space outside its borders. Disneyland is a fantasmatic projection of the history of the American nation, of the way in which this history was conceived with regard to other peoples and to the natural world. Disneyland is an immense and displaced metaphor of the system of representation and values unique to American society.
>
> This function has an obvious ideological function. It alienates the visitor by a distorted and fantasmatic representation of daily life, by a fascinating image of the past and the future, of what is estranged and what is familiar: comfort, welfare, consumption, scientific and technological progress, superpower, and morality. These are values obtained by violence and exploitation; here they are projected under the auspices of law and order. (*U* 240)

Like the Bonaventure, Disneyland is a space that "can be narrated by the visitor (the actor)" (ibid., 247). And the Bonaventure, like the Disney-theater, "transforms reality into its other; fantasy becomes reality, and reality becomes fantasy" (ibid.). As the spectator-actors at Disneyland recreate with their own bodies this historical narrative of American fantasy space, they pass in a circuit from Adventureland (aggressive colonial conquest) to Frontierland (appropriation of the continent) through Fantasyland (which transforms this historical fantasy into a fantasy structure of present and future) to Tomorrowland with its Carousel of Progress. The Bonaventure functions as an extension of this futuristic fantasy of American Progress while it converts the mapped and directed space of Disneyland into the saturated and disorienting space of the Bonaventure Hotel. Jameson's description of this fantasy work of the Bonaventure reads as just such an extension of Marin's study:

> [D]istance in general (including "critical distance" in particular) has very precisely been abolished in the new space of postmodernism. We are submerged in its henceforth filled and suffused volumes to the point where our now postmodern bodies are bereft of spatial coordinates and practically (let alone theoretically) incapable of distantiation; meanwhile, it has already been observed how the prodigious new expansion of multinational capital

ends up penetrating and colonizing those very precapitalist enclaves (Nature and the Unconscious) which offered extraterritorial and Archimedean footholds for critical effectivity. (PM 48–49)

This postmodern hyperspace functions as the figural extension of the narrative of colonization and conquest of Disneyland as it is dialectically transformed under late capitalism.

The point I wish to emphasize here, however, is that the Bonaventure Hotel, far from successfully repelling and absorbing the conflicting spatial coordinates of the Los Angeles that surrounds it, depends on that very space for its intelligibility, for its function as the figural projection of the spectator-actor into another type of space on the order of the figure Althusser develops in *Reading Capital* of a change of terrain. This new terrain takes place on the spot and depends upon while transforming and negating or neutralizing the older terrain. No epistemological break, I am suggesting, is as clean and complete as Althusser and Jameson indicate with these spatial figures. The borders of the enclosed terrain depend on the tower; the tower, in turn, depends on the figural neutralization of the borderland (a sort of figural demilitarized zone) in order to function as such. While the Bonaventure does indeed figure as the explosive and "prodigious expansion of culture throughout the social realm" (ibid., 48), it nevertheless depends on the differential Balkanized pockets of social space making up the urban sprawl of Los Angeles/America/Late Capital. While figuration may produce the image of a vacuum, it cannot function in one.

So what does Jameson mean by the "hysterical" sublime? Hand in hand with the transformation of space under postmodernism is the transformation of our affective response to that space. The Burkean-Kantian sublime was marked by the production of the affects of fear and, subsequently, respect (negative pleasure). These affects have mutated, however, into a form of "hallucinatory splendor," marked by euphoria and oxymoronic "intensities": the postmodern subject finds the bleakest and most horrendous spectacles—such as urban decay or auto wrecks—as objects of exhilaration. The antianthropomorphic nature of postmodern architecture finds its correlate in the fetishism of the body in such various hyperrealistic displays as Duane Hanson's wax figures. The figures of the human are transformed into simulacra, hyperreal figures that outstrip the "realism" of actual human beings and thereby derealize humans themselves. For Kant, an important side-effect of the sublime was the sense of human puniness and insignificance in contrast to the grandiosity of Nature and the

Beyond. But for the postmodern sublime, the human body is eclipsed *by its own images*. Such a move is the correlative response to the eclipse of Nature under late capitalism.

Jameson's point is that for Kant, Nature was the figure of the Other, that unrepresentable system that it was the job of the sublime to present and for teleological judgment to explore and "map out." For postmodernism, on the other hand, the Other is the late capitalist system itself that Jameson wants to encircle in the series of figurations (such as the figure of technology) that would make up the practice of cognitive mapping. Jameson observes "The technology of contemporary society is . . . mesmerizing and fascinating not so much in its own right but because it seems to offer some privileged representational short-hand for grasping a network of power and control even more difficult for our minds and imaginations to grasp: the whole new decentered global network of the third stage of capital itself" (37–38). Cognitive mapping is thus the post-modern correlate for teleological judgment. The question, then—as in the last chapter concerning the distinction between external and determining reflec-tion—is the degree to which Jameson's call for cognitive mapping commits him to a form of subreption, which, we will recall from chapter 2, involves the transcendent extension of a transcendental principle. Does Jameson turn a regulative judgment (cognitive mapping must function as if it were in fact capable of mapping some posited preexisting, yet unrepresentable "real" sub-stratum) into a determining judgment (whereby cognitive mapping gives us some kind of genuine "knowledge" of that substratum).

Jameson, it should be remembered, posits a strategic extension of Althus-ser's definition of ideology in order that it "allows us to rethink these specialized geographical and cartographic issues in terms of social space" (52), while re-minding the reader that "the Lacanian underpinnings of Althusser's theory" can enrich the famous distinction between ideology and science because the "Lacanian system is threefold, and not dualistic. To the Marxian-Althusserian opposition of ideology and science correspond only two of Lacan's tripartite functions: the Imaginary and the Real, respectively. Our digression on cartogra-phy, however, with its final revelation of a properly representational dialectic of the codes and capacities of individual languages or media, reminds us that what has until now been omitted was the dimension of the Lacanian Symbolic itself" (53–54). As we have seen, Jameson gives us the following equations: Ideology = study of the Imaginary; Science = study of the Real; Symbolic = study of "this now enormously complex representational dialectic."

Two features of [Althusser's] definition [of ideology] need to be retained here: first, that ideology must always be necessarily narrative in its structure, inasmuch as it not only involves a mapping of the real, but also the essentially narrative or fantasy attempt of the subject to invent a place for himself/ herself in a collective and historical process which excludes him or her and which is itself basically nonrepresentable and nonnarrative. . . . For the "Real" on this view is conceived, neither as an unknowable thing-in-itself, nor as a string of events or set of facts you can know directly in the form of some "true" or "adequate" representation for consciousness. It is rather an asymptotic phenomenon, an outer limit, which the subject approaches in the anxiety of the moment of truth—moments of personal crisis and of agonizing political polarization of revolutionary situations; and from such an approach to the Real the subject tends to retreat again, at best in possession of abstract and purely intellectual schemata when not of personally charged narrative representations. The narrative apparatus which informs ideological representations is thus not mere "false consciousness," but an authentic way of grappling with a Real that must always transcend it, a Real into which the subject seeks to insert itself through praxis, all the while painfully learning the lesson of its own ideological closure and of history's resistance to the fantasy-structures in which it is itself locked. (FA 12–13)

Cognitive mapping thus does not give us a substantive glimpse of some positive entity called History or Class Struggle or Mode of Production. It presses the representational apparatus to its limits, to the moments of its breakdown that cast up the illusion of the beyond in its current historical state.

THE ACT AND SUBJECTIVE DESTITUTION: POLITICS
BEYOND REPRESENTATION

Let me now return to a recurring motif of this study: Hegel's monarch and Revolutionary Terror. The Terror, according to Žižek, the moment "at which negation ceases to be 'determinate' and becomes 'absolute,'" is the point at which "the subject *encounters itself*, since the subject qua *cogito* is this very negativity prior to every act of exchange" (TWN 27). The Hegelian monarch, on the other hand, functions as the point of subjectivization (interpellation) at the heart of this radical subjectivity. But doesn't the whole notion of the vicious circle and the stupid thing derive from an intensely conservative, perhaps even

fascistic, political impulse? Isn't this turn to the guiding function of the monarch simply a reactionary response to the destabilizing effects of bourgeois
revolution, to the seemingly anarchic condition of democracy as it dissolves the
traditional social ties? Isn't this concern with the Master Signifier that sutures
the social fabric a fascistic call for the father-figure, the *Führer, Il Duce*?

One approach to this problem is to point out that what is involved here is the
logic of symbolization as such. Yes, fascism *is* one response to the desubjectivization inherent in the vacuum of Revolutionary Terror, and as such fascism follows the logic of the insertion of the Thing into the threatening abyss of radical
negativity. But the republican president is also an embodiment of this logic of
symbolization. Who better than Ronald Reagan, for instance, could exemplify
the logic behind Hegel's conception of the monarch, the irrational element at
the heart of the rational totality, the stupid Thing functioning as the point of
symbolic subjectivization, the Subject whose symbolic function—despite that
person's personal, "pathological" qualities—confers on the social whole its subjectivization? The key is simply that whoever occupies this symbolic space of
power must appear to have been found with such qualities as to make him or
her qualified to fulfil this social mandate. The arbitrariness must remain out of
sight, a fact exemplified in the peculiar status of the "teflon president" who,
precisely because he lacked the professionalism and intelligence expected of
someone holding such a position of power in a seemingly rational society,
appeared all the more qualified in a time when traditional notions of leadership
(identified negatively by Reagan as "bureaucracy," "Government," even "politics" itself) no longer fit in a world in which the status of the United States was
increasingly deflated. This Actor and Outlaw—this Rambo figure—embodied
precisely what the American fantasy structure needed at the time, someone
who was willing to break the law in order to uphold the Law.

To get a clearer picture of the issues involved here, let's consider the current
outbreaks of fascist ideology, whether in the United States or Germany or
Bosnia. We have a situation that structurally speaking resembles the moment of
Revolutionary Terror of the 1790s. That situation is capitalism itself. Capitalism
is in its very structure the great destabilizer, the deterritorializer, the abyss of
radical negativity. The structure of the production and circulation of surplus
value is such that no one moment can remain stable. Capitalism by nature
demands the constant revolutionizing of the forces of production and the
destabilization of the vicious circle of circulation; it was Marx who over a
century ago pointed to this inherently crisis-oriented nature of capitalism. As a

result, capitalism constantly destabilizes any attempt at erecting a long-lasting Master figure, for whatever qualities served to legitimize that figure would in due course be outstripped by the further development of capital. Thus the appeal of various forms of corporatism that attempt to heal the wound in the social produced by the excess of capital, the surplus that continuously spins the social order out of itself. Žižek outlines this problem as follows:

> Now, it should also be clear where the corporatist temptation comes from, i.e., why this temptation is the necessary reverse of capitalism. Let us take the ideological edifice of fascist corporatism: the fascist dream is simply to have *capitalism without its "excess," without the antagonism that causes its structural imbalance.* Which is why we have, in fascism, on the one hand, the return to the figure of the Master—Leader—who guarantees the stability and balance of the social fabric, i.e., who again saves us from society's structural imbalance; while, on the other hand, the reason for this imbalance is attributed to the figure of the Jew whose "excessive" accumulation and greed are the cause of social antagonism. Thus the dream is that, since the excess was introduced from outside, i.e., is the work of an alien intruder, its elimination would enable us to obtain again a stable social organism whose parts form a harmonious corporate body, where, in contrast to capitalism's constant social *displacement*, everybody would again occupy his *own place*. The function of the Master is to dominate the excess by locating its cause in a clearly defined social agency: "It is *they* who steal our enjoyment, who, by means of their excessive attitude, introduce imbalance and antagonism." With the figure of the Master, the antagonism *inherent* in the social structure is transformed into a relationship of *power*, a struggle for *domination* between *us* and *them*, those who cause antagonistic imbalance. (TWN 210)

Fascism, nevertheless, is far from the only political response to the radical subjectivity of pure democracy. The point here is that the nature of the political order—monarchical, fascist, democratic, Communist—does not obviate the logic of the symbolic involved in the symbolic function of this Subject in the interpellation of the subjects, the process whereby Substance becomes Subject. The critique, common in contemporary cultural studies, that would seek to subvert this "father-figure" by pointing out how the marginal figures have always already subverted this center, is blind to the fact that this is Hegel's argument itself! To put this in psychoanalytic terms, the symbolic function of the Name of the Father is precisely to domesticate the father as such, the superego figure who, prior to the Law, roams threateningly at the margins himself. He is the obscene figure who questions and thereby hystericizes the subject prior to interpellation. The Name of the Father, on the other hand, is the figure of interpellation, or subjectivization. The Master figure at the heart of the symbolic, then, is a domestication of the "obscene father" by placing him in the inert, meaningless, nonsubstantial center of the social substance. (How can we best contain a megolomaniac's power? Make him or her president!) The question is, rather, *What is to be done*? What stand are we to take in regard to the social fantasy that organizes our desire? Žižek outlines (in psychoanalytic terms) four distinct ethical positions toward this deadlock of symbolic circulation: the hysteric, the obsessional, the pervert, and the unnamed position of psychoanalysis proper, the ethics of the Act. What this suggests is that the real problem is not with the type of "Subject" who occupies the center of power but rather the type of *object* with which the social body identifies.

THE HYSTERIC: As we have seen in chapter 1, the hysteric is the subject for whom no object can ever satisfy his desire—"No, that is not *it*!" But this continuous rejection of potentially satisfying objects conceals the fact that the true aim of this activity is the perpetuation of desire itself. If an object ever did in fact prove satisfying, the desire would at that point cease. As a leftist position, the hysteric would be the radical anarchist for whom no particular articulation of power could prove satisfying, could prove to be *"it."* The hysteric is the subject of fetishistic disavowel: "I know very well that I will never settle on any one object of desire (because that would extinguish my desire as much—which is to be seen by the Other as desiring), but I will continue to act as though I believe that the right object is out there waiting for me to discover it." No political form will ever prove satisfying (because what I really want is to take on the appearance of the one with the purest political principles that no political structure could ever embody). The object of the hysteric is thus *the object of desire as such*.

THE OBSESSIONAL: For the obsessional, on the other hand, the object of desire is too threatening, too saturated with enjoyment. The obsessional's desire, then, is to engage in frenetic activity in order to avoid confronting the abyss of the Other's desire. The obsessional, then, devotes himself or herself to satisfying the Other's demand in hopes that this will preclude exposure of the Other's true desire behind the stated demand ("That is what you demand, but what do you really want as the result of such a demand?"). In leftist political terms, the obsessional would be the Social Democrat, whose ethics is that of compulsively satisfying the Other's (voters) demands by foregoing the achievement of lofty goals in the name of giving the people what they really want. The obsessional's object is the demand of the Other.

THE PERVERT: The pervert devotes himself or herself to working for the Other's enjoyment. In leftist political terms, the pervert is the Stalinist, the one who sees himself or herself as the instrument "serving the enjoyment of the big Other of History (the 'iron Laws of historical Progress,' etc.)" (FTK 272). The Inquisitor, the Puritan, the Sadist, the Stalinist: all are versions of the pervert's ethical stance. The pervert's object is thus the Other's enjoyment.

THE PSYCHOANALYTIC ACT: This is the position that Žižek offers in response to the deadlock of the vicious circle of capital/democracy/representation/subjectivity. The Act is the moment of subjective destitution. Subjective destitution involves the loss of the lost Thing, the sacrifice of the sacrifice—the confrontation with the Real of enjoyment through the giving up of the safety of subjectivization. As a leftist political position, this involves the refusal of symbolic mandates that cover over the trauma at the heart of the social order; it involves instead the perpetual circling around that traumatic wound, the constitutive split that makes the symbolic possible. The object to be identified with in the Act, then, is the object of the *drive*.

But what exactly does this mean? How do we enact this encircling of the traumatic object? In psychoanalytic terms, this means identifying with the kernel of our enjoyment, the stupid rock that gives consistency to our various attempts at symbolization. The passage to the act, the final stage of Lacanian psychoanalysis, means giving up the comfort and stability of our fantasy structure, which provides the "reality" that keeps the Real out of immediate view. But this fantasy is organized around a surplus element (the Thing), an object that resists symbolization, yet paradoxically makes symbolization itself possible by splitting the subject into the subject of representation. Here, we have, then, a final sense of *the beyond of representation*: the identification with the kernel of enjoyment that functions at once as the constituting condition for and the impossibility of representation or symbolization. What we must keep in mind, nevertheless, is that this beyond, as with the other "beyonds" we have examined in this book, is internal to representation itself. What we are beyond is the simple ruse of subjectivization as the staging of the refusal of the Real, the abyss, the crack in the universal that makes any symbolization insufficient. What we are beyond, in a sense, is theater itself, the theatricalization we have observed in its various forms in this chapter.

In order to take a closer look at this beyond of the theater, this beyond of the spectacle, let's look at another dramatic example dear to the hearts of Hegel, Lacan, and Žižek: Antigone. Antigone represents the ethics of the Act par excellence. But how so? In that her "No!" to Creon was not a simple act of disobedience. It was not a hysterical "No! That is not it!" Such hysterical theater is an example of "acting out," which must be distinguished from the Act. Acting out remains within the terms of the symbolic order it addresses. Acting out is, in fact, nothing but an address to the symbolic, to the Other, a staged response of denial that nevertheless keeps the symbolic structure intact, keeps the symbolic circulation within its own orbit. For Žižek, however, Antigone's "No!" is a moment of subjective destitution, of symbolic suicide. While her act is also in a sense literally suicidal (she foresees her death as the result of her act), her literal suicide is not the basis of her act. Suicide in the literal sense is a form of acting out, a message to the Other, and thus maintains the circulation of symbolic capital. Symbolic suicide, on the other hand, is the self-murder of one's own symbolic identity; it is not a symbolized suicide but a suicide that gives up the symbolic itself. When Antigone refuses to follow the orders of the state, she gives up her refuge in her own symbolic identity—her act makes no sense in terms of her identity and destroys that identity itself. Antigone's obstinate persistence even to the point of death and, more traumatically, to the point of subjective destitution is an example of an ethics of the drive.[27]

Žižek's examples from more recent political history include Marshal Tito's "No!" to Joseph Stalin in 1844 and, more recently, the overthrow of Romania's Nicolae Ceauşescu. The power of Tito's act consisted in this refusal by a Communist to accept the symbolic mandate of "Communist." For a brief moment, Tito and Yugoslavia inhabited the space of symbolic destitution wherein their symbolic identity had been sacrificed and not yet resutured into some newer symbolic order. For a Westerner to have renounced Stalin would simply have worked within the already given symbolic structure according which Western renunciation was a constitutive element. Yet what is of crucial importance here is not just an act of denial but the rupture and evacuation of the symbolic order. "What we must bear in mind here is this hiatus" (EYS 45). This hiatus is all the more visible in the Romanian moment of "No!" "The most sublime image that emerged in the political upheavals of the last years—and the term 'sublime' is to be conceived here in the strictest Kantian sense—was undoubtedly the unique picture [of] . . . the rebels waving the national flag with the red star, the Communist symbol, cut out, so that instead of the symbol standing for the organizing principle of the national life, there was nothing but a hole in its center," which was the moment when the "hole in the big Other, the symbolic order, became visible" (TWN 1). Of course we can now cynically look back and comment on how the "Communists" simply changed names and returned to power under another guise. But what is missed in this cynicism is exactly the nature of this openness before "the new guise," the new symbolic order. The hiatus was, for however brief a time, a moment of pure subjectivity before subjectivization and, as such, brought into view the mechanics of subjectivization as such, of its performative dimension in the construction of a new symbolic identity. The point behind the Act, however, is the moment of subjective destitution when all bets are off, when anything is for a moment possible, when the outcome of one's act remains radically undecidable:

> With an act, *stricto sensu*, we can therefore never fully foresee its consequences, i.e., the way it will transform the existing symbolic space: the act is a rupture after which "nothing remains the same." Which is why, although History can always be explained, accounted for, afterward, we can never, as its agents, caught in its flow, foresee its course in advance: we cannot do it insofar as it is not an "objective process" but a process continuously interrupted by the scansion of acts. The new (the symbolic reality that emerges as the aftermath of an act) is always a "state that is essentially a by-product," never the result of advance planning. (EYS 45–46)

But the persistence unto symbolic death of the Act is not the only way to engage in the ethics of the drive. One other method is "the ethical compulsion which compels us to mark repeatedly the memory of a lost Cause" by means of some empty symbolic gesture (FTK 272). This perpetual circling around the traumatic loss—which is nothing but the activity of the drive beyond the desire of fantasy—is not intended to resurrect the lost object—to bring Eurydice back from Hades—which would simply reinscribe the lost object into a new symbolic network, but to keep our eyes focused on the space of the lost itself, the beyond internal to representation, in order to mark its very impossibility. Ideology critique itself must function in this way, as a marking rather than an inscription of the site of the loss:

> And yet in spite of this self-reflective incorporation of the liberal, "socially conscious" ingredients, *the fantasy remains thoroughly the same*, its efficiency in structuring our space of desire intact. The truly radical critique of ideol-

ogy should therefore go beyond the self-congratulatory "social analyses" which continue to participate in the fantasy that sustains the object of their critique and to search for ways to sap the force of this underlying fantasy-frame itself—in short, to perform something akin to the Lacanian "going-through the fantasy." The general lesson to be drawn from it with reference to how ideology works concerns the gap that separates ideology qua discursive formation from its fantasy-support: an ideological edifice is of course submitted to incessant retroactive reconstructions, the symbolic-differential value of its elements shifting all the time, but fantasy designates the hard kernel which resists symbolic "perlaboration," i.e., which as it were anchors an ideology in some "substantial" point and thus provides a constant frame that an ideology cannot be reduced to a network of elements whose value wholly depends on their respective differential position within the symbolic structure. (*TWN* 2/3)

Within these terms, we may begin to differentiate between a Jamesonian and a Žižekian politics concerning the beyond of representation. As I suggested in chapter 1, Jameson's insistence on cognitive mapping seems to be such an attempt mentioned above to submit the Real to some new symbolic system. His imperative to "grow new organs" points to an obsessive impatience with the labor of tarrying with the negative, and appears to work against his own insight—drawn from Hegel—that history is constructed retroactively. Jameson's call to an aesthetics of cognitive mapping appears to operate according to the hysterical fetishistic disavowal that would run something like this: "I know very well that the Real is unrepresentable, but I am going to continue to try to represent it anyway." Certainly Jameson distinguishes between unrepresentability and unknowability:

> What is affirmed is not that we cannot know the world and its totality in some abstract or "scientific" way. Marxian "science" provides just such a way of knowing and conceptualizing the world abstractly, in the sense in which, for example, Mandel's great book [*Late Capitalism*] offers a rich and elaborated *knowledge* of that global world system, of which it has never been said here that it was unknowable but merely that it was unrepresentable, which is a very different matter. The Althusserian formula, in other words, designates a gap, a rift, between existential experience and scientific knowledge. Ideology has then the function of somehow inventing a way of articulating those two distinct dimensions with each other. (*PM* 53)

This "abstract conceptualization" of Marxist science, in the form of cognitive mapping (however we might qualify that term), would then be the level of the symbolic that Jameson claims is missing from Althusser's definition of ideology. Figuration would then take on an active role in the political mandate to give body to the unrepresentable—the postmodern space of late capitalism. "It follows that an aesthetic of cognitive mapping in this sense is an integral part of any socialist political project" (PM 416).

But what of Žižek's claim that Althusser's theory of ideology is already a theory of the symbolic, of subjectivization and interpellation? His Lacanian ethics of the drive would lead him, like Jameson, to the site of the unmappable, the unrepresentable at the heart of the social space. But his insistence, distinct from Jameson's, would be not the obsessional activity of trying to symbolize the Real (at which point we may ask: For whom is Jameson staging this hysterical activity? Who functions as the Other in the Jamesonian fantasy?) but to circle the empty spot in the heart of the symbolic, the trauma that marks the space of the constitutive absence of any comfort beyond representation. What this might mean in a specific political context—the politics of cultural representation—is the subject of my next chapter.

SPIVAK'S SUBLIME SUBALTERN

Like Jameson, Spivak is confronted with a form of the postmodern sublime. The sublime object in this case, however, is not the vast unrepresentable space of global capitalism, although her sublime object is imbricated in just this global capitalist space of the New World Order. The unrepresentable object here is the much-celebrated subaltern. To be more precise—since the subaltern shows up in various guises in Spivak's extended version of her essay, "Can the Subaltern Speak?" now appearing in her book *A Critique of Postcolonial Reason*—the sublime object for Spivak is the possibility of a speaking subaltern. What is at stake is the ability of the critical investigator, such as Spivak herself, to find a way of gaining access to the subaltern, the object of investigation. At issue here is the production of the terms of intelligibility that make a certain object possible within the framework of a certain narrative. For Jameson, as a Marxist, that framework is the narrative of mode of production. But what do we do, Spivak asks (herself sympathetic to and operating within a certain Marxist narrative), with the object that falls out of view in this narrative? And to complicate matters even further, how does one conceive of the object (of study) as the subject (of action, of speech)? The subaltern cannot be other than an impossible subject precisely because it cannot be other than an impossible object from the beginning.

Spivak's initial answer to the question "Can the subaltern speak?" was, as we know, "No." The mode of being that would make the subaltern possible on the stage of Western investigation—speaking—is a mode denied to the subaltern. And while Spivak now admits to an "immediate passion" and despair in her original declaration that "the subaltern cannot speak" (CPCR 308), she nevertheless continues to posit that the subaltern embodies "the sheer heterogeneity of decolonized space" (ibid., 310). As we shall see, the question itself, "Can the subaltern speak?" must be broken down into its implicit assumptions, themselves answers to unspoken questions, such as "What is the subaltern?" "What is speaking?" "What kind of subject speaks?" and "What is the role of the listener in speaking?" All of these questions must be entertained as impossible yet necessary. Behind them is the question of the possibility of writing history— a question privileged by the essay's new title as it appears in *A Critique of Postcolonial Reason*, "History."

WRITING THE RANI

One way Spivak tries to present the (im)possibility of speaking is through an examination of the example of the Rani of Sirmur.[1] Specifically at stake is the question of writing history, especially when the object of investigation exists only in a few scattered accounts—accounts that were written as a way of producing or fabricating the Rani for particular political ends. "In order to construct the Rani of Sirmur as an object of knowledge," Spivak writes, "it should be grasped that she emerges in the archives because of the commercial/territorial interests of the East India Company" (CPCR 227). One such archivist is Robert Ross, a "vulgar-fraction lad" whose brief and racist account of the ancient kingdoms of the hills of northern India was used in the early nineteenth century by the Company to justify its depositions of some leaders and the installation of others more suitable to the Company's imperialist desires. Spivak writes ironically, "He maps the hills cognitively" (ibid.)—a task evidently easier in the premodern landscape of early colonialism than it would prove to be for Jameson in a postmodern cityscape. The relationship here between cognitive mapping and ideological production is nevertheless instructive.

The point Spivak wishes to make here is that history as carried out by the "regular investigative colonial historian," focusing on the grand narrative of great events, neglects the figures in the margins of such narratives. That which remains in the margins of official history is the ordinary or the everyday. "But I want to dwell on this very ordinariness," Spivak writes. "I want to ask what is not considered important enough by the hidden parts of the discipline" (238). As Spivak has learned from Heidegger, the later Foucault, and Derrida, it is in these ordinary moments that the importance of history lies. And yet the ordinary nevertheless remains the *limit* of history writing. That which is most important to historical understanding is beyond history as such. Spivak is driven by an impossible historical imperative: history must be written if we are to remain responsible to those who fall out into the margins of discourse, the fade-out points of our narratives, yet this marginal realm is beyond our grasp. What we learn through acting on such an imperative is not knowledge of the impossible object of history but rather an awareness of the limits of our own history writing. These limits are logical rather than chronological, "logic marking a point beyond which systematic research cannot capture what the everyday sense of self shores up" (229).

One key to understanding Spivak's impossible history writing lies in the following admission: "It must be kept in mind that by the account of these fadeout points, I represent the rhetorical limits of logic, which in turn disclose, by cordoning off, the violent limits of rhetoricity. No one can 'present' them, or to present (them) is to represent" (239). What we have here, then, is another version of Kant's representation through negative presentation. If that is the case, the latter part of her statement above might better be worded as "to represent (them) is to negatively present them." True, no one can present them without representation; but it is exactly this limit of representation that Kant was pointing to in his theory of the sublime. The figure in the margins here functions as the noumenal concept that precisely as noumenal, is beyond (phenomenal) representation and must, then, be presented negatively through the enactment of the breakdown of representation itself. It is the concept of marginality or subalternity itself that is beyond our grasp precisely because such a concept is a logical one, functioning as the negative limits of the "positive" colonial subject. The Other, by its very logical function in hegemonic rhetoric, is nothing but the limits of the Substance of the Subject projected outward onto the bodies of the subaltern. These limits are never stable, however, and must therefore be maintained by a vigilant "rhetorical violence." And here is where both the importance and the impossibility of the gesture toward cultural representation lie.

As mentioned above, one figure Spivak employs in her attempt to flesh out the limits of historical rhetoric is the Rani of Sirmur. Her existence would have passed unremarked—because unremarkable—in the official histories of British

imperialism and Indian nationalism had she not come to function as a rhetorical lever in the construction of British imperial authority in its construction of
India. The Rani fell between two logics, patriarchy and imperialism. As queen,
she was subject to the authority of her husband the king. As mother of the future
"royal" administrator of the British sub-Himalayan colony of Sirmur, she was
subject to the necessities of imperial administration. In neither account was her
own "subjectivity" accounted for, for in its everydayness it fell out of the circuit
of historical narrative. The Rani was only important for the function she played
in competing ideological discourses, a competition that grew heightened when
she declared her intention to be a *sati*, one who sacrifices herself on the funeral
pyre of her husband (234). Her "subjectivity," marked by her "free will," showed
itself in the patriarchal system if she chose to sacrifice herself (such sacrifice was
not prescribed and could thus be seen as an act of volition); her subjectivity in
terms of imperialistc logic showed itself if she "freely chose" not to sacrifice
herself but instead to live up to her duty to her son, the future political administrator. Duty to husband, duty to son—two competing embodiments of her
supposed free will each determined by her duty to a man.[2] "Within the two
contending versions of freedom, the constitution of the female subject *in life*
was thoroughly undermined" (CPCR 235).

TOUCHING THE RANI

So what would the constitution of her female subjectivity *in life* have looked
like? This is the question Spivak feels responsible for. In order to answer it, or to
seek the terms in which an answer might be possible, she embarks on a quest
for traces of the Rani. Interestingly, just as Jameson resorted to a personal
physical itinerary—his "stroll" through the Bonaventure Hotel in Los Angeles—
in order to try to lay out the terms of experience of the postmodern sublime,
Spivak also presents an account of a personal journey into the sublime—an
account marked by a certain narrative pathos. This pathetic nature of cross-
cultural narratives, as we will see below, is not beside the point here but rather
marks the aesthetic space of cultural identification as such:

> The narrative pathos of this unscholarly account is at a great remove from
> the austere practice of critical philosophy. Yet, the differantial contamina-
> tions of absolute alterity (even to utter the words is to differentiate them
> from some other thing, which should of course be impossible) that allow us

to mime responsibility to the other, cannot allow this pathos merely to be faded out. As I approached her house after a long series of detective maneuvers, I was miming the route of an unknowing, a progressive différance, an "experience" of how I could not know her. Nothing unusual here, and therefore never considered worthy of mention, of notice. (241)

"The differantial contaminations of absolute alterity": it is no mere wordplay to point out the etymological connections between "subaltern" and "alterity." The subaltern is defined by its otherness, an alterity that lies below the narrative horizons of Western investigation, both below as in "out of sight" and below as in "substrate" or "foundation." The subaltern is thus the impossible foundation of Western subjectivity as it constructs itself in its "absolute" distinction from its other. It is in this sense, again, that the subaltern marks a logical function rather than a substantive being. And yet Spivak's emphasis on precisely this point does not at all absolve her of her pathetic responsibility to the other, nor does it diminish her desire to "touch" the everyday life of the subaltern. She knows very well that she is miming the route of an unknowing, yet this knowledge does not free her from the imperative to follow through with this impossible miming.[3] Herself contaminated by the *différance* of absolute Alterity—that other that is constantly different from what it had seemed to be, constantly deferred by another series of obstacles—Spivak nevertheless devotes herself to this "experience" of impossible knowing. And this is what marks the drive toward cultural identification as pathetic, both in its technical sense as *pathos* or emotional identification and in its colloquial sense as hopelessly impossible. We are implicated in a kind of Pascalian wager according to which action rather than truth determines the effectivity of our practice.

Spivak specifically invokes the discourse of the sublime as she continues her narrative. As she encounters the palace as space, she tries to account for her aesthetic experience in terms of the sublime:

> The palace was a legend of this deferment and difference. On the south, past the open terrace and directly below it, stretched the peaks and waves of the foothills of the Himalayas as far as the eye could see. I was halted by the discourse of the European sublime and, percolated through it, Kalidasa, the fifth-century Sanskrit court-poet beloved of Goethe, both out of the Rani's reach. To the East, the less lofty two-storied Mughal wing of the women's quarters, with the stucco jalousies, now permanently locked, undoubtedly the Rani's habitation. I was lodged in the men's wing, added on in the

nineteenth century, with its floor-to-ceiling tarnished mirrors and life-size portraits of indifferent quality. Here I was halted by my own ideological formation as child of a Kali-worshipping sect, an East Indian phenomenon imbricated with the so-called Bengal Renaissance, as clearly out of the Rani's reach. There were no papers, the ostensible reason for my visit, and of course, no trace of the Rani. Again, a reaching and an un-grasping. (CPCR 242–43)

Is it an accident that Spivak invokes the sublime at the moment she is about *not so see* signs of the Rani? As far as the eye can see: the mountains and foothills stretch out beyond the limits of her perception, just as Kant describes the experience of the sublime. But why is she "halted" by this discourse? What Spivak realizes is that her own experiences, here in the place where the Rani experienced her everydayness, are informed by experiences that were never available to the Rani. How much of the Western(ized) experience of the sublime is conditioned by eighteenth-century European aesthetic discourse? Even when that Western discourse is supposedly conditioned by an Indian source—Kalidasa—this ancient Bengali form of "Indian" experience too is out of reach of the Rani. Even as another "Indian" "woman," Spivak's own experiences take her out of the everyday world of the Rani. Spivak's own "Indianness," marked by her upbringing in a foreign religious world not available to inhabitants of Sirmur, is no passport at all into the world of the Rani. All of these educational experiences are halting rather than impelling. "Again, a reaching and an un-grasping."

"Grasping," of course, is the literal translation of the German Idealist word for conceptualizing, for grasping or getting hold of a concept—begreifen. The experience of the sublime is that of the breakdown not only of conceptualizing but of perceiving. Ironically, then, Spivak's own education in the discourses of the sublime has transformed the Rani for her into an inverted form of the sublime object itself. For Kant, the experience of the sublime grows out of our encounter with phenomena too great to perceive in their totality. There is too much perceptual information to take in at one time. Just the opposite seems to be the problem here with the Rani. The Rani is forever just beyond the horizon, just around the corner, always differed and deferred. And yet it is precisely in her absence that she comes to take on her full significance. The effects of the imperialist system that produced her are everywhere. What is at stake here is the possibility of conceiving of the sublime expansiveness of the global system of late capitalism by means of its other, the subaltern. What makes the nonpresence of the Rani sublime in a world that constantly promises yet never actually provides traces of her is that she comes to embody the nonrepresentability—in terms of Western capitalist logic—of the subaltern as such. The implied point of sadness in Spivak's account is that if only she had been able to see and speak with the Rani, she could then come to know her, to represent her, to rescue her from historical obscurity.

This fantasy of knowing-through-presence—despite all the deconstructive assurances that this trip could never be anything more than a miming of an unknowing—finds its truth in the scene following this account of the Rani's palace—a scene that chronologically took place prior to Spivak's arrival at the palace, but that takes on its full significance in Spivak's subsequent moment of failure. This encounter took place on the first of five visits in her attempt to track down the Rani:

> I made five visits in all. This was the last. On the very first try, in search of the palace, I had walked about in the hills where buses did not go. Shy hardy women gathered leaves and vegetation from the hillside to feed their goats. They could not have had a historical memory of the Rani. And they are, have been historically, at a distance from the culture of imperialism, and from the relay between princely state and nation-state that swept the Rani's descendants into its currents and whirlpools. They were the rural subaltern, the real constituency of feminism, accepting their lot as the norm, quite different from the urban sub-proletarian in crisis and resistance. If I wanted to touch their everyday without the epistemic transcoding of anthropological field work, the effort would be a much greater undoing, indeed, of life's goals, than the effort to catch the Rani in vain, in history. These are the familiar limits of knowing; why do we resist it when deconstruction points at them? (243)

Here Spivak recognizes the "true" representation of the subaltern within the current conditions of global capital. The figure that could embody the subaltern as such progressively recedes from view in Spivak's chapter. Each figure held up as its embodiment is found to be *not quite it*, not quite subaltern enough, until the author confronts these women of the hills. As a representative of cultural otherness when otherness is from the point of view of the West, any non-Westerner would seem to do. But when seen within the dynamics of a more regionalized context, the native elite—in contrast to those under them at home—are far from subaltern. Any woman is subaltern in relation to males in general, but a privileged Indian woman is not subaltern in relation to others not so privileged in the Indian caste system. But here, in the women of the sub-Himalayan rural country, is the "real subaltern," the "real constituency of feminism," a group even more subaltern than the urban female subproletarian (242).[4] Spivak failed to grasp the everyday existence of the Rani; she would have to give up on her previous life goals to even begin to be able to "touch" the lives of these women.

It is crucial to recognize that Spivak's desire when confronted with the women of the hills, forever beyond the limits of her knowing, is a desire to "touch their everyday." She does not desire to "know what they think" or to "grasp their consciousness," at least not in the ordinary senses in which we say these things. The everyday and consciousness operate according to different critical itineraries. As a good deconstructionist, versed as well in Marx and Freud, Spivak cannot hope to know another's consciousness precisely because the whole notion of a self-present consciousness is never fully available even to the one whose "consciousness" we are investigating. Nevertheless, even the everyday operates according to a code, one that would take a lifetime to begin to crack—all in vain even more than her desire to grasp the sublime nature of the Rani.[5]

"The everyday" necessarily remains a rather vague concept for Spivak. What she is *not* aiming at is some kind of ontological ground or prediscursive experience: "I am speaking of a history that can attend to the details of the putting together of a continuous-seeming self for everyday life. This may well be the limit of history-*writing*" (CPCR 238). Spivak is after a certain poetics, then, a certain mode of putting together of a "continuous-seeming self" for everyday life. This self, which only "seems" continuous—but has to seem as such for everyday functioning—has been put together for just such a seeming, "despite the chanciness that must be reined in in the necessary production of this continuity" (ibid.). And yet even this hope seems rather Utopian, given the unrepresentability of subalternity as such.

Interestingly, despite all of Spivak's claims that the subaltern is unrepresentable, she does manage to identify (if not represent) them. "Development studies of Indian women tell us," Spivak writes, "that this group of women, unorganized landless female labor, is one of the targets of super-exploitation where local, national, and international capital intersect" (242). She expands on this claim in a note as follows: "Upon the registers of great apparatuses, as World

Trade becomes secondary to finance capital, the peculiar phenomenon of credit-baiting without infrastructural involvement or involvement in social redistribution creates a general subaltern will for the financialization of the globe. This is the new globalized subject, rather different from the visible violence of super-exploitation" (243 n. 70).[6] Spivak registers the crux of the representational abyss opened up by the object of subaltern studies by claiming that these "women outside the mode of production narrative mark the points of fadeout in the writing of disciplinary history even as they mime 'writing as such,' footprints of the trace (of someone? something?—we are mistakenly obliged to ask) that efface as they disclose" (244). Effacement in disclosure: this is the mode of phenomenality that characterizes subaltern consciousness for Spivak.

OVERDETERMINATION AND *ENTSTELLUNG*

Elsewhere Spivak has spoken of this problem as it has surfaced in the work of the Subaltern Studies group. For the group, the discussion of consciousness "is not consciousness-in-general, but a historicized political species thereof, subaltern consciousness" (*IOW* 203). She elaborates on this point:

> Because of this bestowal of a historical specificity to consciousness in the narrow sense, even as it implicitly operates a metaphysical methodological presupposition in the general sense, there is always a counterpointing suggestion in the work of the group that subaltern consciousness is subject to the cathexis of the élite, that it is never fully recoverable, that it is always askew from its received signifiers, indeed it is effaced even as it is disclosed, that it is irreducibly discursive. (ibid.)

This always-askew movement of effacement-in-disclosure is what Spivak aims at in her adoption of one of Freud's metaphors from *The Interpretation of Dreams*. It is there that Freud develops his notion of overdetermination as a way of accounting for the peculiar operations of the production of dream images. The importance here for Spivak is that Freud attempts to find a term that will do justice, *all at once*, to the interaction of two different figurative processes in the production of a single image. The two processes at work, Freud claims, are wish-fulfillment and dream-work. The beauty of this relationship, according to Spivak, is that the notion of overdetermination attempts to think these two processes at once in a single term, one process—wish-fulfillment—

referring to subjective will and desire (or "consciousness") and the other—dream-work—referring to some *other* process operating outside the site of conscious will: "the desire to hold in one thought something like a wish *and* an economy" (CPCR 219). "Wish-fulfillment" accounts for the subjective process "where the psychic agency seems close to the deliberative consciousness that we colloquially identify as our 'self' " (ibid., 218). The dream-work, on the other hand, marks a site of figurative production operating outside the realm of consciousness, a radically *other* process at work along with the will in the production of a single image. This image, then, cannot be attributed simply to "consciousness," but neither can "consciousness" simply be dismissed as mere subjectivism. The beauty of such a concept of overdetermination is that it allows Spivak to posit a subaltern consciousness while at the same time recognizing the radical Alterity at work at the heart of such a consciousness (and at the heart of consciousness as such). Consciousness must be seen as something produced or constructed, yet this awareness must not obscure the fact that consciousness itself still has determinate effects in the world.[7] Spivak writes:

> Using the Freudian concept-metaphor as a formal rather than methodological model, then, I am going to suggest that to disclose only race-class-gender determinations of social practices is to see overdetermination as only many determinations. If we notice that explanations and discourses are irreducibly fractured by an epistemic violence of monopoly imperialism, we begin to entertain the possibility of a determination whose ground is itself a figuration: a "determination otherwise." Of course Freud never speaks of imperialism. But the notion of figuration at the ground (rather different from *non*-foundationalism) surfaces in the pervasive Freudian discourse of *Entstellung*: displacement as grounding in the emergence of significance. (CPCR 219)

Entstellung, then, is the process at work in Spivak's claim above that "women outside the mode of production narrative mark the points of fadeout in the writing of disciplinary history even as they mime 'writing as such,' footprints of the trace . . . that efface as they disclose." Entstellung, like *Entäußerung* or alienation, is a process marked by a radical Alterity, an Alterity that nevertheless functions as the ground of being of the figure as such. This is a figure that breaks-off-from (Ent-) at the same time as it presents or places (stellen) in view.

This desire to hold both a will and an economy in the mind at once by way of an appropriation of the concept of overdetermination presents a move beyond or away from Spivak's earlier emphasis on the poststructuralist notion of "subject-effect" and of "strategic essentialism." In discussing the notion of subject-effect, she writes:

> A subject-effect can be briefly plotted as follows: that which seems to operate as a subject may be part of an immense discontinuous network ("text" in the general sense) of strands that may be termed politics, ideology, economics, history, sexuality, language, and so on. (Each of these strands, if they are isolated, can also be seen as woven of many strands.) Different knottings and configurations of these strands, determined by heterogeneous determinations which are themselves dependent upon myriad circumstances, produce the effect of an operating subject. Yet the continuist and homogenist deliberative consciousness symptomatically requires a continuous and homogeneous cause for this effect and thus posits a sovereign and determining subject. This latter is, then, the effect of an effect, and its positing a metalepsis, or the substitution of an effect for a cause. (*IOW* 204)

This turn to the "subject-effect" grows out of the desire among hegemonic radicals to avoid the "essentialism" behind the concept of a sovereign and determining subject. Yet as Spivak warns, some of "the most radical criticism coming out of the West in the eighties was the result of an interested desire to conserve the subject of the West, or the West as Subject. The theory of pluralized 'subject-effects' often provided the cover for this subject of knowledge" (*CPCR* 248). Such is the case, for instance, with Foucault and Deleuze when they attempt to provide the stage upon which the workers or students or prisoners or other "subaltern" groups can speak for themselves.[8]

Spivak's primary reference here is a published conversation between Foucault and Deleuze in which they discuss the relationship between intellectuals and power.[9] It is in this conversation that Spivak sees the relationship between representation and the subaltern tied up with the empowerment of the investigator. To their credit, the two Western intellectuals recognize the need to "disclose and know the discourse of society's other" (*CPCR* 249), but their problem is that they are blind to their own complicity in the policing of this other. The concept of desire is meant to displace the sovereign subject and replace it with the heterogeneous libidinal flow of desire as such. One problem here, Spivak claims, is that this "parasubjective matrix, cross-hatched with heterogeneity, surreptitiously ushers in the unnamed Subject, at least for those intellectual workers influenced by the new hegemony of pure catachresis" (253–54). This newly ushered in Subject looks and operates curiously like the heterogeneous flow of the Subject of global capitalism—namely, the Subject of Europe.

Another problem with the unacknowledged production of this Subject as Desire is the related urge on Foucault and Deleuze's part to deny the role of ideology in the mechanisms of oppression of the Other. This relationship between ideology and interest ("a theory of which is necessary for an understanding of constituted interests within systems of representation") disappears and is replaced by a kind of ventriloquism through which the Left intellectual will let the subaltern speak for itself. It is not surprising that the notion of representation itself must go if the subaltern is to speak so ably and without mediation. A passage particularly interesting to Spivak reads as follows:

> A theorizing intellectual, for us, is no longer a subject, a representing or representative consciousness. Those who act and struggle are no longer represented, either by a group or a union that appropriates the right to stand as their conscience. Who speaks and acts? It is always a multiplicity, even within the person who speaks and acts. . . . Representation no longer exists; there's only action—theoretical action and practical action which serve as relays and networks.[10]

This effacement of representation leads to one of Spivak's most important points. When theorizing intellectuals posit the transparency of the subaltern will as it speaks and acts, they run together two different senses of the word "representation." The question of representation and consciousness or knowledge is a question of subject-predication, whereas the question of speaking for (wherein the masses speak for themselves, not needing intellectuals to represent them or to speak for them) concerns the question of representation as standing-in-for. The claim that "the masses . . . know far better than [the intellectual] and they are certainly capable of expressing themselves" runs knowledge and expression together.[11] The danger here, beyond the simplistic notion of consciousness and action as well as the relationship between the two, is that a strategic understanding of the relationship between hegemonic representatives and the subaltern depends on keeping these two senses of representation separate. Ideological domination itself in the New World Order depends on conflating these two senses in order to legitimize bourgeois patriarchal neocolonial power. It is the task of the intellectual involved in ideological critique, then, to be able to distinguish between them: "Radical practice should attend to this double session of representations rather than reintroduce the in-dividual subject through totalizing concepts of power and desire" (CPCR 264).

REPRESENTATION VERSUS REPRESENTATION

Spivak develops her argument by noting that these two senses of representation are referred to by two separate words in German, vertreten ("to represent" in the sense of political proxy) and darstellen (which Spivak first identifies as to "re-present" in the sense of subject-predication). One reason for drawing atten-tion to this German distinction is that her primary example comes from a reading of Marx's *The Eighteenth Brumaire of Louis Bonaparte* in the German.[12] Marx's argument turns on his emphasis on the distinction between class con-sciousness and class interest. His point is that under certain historical condi-tions, a group that forms a class (in that it exists under different conditions than other classes) might lack a clear sense of itself *as a class* (that is, in relation to the system of relations of production within which it comes into being) and there-fore not be able to recognize its own class interests. When this is the case, members of that class might see their interests as embodied by a member or members of another class. In Spivak's terms, when a class cannot form a picture of itself as a class (re-present as darstellen), it turns to others to speak for its interests (represent as vertreten). Marx's example was the French small peasant proprietors who, because they could not form a picture of themselves as a class, turned to Bonaparte as the representative of their interests. "The small peasant proprietors," Marx writes, "form an immense mass, the members of which live in the same situation but do not enter into manifold relations with each other. Their mode of operation isolates them instead of bringing them into mutual intercourse" (EB 238). Due to their organization around the isolated family farm rather than the town, "the great mass of the French nation is formed by the simple addition of isomorphous magnitudes, much as potatoes in a sack form a sack of potatoes" (239). The passage especially crucial for Spivak's argument is the following:

> In so far as these small peasant proprietors are connected on a local basis, and the identity of their interests fails to produce a feeling of community, national links, or a political organization, they do not form a class. They are therefore incapable of asserting their class interest in their own name,

whether through a parliament or through a convention. They cannot represent themselves; they must be represented. Their representative must appear
simultaneously as their master, as an authority over them, an unrestricted
governmental power that protects them from the other classes and sends
them rain and sunshine from above. The political influence of the small
peasant proprietors is therefore ultimately expressed in the executive subor-
dinating society to itself. (ibid.)

Marx's word for "represent" in the statement "They cannot represent themselves; they must be represented," Spivak emphasizes, is vertreten. Because they
cannot form a Darstellung of themselves, they must resort to a Vertretung who
will represent them for themselves. Or more accurately, because the Darstellung
they form of themselves is not one of a class united by common interests but
rather a mass of isolated individual families, they turn to the Vertretung that
best appears to speak for their perceived interests. Neither Marx nor Spivak
suggests that there is no relationship between Darstellung and Vertretung—in
fact, the complicity between the two is exactly their point. Spivak's emphasis is
that the failure to distinguish between the two modes of representation blinds
us to a crucial dimension of ideological production. The image a class has of
itself will determine (in the sense of "de-limit") the particular representative
that class will accept as representing its best interests. It should also be pointed
out here that Marx is not claiming that the problem is that the small peasant
proprietors sought a representative outside their own class to represent their
interests. In fact, according to Marx this is exactly what they needed to do if
they were to work in the name of their own interests. The problem for Marx
was that they chose Bonaparte rather than the proletariat as their representative: "This point should be clearly understood: the Bonaparte dynasty represents [repräsentiert] the conservative, not the revolutionary peasant: the
peasant who wants to consolidate the condition of his social existence, the
smallholding, not the peasant who strikes out beyond it" (240). The first alliance between the peasantry and a Bonaparte was a revolutionary one; the
second was a reactionary one. "The interests of the peasants," Marx continues,
"are therefore no longer consonant with the interests of the bourgeoisie, as they
were under Napoleon, but in opposition to those interests, in opposition to
capital. They therefore find their natural ally and leader in the urban proletariat, whose task is the overthrow of the bourgeois order" (242).

Spivak's point in relation to Foucault and Deleuze is that the conflation of these two forms of representation (not to mention the outright rejection of both) has to be taken into account if the history of "this unfortunate marionette," the unheeded subaltern in the shadows of hegemonic theorizing, is to unfold (*CPCR* 259). The notion of a self-conscious subaltern who speaks for himself (the pronoun here is deliberate—one of Spivak's assertions is that the subaltern *woman* is doubly in the shadows of this puppetry) on the stage prepared by the (invisible) theorist adheres to a notion of the speaking subject that merely masks the production of the subject of global finance capital. This is one of the dangers, then, of Foucault and Deleuze's notion of the speaking masses: "Without a theory of ideology," Spivak argues, "it can lead to a dangerous utopianism. And, if confined to migrant struggles in Northern countries, it can work against global social justice" (ibid., 279) by ignoring the international division of labor (250).

It is in this context that Spivak asks her now infamous question, "Can the subaltern speak?" As mentioned earlier, her initial answer was no. "I was so unnerved by this failure of communication that, in the first version of this text, I wrote, in the accents of passionate lament: the subaltern cannot speak! It was an inadvisable remark" (308). Spivak makes a similar clarification in an interview for *Socialist Review*:

> When I hear people say to me, "You say that the subaltern cannot speak," I feel that people have forgotten to read. . . . Don't they see where the claim comes in the essay? . . . The rhetoric of the ending is a rhetoric of despair. It was at that moment, right after the story [of Bhaduri's suicide], when I said, throwing up my hands, "The subaltern cannot speak." And it's read as me opining about all subalterns in the world, saying in a deconstructive way that there is no subject.[13]

Beyond the suggestions for a certain protocol of correct reading, Spivak seems to suggest here that, despite her earlier claim uttered in a moment of despair, the subaltern *can* speak. This is clearly not the case, however, as she continues to make comments such as "If, in the contest of colonial production, the subaltern has no history and cannot speak, the subaltern female is even more deeply in the shadow" (*CPCR* 274). Her protocol of reading, on the other hand, demands that we read this statement in the context of the economy of her text. In that case, the key element is not so much that the subaltern *as such* ("all subalterns in the world") cannot speak but that the subaltern subject constructed *in the contest of colonial production* cannot speak. The claim is historical, contextual, and furthermore, gendered. The problem facing us today in this New World Order is "the problem of the muted subject of the subaltern woman" (ibid., 260). It is in this context—and against the "benevolent" intentions of Foucault and Deleuze as well as the metropolitan "third world feminist" who posit an oppressed who can speak and know their conditions—that Spivak's infamous question arises: "We must now confront the following question: On the other side of the international division of labor from socialized capital, inside *and* outside the circuit of the epistemic violence of imperialist law and education supplementing an earlier economic text, *can the subaltern speak?*" (269).

Clearly, then, one issue at stake is the definition of the subaltern. This was one of the stakes in the Subaltern Studies group. For Ranajit Guha, the term "subaltern" becomes exchangeable with the term "the people," which in turn is exchangeable for "the peasantry" (obviously not the same "people" as "We the people" in the context of U.S. republicanism). Concerned with the development of "Indian" nationalist insurgency opposed to British imperialism, Guha finds the need to narrow the Indian-British opposition to one between different segments of Indian society itself, in particular the elite versus the people, with an important yet ambiguous buffer group operating in between. The subaltern, then, is defined as someone "of inferior rank," and the word will be used "as a name for the general attribute of subordination in South Asian society whether this is expressed in terms of class, caste, age, gender and office or in other way" (sss 35). Subordination is not a positive characteristic, however, but one established through difference; that is, the "identity-in-difference" of the subaltern (CPCR 271) is predicated on its not being hegemonic: "*The demographic difference between the total Indian population and all those whom we have described as the 'elite'*" (ss 1:8; sss 44).[14]

In her analysis of Guha's definition, Spivak makes the following curious statement:

> For the (gender-unspecified) "true" subaltern group, whose identity is its difference, there is no unrepresentable subaltern subject that can know and speak itself; the intellectual's solution is not to abstain from representation. The problem is that the subject's itinerary has not been left traced so as to offer an object of seduction to the representing intellectual. (CPCR 272)

Part of the problem Spivak sees is that the "gender-unspecified" group in actuality means that women have become invisible in the group. As problematic as this situation was during the earlier days of nationalist insurgency, this problem is all the more extreme with the feminizing of the subaltern in the "gradual emergence of the new subaltern in the New World Order" (ibid., 274). It is the hill women of Sirmur, for example, women outside the mode of production narrative, who are "insufficiently represented or representable in that narration. We can docket them, but we cannot grasp them at all. The possibility of possession, of being haunted, is cut by the imposition of the tough reasonableness of capital's mode of exploitation" (244) as it shifts from urban industrial exploitation to rural credit-baiting.

What we need to grasp here is that the issue of representation does not hinge on a simple question of epistemology—that is, of some kind of pure state of subject-object relation between the subaltern and the investigator. The difficulty is neither that the subaltern by its very nature is unrepresentable nor that the investigator by his or her nature is incapable of grasping the subaltern as an object of knowledge. The problem, rather, is that under the current historical situation in which such investigations must operate, the itinerary of the trace of a sexed subaltern subject has been effaced. Spivak will go on to say both that "knowledge of the other subject is theoretically impossible" (283) and yet that this question of the subaltern woman as subject is "not an idealist red herring" (282).

Here I return to the problem of representation Spivak outlined in her vertreten-darstellen distinction. How are we to represent (as proxy) the subaltern if we cannot represent her (in portraiture)? Let us return to the passage quoted above, particularly the line, "For the (gender-unspecified) 'true' subaltern group, whose identity is its difference, there is no unrepresentable subaltern subject that can know and speak itself." What is the meaning of the double negative in "no unrepresentable subaltern subject"? Is Spivak suggesting that there *is* a representable subaltern subject? This is clearly at odds with her argument throughout the various versions of her essay. Furthermore, if there were a representable subaltern subject, then the problem of representation of the subaltern that Spivak continually points to would disappear and there would be no need for the following statement: "The intellectual's solution is not to abstain from representation." The need for a solution implies the existence of a problem. The problem can be stated perhaps more clearly as "The subaltern subject is unrepresentable and, as such, cannot speak and know itself." The reason for its being unrepresentable is that "the subject's itinerary has not been left traced so as to offer an object of seduction to the representing intellectual."

The implication seems to be that the subaltern subject's "itinerary" could be traced under different conditions and, in that case, then offer up an object of seduction to the representing intellectual. But why is there no trace of the subaltern subject's itinerary? This is the crux of Spivak's chapter.

THE ITINERARY

The following passage marks a representative move of Spivak's:

> Within the effaced itinerary of the subaltern subject, the track of sexual difference is doubly effaced. The question is not of female participation in insurgency, or the ground rules of the sexual division of labor, for both of which there is "evidence." It is, rather, that, both as object of colonialist historiography and as subject of insurgency, the ideological construction of gender keeps the male dominant. If, in the contest of colonial production, the subaltern has no history and cannot speak, the subaltern female is even more deeply in shadow. (274)

"Itinerary" here refers to the production of the subject within a particular ideological discourse. Within various discourses, the subaltern figures both as subject and object. Within the discourse of colonialist historiography, the subaltern is constructed as the object of study, as the other of the colonial subject. For example, Spivak writes that "the itinerary of recognition through assimilation of the Other can be more interestingly traced, it seems to me, in the imperialist constitution of the colonial subject and the foreclosure of the figure of the 'native informant'" (280). Even in the imperialist construction of a colonial subject, however, the figure of the woman remains invisible until constructed as the object of benevolent imperialist protection. Within Indian nationalist discourse, on the other hand, the subaltern is inscribed as the insurgent subject, in the process of which the figure of woman is again effaced.

In her discussion of *sati* or widow sacrifice, Spivak focuses on the competing constructions of the figure of woman in the discourses of imperialism and nationalism. The British, who believe themselves usually neutral in the internal cultural affairs of the colony, violate this neutrality in order to oppose widow sacrifice in the name of a higher humanity. The protection of woman in India is carried out in the name of the civilizing project of empire. On the other hand, Indian nationalists, operating under a patriarchal logic, construct the self-sacrificed woman as a patriotic hero, as the subject of free will. The same act is

coded as victimage in one discourse and heroism in another. Once the definition of woman as subject of free will takes hold, then her construction becomes
a contest between different versions of free will—the free choice to reject "bar-
barism" or to accept "heroism." "Paradoxically," Spivak notes, "these same
moves allow us to witness the unfixed place of woman as signifier in the
inscription of the social individual" (291). "The task of recovering a (sexually)
subaltern subject," she adds, "is lost in an institutional textuality at the archaic
origin" (300). Nevertheless, as we saw above, "the intellectual's solution is not
to abstain from representation." So what is the intellectual's solution?

Spivak first begins by calling for an articulation of our participation in the
formation of the figure of the sexed subaltern subject and to recognize, at the
same time, the dangers inherent in this participation. Spivak's answer here is
not to call for the development of some new perceptual organ that will allow us
to grasp what is currently ungraspable. Her answer instead is to construct a
certain sentence, a sentence that will replace (while marking the space of production of) the impossible question of the speaking subaltern. This sentence
will be posited as the trace of a history of repression: "It is in acknowledg-
ment of these dangers rather than as solution to a problem that I put together
the sentence 'White men are saving brown women from brown men'" (284).
The function of this sentence is strategic rather than declarative. Drawing on
Freud's discussion of his construction of the sentence "A child is being beaten,"
Spivak sees the sentence as the screen covering over a scene of repression. What
is repressed is the history of the production of the subject. Her sentence functions, then, as a metonym for the repressed imperialist ideology that constructs
the subaltern woman as victim-to-be-saved. Against this sentence she poses a
countersentence, the Indian nativist statement: "The women wanted to die"
(287). Spivak's strategy, beyond condensing opposing ideologies into opposing
sentences that speak the place of woman in conflicting ways, is to pose the
question of the space between the sentences, the space of the differend. "The
differend" is Lyotard's term for the condition in which one is faced with phrases
operating according to incompatible logics, both of which are true in their own
terms but cannot be resolved according to a general logic that could account for
both phrases or statements at once.[15] Spivak's point is that the sexed subaltern
subject is lost in this space between sentences: "Between patriarchy and imperialism, subject-constitution and object-formation, the figure of the woman
disappears, not into a pristine nothingness, but into a violent shuttling that is
the displaced figuration of the 'third-world woman' caught between tradition

and modernization, culturalism and development" (CPCR 304).[16] It is in this sense of the history of repression that the notion of the itinerary of the trace of the production of the sexed subaltern subject must be read. This itinerary is effaced in that it falls out into the space between competing repressed logics.

So what of a logic that could account for this itinerary? What of a third sentence that could metonymically represent the itinerary of the trace? Spivak is rather sober about the conditions of possibility for such a sentence: "The two sentences go a long way to legitimize each other. One never encounters the testimony of the women's voice consciousness. Such a testimony would not be ideology-transcendent or 'fully' subjective, of course, but it would constitute the ingredients for producing a countersentence (CPCR 287). Such a testimony, though, is not immediately forthcoming because the effacement of the itinerary of the trace of the sexed subaltern subject continues today under the terms of a neocolonialist New World Order that attracts the unwitting complicity of academic feminists and multiculturalists.[17] Recognizing nevertheless the practical importance "of being upbeat" (CPCR 309), Spivak continues to wonder "if a perception of the origin of my sentence might contain interventionist possibilities" (290), presumably by pointing toward these repressed histories.[18]

THE ABYSS OF HETEROGENEITY

Whatever itineraries of the subject we might imagine capable of offering themselves up as objects of intellectual seduction, we must, it seems, content ourselves with the impossible demand to continue on the quest to represent the unrepresentable. We must, it seems, continue—whether out of curiosity, political motivation, or moral love (more on this later)—to mime the route of an unknowing. Despite the important deconstructive interventions we might entertain, according to Spivak we remain on the other side of subalternity and have no hopes of crossing over to the other side, the side of the other: "It is not a mere tautology to say that the colonial or postcolonial subaltern is defined as the being on the other side of difference, or an epistemic fracture, even from other groupings among the colonized. What is at stake when we insist that the subaltern speaks?" (CPCR 309).

I would argue that Spivak's presentation of the subaltern in her concluding pages condemns us to an impossible injunction that is at odds with one movement of her essay. That injunction or imperative is not one that demands that we continue to try to represent the unrepresentable subaltern, although on a certain level this imperative does operate here. Her injunction, rather, is to keep the space of subalternity open and indeterminate. Subalternity, as Spivak constructs it, is the space of radical negativity that must by definition remain unfilled by any particular "trace of the subject," whether that is the (unsexed) peasant insurgent or the migrant intellectual or the First World minority. Spivak closes her essay with three points, the first of which reads:

> 1. Simply by being postcolonial or the member of an ethnic minority, we are not "subaltern." That word is reserved for the sheer heterogeneity of de-colonized space. (310)

Spivak earlier commented that "the colonized subaltern *subject* is irretrievably heterogeneous" (270). We find here that such heterogeneity marks the space of the *de*colonized subaltern subject as well. While we might hope that through historical development beyond our current decolonized space the subaltern might then appear on this side of difference, that can never happen because the subaltern as such is the name for the space of radical difference. This becomes clear in Spivak's second claim:

> 2. When a line of communication is established between a member of sub-altern groups and the circuits of citizenship or institutionality, the subaltern has been inserted into the long road to hegemony. Unless we want to be romantic purists or primitivists about "preserving subalternity"—a contradiction in terms—this is absolutely to be desired. (ibid.)

The key here is that when a figure who currently occupies the space of subalternity can be reached through a line of communication (when the subaltern can speak?), that figure is already on the side of hegemony and no longer subaltern. The subaltern, again, is by definition beyond the line of communication. The point about the "contradiction in terms" seems to imply that one must already have something to preserve it; the subaltern, by definition, is beyond our grasp—we cannot preserve what we never had in the first place. The question remains, however, how such a line of communication with a member of the subaltern can be opened to begin with, given that the subaltern is beyond representation and, therefore, beyond recognition. Where do we find this member in order to dismember him or her from the space of subalternity? Such a move might indeed be desirable, but it is—within Spivak's terms—impossible.

This leaves us with an important practical question about the effectivity of hegemonic struggle within these terms—a question to which I will return.[19]

Her third point marks the point of despair Spivak has reached:

> 3. This trace-structure (effacement in disclosure) surfaces as the tragic emotions of the political activist, springing not out of superficial utopianism, but out of the depths of what Bimal Krishna Matilal has called "moral love." (CPCR)

This is the end result of our one-hundred page engagement with Spivak as she mimes the route of an unknowing along this trace-structure: the call for seeing moral love as the source of tragic emotions. This is Spivak in her most Kantian moment—when the representational apparatus breaks down in the face of the sublime and throws us into tragic despair, out of the depths rises the Idea of Moral Love as compensation for all of our pathetic human shortcomings. The breakdown of the Imagination presents us with the priority of Practical Reason.

I would rather turn to Spivak's *other* answer to this epistemological aporia: her turn to the transformative dialectical interplay of sentences in dispute. This transformation involves the transition from a logical aporia to a historical repression. "This gesture of transformation [of a sentence into the object of simple semiosis] marks the fact that knowledge of the other subject is theoretically impossible" (283). This is the practical turn to the logic of hegemony as carried out by Laclau and Mouffe and as implicit throughout Spivak's essay. What is Spivak's contest of sentences in dispute but an example of hegemonic struggle over the empty signifier of the subaltern? When Spivak describes the contest between imperialist and patriarchal constructions of the sexed subaltern as woman as one in which the figure of woman is "ideologically cathected" (296), she is describing the process of hegemony, the struggle over the production of the definition of the signifier—in this case, the good woman (the woman who freely chooses to live up to her symbolic mandate)[20]—which will confer a particular ideological identity onto those to whom the signifier supposedly refers. In her discussion of the development of (impossible) "full class agency," Spivak describes this process of hegemony: "It is a contestatory *replacement* as well as an *appropriation* (a *supplementation*) of something that is 'artificial' to begin with" (CPCR 261). This process is, in fact, that which lies at the heart of Spivak's analysis of imperialist ideological production: "This is not to describe 'the way things really were' or to privilege the narrative of history as imperialism as the best version of history. It is, rather, to continue the account of how *one* explanation and narrative of reality was established as the normative one" (267).

WHOSE "PEOPLE"? HEGEMONIC STRUGGLE IN NICARAGUA

This political application of Spivak's text is developed in an important essay appearing in *Socialist Review* titled "Can the Subaltern Vote?"[21] The authors— Leerom Medovoi, Shankar Raman, and Benjamin Robinson—take as their example the Nicaraguan elections of February 1990 when Violeta Chamorro defeated Daniel Ortega. Arguing that the "issue of representation lies at the heart of neocolonial aggression" (csv 133), they go on to discuss the ways in which the very notion of elections itself frames the narrative not just of what was at stake in the elections but of the nature of the Nicaraguan "people" themselves. They analyze this hegemonic construction as follows:

> What underpins both these representations [of Ortega and Chamorro by the mainstream U.S. press] is the constructed and assumed notion of "the people" who can then "speak" through either Ortega or Chamorro. Indeed, the discursive web spun by the right denies the possibility of the subaltern position: "the people" are represented as always knowing their own interests and being able to speak them. The question of a gap between "the people's" desires and their interests never arises. The point here is not to deny the existence of "the people" as a collection of individuals who talk and act (that is, not to deny people their lived existence), but to see that these individuals receive their identities only within historically determinate systems of social, political, and economic representation. Not only are these systems non-congruent, they also necessarily abstract from the hybrid multiplicity of "the people's" lived existence. The discourses of the right refuse to recognize the possibility of an incongruence between lived existence and representational identity. We can uncover the traces of this refusal in both the representations of Ortega and Chamorro, as well as in the notion of "the people" that underwrites those representations. (ibid., 141)

This, of course, is the parallel situation to Marx's analysis of the peasants in *The Eighteenth Brumaire*. The authors, going beyond Spivak's political paralysis, argue not simply for a deconstructive reading of hegemonic narratives but the construction of alternative narratives: "Unless it disrupts the right's construction of the subaltern, the left will be forced to concede that in the referendum on anti-imperialist struggle [Ortega] versus day-to-day welfare [Chamorro], the latter are the democratic issues" (147). In relating this intervention to Spivak's vertreten-darstellen distinction, the authors remark that it is the Left's task "to disrupt the process of portraiture whereby the subaltern was represented" by the Right. In the struggle for hegemony, the choice of a figure of political representation (Vorstellung) depends on the success of a given staging of the figuring process of representation (Darstellung).

Spivak's turn from the epistemological aporia (of the question) to the speculative positioning (of sentences in dispute—the differend) appears to be her final, strategic response to the inevitably sublime nature of the notion of the subaltern. But in her closing remarks, when she returns to the definition of the subaltern as "sheer heterogeneity," Spivak returns to the moment of logical aporia and undoes the progress of her turn to the differend and, by extension, the process of hegemony. It is the term "subaltern" itself that ultimately makes the task of engaging in the contest of globalized hegemony impossible. The whole apparatus of the darstellen-vertreten distinction is ultimately useless when the definition of subaltern makes both Darstellung and Vertretung theoretically impossible. As such, then, Spivak's argument falls in line with Foucault and Deleuze's, but for the opposite reason.

This is where the Vorstellung-Darstellung distinction makes itself felt. The Darstellung of Spivak's essay is in fact a Vorstellung, an image, a picture. In her move to the differend, on the other hand, she engages in the process of Darstellung as staging—more specifically, stagings-in-dispute. As we learned from Hegel, however, representation must move beyond the level of the mere image or Vorstellung (the night in which all cows are black) to the staging of the system of representation itself as Darstellung. To echo Spivak, it is not as though the two are not related; just the opposite, Darstellung (the staging of system) depends on the privileging of a given Vorstellung (the privileged signifier excluded from the circuit of signification) that embodies the radical negativity of the system as such.[22] The relationship to be deconstructed is not two-way but three-way: we must examine the intricate complicities between the representative image or portrait, the system of representation in which that image circulates, and the choice of representative who will embody the negativity at the heart of that system. This is Marx's point when he talks of the power of the sublime name of Bonaparte as it is manipulated by Louis: "Driven on by the contradictory demands of his situation, Bonaparte, like a conjurer, has to keep the eyes of the public fixed on himself, as Napoleon's substitute, by means of constant surprises, that is to say by performing a coup d'état in miniature every day" (EB 248). What else is the process of hegemony but this process of a coup d'état in miniature every day?

The Subaltern of Spivak's system (with a capital S to mark its sublime transformation from the figure that indicates the impossibility of representation to the Idea as the representation of Impossibility as such) is nothing other than the space of radical negativity at the heart of the global order. As such, the position of the subaltern is always impossible, always empty by definition. That is, once a particular person enters into this space, he or she is already alien to it, already co-opting its radical Alterity by staining it with some excessive corporeality. Nobody can inhabit the sublime space of the subaltern; more specifically, no Body can embody the subaltern. The Spivakian Subaltern is thus coterminous with the subjectivity of Jacobin democratic revolution and, therefore, just as impossible. The Spivakian Subaltern, then, is not only *not* opposed to globalization but functions as its very subjective core.

ANTAGONISM AND ITS SYMPTOM: LACLAU AND MOUFFE PLUS ŽIŽEK

The key concept behind Laclau and Mouffe's theory of hegemony is articulation. They define articulation as a practice that "consists in the construction of nodal points which partially fix meaning; and the partial character of this fixation proceeds from the openness of the social, a result, in its turn, of the constant overflowing of every discourse by the infinitude of the field of discursivity" (HSS 113). What this means is that articulation consists of taking hold of empty, ambiguous, "floating" signifiers—such as freedom, democracy, the people—and weaving them into a particular ideological context (suturing them into a political discourse). The significance of any of these terms depends on the work they have to do in a given discourse; and the work that a given concept does in one context can be completely opposite that which it does in another context. A good example would be the use of the word "democracy" during the U.S.-Nicaragua confrontations of the 1980s. Both Reagan and Ortega could at the same time claim to be fighting for democracy while supporting mutually exclusive political campaigns. What this means, of course, is that these floating signifiers have no essential meaning of their own. It would be futile to argue that Reagan's democracy or Stalin's communism or Clinton's humanitarianism are not true to their concepts, since the truth of these concepts lies only in their use. As we will see in my discussion of Chicano politics, the same is true for the concepts "Chicano," "American," and "citizen." Each of these terms gains its proper identity through the particular ways in which it is articulated toward particular ideological ends.

It is important to keep in mind that articulation is more than simply weaving a concept into an ideological matrix; it is the construction of an ideological nodal point by way of that concept that itself brings the ideological discourse into being. The empty concept (precisely because of its emptiness) stands in as the master signifier for a host of other ideological signifiers, bestowing on each signifier its differential identity. A given discursive object might exhibit the same empirical qualities as it passes from one discourse into another, but it is the new name that confers on these qualities their newly baptized nuance. For instance, "Mexican-American," "Wetback," and "Chicano" might refer to a more or less continuously recognizable set of qualities, but it is the name that does the ideological work, that constitutes the foundation of identity and articulates those qualities into a given ideological discourse.

One crucial distinction here is that between elements and moments: a signifier that is unattached to a particular discourse is referred to as an "element"; the element is a free-floating signifier. Once the signifier is articulated into a discursive totality, it is then referred to as a "moment." Two different logics are operating here: elements operate according to the logic of equivalence, whereas moments operate according to the logic of difference. As in Saussurean linguistics, the relationship between moments in a discourse is differential—each moment functions in its particularity insofar as it differs from all the other moments in the discourse. In the process of hegemony, however, these elements can be wrenched from their differential function and aligned to other elements as equivalents. That is, in revolutionary moments a given moment is broken from its differential function and symbolically conflated with other elements, each one of which symbolically represents opposition to the hegemonic power. In racial politics, for instance, members of different oppressed racial groups might each function as the oppositional term to white hegemony, just as the various European ethnic groups will all be reduced to "white" in opposition to "colored." In the same way, the term "Chicano" tends to reduce the heterogeneous makeup of Americans of Mexican descent in opposition to the Anglo (a term that in extreme contexts, such as New Mexico, includes African Americans, although the term "Hispano" more often replaces "Chicano").

Another way of viewing this, as we saw in the last chapter, is in light of the metaphor/metonymy distinction: like metaphor, equivalence works as a point of condensation where the differences between moments are dissolved to the point that the social breaks down into two opposing camps; the identities of these two camps are established through a relation of negativity, the one defined simply as the negation of the other, as with colonizer versus colonized, black versus white, or male versus female.[23] Like metonymy, on the other hand, difference works as contiguity and displacement, and a moment's identity derives from its differential position in a given field. Yet neither logic is ever complete unto itself, for then there could be no floating elements, and thus no space for articulation, rupture, and change. What becomes crucial here is to recognize the proliferation of nonarticulated spaces, interstitial spaces of no-man's-land at the limits of the established fields. These sites provide the potential for local struggles as nodal points of articulation that can subvert the established fields at their margins.

This articulatory practice is possible, Laclau and Mouffe assert above, because of the "openness of the social." "Society" is impossible, they claim. That is, the discourse ("the structured totality resulting from an articulatory practice" [HSS 105]) articulating any given conception of "society" is never completely closed; if it were, politics would be impossible. But a given ideological totality never exists in isolation, and the signifiers that it sutures into itself are never totally pinned down to one given meaning. This is because the boundaries of a given discourse are fluid and open to the polysemous overflow of signification of particular elements that are not tied to a single discourse but float around in a field of discursivity, a "no-man's land" (ibid., 111) in which elements are never entirely transformed into moments. It is within this field, marked by the overdetermined character of any identity, that articulation is possible. Laclau and Mouffe write that overdetermination is "constituted in the field of the symbolic, and has no meaning whatsoever outside it" (97). All identity, then, is symbolic, and every identity is "overdetermined inasmuch as all literality appears as constitutively subverted and exceeded; far from there being an essentialist *totalization*, or a no less essentialist *separation* among objects, the presence of some objects in the others prevents any of their identities from being fixed" (104). But the hegemonic function of each discourse is precisely to *fix* identity after subverting its function within a competing discourse.

Laclau and Mouffe, in summarizing these points, comment:

> We now have all the necessary analytical elements to specify the concept of articulation. Since all identity is relational—even if the system of relations does not reach the point of being fixed as a stable system of differences— since, too, all discourse is subverted by a field of discursivity which overflows it, the transition from "elements" to "moments" can never be complete. The status of the "elements" is that of floating signifiers, incapable of being wholly articulated to a discursive chain. And this floating character finally penetrates every discursive (i.e. social) identity. But if we accept the non-complete character of all discursive fixation and, at the same time, affirm the relational character of every identity, the ambiguous character of the sig-nifier, its non-fixation to any signified, can only exist insofar as there is a proliferation of signifieds. It is not the poverty of signifieds but, on the contrary, polysemy that disarticulates a discursive structure. That is what establishes the overdetermined, symbolic dimension of every social identity. Society never manages to be identical to itself, as every nodal point is con-stituted within an intertextuality that overflows it. (113)

This all points to the role of antagonism in the process of hegemony. The overflow of signification mentioned above keeps the social from ever achieving complete disclosure, complete self-identity. "Antagonism, far from being an objective relation," Laclau and Mouffe argue, "is a relation wherein the limits of every objectivity are shown. . . . Antagonism, as a witness of the impossibility of a final suture, is the 'experience' of the limit of the social" (125). This is the experience Jameson points to in his claim that History (as the Real) is beyond representation and that History is what hurts. It is unrepresentable because it is the experience of the failure of representation itself (*PU* 102). This is what Laclau and Mouffe indicate when they write that "every language and every society are constituted as a repression of the consciousness of the impossibility that penetrates them. Antagonism escapes the possibility of being apprehended through language, since language only exists as an attempt to fix that which antagonism subverts" (*HSS* 125). "Society," then, is the ideological illusion of a domesticated discursive order that has repressed its founding antagonism. An-tagonism is thus both the possibility and the impossibility of society in that no social order is possible without the prior irruption of antagonism—the dissolution of the differential logic of the previous social order that made the present social order possible—and yet that very antagonism remains as the source of the perpetual impossibility of the present social order to achieve full identity.

This is precisely what makes politics possible. Antagonistic articulatory practices operate in the margins of discourses—that is, in the field of discursivity and overdetermination—where the heterogeneity of moments within the differential logic of the seemingly-sutured totality break apart from the dominant discourse and are conflated into a homogeneous equivalential bloc that represents the negativity of the social itself as the production of "frontier effects" (ibid., 136). This process of hegemony is at once the deconstruction of the dominant discourse and the traumatic founding gesture of the Law that must be repressed in the newly articulated discourse and foundation of identity itself.[24]

THE MASTER SIGNIFIER AND THE SYMPTOM

Žižek's project can be seen as a Lacanian translation and augmentation of Laclau and Mouffe's conception of hegemony.[25] In fact, Žižek often uses the language of suture, articulation, and hegemony that we find in the latter theorists. They themselves were influenced, of course, by the Lacanian twist of the post-Althusserian theory of the *Screen* group, for whom "suture" became a key motif in theorizing the interpellative mechanisms of film.[26] For Žižek, the notion of suture becomes key for translating the Lacanian theory of subjectivization into the terms of Marxist ideological critique. Ideological suture functions by way of what Lacan referred to as the *point de capiton* or quilting point— what Laclau and Mouffe call a nodal point. That is, a given ideology is inflected by a master signifier, the signifier that provides the point of unity and consistency to a given symbolic order as a whole. This signifier, abstracted from the play of difference of the symbolic, is emptied of its particular content and functions as the stand-in for the universal. "The universal emerges out of the particular," Laclau remarks in *Emancipation(s)*, "not as some principle underlying and explaining the particular, but as an incomplete horizon suturing a dislocated identity."[27] One crucial moment of ideology critique, then, is the identification of the particular that functions as the universal, the master signifier that "quilts" the discursive order into a consistent system.

One point of difference between Žižek and Laclau and Mouffe concerns exactly this relationship between the particular and the universal. Žižek accepts the notion that the universal is nothing but a particular signifier, emptied of its signified, occupying (like Hegel's monarch) the empty place of the universal. This is exactly the point behind Lacan's notion of the master signifier or Marx's general equivalent. Where Žižek differs is that, as with Lacan, he sees this relationship as involving a third, repressed term: the symptom. The symptom is the truth of the master signifier—that is, the particular that subverts its own universal principle. As Žižek writes

> The gap between the empty signifier and the multitude of particular contents which, in the fight for hegemony, endeavor to function as the representatives of this absent fullness, is thus reflected within the Particular itself, in the guise of the gap that separates the particular hegemonic content of an ideological universality from the symptom that undermines it (say, the bourgeois notion of "just and equivalent exchange" from the exchange between capital and workforce as the particular exchange that involves exploitation precisely in so far as it is "just" and "equivalent"). We should therefore consider three, not just two, levels: the empty *Universal* ("justice"), the *particular* content which hegemonizes the empty universal ("just and equivalent exchange"), and the *individual*, the symptomatic excess which undermines this hegemonic content (exchange between capital and workforce). One can see immediately in what sense the individual is the dialectical unity of Universal and Particular: the individual (symptomatic excess) bears witness to the gap between the Universal and the Particular: to the fact that the Universal is always "false" in its concrete existence (hegemonized by some particular content which involves a series of exclusions). (*TS* 180–81)

Žižek's point is that the master signifier and its symptom are two sides of the same Universal: the Universal itself is always already split, always internally antagonistic. Here is the Hegelian "proof" of Laclau and Mouffe's anti-Hegelian theory of hegemony—the very principle that functions as the point of unity for the antagonistic social symbolic order is perfectly appropriate in that its entire existence is due to the constitutive nature of antagonism as such. The One (the Universal) is at its core already two, not just because a particular functions as the Universal but rather because it is fundamentally split between its master signifier (which guarantees the consistency of the social order) and its symptom (which perpetually embodies that social order's internal antagonism). Every symbolic system, then, depends on two exclusions: the exclusion from the differential circuit of subjectivization of one particular that stands in as the empty subjectivizing Universal, and the exclusion to the periphery of that particular that functions as the embodiment of internal negativity—the symptom. But what exactly is the symptom?

The symptom (or more appropriately in its Lacanian terms, the *sinthome*) as Žižek uses it is different from the colloquial conception of symptom (the sign of some underlying reality). One example would be undocumented workers, who function as the symptom of American nationalist economy in that they appear as a foreign parasite on the national body. This conception of the symptom is quite different from the everyday sense of symptom that sees it as a sign of an underlying cause—a fever, for example, being the symptom of an underlying illness. First of all, in terms of racist Anglo-American ideology (the parasite model) the undocumented worker is not the symptom but the cause—it is that which is at the root of our social malaise. The symptom would be, say, high unemployment or urban poverty, and the cause would be the immigrant-scapegoat. Žižek inverts this model by showing that the particular element that we single out as the cause of our woes is in actuality the symptom—symptom in the sense that the particular element (the scapegoat) embodies (gives body to) the antagonistic split of economic culture. To put this in Hegelian language, the symptom is the speculative truth of the national notion; that is, the truth of society is embodied by its immanent negation.

In *The Sublime Object of Ideology*, Žižek writes about this, using the example of anti-Semitic ideology: for Fascism the Jew functions as "the element which represents within it its own impossibility. Society is not prevented from achieving its full identity because of Jews: it is prevented by its own antagonistic nature, by its own immanent blockage, and it 'projects' this internal negativity into the figure of the 'Jew.' In other words, what is excluded from the Symbolic (from the frame of the corporatist socio-symbolic order) returns in the Real as a paranoid construction of the 'Jew' " (*SOI* 127). In Laclau and Mouffe's terms, because the antagonism lies at the heart of the social (as its impossible ground of existence), Society (a coherent, nonantagonistic social body) does not exist. The symptom is the excluded element that embodies this inherent antagonism.

The key progression from this point is to recognize that the symptom itself is what gives the social body its sense of consistency:

> What we must bear in mind here is the radical ontological status of symptom: symptom, conceived as sinthome, is literally our only substance, the only positive support of our being, the only point that gives consistency to

the subject. In other words, symptom is the way we—the subjects—"avoid madness," the way we "choose something (the symptom-formation) instead of nothing (radical psychotic autism, the destruction of the symbolic universe)" through the binding of our enjoyment to a certain signifying, symbolic formation which assures a minimum of consistency to our being-in-the-world. (ibid., 75)

In other words, without the undocumented workers, "America" (the conception of the whole, intact socioeconomic body minus its immigrant-parasite) would cease to exist.

THE POLITICS OF THE UNIVERSAL

This question of the relationship between the particular and the Universal lies at the heart of the question of politics. The foregrounding of the particular at the expense of the Universal lies at the base of rightist politics (which is ultimately the target of the postmodern critique of essentialism). The foregrounding of the empty Universal, on the other hand, lies at the base of the Enlightenment liberal tradition. Where, then, does a properly leftist position find its base? To return to Spivak's example, the problem with Foucault and Deleuze was the ironic reversal of their privileging of the vast multitude of particulars—letting the various oppressed groups speak for themselves—in that the subjective position behind such a gesture was the unavowed empty Universalism of Eurocentric Enlightenment liberalism from whose perspective all the heterogeneous particular demands could be leveled out into an apparently benign neutral space. The constitutive antagonism at the heart of both the particular and the Universal remained hidden from view, externalized into the hypostatized conception of Power or Desire. Such an empty "Universal" position was at one with the empty subject position of global capitalism. As I suggested above, however, Spivak's own position remains caught in the aporetic space of abstract antagonism, the position from which all political gestures will be doomed in advance as falling back into the trap of essentialism since no particular can legitimately represent itself as the Universal point of enunciation. To put this in Laclau and Mouffe's terms, Spivak refuses to consider a logic outside that of difference because for her, any gesture toward a logic of equivalence—whereby the social will be split into two antagonistic camps—will simply reduce the sheer heterogeneity of différance into one more binary opposition.

Such a reduction is nevertheless exactly what is required according to the theory of hegemony in order for "politics proper" (Žižek) to take place.

This problem is also what limits Spivak's conception of politics as the interplay of Vertretung and Darstellung. Ultimately, no politics is possible because no particular representation or Darstellung can stand in as the appropriate universalized representative or Vertretung that would speak for the people, the proletariat, the subaltern, and so on. What is missing, as I have already suggested, is the Hegelian moment whereby—as Žižek put it above—the particular and Universal find their truth in the individual. This, for Hegel, was what characterizes the dialectical move from Vorstellung (what Spivak speaks of as Darstellung) to Darstellung as the movement of the antagonistic split of the Universal into its empty signifier and excluded symptom. A properly politicized Vertretung, then, bases itself neither on the empty signifier nor some positive particular but rather the symptom, the particular that is none, the particular that functions not in the name of its own particular "essence" but as the embodiment of antagonism as such. In this way, the reduction of différance to equivalence is just the opposite of so-called essentialism.

The issue of the relationship between globalization and multiculturalism can clarify this strategic difference. Interestingly, both Spivak and Žižek denounce Western academic liberal multiculturalism for its complicity with global capitalist hegemony, just as both insist on a Marxist reading of global cultural politics. One should insist, Žižek emphasizes, "that the socioeconomic logic of Capital provides the global framework which (over)determines the totality of cultural processes" (*τ*s 243 n. 46). Žižek's starting point is the distinction between globalization and universalization:

> Globalization (not only in the sense of global capitalism, the establishment of a global world market, but also in the sense of the assertion of "humanity" as the global point of reference for human rights, legitimizing the violation of State sovereignty, from trade restrictions to direct military interventions, in parts of the world where global human rights are violated) is precisely the name for the emerging post-political logic which progressively precludes the dimension of universality that appears in politicization proper. (ibid., 201)

Universalization, on the other hand, involves not some positing of "neutral," pluralistic space within which each different particular is accorded its unique and benign identity but rather the identification with the symptom, "of *identifying universality with the point of exclusion*" (224). The problem with liberal multiculturalism, from Žižek's point of view, is the lack of just such an identification operating within a logic of equivalence. In the face of the increasing cultural homogenization brought about by global capitalism, the multiculturalist—conferring upon the multiple cultural groups their differential identities—functions as the other face of the fundamentalist who accepts his or her own particularity at the expense of all others.[28] Multicultural openness and xenophobia, in other words, are two sides of the same coin, both made possible by the evacuation of particular content resulting from Capital itself as each group is rendered equally exploitable. This cultural logic of late capitalism (as Jameson has put it) is the overdetermined result of the transformation of imperialism based on the nation-state into imperialism marked by an "auto-colonization" (TS 215) by means of which the multinational corporation treats its "mother country" as just one more colony to exploit. Žižek continues:

> The ideal form of ideology of this global capitalism is multiculturalism, the attitude which, from a kind of empty global position, treats *each* local culture as the colonizer treats colonized people—as "natives" whose *mores* are to be carefully studied and "respected." That is to say: the relationship between traditional imperialist colonialism and global capitalist self-colonization is exactly the same as the relationship between Western cultural imperialism and multiculturalism—just as global capitalism involves the paradox of colonization without the colonizing nation-state metropolis, multiculturalism involves a patronizing Eurocentrist distance and/or respect for local cultures without roots in one's own particular culture. (ibid., 216)

Žižek's answer to this deadlock of multicultural liberalism, as we have seen, is to identify with the symptom. But what exactly does this mean?

IDENTIFICATION WITH THE SYMPTOM

Žižek claims that the "leftist political gesture par excellence" is "identifying with the symptom" (224). If the symptom is "the part which, although inherent to the existing universal order, has no 'proper place' within it (say, illegal immigrants or the homeless in our societies)," then this means that leftists must identify with these excessive, "improper," excluded particulars. "Identification with" functions as the positing of subjective identity with the symptom, the propositional form of which would be "I am the symptom." More concretely, this identity takes the form of slogans such as "We are all citizens of Sarajevo" or

"We are all undocumented workers." Yet the consequences of this identification are hardly given in advance; or as Žižek puts it, "The authenticity of the pathetic identification lies in its sociopolitical efficiency" (230).[29] At issue are two different modes of identification: metaphoric and speculative. Metaphoric identification posits a relationship of equivalence, an equation of A = B according to which both A and B share equivalent conditions of existence. While metaphoric identification has the benefit of causing A (the privileged subject) to imagine the conditions of oppression that B (the oppressed subject) suffers, this same identification can nevertheless function as yet one more form of appropriation—A can comfortably take on the prestige of B's suffering without actually having to suffer the oppressive conditions that B experiences. In this way, identification with the symptom can "induce a hasty claim that our own predicament is in fact the same as that of the true victims" (TS 229). There is "something fundamentally faked," for example, "in the pathetic statement of a radical upper-middle-class student that 'the Berkeley campus is also a gigantic *Gulag*'" (ibid.). Spivak, in her essay "Poststructuralism, Marginality, Postcoloniality, and Value," warns of this danger when she argues that claims such as "We are all postcolonials" can produce a "new orientalism" that through a catachresis (the false metaphoric universalization of the excluded that Žižek points to), views the world as immigrant (PMPV 207). "The radicals of the industrial nations," Spivak writes, "want to *be* the Third World" (ibid., 201).

The answer to this catachrestic or "false" metaphoric identification is not the positing of some true, positive, nonmetaphoric identification but instead the recognition that the identity posited in "We are the symptom" must be a negative, speculative one. In other words, the statement of identification must function as a Hegelian speculative proposition—a proposition, that is, according to which the subject ("We") is nothing but the empty point of universality that must be filled out by some particular content ("the symptom"). The key to seeing this as a speculative proposition is the understanding that the predicate is the negation of the subject, that our true universal identity is embodied in a particular excluded element, "a universal which comes to exist," Žižek argues, " . . . only in a particular element which is structurally displaced" (TS 224). What we identify with, then, is this point of exclusion as the rock of our very being, as that which fleshes out the negativity at the heart of our existence. Such is the Hegelian basis for the psychoanalytic conception of identification with the symptom that Žižek calls for here. Without the symptom we lose our symbolic consistency: "If the symptom in this radical dimension is unbound, it means literally 'the end of the world'—the only alternative to the symptom is nothing: pure autism, a psychic suicide, surrender to the death drive even to the total destruction of the symbolic universe. That is why the final Lacanian definition of the end of the psychoanalytic process is identification with the symptom. The analysis achieves its end when the patient is able to recognize, in the Real of his symptom, the only support of his being" (SOI 75). It is in this speculative light that one must read Žižek's following claim: "This procedure of identifying with the symptom is the exact and necessary obverse of the standard critical and ideological move of recognizing a particular content behind some abstract universal notion ('the "man" of human rights is effectively the white male owner . . . '): one pathetically asserts (and identifies with) *the point of inherent exception/exclusion, the 'abject,' of the concrete positive order, as the only point of true universality*, as the point which belies the existing concrete universality" (TS 224).

The question Žižek neglected to ask in his earlier version of this argument is from whose perspective is the symptom the symptom? Who exactly is it who is to identify with the symptom? Here is a twist in the logic operating in Foucault and Deleuze's transparent subject-position as they make a space for the other to speak. Žižek, certainly, is careful not to assume the transparency of his own "properly leftist" position in relation to the symptom; if anything, the subject position he identifies with (the identifying subject itself) is all too visible in that the subject position of the symptom itself with which he would have us (which "us"?) identify remains unthought. What is involved, in other words, from the point of view of the symptom? How does the symptom identify with the symptom? This is perhaps the limit of the Lacanian (and Hegelian) apparatus as a model for conceiving of global relations.[30] The problem with Lacan's model is that it only allows us to think one system or symbolic order at a time. Hegel's master-slave dialectic, for example, provides a model for thinking the effectivity of the other, but only in terms of a given symbolic order—which for Hegel, of course, is the order of the Western spirit as it moves beyond other historically "defunct" cultures. And for all of Lacan's obsessions with the other—both Big and petit—his others remain the others of the system itself. Here is where Spivak's model at least allows us to imagine an Alterity external to the ideological order of the West, even though in her system that other must remain perpetually out of reach, radically untouchable.

The point here is not to reintroduce some benign notion of pluralism—all these happy coexisting symbolic orders safely existing in their exteriority to each other—but rather to suggest that the metasystem that may or may not be at work in capitalist globalization, while driven by a given ideological order, cannot be reduced to that order. Here is where Jameson's notion of a cultural dominant can be usefully adapted, allowing us to think of a global dominant that increasingly colonizes the heterogeneous pockets of Alterity around the globe, yet cannot be thought of as a closed, sutured, differential system. This "cannot," however, should not be seen as a moral imperative—"It's not nice to totalize!"—but rather as a limit to logic, a frontier effect not only internal but also external to the system. In other words, I am not offering another version of Althusser's notion of a structure and its other but of an other outside that system—another system.

My distinction between *the* other and *an*-other can also be seen in Enrique Dussel's distinction between *lo otro* and *el otro*. Walter Mignolo, drawing on and modifying Dussel's work, explains the difference between the two otros as follows:

> In 1971 Dussel, starting and departing from Lévinas, conceived totality as composed by "the same" and "the other." Describing the totality formed by "the same" and "the other," Dussel called it "the Same." And we'll see soon why. Outside totality was the domain of "the other." The difference in Spanish was rendered between *lo otro*, which is the complementary class of "the same," and *el otro* relegated to the domain exterior to the system. I am tempted to translate this view today as "interior" and "exterior" subalternities. Socially and ontologically, the exteriority is the domain of the homeless, unemployed, illegal aliens cast out from education, from the economy, and the laws that regulate the system. Metaphysically, "the other" is—from the perspective of the totality and the "same"—the unthinkable that Dussel urges us to think.[31]

Lo otro, then, is the dialectical other operating in terms of the symbolic other while el otro is the exterior other. With the eclipse of the Iberian world order (characterized by its trans-Atlantic network of power) by the construction of the hegemonic modern world system led by northern Europe, and, eventually, the U.S. and the Soviet Union, Latin America was transformed from lo otro to el otro, becoming the unthinkable Other for the Same.[32] Mignolo's point, which he earlier developed in *The Darker Side of the Renaissance*, is that the Other has to be conceived of as "speaking" from an alternative locus of enunciation.[33]

Laclau and Mouffe introduce a helpful concept—the hegemonic formation:

> The hegemonic formation, as we have conceived it, cannot be referred to the specific logic of a single force. Every historical bloc—or hegemonic formation—is constructed through regularity in dispersion, and this dispersion includes a proliferation of very diverse elements: systems of differences which partially define relational identities; chains of equivalences which subvert the latter but which can be transformistically recovered insofar as the place of opposition itself becomes regular and, in that way, constitutes a new difference; forms of overdetermination which concentrate either power, or the different forms of resistance to it; and so forth. (HSS 142)

As with Nicos Poulantzas's concept of social formation as an advance on the Althusserian insistence on structure, the concept of the hegemonic formation allows us to conceptualize the relationship between alterior systems.

Žižek makes a start at addressing this problem in his newer version of the argument appearing in *The Ticklish Subject*:

> The further distinction to be made here is between the two opposed subjects of enunciation of the statement that asserts the *universel singulier*: is this statement the direct statement of *the excluded victim itself* (of *demos* in old Athens; of the *troisième état* in the French Revolution; of Jews, Palestinians, Blacks, women, gays . . . today), which proposes its particular plight as representative of the universality of "humanity," or is it the statement of solidarity made by *others*, the concerned "enlightened public"? How do these two modes of functioning relate to one another? (TS 230–31)

The problem is that Žižek never develops this question of the relationship between these "two modes of functioning" except by introducing yet another Marxist-Hegelian take on the form of the question itself: "The difference in question is the difference between the universal Public claiming: 'We are all them (the excluded non-part)?' and the excluded non-part claiming: 'We are the true Universal (the People, Society, Nation . . . !)'—this reversal, although apparently purely symmetrical, never produces direct symmetrical effects. . . . [T]he symmetrical reversal . . . produces an asymmetrical result" (ibid., 231). After this point Žižek is off on a discussion of Marx's theory of fetishism and Hegel's musing on the symmetrical reversal of Self and Substance. My point is not that this view of the asymmetrical transformation of loci of enunciation is unimportant—it is crucial, as my chapter on Hegel's speculative proposition should make clear—but that Žižek ends up totally evading the issues involved in the claim that " 'We (the nation) are all immigrant workers' is not the same as 'We (immigrant workers) are the true nation' " (232)—a claim that is radically different from Homi Bhabha's statement that "the paranoid threat from the hybrid is finally uncontainable because it breaks down the symmetry and duality of self/other, inside/outside."[34] One way to address these issues is to explore this question of another locus of enunciation, the locus of the symptom itself. The specific locus I have in mind is that of the Mexican, a species of "American" who, in relation to the idea of the nation, functions simultaneously as lo otro and el otro.

THE MEXICAN AS SYMPTOM OF THE NATION

Let's look now at the logic involved in the claim that the Mexican is the symptom of the nation. It is important to note up front that the analysis of the symptom does not operate under the assumption that the symptom is the cryptic, encoded cypher for some more authentic underlying social reality. If this were the case, then the job of the cultural analyst would be to interpret that symptom back into its "original" social terms, to recognize the contradictions that gave birth to this symptom, and then to focus on the potential cure for that contradiction itself. But to put this in Hegelian terms, quite the opposite is true: the symptom is the truth of that reality itself. It is not society's truth in the sense of having somehow sublated and synthesized elements of the contradictions threatening the stability of that society but rather that that social reality depends on the symptom for its own consistency and effectivity. Without the symptom, there would be no reality. This is so because the symptom exists as the founding exclusion whose function is to cover over the inherent impossibility of that society. In other words, a given society is impossible in the sense that it is split from the start by an internal contradiction; it is only with the exclusion of one of its defining elements or species that it can operate under the necessary misunderstanding that it is in fact a consistent and universal totality. Once this symptom has been recognized as the true ground of that society, that symptom dissolves—and yet so does the society that depended on its exclusion. As we saw above, the job of the leftist cultural critic, then, is not to interpret the symptom but to identify with it: to recognize that the properties attributed to the symptom are in fact the defining properties of that society itself—properties that must be externalized if that society is to maintain its consistency.

The figure of the Mexican functions in exactly this way in American culture. The problem with the concept of the American Nation is that the consistency of such a construct is constantly threatened by its own heterogeneity. The only way to pose that national identity as truly universal—as truly open to and representative of all its citizens, despite the particularities of their existence (such as class, ethnicity, gender, and so forth)—is to displace this radical and incommensurable heterogeneity, to locate it outside the system, excluded as an extraneous and threatening excess that hinders the operation of that universality. This process, whereby the Mexican has to be identified as a foreign body within the body of the Nation, can be seen as early as the 1840s when, in the name of Manifest Destiny, the Anglo-American Nation came up against a force that contradicted its claim to universality: Mexico. While Anglo-American national ideology had long been operating under various logics of exclusion in order to make sense of the indigenous peoples and African slaves, it now confronted a new problem in its annexation of the Southwest under the Treaty of Guadalupe Hidalgo in 1848, that problem being the preexistence of a people—part European, part indigenous, part African—who now under the terms of the Treaty were to be considered as U.S. citizens. The answer was instead to consider *them* as foreigners, as immigrants in the land where they had lived and carried out their own imperialist conquest and subjugation long before the Anglo-American's arrival. The construction of national identity thus demanded as its founding gesture in the Southwest the invasion and conquest of a foreign land and culture that, in too uncanny a way, resembled the suppressed nature of the new invaders. In a necessary reversal, then, the Mexican-American had to be identified as the foreigner, the invader, the threat to cultural and linguistic identity and integrity. Especially because of their hybrid ethnicity, culture, and language, the "Mexicans" functioned as the symptom of the Nation's own internal heterogeneity and hybridity—the Southwest, in other words, functioned as a third entity that could unite antebellum North and South as a single national notion.

As I use it here, the term "Chicano"—an inherently politicized term in any context—functions as a self-inscribed oppositional marker for the symbolic or discursive indeterminateness and internal contradiction that lies at the base of the ideological construction of American national identity.[35] "Chicano," then, is the obverse of "Illegal Alien," the signifier through which Anglo-American ideology reduces the particularity and heterogeneity of Mexican-American citizens to the status of illegal immigrant.[36] The "Illegal Alien," in other words, points to that element of American society that has to be excluded in order for American national identity to function. It does not refer, then, to the supposedly empirical existence of U.S. citizens of Mexican descent but rather to a construct necessary for the maintenance of the ideology of the American Nation-State itself.[37] The Chicano is thus the marker for the hegemonic inversion of the symptom of American nationalism, the embodiment of the inherent impossibility of national identity whereby the alienated other speaks back to the nation. My argument is that this particular performative function of the Chicano is what makes the politics of Chicano cultural politics possible in the first place.[38] If the Chicano were fully incorporated into the American Nation-State, both the Chicano-construct as such and the current Anglo-centric notion of "America" would cease to exist. The effectiveness of any current politics of Chicanismo depends, in other words, on the already existing racist construct of the Mexican in the American imaginary. The Mexican-Chicano dyad thus functions as the embodiment of this dialectical tension in all of its enabling and destabilizing effects.[39]

One of the poets most often associated with the question of the politics of *mestizaje* or cultural hybridity, of course, is Gloria Anzaldúa. And one of the most famous passages from her book, *Borderlands/La Frontera: The New Mestiza*, cited in part above, reads:

> The U.S.-Mexican border *es una herida abierta* where the Third World grates against the first and bleeds. And before a scab forms it hemorrhages again, the lifeblood of two worlds merging to form a third country—a border culture. . . . A border is a dividing line, a narrow strip along a steep edge. A borderland is a vague and undetermined place created by the emotional residue of an unnatural boundary. It is in a constant state of transition.[40]

The political charge of the figure of the borderland, then, in its distinction from the figure of the border, is that the borderline of demarcation—which is to separate the space of the American Nation from its defining excluded object—now functions as an amorphous and unstable third entity that threatens the neat, defining limit of the Nation. American identity is here confronted with its dissolution, its miscegenation, its loss of purity. A new Thing threatens the Nation on two counts: this Thing invades the Nation-space at the same time that it joins that space to the foreign space of Mexico; both Nations are wounded and bleed into one another. This third Thing, and not the original border, is the true defining feature of American national identity, for this amorphous, oozing mass gives body to the instability of national identity itself. It is this stain, marking both the inside and the outside of the national body, that is the truth of the Nation in its inherent impossibility. From the beginning, the National-Substance is already internally split and incommensurate with itself. This incommensurability *is* its identity.[41]

AZTLÁN AND A COUNTER-NATIONALIST POETICS: RODOLFO "CORKY" GONZALES AND ALURISTA

One response to this exclusionary gesture that founds American identity is to oppose to it an alternative national construct. This was, in fact, the motivation behind the early poet-activists of the Chicano movement of the late 1960s. Early in 1967, Rodolfo "Corky" Gonzales published his epic poem *I Am Joaquín*. By March, the poem had already been adapted for film by the traveling activist troupe Teatro Campesino. The poem was mimeographed and widely circulated in order to be read during public demonstrations and organizing campaigns of what would come to be known as *El Movimiento* or the Chicano Movement. Beyond its immediate public activist function, however, *I Am Joaquín* also functioned as the inaugural work of what is now seen as the Chicano Literary Renaissance, lasting from the late 1960s to the mid-1970s.[42] *I Am Joaquín* provided the groundwork, then, for all Chicano poetry to come. Yet what is perhaps more interesting is its role in serving as the founding literary work for all previous Chicano literature. What I am saying is that before 1967 Chicano literature did not exist, but after 1967 the whole history of Chicano literature from the 1600s to the 1960s suddenly, retroactively came into being. Moreover, I contend that prior to 1967 and the publication of *I Am Joaquín*, Chicanos did not exist, and yet after that moment we can see that they had been around for centuries.

I Am Joaquín was able to perform this magic because through this poem the various elements that would make up Chicano identity came together for the first time under the name "Chicano." Prior to this, all of the work for justice, civil rights, farm labor laws, and cultural recognition for Mexican Americans had been carried out by Mexican Americans. But it wasn't until *I Am Joaquín*— which embodied all these elements under the blanket concept of Chicanismo— that these elements could come into concert in the revolutionary subjectivity of the Chicano as the founding gesture of Chicano identity itself. The term "Chicano" as it functions in *I Am Joaquín* brought the Chicano as such into being. This is not to say that the term "Chicano" became an effective label for an already existing entity; it is to say, rather, that the entity itself only came into being with the use of the word in the particular context of the poem.

The term "Chicano," which many scholars suggest derives from a shortened version of the Indian pronunciation of "Mexicanos," was initially used as an insult, signifying a person of lower status and culture.[43] This is in fact the way Mexican Americans were viewed by both Americans and Mexicans. Prior to the late 1960s, even within the Mexican American community the term "Chicano" was reserved for recently arrived immigrants. New arrivals from Mexico—often poor and more visibly "Other" than the more assimilated earlier Mexicans in America—threatened the status of those Mexican Americans who often fought hard to prove their American identity by distancing themselves from their Mexican and Indian roots. Later, however, the term was appropriated by Mexican American activists during the 1960s as a way of transforming an insult into a signifier of ethnic strength and pride and as a refusal to assimilate into mainstream white culture. Now "Chicano" came to serve as a badge of militant identity within and against mainstream Anglo-America.

After 1967, then, the term "Chicano" served a consciously ideological function among young radicals as a designator of oppositional identity. The beauty of the poem *I Am Joaquín* lay in the way Gonzales wove together a wide variety of cultural and historical tropes into one emergent identity. Gonzales recounts the roots of Chicano identity in the long history of Mexican miscegenation through Spanish and Indian contact on up through the U.S. occupation and annexation of northern Mexico. The poem also displays the mytho-cultural icons of Chicano identity growing out of pre-Columbian Amerindian cultures. Then the poem surveys the history of Mexican American oppression, and ends by imagining the future liberation of the Chicanos and their homeland. Through this poem, which was staged (and even filmed) as part of the public presentations of the Chicano civil rights movement, Mexican Americans were transformed into Chicanos.

The poet Alurista also played a key role in constructing a national allegory to compete with that of the "Gringo." In "El Plan Espiritual de Aztlán," the founding manifesto of the Chicano Movement, Alurista, working with Gonzales, writes, "Brotherhood unites us, and love for our brothers makes us a people whose time has come and who struggles against the foreigner 'gabacho' who exploits our riches and destroys our culture. With our heart in our hands and our hands in the soil, we declare the independence of our mestizo nation."[44] "The Spiritual Plan of Aztlán," written in 1969, made explicit the connection between national and cultural politics:

> CULTURAL values of our people strengthen our identity and the moral background of the movement. Our culture unites and educates the family of La Raza towards liberation with one heart and one mind. We must insure that our writers, poets, musicians, and artists produce literature and art that is appealing to our people and relates to our revolutionary culture. Our cultural values of life, family, and home will serve as a powerful weapon to defeat the gringo dollar value system and encourage the process of love and brotherhood.[45]

Chicano poets and artists, in other words, must help in the construction of a united and revolutionary Chicano identity in opposition to the capitalist values of the "foreigner gabachos," the Anglo-Americans who, with the Treaty of Guadalupe Hidalgo of 1848, took possession of almost half of Mexico's territory, the present-day American Southwest. Key to this counternationalist politics and poetics is the image of Aztlán, the original ancestral homeland of the Aztecs (and presumably most of today's Native Americans of the Southwest), an area comprising much of the four-corners states. What the image of Aztlán affords is a claim to territorial priority and a reversal of the logic of American national identity: it is not the Chicano who is a stranger on this land but the Anglo-American. The Chicano can now claim an ancestral heritage in the Southwest dating back over a thousand years.

The key elements characteristic of Alurista's Chicano nationalism are displayed in the poem "A Child to Be Born," which opens with these lines: "a child to be born/pregnant is the continente/el barro y la raza [the clay and the race]/to bear Aztlán on our forehead" (ll. 1–4).[46] This poem about the fusion of people and earth displays that fusion with compound neologisms such as "una madretierraroja" (a redmotherearth) and "el continentetierraroja" (the redearthcontinent). It is the identification with this fusion that marks Alurista's production of Chicano consciousness, imagined as the child of "madrecontinentetierra" (Aztlán as motherearthcontinentearth) and the fatherly gods Quetzalcóatl and Kukulcán (who synthesize the Aztec and Mayan people).

As Alfred Arteaga has pointed out, Alurista "emphasizes the form of the form, that is, he focuses on hybridization itself."[47] And while this hybrid form certainly functions in opposition to the naturalized universality of the Anglo-American conception of National space, it cannot be reduced to this oppositional stand. Alurista's poetics is as positive as it is oppositional. His emphasis on Chicano nationalism signals an attempt to construct a positive and authoritative Chicano identity based on the revival of an Amerindian ethos in which poetry functions as a social and spiritual foundation of communal, ethnic identity. In other words, Alurista's poetics is a form of social and cultural articulation. It should be kept in mind that the "oppressive" sense of hegemony determines the "positive" in that any positive construction of an alternative identity takes place within the field of the dominant force. In this case, any construction of Chicano nationalism takes place within the determining context of the American Nation as defined by Anglo-American ideology.

The hegemonic process that Alurista sets in motion involves the deliberate hybridization of form. For example, in "A Child to Be Born" and much of his other poetry, Alurista develops a counter-syncretism. The Spanish invaders translated the religious beliefs, practices, and iconography into a Christian context, but the result was a hybrid or syncretistic form in which Tonantzin, the sacred mother goddess of the Aztecs, still shows through the Virgin of Guadalupe.[48] Alurista reverses this syncretism by translating Christian motives back into Aztec, Toltec, and Mayan ones. In the poem, Tonantzin appears as "red-motherearth," a critical conceptual as well as linguistic fusion for Alurista since his whole symbology depends on reclaiming a territorial priority denied by the Anglo-American construct of the Nation. This priority gets its force, in part, through the identification of the Chicano Raza with its Amerindian roots in the red-earth ancestors of Mexican and Southwestern American Indians, who presumably resided in Atzlán. The Southwest, as we have seen, is thus the homeland of the indigenous peoples of the countries on both sides of the border, and the Chicanos are the ones who continue to occupy that homeland.

While Alurista has been criticized for constructing a romantic, Utopian figure dependent on a nostalgia for past origins, the title of the poem contradicts that claim.[49] This child's birth is a future event and condition, not a past one. Just as Alurista reverses the syncretism of the Spanish-Amerindian hybrid, he also reverses the time scheme. This hybrid "red" race is a promise of the future—one that depends on the hegemonic struggles of the Chicano people themselves. In this sense, Alurista reverses the temporality of Aztlán as well, now to be seen as a political goal realized through the poeticization of Chicano culture. And Alurista's fusion of Spanish, English, and Amerindian languages—

otherwise known as code-switching—is part of this process.[50] While he works his way in and out of both Spanish and English rather fluidly without designating either language as representative of any particular realm of content, he nevertheless continually refers to the father of this child in either Náhuatl (Quetzalcóatl) or Mayan (Kukulcán) (Kukulcán is the Mayan rendering of Quetzalcóatl);[51] the mother is always referred to in Spanish (continentetierraroja); and the niño is most often in English (the "nationchild" of the book's title). While the substance of its rendering is both spiritual and earthly, the child itself is a political concept—the nation itself. Ironically, then, this new Chicano national space appropriates the dominant Anglo-American language in order to appropriate the discursive space of the Nation.

The substitution of one nationalism for another, of course, does not in itself challenge the political dangers inherent in any nationalism, such as the various forms of racist, ethnic chauvinisms that mark the resurgence in the 1990s of nationalisms in the Balkans. And a counter-nationalism will always be defined, in part, in terms of the nationalism it opposes and, to that extent, depend on the logic and definitions of that former nationalism. Such a Chicano counter-nationalism could, in fact, function as part of a broader conservative populism, as Ignacio M. García has pointed out. This particular form, with its emphasis on preserving the familia and the barrio against the decadent effects of gringo capitalism, "sought to turn back time and to slow down the urbanization of the Chicano family, which [Rodolfo "Corky" Gonzales] saw as leading to broken homes, parents who could not control their children, and rebellious youth who found camaraderie and family in gangs."[52] For Rafael Pérez-Torres, Alurista's nationalism, at least as it is defined in "El Plan Espiritual de Atzlán," suggests "through the 'call of our blood' an essentialized and biologically determined nationalism."[53] It seems curious, nevertheless, that such a hybridized conception of "blood" could be seen as essentialist when from the start it was posed as a consciously constructed cultural and political reaction to the "essentialist" claims of Anglo-American nationalism. The "call of our blood" could never have been anything but a foregrounding of the specious claim to authority of Anglo-American blood when the latter is itself a hybrid and artificial formation. Nothing underscored this nonessentialist nature of Chicano identity more than code-switching, and Alurista was the pioneer in this poetic form. Rightful ownership of Atzlán, Alurista will later claim, "is not established . . . on the basis of lineage, but rather on the basis of 'those who work it.' "[54] At any rate, in this postnationalist age of multinational capitalism, such arguments may now be beside the point. The problem can no longer be one of essentialism since the logic of capital itself has long ago eroded the authority behind such claims.

While Pérez-Torres is critical of the nationalist gesture behind the earlier uses of the concept of Aztlán, he does find a critical use for that trope if it is conceived of not as homeland but as borderland:

> The transformation of "Aztlán" from homeland to borderland signifies an opening within Chicano cultural discourse. It marks a significant transformation away from the dream of origin toward an engagement with the construction of cultural identity. As the U.S.-Mexican border represents a construction tied to histories of power and dispossession, the construction of personal and cultural identity entailed in any multicultural project comes to the fore in Chicano cultural production. The move represents at this point a liberating one that allows for the assumption of various subject positions. The refusal to be delimited, while simultaneously claiming numerous heritages and influences, allows for a rearticulation of the relationship between self and society, self and history, self and land. The geographic Aztlán as a site of origins and nation has been rejected. But Aztlán as a realm of historical convergence and discontinuous positionalities becomes another configuration embraced and employed in the borderlands that is Chicano culture.[55]

The degree to which these discontinuous positionalities are the result of a conscious and politically determined "refusal to be delimited" is up for questioning. It could be argued that borderlands culture is delimited by Anglo culture *precisely as discontinuous*. The borderlands by definition are the space of externalized discontinuity necessary for the internal continuity of the Anglo-American Nation. Žižek remarks that

> a nation exists only as long as its specific enjoyment continues to be materialized in a set of material practices and transmitted through national myths that structure these practices. To emphasize in a "deconstructionist" mode that Nation is not a biological or transhistorical fact but a contingent discursive construction, an overdetermined result of textual practices, is thus misleading: such an emphasis overlooks the remainder of some real, nondiscursive kernel of enjoyment which must be present for the Nation qua discursive entity-effect to achieve its ontological consistency. (*TWN* 202)

The acceptance and repetitious display of this discontinuous identity, however, can function as a subversive response to that delimitation by looming up as the radical excess of enjoyment threatening to initiate a reverse colonization of the Nation.

THE TEMPORALITIES OF HYBRIDITY

The Chicano emphasis on cultural and linguistic mestizaje offers a point at which Chicano studies and what could be called hybridity studies might productively converge. This is especially so when paired with the theoretical works of Homi Bhabha and Néstor García Canclini. And it is this potential point of convergence (or at least of distinction) that might offer another view of the logic at work in the notion of the Mexican as symptom of American National identity. Both Bhabha and García Canclini offer analyses of hybridity and national identification that resonate with this book; but the implicit politics of all three positions cannot so neatly converge. Such a comparison might also go a long way toward specifying the politics at work in Chicano poetry.

Bhabha's work, of course, operates within the field of Postcolonial studies. To the extent that the internal-colonialism model works as a description of the Mexican in American culture, there is certainly a space for interchange here. Key to understanding Bhabha's conception of hybridity is his distinction between symbol and sign. The symbol is the representational construct that the dominant power poses as its authenticating and authorizing image—a symbol that operates as a synchronous, naturalized, homogeneous object. The Nation is just such a symbol, posited as the natural and transparent representation of universal American culture. The fantasy at work here is that all "cultures"—all ethnic and sexual particularities—can find their meaning in this universal culture. What this universalizing symbol covers over is its concurrent function as a sign, that is, as a representation of cultural difference—an inescapable function, given the differential nature of the sign. In other words, in positing itself as the universal culture in distinction to all particular cultures, the "universal" is nothing but a privileged particular to which all other particulars are expected to conform. To put it more strongly, culture itself is nothing but the space of the dislocation of the symbol by the sign. And herein lies the answer to the question implied in the title of Bhabha's book: the location of culture is in the splitting of the National-Colonial subject between its function as authorizing symbol and differentializing sign; to put this in Hegelese (something Bhabha himself would be averse to doing), culture is nothing but this split internal to the Nation itself.[56] The name for the doubling produced by this split is hybridity:

> Hybridity is the name of this displacement of value from symbol to sign that causes the dominant discourse to split along the axis of its power to be representative, authoritative. Hybridity represents that ambivalent 'turn' of the discriminated subject into a terrifying, exorbitant object of classification—a disturbing questioning of images and presences of authority. (*LOC* 113)

The hybrid should not be thought of simply in terms of space, though, for space is the provenance of the symbol in its self-representation as a synchronous, unified field. The hybrid is the effect of the temporalization of this space, of the production of a time-lag between the synchronous time of the universal and diverse times of differentiation set in motion by the work of the sign.

The implied politics here, then, is that of displacement and decentering. Bhabha proposes no general theory, "only a certain productive tension of the perplexity of language in various locations" in order to suggest "no salvation, but a strange cultural survival of the people. For it is by living on the borderline of history and language, on the limits of race and gender, that we are in a position to translate the differences between them into a kind of solidarity" (ibid., 170). Interestingly, "the people" has been transported from the universalized "center" of the Nation to the borderlines where all differences will be translated into solidarity. Is this not simply a shift in liberal politics, where the point of universality (translation into solidarity) has now been moved to the margins? And what mechanism could provide the conditions of translatability necessary for this new union—a mechanism working no longer according to the logic of centralization but of dispersion? Perhaps the logic of late capitalism itself in its homogenization of the peripheries as part of its globalizing project. Doesn't this translatability of differences into solidarity signal the ultimate colonization of the margins into a new universal language?

To a certain degree these questions are unanswerable, and I will turn to them again below. But one should not overlook the Utopian nature of this marginal translation offered by Bhabha, for such solidarity must certainly be the goal of a leftist as well as a liberal politics. For the moment, I simply want to complicate the optimism of Bhabha's deconstructive politics, according to which the ultimate (and perhaps only) political act available is the destabilization of normative narratives. Bhabha's postmodern optimism leads him to write the following: "Counter-narratives of the nation that continually evoke and erase its totalizing boundaries—both actual and conceptual—disturb those ideological

manoeuvres through which 'imagined communities' are given essentialist identities" (149). The problem is that such counternarratives actually *provoke* rather
than simply *evoke* those totalizing boundaries, and therefore in no way erase
them. They might offer alternative boundaries, such as the ambiguous and
exoticized boundary of Aztlán, but such disturbances often serve to provoke
ever more rigid National identifications. Nevertheless, Bhabha is correct to note
the critical function of concepts such as Aztlán: "What is more significant and
in tension with the exoticism, is the emergence of a hybrid national narrative
that turns the nostalgic past into the disruptive 'anterior' and displaces the
historical present—opens it up to other histories and incommensurable narrative subjects" (167). These other histories and incommensurable subjects grow
out of the time lag inherent in the dislocation of the National symbol by the
differential sign. This time lag offers a space within which modernity—the
condition of symbolic universalism making possible the identification of the
Nation with "the People" ("*E Pluribus Unum*")—can be used against itself:
"Modernity, I suggest, is about the historical construction of a specific position
of historical enunciation and address. . . . It gives [the historically displaced] a
representative position through the spatial distance, or the time-lag between
the Great Event and its circulation as a historical sign of the 'people' or an
'epoch,' that constitutes the memory and the moral of the event as a narrative, a
disposition to cultural communality, a form of social and psychic identification" (243).

Bhabha turns to the concept of the time lag in order to theorize a position of
representation for those displaced by the grand narratives of modernity. This
time lag, as we have seen, is the temporal space opened up by the self-splitting
of the dominant ("colonial") discourse—a split between its symbol (as narrative unity and universality) and its sign (the significatory breach separating the
speaker and the spoken). The symbol occurs as a synchronous temporality in
which all subjective identification presumably takes place in the homogeneous
empty space of universality ("the people") whereas the sign operates according
to a temporality of interruptive repetition (multiple "peoples" operating according to nonsynchronous temporal logics), the subjective split opened up
between signifier and signified:

> The possibility of inciting cultural translations across minority discourses
> arises because of the disjunctive present of modernity. It ensures that what
> *seems* the same within cultures is negotiated in the time-lag of the 'sign'

which constitutes the intersubjective, social realm. Because that lag is indeed the very structure of difference and splitting within the discourse of modernity, turning it into a performative process, then each repetition of the sign of modernity is different, specific to its historical and cultural conditions of enunciation. (247)

It is this temporal and cultural hybridity, opened up by the split internal to dominant discourse itself, that offers *precisely in the space of that splitting* a political space to articulate and negotiate culturally distinct and contested identities. "What is in modernity *more* than modernity," Bhabha concludes in his paraphrase of Lacan, "is the disjunctive 'postcolonial' time and space that makes its presence felt *at the level of enunciation*" (251).

One might say that Bhabha offers a general theory of hybridity, and that the temporality of the time lag is also general and presumably universal to all postcolonial hybrid experience. García Canclini, on the other hand, is not interested in a general temporality of hybridity but rather a heterogeneous array of hybrid temporalities. The value of García Canclini's study of hybridity in Latin American culture is his refusal to isolate any one logic determined by any one power structure or cultural condition. His point is, rather, that what characterizes the hybrid nature of Latin American culture is the "multitemporal heterogeneity of each nation" (HC 3). This conception of multiple temporalities is helpful in making sense of the complex cultural negotiations demanded of the Chicano.

García Canclini sees modernity as a social process of disenchantment—that is, of the desacralization of traditional ties, beliefs, and cultural systems. The crucial point to grasp, he claims, is that modernity has never been widely successful in Latin America, having been the provenance primarily of an educated elite (many of whom were educated in Europe or the United States). Alongside the signs of modernity coexist the still-thriving elements of traditionalism. Such a condition qualifies the status of postmodernity in Latin America since it cannot be conceived of in any evolutionist sense in a culture that has never yet fully experienced modernity. Thus García Canclini is driven to "conceive of postmodernity not as a stage or tendency that replaces the modern world, but rather as a way of problematizing the equivocal links that the latter has formed with the traditions it tried to exclude or overcome in constituting itself" (ibid., 9). In a similar way, current Chicano culture must be seen as "the result of the sedimentation, juxtaposition, and interweaving of indigenous traditions . . . , of Catholic colonial hispanism, and of modern political, educational, and communicational actions" (46). This hybrid temporal condition affects Chicano aesthetics as well, connecting the Chicano to a new generation of Mexican artists: "Far from being concerned with indoctrinating, with defining *one* symbolic universe, as was the case in earlier generations, they [young Mexican painters such as Arturo Guerrero and Marisa Lara] are more freely linked to the ambiguities of the past and of immediate life. They accept naturally the coexistence of the Virgin of Guadalupe with the television set, the proliferation of artifacts and modern gadgets together with the 'poor,' the downtrodden, brilliant, boisterous taste of the popular sectors, which brings them close to the Chicano aesthetic" (84–85).

It is important to point out, however, that one feature distinguishing the Chicano artist from these younger Mexicans is that these younger Mexicans are themselves reacting against an entrenched and institutionalized tradition of cultural nationalism, whereas those nationalist Mexican icons still provide great conjuring power in the Chicano community. While the commodification of Frida Kahlo and Diego Rivera in mainstream U.S. culture is disturbing to many Chicanos, and leads some to engage in parodic reinscriptions of the Kahlo-Rivera iconography, these emblems of a revolutionary nationalist *mestizaje* cannot yet be relegated to the past. What this means, then, is that this layer of temporal incongruency operates within Chicano culture in a unique way. Because Mexican nationalism offers the Chicano another way of negotiating Anglo-American cultural space, it remains politically potent in a way it might not in Mexico itself.[57] And Mexico's example is itself unique among Latin American nations in that "it had the *earliest* experience of modern revolution in a society that did not try to renounce its pre-Columbian and colonial traditions, an experience that could be more *radical* and *prolonged* because it manifested a continuous policy destined to popularize culture and develop its own symbolic sources, with changes in direction without the abrupt alterations of coups d'état suffered by other countries" (HC 103).

In *Emancipation(s)*, Laclau addresses the relationship between a democratic politics and hybridity:

> It tries to inscribe this plurality in equivalential logics which make possible the construction of new public spheres. Difference and particularisms are the necessary starting point, but out of it, it is possible to open the way to a relativization of values which can be the basis for a popular hegemony. This

universalization and its open character certainly condemns all identity to an unavoidable hybridization, but hybridization does not necessarily mean decline through the loss of identity: it can also mean empowering existing identities through the opening of new possibilities.[58]

Both Spivak and Žižek, on the other hand, have criticized the overgeneralization of the politics of hybridity. For Spivak, the danger with the valorization of the hybrid migrant is that it extends the logic of colonialism by further occluding the native (CPCR 255–56). The migrant as the other of the West (or more accurately, as Spivak insists, the North) still functions within the terms of Eurocentric identity. The result is that the external other (el otro rather than lo otro) remains hidden from view, a condition that works in favor of Eurocentric hegemony as the "new proletarian"—women in the periphery—is silently and invisibly exploited. This "unexamined metropolitan hybridism" functions as yet one more "itinerary of recognition through assimilation of the Other" (ibid., 281). We thus have a "new Orientalism" that views the world as immigrant. "It is meretricious to suggest that this reminder undervalues the struggle of the marginal in metropolitan space. It is to remember that that struggle cannot be made the unexamined referent for all postcoloniality without serious problems. No 'two-way dialogue' in 'the great currents of international culture exchange' forgets this" (PMPV 207).[59]

> This ever-growing flowering of groups and subgroups in their hybrid and fluid, shifting identities, each insisting on the right to assert its specific way of life and/or culture, this incessant diversification, is possible and thinkable only against the background of capitalist globalization; it is the very way capitalist globalization affects our sense of ethnic and other forms of community belonging: the only link connecting these multiple groups is the link of Capital itself, always ready to satisfy the specific demands of each group and subgroup (gay tourism, Hispanic music . . .). (TS 209–10)

Of course, the "truth" of Žižek's rather dismissive statement regarding the specific demands of each subgroup can be seen in the commercialization of Hispanic music into a national pop phenomenon in which anything specifically "other" is reduced to the sexualized commodities of Latino bodies as represented by Jennifer Lopez and Ricky Martin—both of whom are Puerto Rican, not Chicano, this fact itself giving witness to the conversion of a strategic pan-Latino coalition politics (according to the logic of equivalence) into a generalized "Hispanic" object for sale, not to mention the politics of representation of Hispanic music itself, with Tropical music squeezing out Norteño music at the 2000 Latin Grammies (ibid., 225).

COUNTERDISCOURSE OR CAPITAL LOGIC?

Žižek's point—as well as Spivak's—not to be missed here, however, is that theories of hybridity all too often end up playing into the hands of the very globalizing forces they are supposed to challenge. This is due in part to hybridity theory's tendency to rely on the work of Foucault and Deleuze. In the same way, the tropes used to characterize the politics of Chicano poetry often come from the lexicon of poststructuralism. Predominant among these tropes is Foucault's "discourse" along with Deleuze and Guattari's "deterritorialization." Implicit in this adherence to a poststructuralist vocabulary, Spivak has observed, is a politics not of class struggle (as in Marxism) but one of opposition through "counterdiscourses" that serve to decenter, destabilize, and de-essentialize the hegemonic discourse of the white power structure. Such a politics is implicit in Pérez-Torres's comment:

> The deployment of the various vernaculars current in Chicana communities by Chicana poetic texts connects on an aesthetic level—through the incorporation of 'standard' forms of English and Spanish, mexicanismos, slang and working class English, caló, regional Mexican Spanish, chicanismos, regional Chicano Spanish, indianismos—the processes of deterritorialization and reterritorialization evident on a socioeconomic and political level within Chicano communities.[60]

One critique (from a certain Marxist perspective) of the celebration of marginalization and hybridity is that any poetics based on these destabilizing rhetorical effects is unwittingly contributing to the culture of late capitalism. The purpose of such a critique, though, is not to dismiss hybridity theory out of hand nor to proclaim the need for some renewed stable entity beyond the movement of différance, as Spivak's reliance on aspects of Derrida's theory should remind us, herself being one of the major critics of essentialism. Žižek, in a Heideggerian moment, writes:

> We can see, now, in what precise way the dimension of the Universal is opposed to globalism: the universal dimension "shines through" the symp-

tomatic displaced element which belongs to the Whole without being properly its part. For this reason, criticism of the possible ideological functioning of the notion of hybridity should in no way advocate the return to substantial identities—the point is precisely to assert *hybridity as the site of the Universal.* (TS 225)

This also applies to the notion of the Nation. The supposed disruption of national identity by a code-switching poetry at a certain level simply replicates the disruptive process of capitalism itself in its latest, multinational phase. One sees this critique, for example, in the work of Jameson, for whom the whole emphasis on the so-called New Political Movements (those radical movements that have shifted attention away from a strict class analysis in order to include questions of race, gender, and sexuality) misses the mark when making radical claims for oppositional strategies aimed at destabilizing such rigid and oppressive concepts such as nationality. Žižek puts it this way:

> The fear of "excessive" identification is therefore the fundamental feature of late-capitalist ideology: the Enemy is the "fanatic" who "over-identifies" instead of maintaining a proper distance toward the dispersed plurality of subject-positions. In short: the elated "deconstructionist" logomachy focused on "essentialism" and "fixed identities" ultimately fights a straw-man. Far from containing any kind of subversive potentials, the dispersed, plural, constructed subject hailed by postmodern theory (the subject prone to particular, inconsistent modes of enjoyment, etc.) simply designates *the form of subjectivity that corresponds to late capitalism.* Perhaps the time has come to resuscitate the Marxian insight that Capital is the ultimate power of "deterritorialization" which undermines every fixed social identity, and to conceive of "late capitalism" as the epoch in which the traditional fixity of ideological positions (patriarchal authority, fixed sexual roles, etc.) becomes an obstacle to the unbridled commodification of everyday life. (TWN 216)

The point here is that in terms of the logic of late capitalism itself, the nation-state no longer functions as the arena in which capitalism is played out. Capitalism in this era of globalization has become multinational, thereby making the emphasis on national boundaries seem rather quaint. Jameson describes this process as follows:

> [Ernest] Mandel's intervention in the postindustrial debate involves the proposition that late or multinational or consumer capitalism, far from

being inconsistent with Marx's great nineteenth-century analysis, constitutes, on the contrary, the purest form of capital yet to have emerged, a prodigious expansion of capital into hitherto uncommodified areas. This purer capitalism of our own time thus eliminates the enclaves of precapitalist organization it had hitherto tolerated and exploited in a tributary way. One is tempted to speak in this connection of a new and historically original penetration and colonization of Nature and the Unconscious: that is, the destruction of the precapitalist Third World agriculture by the Green Revolution, and the rise of the media and the advertising industry. (*PM* 36)

Jameson relates this process to what he refers to as the rise in "neoethnicity"—that is, a stress on the politics of ethnic identity long after ethnicity has ceased to function (at least between nations) in its nationalist phase: "Much of what passes for a spirited defense of difference is, of course, simply liberal tolerance, a position whose offensive complacencies are well known but which has at least the merit of raising the embarrassing historical question of whether the tolerance of difference, as a social fact, is not the result of social homogenization and standardization and the obliteration of genuine social difference in the first place" (ibid., 341).

In this view, then, the North American Free Trade Agreement between Mexico, the United States, and Canada could be seen as the ultimate agent of hybridity, breaking down in its own way the "artificial constructs" of nation and ethnicity in order to make the world safe for capitalism. The cultural equivalent to multinational capital would then be depoliticized multiculturalism, according to which all cultural differences can meet together and be celebrated, not in spite of but precisely because of their differences, in a new, neutralized political space—the predominant manifestations of such spaces being the academic classroom and corporate boardroom.[61] The problem is—as Spivak endlessly argues—that in addition to replicating the logic of late capitalism, such multicultural spaces render the privileged position of the upper-middle-class Anglo-American invisible or transparent, for it is only from such a perspective that the present-day effects of nationalism and racism could appear to be resolved or, at least, resolvable. "The conclusion to be drawn," Žižek writes, "is thus that the problematic of multiculturalism—the hybrid coexistence of diverse cultural life-worlds—which imposes itself today is the form of appearance of its opposite, of the massive presence of capitalism as *universal* world system: it bears witness to the unprecedented homogenization of the contemporary world."[62]

There are some key distinctions to make at this point, however. First, the reduction of Chicano poetics to a poststructuralist strategy of decentering is off the mark. While the use of code-switching does function in opposition to the Anglo-American conception of nationality, this opposition is not carried out through the simple "bad infinity," as Hegel would call it, of a constantly self-subverting textuality that presumably threatens the metaphyscial nature of racist ideology. Such a claim is insufficient on at least two counts: racist ideology, first of all, cannot in itself be reduced to merely a question of discursive hegemony but must also be seen as a particular mode of organizing the fantasy screen whose function it is to cover over the constitutive lack at the heart of the Nation; second, such code-switching is anything but the textual evacuation of meaning. It must be seen instead as the saturation of meaning, the production of an excess of meaning through the use of multiple codes. Code-switching does not deconstruct codes; it embeds them into a palimpsestic terrain that contests borders not by undoing them but by multiplying and overlaying them on different planes laid across the same space, just as the invocation of Aztlán constructs a national boundary that writes over the currently existing national border between Mexico and the United States. The use of Spanish does not obliterate the functionality of English, in other words, but instead heightens this functionality exponentially by covering the same field of content with several different codes. The result, then, is not the deconstruction of a given discourse but the setting into motion of a hyperdiscourse that produces an excess of signification.

Another distinction that has to be made is that the existence of capital logic does not obliterate other logics. In other words, while an emphasis on "neo-ethnicity" and the construction of contesting nationalities might seem to be working hand in hand with the destabilization of the national function through the globalization of capitalism, this claim is effective only in terms of capital logic itself, which never exists in isolation. That is, the logic of nationalism, while complicated and altered by the expansion of multinationalism, does not cease to be effective. Jameson's theory of postmodernism, after all, claims postmodernism is the cultural dominant—the cultural form that presumably regulates the effectivity of other cultural forms. But such a claim by definition suggests that other cultural forms are still operative according to their various relatively autonomous logics. This brings us back to Laclau and Mouffe's distinction between elements and moments, or to Dussel's distinction between el otro and lo otro.

This perhaps can be seen more clearly by asking the following questions: If national identity no longer functions as the ideological masking of the logic of capital, then what about the apparent rise in recent years of ultraright-wing neonationalism? What about the virulent racism that marks not just neofascist hate groups but also legislative initiatives such as the English-only movement and the various anti–affirmative action propositions in California, Texas, and elsewhere? And what about the increased militarization of the border patrol under the guise of the so-called war on drugs? Paradoxically, all of these ultranationalist phenomena are proof that American national identity has ceased to function as the alibi for capitalist exploitation. These movements, in short, are themselves symptoms of the dissolution of the national imaginary bond that previously sustained American identity in its expansionist phase. Now that capital has outgrown the nation-state model, those who earlier found their identity in that model are fighting hysterically to reassert just that national identity in such a violent and frantic way that they raise to the fore the logic of identity formation itself, with its dependence on the excluded element. Ironically, then, the more these neonationalist movements fight to reassert their identity through the exclusion of the Spanish-speaking immigrant, the more they draw attention to the dissolution of that identity itself. Yet this dissolution in no way obliterates the very real racist and Utopian effects of neonationalism. "The structural dialectic of imperialism," Aijaz Ahmad writes, "includes, in other words, the deepening penetration of all available global spaces by the working of capital and intensification of the nation-state form simultaneously."[63]

CAN THE SYMPTOM SPEAK?

In an interview published in 1998, Herbert Siguenza, one of the current members of the Chicano political comedy troupe Culture Clash, said the following: "Although Richard [Montoya] is Chicano, there's still that sense that one is an immigrant in this country—there's that rage of being left out, disenfranchised."[64] This point echoes one made by Alurista in an interview in 1975:

> Some people say my poetry is protest poetry. *No. It's also about reconstructing.* To reconstruct ourselves, *because being colonized people*, the self that we possess, the view that we have, is colored by the colonization that we suffered, by the schooling that we have been subjected to. *We have to expel the Yankees*

from our heart. We have to give ourselves the responsibility of constructing a vision of the world that is truly ours, not a colonized version of the world.[65]

The status of Mexican as symptom appears as strong today as it did in 1968 in the early days of El Movimiento. While Chicano literary studies is making its mark in the academy, anti-immigration sentiment—and the conflation of the Chicano to the status of immigrant—continues unabated and, if anything, is on the increase, as political developments in California and around the country indicate. The suggestion of English-only legislation has been raised even in Kansas, in the heart of the Midwest, where one could hardly be further from a national border anywhere else in the United States.

There is a real danger here, however, if the symptom is conceived of as a wrongfully excluded element that simply needs to be accorded its rightful claim to citizenship. Rather, the symptom can never be integrated into the Nation because the Nation's existence itself is a function of the symptom. A further danger is to construe "identification" in the liberal sense of projecting one's own (presumably transparent and benign) sense of identity onto the symptom or the concomitant belief that one can take on the identity of the symptom. Spivak highlights this danger when she remarks: "In the hands of identitarians, alas, this can lead to further claims of marginality. 'We are all postcolonials'" (*PMPV* 206). "To 'identify with the symptom,'" Žižek explains, "means to recognize in the 'excesses,' in the disruptions of the 'normal' way of things, the key offering us access to its true functioning" (*SOI* 128). Or again in Spivak's words: "In that sense 'postcoloniality,' far from being marginal, can show the irreducible margin in the center" (*PMPV* 206).

Despite these cautions, though, Žižek insists that the claim "We are all immigrant workers" is more productive than simply noting that the universal position from which the immigrant is excluded is that of the privileged white middle-class citizen. For such a statement of identification as Žižek proposes functions as a type of what Hegel referred to as the speculative proposition, meaning that the form of the proposition itself subverts its content by presenting an absurd and impossible subject-predicate relationship. The speculative proposition functions in the same way as Jacques Rancière's "singular universal": It is the "assertion," Žižek continues, "of the singular exception as the locus of universality which simultaneously affirms and subverts the universality in question. When we say, 'We are all citizens of Sarajevo,' we are obviously making a 'false' nomination, a nomination which violates the proper geopolitical disposition; however, precisely as such, this violation gives word to the injustice of the existing geopolitical order" (*soi* 128). In the same way, when we say "We are all immigrants," the form of the proposition itself underscores the impossibility of the social relationship from which the immigrant (and by extension the Chicano) is excluded.

A question still remains, however: What happens when the Chicano says, "We are all Mexicans"? In other words, is the Chicano included in this royal "we" or is the "we" by definition non-Chicano? To the extent that the term "Mexican" functions in the American imaginary as the condensation of all Mexican-Americans to the status of illegal immigrant, then this statement, even when uttered by the Chicano, by its very seeming tautology underscores the absurdity inherent in the Nation itself. If the statement were posed as "We (Mexicans) are all Mexicans," then it would fail to function as the indication of the particular that appropriately fleshes out the universal subject, instead presenting the universal subject with its own vacuity, confronting it with the abyss of radical negativity at the heart of the subject of the Nation, the abyss that was to have been covered up by the existence of the symptom in the first place. The conversion of the symptom to the Chicano, though, undoes the universal that exists in mute and interminable silence. The proposition "Chicano is Mexican" hegemonically discolors the implied whiteness of the "we," thereby speaking the darker side of the Nation as a positive political alternative to the aporia opened up by the abyss of representation.

NOTES

ONE REPRESENTATION AND THE ABYSS OF SUBJECTIVITY

1 I am thankful to Lawrence Kramer for providing me a way into this poem with his essay " 'Syringa': John Ashbery and Elliott Carter," in *Beyond Amazement: New Essays on John Ashbery*, ed. David Lehman (Ithaca, N.Y.: Cornell University Press, 1980).

2 See Ernesto Laclau and Chantal Mouffe, *Hegemony and Socialist Strategy* (London: Verso, 1985).

3 Slavoj Žižek, *Tarrying with the Negative: Kant, Hegel, and the Critique of Ideology* (Durham, N.C.: Duke University Press, 1993), 30.

4 Louis Althusser, "Ideology and Ideological State Apparatuses," in *Lenin and Philosophy* (London: Monthly Review Press, 1971), 162.

5 For one attempt to relate this notion of "imaginary relations" to Althusser's aesthetics, see Michael Sprinker, *Imaginary Relations: Aesthetics and Ideology in the Theory of Historical Materialism* (London: Verso, 1987), chap. 10. I turn to Sprinker's account below in chapter 6.

6 See chapter 6 below for an elaboration of Althusser's "theoretical theater."

7 In the preface to the *Phenomenology of Spirit*, Hegel writes:

> The activity of dissolution is the power and work of the *Understanding*, the most astonishing and mightiest of powers, or rather the absolute power. The circle that remains self-enclosed and, like substance, holds its moments together, is an immediate relationship, one therefore which has nothing astonishing about it. But that an accident as such, detached from what circumscribes it, what is bound and is actual only in its context with others, should attain an existence of its own and a separate freedom—this is the tremendous power of the negative; it is the energy of thought, of the pure "I." Death, if that is what we want to call this non-actuality, is of all things the most dreadful, and to hold fast what is dead requires the greatest strength. Lacking strength, Beauty hates the Understanding for asking of her what it cannot do. But the life of Spirit is not the life that shrinks from death and keeps itself untouched by devastation, but rather the life that endures it and maintains itself in it. It wins its truth only when, in utter dismemberment, it finds itself. It is this power, not as something positive, which closes its eyes to the negative, as when

we say of something that it is nothing or is false, and then having done with it, turn away and pass on to something else; on the contrary, Spirit is this power only by looking the negative in the face, and tarrying with it. This tarrying with the negative is the magical power that converts it into being. This power is identical with what we earlier called the Subject, which by giving deter- minateness an existence in its own element supersedes abstract immediacy, i.e. the immediacy which barely is, and thus is authentic substance: that being or immediacy whose mediation is not outside of it but which is this mediation itself. (§32, p. 19)

8   See chapter 3 below for an elaboration on this concept of the speculative proposition in Hegel.

9   Again, this same structure pertains to Hegel as well as Lacan, as Žižek illustrates:

First, we must bear in mind that with Hegel this subjectivization of the object never "turns out": there is always a remainder of the substance which eludes the grasp of "subjective mediation"; and far from being a simple impediment preventing the subject's full actualization, this remainder is *stricto sensu* cor- relative to the very being of the subject. We reach thereby one of the possible definitions of *objet a*: that surplus of the Substance, that "bone," which *resists subjectivization*; *object a* is correlative to the subject in its very radical incom- mensurability with it. (*TWN* 21)

10   As Žižek puts it,

So we are here again at the tension between the public Law and its obscene superego underside: the ideological recognition in the call of the Other is the act of identification, of identifying oneself as the subject of the public Law, of assuming one's place in the symbolic order; whereas the abstract, indetermi- nate "guilt" confronts the subject with an impenetrable call that precisely prevents identification, recognition of one's symbolic mandate. The paradox here is that the obscene superego underside is, in one and the same gesture, the necessary *support* of the public symbolic Law and the traumatic vicious circle, the impasse that the subject endeavors to *avoid* by way of taking refuge in public Law—in order to assert itself, public Law has to resist its own foundation, to render it invisible.

What remains "unthought" in Althusser's theory of interpellation is thus the fact that prior to ideological recognition we have an intermediate moment of obscene, impenetrable interpellation without identification, a kind of "van- ishing mediator" that has to become invisible if the subject is to achieve symbolic identity—to accomplish the gesture of subjectivization. In short, the "unthought" of Althusser is that there is already an uncanny subject that *precedes* the gesture of subjectivization. (*ME* 61)

11 Jacques Lacan, *The Four Fundamental Concepts of Psycho-Analysis* (New York: W. W. Norton, 1981), 34.

12 Žižek asks,

> Wherein lies the kernel of the obsessional's economy? The obsessional partici-
> pates in frenzied activity, he works feverishly all the time—why? To avoid some
> uncommon catastrophe that would take place if his activity were to stop; his
> frenetic activity is based on the ultimatum, "If I don't do this (the compulsive
> ritual), some unspeakably horrible X will take place." In Lacanian terms, this
> X can be specified as the barred Other, i.e., the lack in the Other, the inconsis-
> tency in the symbolic order. . . . We must be active all the time so that it does
> not come to light that "the Other does not exist" (Lacan). (*LA* 35)

TWO PRESENTATION BEYOND REPRESENTATION: KANT AND THE
LIMITS OF DISCURSIVE UNDERSTANDING

1 See Georg Lukács, *History and Class Consciousness* (Cambridge, Mass.: MIT Press, 1971). I am not alone, of course, in making claims to the lingering legacy of Kant in contemporary Marxist theory. Jameson himself points to the relationship—however tortured it may be—between Kant and Theodor Adorno in his *Late Marxism: Adorno, or, the Persistence of the Dialectic* (London: Verso, 1990); and Žižek builds his Lacanian ethics on a renewed reading of Kant in most of his works since *Tarrying with the Negative: Kant, Hegel, and the Critique of Ideology* (Durham, N.C.: Duke University Press, 1993). See also Alenka Zupancic, *Ethics of the Real: Kant, Lacan* (New York: Verso, 2000); and Robert Kaufman, "Red Kant, or the Persistence of the Third Critique in Adorno and Jameson," *Critical Inquiry* 26, no. 4 (summer 2000): 682–724. For a helpful discussion of Kant's antinomies in the *Critique of Pure Reason*, see John Sallis, *The Gathering of Reason* (Athens: Ohio University Press, 1980), 102–31. Sallis emphasizes Kant's point that the antinomies concern "cos-mological ideas"—questions of totality that remain at the heart of Jameson's concept of cognitive mapping. See Jameson's own postmodern update of Kant in his chapter "The Antinomies of Postmodernity," in *The Seeds of Time* (New York: Columbia University Press, 1994), 1–71.

2 It is my position that just as Marxist theory remains caught up in its Kantian traces, it still remains indebted to Althusser, despite the thirty-five years that have passed since Althusser's rise to prominence and later fall from grace. In this way, Jameson would perhaps be seen as Althusserian (to signify his continuing indebtedness to

Althusserian theory) as distinct from the more restricted sense of post-Althusserian as a reference to the work of, say Barry Hindess and Paul Q. Hirst or Laclau and Mouffe, for whom the "post" signifies a supposed move beyond Althusser's limitations. I should make it clear up front, then, that I do not believe that the necessary explorations of Althusser's limitations have yet been exhausted. Even though Žižek, for example, poses Lacan as a move beyond Althusser, that move still operates within terms laid out by Althusser himself (and by Marx, by Hegel, by Kant . . .). Many references to these works appear in the pages that follow.

3 Marxism, of course, had been plagued by its Kantian ghost long before Jameson. For Vladimir Lenin, neo-Kantianism was one major source of Marxist revisionism (see "Marxism and Revisionism," Vladimir Ilich Lenin, *Collected Works, Volume 15* (Moscow: Foreign Languages Publishing House, 1960–), 29–39. The Frankfurt school also had to wrestle with Kant. It is Jameson, in fact, who in his *Late Marxism* characterizes Adorno's *Negative Dialectics* as an imitation of "the plan of Kant's *Critique of Pure Reason*" (73) and *Aesthetic Theory* as a rewriting of the *Critique of Judgment*: "As for Kant, Adorno's dealings with him are brilliantly unprincipled and suggestive: some guerrilla raids into the *Critique of Judgment* turn it inside out and rewrite it as a virtual Copernican revolution of the new anti-subjective aesthetic" (127).

4 This question of the bridge is one of the key problems explored in Salim Kemal, *Kant's Aesthetic Theory* (New York: St. Martin's Press, 1992).

5 It is for this reason that Terry Eagleton sees Kant's notion of purposiveness as thoroughly ideological: "That things are conveniently fashioned for our purposes must remain a hypothesis; but it is the kind of heuristic fiction which permits us a sense of purposiveness, centredness and significance, and thus one which is of the very essence of the ideological" (*The Ideology of the Aesthetic* [Oxford: Basil Blackwell, 1990], 85). Drawing on Althusser, Eagleton goes on to say: "In the 'imaginary' of ideology, or of aesthetic taste, reality comes to seem totalized and purposive, reassuringly pliable to the centred subject, even though theoretical understanding may more bleakly inform us that this is a finality only with respect to the subject's faculty of cognition" (87).

6 Gilles Deleuze, *Kant's Critical Philosophy: The Doctrine of the Faculties*, trans. Hugh Tomlinson and Barbara Habberjam (London: Athlone Press, 1984), 58, 64.

7 John H. Zammito, *The Genesis of Kant's Critique of Judgment* (Chicago: University of Chicago Press, 1992), 151.

8 "One must necessarily respect Kant's emphasis upon the subjective and moral resonances of the judgment of the sublime, and of aesthetic judgments generally," writes J. N. Findlay in *Kant and the Transcendental Object: A Hermeneutic Study* (Oxford:

Clarendon Press, 1981), 345. Findlay goes on to add that Kant's reservations about objective subreption do not do justice to the stupid sublimity of being:

> One may, however, make the suggestion that there is also something of the sublime in the *disregard* for everything subjective and even moral shown by certain great natural existences and forces. They are magnificent in their total unawareness of what they are, and of what they are doing, in their contentment, as it were, simply to be what they are, and to function as they do function. And God likewise, as many good theologians have taught us, may only be said to know or will anything, not as some extraneous subjective exercise, but solely by *being* the comprehensive reality that He is. There certainly is a sublimity of being which transcends the restless sublimity of thought and consciousness. (ibid.)

This utter disregard of being for everything subjective also marks the Lacanian notion of the sublime Real.

9   "To be sure," Ernst Cassirer comments,

> "this critical solution of the problem of the sublime, when looked at more closely, carries a new critical question within itself. For through the relation of the sublime to the idea of self-legislation and the free personality the sublime seems, since it is cut loose from nature, to fall wholly into the realm of the ethical. Its special aesthetic character and its independent aesthetic value, however, would be equally erased in either case. In fact, the execution of Kant's analysis reveals how near we are to this peril. For the psychology of the sublime leads us back to that basic emotion of awe, which we have already recognized as the universal form in which the consciousness of the moral law presents itself to us. (*Kant's Life and Thought*, trans. James Haden [New Haven, Conn.: Yale University Press, 1981], 330)

10   Jacques Derrida speaks of the recuperative value of this conversion of pain into pleasure:

> Although repulsive on one of its faces, the sublime is not the absolute other of the beautiful. It still provokes a certain pleasure. Its negativity does indeed provoke a disagreement between the faculties and disorder in the unity of the subject. But it is still productive of pleasure and the system of reason can account for it. A still internal negativity does not reduce to silence; it lets itself be spoken. The sublime itself can dawn in art. The silence it imposes by taking the breath away and by preventing speech is less than ever heterogeneous to spirit and freedom. The movement of reappropriation on the contrary is even

more active. That which in this silence works against our senses or in opposition to the interest of sense (hindrance and sacrifice, says Kant) keeps the extension of a domain and of power in view. Sacrifice [*Aufopferung*] and spoilation [*Beraubung*], through the experience of a negative *Wohlgefallen*, thus allows for the acquisition of an extension and a power [*Macht*] greater than what is sacrificed to them. . . . Economic calculation allows the sublime to be swallowed. ("Economimesis," *diacritics* II, no. 2 [June 1981]: 21–22)

Here it becomes apparent how the Kantian sacrifice functions to maintain a certain symbolic economy.

11 Deleuze, *Kant's Critical Philosophy*, 65.

12 It is this move from epistemology to metaphysics to which Paul Guyer objects in his *Kant and the Claims of Taste*, 2d ed. (Cambridge: Cambridge University Press, 1997). Guyer writes that "the indeterminate idea of a supersensible substratum can resolve the antinomy of taste and provide the ultimate deduction of aesthetic judgment only if it is accepted. That the sceptic who has been unpersuaded by Kant's earlier arguments will be even more suspicious of this idea, and that no modern reader will find it very attractive, are, I think, too obvious to require any argument; Kant's theory of taste must survive by its epistemological analysis of aesthetic judgment if it is to survive at all" (309). Guyer qualifies his position in his foreward:

I argue that the introduction of this "supersensible substratum" is superfluous, because the notion of the harmony of the faculties as an intersubjective ground of aesthetic response is already an "indeterminate concept," and that Kant's new notion of a noumenal ground of aesthetic experience is an unnecessary flight of metaphysical fancy. Given a narrow concern with the justifiability of judgments of taste, these strictures may be right; but I would now be inclined to say that we should not see this line of argument as an *alternative* to the more purely epistemological arguments Kant earlier offered but rather as an *additional* level of meaning, parallel to and preparatory for a similar line of thought Kant will introduce in the "Critique of Teleological Judgment," where he will argue that it is natural for us to posit a supersensible source for systematic order in nature but then also go on to argue that this natural thought will be merely a natural illusion unless we recognize it as merely a regulative ideal that is ultimately valid only from a practical point of view. (xix–xx)

13 Cathy Caruth, "The Force of Example: Kant's Symbols," *Yale French Studies* 74 (1988): 30.

14 Cited in ibid., 30.

15 Caruth, "The Force of Example," 35.

THREE THE SPECULATIVE PROPOSITION: HEGEL AND
THE DRAMA OF PRESENTATION

1 For a recent attempt to rescue Hegel's ethical thought from his own speculative apparatus, see Allen W. Wood, *Hegel's Ethical Thought* (Cambridge: Cambridge University Press, 1990).

2 For another elaboration on the distinction between these two terms, see Andrej Warminski, "Pre-positional By-play," *Glyph* 3 (1978): 105–6.

3 Terry Eagleton points to (but does not develop) this distinction between representation and presentation in *The Ideology of the Aesthetic* (Oxford: Basil Blackwell, 1990):

> Wisdom for Hegel is finally conceptual, never representational: the whole can be grasped through the labour of dialectical reason, but not *figured* there. Art and religious faith are the closest approximations we have to such concrete imaging; but both involve sensuous representations which dilute the clarity of the concept. Dialectical reason can render us reality as an indivisible unity; but in the very act of doing so it is condemned from the viewpoint of aesthetic immediacy to the division, linearity and periphrasis of all rational discourse, disarticulating the very substance it seeks to totalize. Only the *structure* of philosophical discourse can suggest something of the synchronic truth of the Idea it strives to explicate. (150)

4 I am, of course, anachronistically imposing a Marxist terminology here onto Hegel's conception of externalization [Entäusserung]. For two classical Marxist readings of this concept, see Georg Lukács, *The Young Hegel*, trans. Rodney Livingstone (Cambridge, Mass.: MIT, 1976), esp. 537–68; and Herbert Marcuse, *Hegel's Ontology and the Theory of Historicity*, trans. Seyla Benhabib (Cambridge, Mass.: MIT, 1987), 305–18.

5 See also Jacques Derrida's helpful reading of this moment in "The Pit and the Pyramid: Introduction to Hegel's Semiology," in *Margins of Philosophy*, trans. Alan Bass (Chicago: University of Chicago Press, 1982).

6 John McCumber, *The Company of Words: Hegel, Language, and Systematic Philosophy* (Evanston, Ill.: Northwestern University Press, 1993), 222.

7 Jacques Lacan, *The Seminar of Jacques Lacan: Book I*, trans. John Forrester (New York: W. W. Norton, 1988), 223.

8 For an analysis of this relationship between Hegel and Lacan on the Master-Slave relationship through the Thing, see Eckhard Hammel, "Hegel und die Dingproduktion: Ein Einblick in Lacans Hegel-Rezeption," *Hegel-Studien* 23 (1988): 227–44.

9   Žižek points out that Lacan also depended on a form of the speculative proposition: "Metalanguage is not just an Imaginary entity. It is *Real* in the strict Lacanian sense—that is, it is impossible to *occupy* its position. But, Lacan adds, it is even more difficult simply to *avoid* it. One cannot *attain* it, but one also cannot *escape* it. That is why the only way to avoid the Real is to produce an utterance of pure metalanguage which, by its patent absurdity, materializes its own impossibility: that is, a paradoxical element which, in its very identity, embodies absolute otherness, the irreparable gap that makes it impossible to occupy a metalanguage position" (*SOI* 156).

10 Allen W. Wood, "Hegel's Ethics," in *The Cambridge Companion to Hegel*, ed. Frederick C. Beiser (Cambridge: Cambridge University Press, 1993): 211–33.

11 The "speculative" reading of Hegel's proposition that I have been forwarding here appears especially perverse when operating with terms such as "reconciliation" (*Versöhnung*). What is thus "reconciled" is the impossibility of such adequation; that is, each term to be reconciled must in itself be seen as internally bifurcated, negated, impossible. It is the dialectical concretization of this impossibility that Hegel is pointing out in his model of the state. For an opposed reading of the role of reconciliation in Hegel's political thought, see Michael O. Hardimon, *Hegel's Social Philosophy: The Project of Reconciliation* (Cambridge: Cambridge University Press, 1994).

FOUR   MARX'S KEY CONCEPT? ALTHUSSER AND
THE *DARSTELLUNG* QUESTION

1   This question of what Althusser means by "structural causality" is hardly a new one and has been discussed in depth over the past thirty years. But because of the complexity of the details of the Darstellung question, and because of the relative neglect of Althusser's work over the past five years, I believe such an overview to be necessary at this point. Alex Callinicos's studies of Althusser on structural causality remain among the best; see his *Althusser's Marxism* (London: Pluto, 1976), and *Is There a Future for Marxism?* (London: Macmillan, 1982). For an early, hostile response to Althusser's structuralism as well as his theory of the relationship between Darstellung and structural causality, see André Glucksmann, "A Ventriloquist Marxism," *New Left Review* 72 (March–April 1972): 68–92.

2   As Jameson has argued, "Mechanical causality is . . . less a concept that might be evaluated on its own terms, than one of the various laws and subsystems of our peculiarly reified social and cultural life" (*PU* 26).

3   These are the terms that Ernest Mandel uses in his account of a proper Marxist method:

> The *combination* of all these uneven tendencies of development of the fundamental proportions of the capitalist mode of production—the combination

of these partially independent variations of the major variables of Marx's system—will enable us to explain the history of the capitalist mode of production, which we shall call "late capitalism," by means of the laws of motion of capital itself, without resort to exongenous factors alien to the core of Marx's analysis of capital. In this way the "life of the subject matter" should emerge in the interplay of all the laws of motion of capital: in other words, it is their totality which yields the mediation between the surface appearances and the essence of capital, and between "many capitals" and "capital in general" (*Late Capitalism*, trans. Rodney Livingstone [Cambridge, Mass.: MIT, 1972], 42).

4 "For Marx, the social relations of production do not bring *men alone* onto the stage, but the *agents* of the production process and the *material conditions* of the production process, in specific 'combinations' " (RC 174).

5 Žižek makes the following critique of Althusser's position on Hegel:

> It should be clear, now, that the Althusserian critical attribution to Hegel of "expressive causality" misses the target: Hegel himself articulated in advance the conceptual framework of Althusser's critique; i.e., his triad of formal, real, and complete ground corresponds perfectly to the triad of expressive, transitive, and overdetermined causality. What is "complete ground" if not the name for a "complex structure" in which the determining instance itself is (over)determined by the network of relations within which it exerts its determining role? . . . Hegel outlined in advance the contours of the Althusserian critique of (what Althusser presents as) "Hegelianism"; moreover he developed the element missing in Althusser and prevents him from thinking out the notion of overdetermination—the element of subjectivity which cannot be reduced to imaginary (mis)recognition qua effect of interpellation, that is to say, the subject as [split] S, the "empty," barred subject. (TWN 140)

6 Pierre Vilar comments briefly on this theatrical image for structural causality:

> This is a seductive notion, and reinforces my conviction . . . that no global structure can exist unless all its effects are present. Yet I do not like Althusser's arguments. They are too close to images. The image of the Darstellung is that of a theatrical representation. It was first proposed by Marx and while I appreciate its suggestive force, I can also see its vagueness and incoherence. Elsewhere Marx compares a mode of production to "a general illumination which bathes all other colors and modifies their particularity" and then to "a particular ether which determines the specific gravity of every being which has materialized within it." (A: CR 36)

7   See chapter 10 of Michael Sprinker, *Imaginary Relations: Aesthetics and Ideology in the Theory of Historical Materialism* (London: Verso, 1987), 288–95.

8   See my chapter 7 below for an elaboration of the dramatic metaphor.

9   MEW 1: 201–333; and Karl Marx, *Contribution to the Critique of Hegel's Philosophy of Right: Early Writings*, trans. and ed. T. B. Bottomore (New York: McGraw-Hill, 1964), 57–198.

10   Louis Althusser, *For Marx*, trans. Ben Brewster (London: Verso, 1990).

11   It is on this point that Mandel disagrees with the Althusserian emphasis on this passage of the *Grundrisse* in order to arrive at Marx's method:

> The difference between Marx's and Althusser's conception comes out most clearly in Marx's *Marginal Notes to Wagner*, where he states explicitly: "At the very outset *I do not start from 'concepts.'* Therefore I do not start out from the concept of value either, and hence I do not 'introduce' it in any way." . . . Althusser thus sanctions only a relationship between economic theory and historical theory; the relationship between economic theory and concrete history is by contrast declared a "false problem," "non-existent" and "Imaginary." (*Late Capitalism*, 18–19).

12   For Engel's text, see his forward to volume 2 of *Capital* (MEW 24, 21–24).

13   On the subject as superadequation, see Gayatri Chakravorty Spivak, "Scattered Speculations on the Question of Value," in *In Other Worlds: Essays in Cultural Politics* (New York: Routledge, 1987): 154–75.

> The moment [of the full development of capital], as Marx emphasizes, entails the *historical* possibility of the definitive predication of the subject as labor-power. Indeed, it is possible to suggest that the "freeing" of labor-power may be a description of the social possibility of this predication. Here the subject is predicated as structurally superadequate to itself, definitively productive of surplus-labor over necessary labor. And because it is this necessary possibility of the subject's definitive superadequation that is the origin of capital as such, Marx makes the extraordinary suggestion that Capital consumes the *use*-value of labor-power. If this critique of political economy were simply a question of restoring use-value [as is the case with the utopian socialists], this would be an aporetic moment.

14   The collection of essays titled *Value: The Representation of Labor in Capitalism*, ed. Diane Elson (London: CSE Books, 1979) is representative of this tendency (no pun intended).

15   Gayatri Chakravorty Spivak, "Can the Subaltern Speak?" in *Marxism and the Inter-*

pretation of Culture, ed. Cary Nelson and Lawrence Grossberg (Urbana: University of Illinois Press, 1988), 271–313.

16   Ibid., 276.

17   It is also precisely this complicity of Darstellung and Vertretung in interpellation that suggests that Spivak is off the mark in rejecting the efforts of Jean-Joseph Goux in constructing a homology of effects between the Marxist and the psychoanalytic models of (re)presentation (*IOW* 156–57). I would nevertheless champion her criticism of the "continuist" urge she sees in Goux's construction of this model. Žižek's version of this homology should lay to rest the "necessity" of this continuism.

18   On this question of Althusser's continuing relevance for contemporary theory, see E. Ann Kaplan and Michael Sprinker, eds., *The Althusserian Legacy* (New York: Verso, 1993).

19   This function of the Name of the Subject is precisely what Spivak refers to in her discussion of Vertretung (see above). It is the relationship between the Vertretung function of the Name and the Darstellung function of the valorization process itself that Spivak wants to keep in play. I elaborate on this opposition further in chapter 7.

20   I cannot accept the characterization of the subject of structural causality posed by Anthony Cutler, Barry Hindess, Paul Hirst, Athear Hussein: "The empty subject necessary for the capitalist process of representation can be conceived as a subject emptied of its potential by alienation, an alienation which is the condition of existence of this process. The empty (passive) subjects necessary to commodity production and capitalism will be replaced in socialism by the full constitutive subject, the members of humanity linked in conscious collectivity" (*MC* 80). The authors overlook the crucial distinction between the theories of alienation and fetishism in Marx, and thus cannot conceive of anything other than a "full" subject as the stand-in for the "empty" ones of capitalism.

21   An additional difficulty lies in the fact that "terrain" was not Marx's trope but the result of the French translation of *Capital.* Althusser writes the following: "But recently, reading the chapter of *Capital* on wages, I was stupefied to see that Marx used the very expression 'change of terrain' [*changement de terrain*] to express this change of theoretical problematic. Here again, the question (or its concept) which I had laboriously reconstituted out of its *absence* in one precise point of Marx's, Marx himself gave in black and white [*en toutes lettres*] *somewhere else* in his work" (*RC* 29 n. 10; *LC* 30). The problem is that Marx did not use this phrase in the German; this phrase is from M. J. Roy's French translation. The sentence in question reads as follows in Roy's translation: "*A son insu, elle changeait ainsi de terrain, en substituant à la valeur du travail, jusque-là l'objet apparent de ses recherches, la valeur de la force du travailleur*" (cited in *LC* 18). The

English translation of the French as it appears in *Reading Capital* is: "It thus unwittingly changed terrain by substituting for the value of labor, up to this point, the apparent object of its investigations, the value of labor power" (RC 20). But the English translation from the German is quite different: "The political economists unconsciously substituted this question [of the cost of producing or reproducing the worker] for the original one [of the cost of the production of labor], for the search after the cost of production of labor as such turned in a circle, and did not allow them to get any further forward at all" (C1 678). The German itself reads: "*Diese Frage schob sich der politischen Ökonomie bewußtlos für die ursprüngliche unter, da sie mit den Produktionskosten der Arbeit als solcher sich im Kreise drehte und nichte vom Flecke kam*" (560). Marx's language refers to an unconscious substitution of questions, not a change of terrain.

FIVE   FIGURATION AND THE SUBLIME LOGIC OF THE REAL: JAMESON'S LIBIDINAL APPARATUSES

1   For collections that record a range of approaches to and interpretations of Jameson's work, see *New Orleans Review* 11, no. 1 (spring 1984), guest ed. Michael Clark; *diacritics* 12, no. 3 (fall 1992); and Douglas Kellner, ed., *Postmodernism/Jameson/ Critique* (Washington, D.C.: Maisonneuve Press, 1989). The latter collection is largely representative of the "poststructuralist" responses to Jameson's work, which for the most part attack his "logocentric" teleological and totalizing Marxist narrative that presumably reduces the heterogeneous flows and dispersals of our postsubject existence. I would argue that Jameson's task in *The Political Unconscious* was to challenge while engaging in and appropriating key elements of precisely this trend in literary-cultural criticism (see especially Jameson's concluding chapter of his *Postmodernism*, which is in part a response to the Kellner collection). To my mind, both positions receive a necessary qualification in Žižek's articulation of a Lacanian Marxism (to which I refer throughout this book).

2   Thus, I attempt to provide here a response to critics who rightly claim the following:

> But unfortunately Jameson fails to provide a clear-cut working definition of his key concept—that of a "political unconscious" which acts as a determinant of the "socially symbolic act" which is the text. It remains unclear just how the political unconscious differs from the object of psychoanalysis, to which Jameson refers as "the genuine Unconscious." We are left to wonder if Jameson's terminology is intended to function literally or figuratively: is the object of his study the political component of the Freudian Unconscious, or is he using the term "unconscious" metonymically, to indicate a mere displacement

of form or function?" (Jerry Anne Flieger, "The Prison-House of Ideology: Critic as Inmate," *diacritics* 12, no. 3 [fall 1992]: 50).

3 For an early study of Jameson's use of Althusser, see William C. Dowling, *Jameson, Althusser, Marx: An Introduction to the Political Unconscious* (Ithaca, N.Y.: Cornell University Press, 1984).

4 Eric Auerbach, *Mimesis* (Princeton, N.J.: Princeton University Press, 1953), 29.

5 Cornel West discusses the role of Frye in Jameson's book as follows: "Frye's conflation of ethics and politics gives Jameson the opportunity both to congratulate and to criticize him. Jameson congratulates Frye—the North American version of structuralism—because Frye conceives the central problem of criticism to be not epistemological but rather ethical, namely the relation of texts to the destiny of human communities . . . since he understands that there is a crucial relationship among desire, freedom, and narrative. Jameson criticizes Frye because Frye understands this relationship too idealistically and individualistically" ("Ethics and Action in Fredric Jameson's Marxist Hermeneutics," in *Postmodernism and Politics*, ed. Jonathan Arac [Minneapolis: University of Minnesota Press, 1986], 132).

6 The question of Jameson's "style" has long intrigued his critics. For various readings of this issue, see Terry Eagleton, "Fredric Jameson: The Politics of Style," in *Against the Grain: Selected Essays, 1975–1985* (London: Verso, 1986), 65–78; Clint Burnham, *The Jamesonian Unconscious: The Aesthetics of Marxist Theory* (Durham, N.C.: Duke University Press, 1995), 31–75, for whom Jameson's writings of the early 1990s function as a kind of "sublime quilt" (164–66); and Sean Homer, *Fredric Jameson: Marxism, Hermeneutics, Postmodernism* (New York: Routledge, 1998), 13–35.

7 I critiqued Jameson's reading of postmodern poetry in my *Textual Politics and the Language Poets* (Bloomington: Indiana University Press, 1989). See chapter 3, "Jameson's Perelman: Reification and the Material Signifier," 42–52. An earlier version of that chapter appeared in *Poetics Journal* 7 (September 1987): 52–62. That work was the germ of the present chapter, the latter being a necessary qualification to my earlier reading.

8 In more properly Marxist terms we would be dealing here with the question of the relationship between figuration and the base-superstructure binary. In a discussion of Adorno's theory of culture, though, Jameson inverts this moment by pointing out the figural nature of the base-superstructure model itself: "But we must initially separate the figuration of the terms base and superstructure—only the initial shape of the problem—from the type of efficacity or causal law it is supposed to imply. *Überbau* and *Basis*, for example, which so often suggest to people a house and its foundations, seem in fact to have railroad terminology and to have designated the rolling stock and the rails respectively, something which suddenly jolts us into a

rather different picture of ideology and its effects" (*Late Marxism: Adorno, or, the Persistence of the Dialectic* (London: Verso, 1990), 46. See also "Base and Superstructure," in Raymond Williams, *Marxism and Literature* (Oxford: Oxford University Press, 1977), 75–82.

9 For an early attempt to explore Jameson's relationship to Lacan, see Michael Clark, "Imagining the Real: Jameson's Use of Lacan," *New Orleans Review* 11, no. 1 (spring 1984): 67–72. Sean Homer argues that "we may say that Jameson's horizons of interpretation trail Lacanian resonances but there is no correspondence between them in any meaningful sense; Jameson does not reproduce Lacanian categories in a precise sense and this serves to obfuscate the specific nature of the analogy being made" (*Fredric Jameson*, 55). I would argue that such noncorresponding trailings and obfuscations do not in themselves preclude a "meaningful" relationship between Jameson's horizons and Lacan's trailings. We are confronted with a question of strategic appropriation rather than coherent correspondence.

SIX THE THEATER OF FIGURAL SPACE

1 Louis Althusser, "The 'Piccolo Teatro': Bertolazzi and Brecht," in *For Marx*, trans. Ben Brewster (London: Verso, 1990), 129–51.

2 Notice the similarity between this turning back and assailing and that of Althusser's "Ideology and Ideological State Apparatuses" essay: When the police hail us, we are transformed into subjects. "Assuming that the theoretical scene I have imagined takes place in the street, the hailed individual will turn round. By this mere one-hundred-and-eighty-degree physical conversion, he becomes a *subject*" (LP 174). Let us keep in mind, however, the earlier distinction between subject and subjectivization (as discussed in chapter 1).

3 Other examples of such judgments include "the non-observability of an ideally competent native speaker of any language to generative grammar" and the lack of "a pure instance of a capitalist social formation (not even Holland in the 17th century)" to prove the existence of capitalism (IR 292). Sprinker hastens to add in a note that his "only claim here is that empirical hypotheses . . . may be subject to confirmation once adequate data are made available" (ibid., 293 n. 20). Whatever the merits of such a claim, we are no longer operating in terms of reflective judgment, for which such confirmation is by definition impossible.

4 "Before its birth, the child is therefore always-already a subject, appointed as a subject in and by the specific familial ideological configuration in which it is 'expected' once it is conceived" (LP 176).

5 This is precisely the job Terry Eagleton gives himself in *Criticism and Ideology* (London: Verso, 1976).

6 This distinction between insertion and performative production would go a long way in responding to the charges of Barry Hindess and Paul Hurst that Althusser's model of interpellation depends on an already constituted subject that would be able to recognize itself in its call.

7 For a review of works from the 1970s and 1980s that in one way or another attempted to work out an Althusserian theory of aesthetics, see James Kavanagh, "Marxism's Althusser: Towards a Politics of Literary Theory," *diacritics* (fall 1982): 25–45.

8 *diacritics* (winter 1985): 37–56.

9 Lewis borrows the notion of tropic-concept from Jacques Derrida's "White Mythology" (in *The Margins of Philosophy*, trans. Alan Bass [Chicago: University of Chicago Press, 1982]). Lewis is careful to point out, however, that Derrida's own position in regard to metaphor remains at the level of metaphor as resemblance, whereas Althusser's display of tropic-concepts points toward a sense of metaphor as production.

10 The canonical source for this argument is, of course, Roman Jakobson, "Two Aspects of Language and Two Types of Aphasic Disturbances," in *Fundamentals of Language*, Roman Jakobson and Morris Halle (The Hague: Mouton, 1956), 55–82.

11 See Gilles Deleuze and Félix Guattari, *Kafka: Toward a Minor Literature*, trans. Dana Polan (Minneapolis: University of Minnesota Press, 1986).

12 John Sallis, *Crossings: Nietzsche and the Space of Tragedy* (Chicago: University of Chicago Press, 1991), 25–26.

13 "If we could imagine dissonance become man—and what else is man?—this dissonance, to be able to live, would need a splendid illusion [*Illusion*] that would cover dissonance with a veil of beauty. This is the true artistic aim of Apollo in whose name we comprehend all those countless illusions of the beautiful Schein [*Illusionen des schönen Scheins*] that at every moment make Dasein worth living at all and prompt the desire to live in order to experience the next moment" (BT 143).

14 Derrida, "White Mythology," 250–51.

15 See chapter 6 of Slavoj Žižek, *For They Know Not What They Do* (London: Verso, 1991).

16 Sallis, *Crossings*, 93.

17 Martin Heidegger, "What Are Poets For?" in *Poetry, Language, Thought*, trans. Albert Hofstadter (New York: Harper and Row, 1971), 106.

18 Ibid., 134.

19 "On the other hand, we need not conjecture regarding the immense gap which separates the *Dionysian Greek* from the Dionysian barbarian. From all quarters of the ancient world—to say nothing here of the modern—from Rome to Babylon, we can point to the existence of Dionysian festivals, types which bear, at best, the same relation to the Greek festivals which the bearded satyr, who borrowed his name and attributes from the goat, bears to Dionysus himself. In nearly every case the festivals

centered in extravagant sexual licentiousness, whose waves overwhelmed all family life and its venerable traditions; the most savage natural instincts were unleashed, including even that horrible mixture of sensuality and cruelty which has always seemed to me to be the real witches' brew" (BT 39).

20   "Beside this isolated insight, . . . there is, to be sure, a profound illusion [*tiefsinnige Wahnvorstellung*] that first saw the light of the world in the person of Socrates: the unshakable faith that thought, using the thread of causality, can penetrate the deepest abyss of being, and that thought is capable not only of knowing being but even of correcting it. This sublime metaphysical illusion accompanies science as an instinct and leads science again and again to its limits at which it must turn into art—which is really the aim of this mechanism" (BT 95–96).

21   Charles Shepherdson works with this problem in his on-line essay, "History and the Real: Foucault with Lacan," *Postmodern Culture* 5, no. 2 (January 1995) (http://www.iath.virginia.edu/pmc/text-only/issue.195/shepherd.195).

22   "The Greek words for 'truth' (η αληθεια, το αληθσ) are compounded of the privative prefix α- ('not') and the verbal stem -λαθ- ('to escape notice,' 'to be concealed'). The truth may thus be looked upon as that which is un-concealed, that which gets discovered or uncovered ('entdeckt') (Martin Heidegger, *Being and Time*, trans. John Macquarrie and Edward Robinson [San Francisco: Harper and Row, 1962], 57 n. 1).

23   "The Greek expression fainomenon, to which the term 'phenomenon' goes back, is derived from the verb φαινεσθαι, which signifies 'to show itself.' Thus φαινομενον means that which shows itself, the manifest [*das, was sich zeigt, das Sichzeigende, das Offenbare*]. φαινεσθαι itself is a *middle-voiced* form which comes from φαινω—to bring to the light of day, to put in the light. Φαινω comes from the stem φα—; like φως, the light, that which is bright—in other words, that wherein something can become manifest, visible in itself. Thus we must *keep in mind* that the expression 'phenomenon' signifies *that which shows itself in itself*, the manifest. Accordingly the φαινομενα or 'phenomena' are the totality of what lies in the light of day or can be brought to the light—what the Greeks sometimes identified simply with τα οντα (entities). Now an entity can show itself from itself [*von ihm selbst her*] in many ways, depending in each case on the kind of access we have to it. Indeed it is even possible for an entity to show itself as something which it is not. When it shows itself in this way, it 'looks like something or other' ['*sieht* . . . '*so aus wie . . .*']. This kind of showing-itself is what we call 'seeming' [Scheinen]. Thus in Greek too the expression φαινομενον ('phenomenon') signifies that which looks like something, that which is 'semblant,' 'semblance' [*da 'Scheinbare,' der 'Schein'*]. Φαινομενον αγαθον means something good which looks like, but 'in actuality' is not, what is designated in the first signification of φαινομενον ('phenomenon' as that which shows itself)

and what is designated in the second ('phenomenon' as semblance) are structurally interconnected" (Heidegger, *Being and Time*, 51).

24 Plato's *Phaedrus* provides an elaborate unfolding of the relationship between the beautiful, the shining forth of the ειδη, and truth as αληθεια. See also Sallis, *Being and Logos*, chap. 3.

25 Jameson specifically refers to this problem of the postmodern sublime as a representational drama: "The representation of individual items is at best a matter of aesthetic appreciation or belletristic interest; nor does representation really emerge as an issue and a dilemma in its own right when the possibility of some realistic access to the social totality is taken for granted and given in advance. It is only with the second or monopoly stage of capitalism, and the emergence of a classical imperialist system beyond the confines of the various national experiences, that a radical aesthetic and epistemological doubt about the possibility of grasping society as a whole begins to be felt: and it is precisely this radical doubt that inaugurates modernism as such and constitutes the representational drama specific to it" (*Late Marxism: Adorno, or, the Persistence of the Dialectic* [London: Verso, 1990], 244).

26 See Louis Marin, *Utopics: Spatial Play*, trans. Robert A. Vollrath (Atlantic Highlands, N.J.: Humanities Press, 1984), 239–57.

27 For a suggestive critique of this existential politics, see James S. Hurley, "Real Virtuality: Slavoj Žižek and 'Post-Ideological' Ideology," *Postmodern Culture* 9, no. 1 (September 1998):

> What bothers me about this move, and in this it is rather typical of Žižek's work, is its implication that it is ultimately the intrapsychic where the ideological action is, including, presumably, the action that can problematize and constructively modify ideology's interpellative precepts. In reframing the larger structural questions he has so frequently and provocatively raised in *Plague of Fantasies* in terms of the individual subject's ethical choice, Žižek achieves a position at the end of the book that is, curiously, a kind of "Lacanized" existentialism: what is imperative for the subject is a self-constitutive choice in the face of a spiritually impoverished and politically disempowering life-world; but unlike the autonomous, self-identical subjectivity that is the Sartrean ideal, the Žižekian subject's self-constitution results from an act of willing self-destitution, an acceptance of the primordial splitting that is subjectivity's necessary condition of existence. In the context of the dropping from Žižek's discussion of the "global" issues he has raised, the famous Lacanian symbol for this split subjectivity—$—seems, unfortunately, all too appropriate: Žižek's theorization of postmodern subjectivity may finally accord even better with the privatizing logic of postmodern capitalism and liberal

democracy than does the neo-Gramscian model of left-alliance politics he criticizes. (¶ 18)

SEVEN CAN THE SYMPTOM SPEAK? HEGEMONY AND THE
PROBLEM OF CULTURAL REPRESENTATION

1 An earlier version of this portion of Spivak's "History" chapter appears as "The Rani of Sirmur: An Essay in Reading the Archives," *History and Theory* 24 (1985): 247–72.

2 "Consequently," writes Gyan Prakash, " . . . the debate left no room for the widow's enunciatory position. . . . The problem here is not one of sources (the absence of the woman's testimony) but of the staging of the debate: it left no position from which the widow could speak" ("Subaltern Studies as Postcolonial Criticism," *American Historical Review* 99, no. 5 [December 1994]: 1487). As we shall see, however, it is the possibility of positioning and speaking themselves that haunts Spivak in her ruminations on the investigator's lack of access to the widow's speech.

3 Spivak speaks on an upbeat note of this condition elsewhere: "This is the greatest gift of deconstruction: to question the authority of the investigating subject without paralysing him, persistently transforming conditions of impossibility into possibility" ("Subaltern Studies: Deconstructing Historiography," in *In Other Worlds* [New York: Routledge, 1987], 201). I will refer to this essay as *IOW*.

4 Note here the language of representative politics in the term "constituency." According to the logic of Spivak's dominant tropes, though, the relationship between "feminism"—however one might conceive of the subject of *this* term—and its constituency remains fundamentally incommensurate.

5 Heidegger writes in a similar vein: "Consequently, despite all its historiographical interests and all its zeal for an Interpretation which is philologically 'objective' ['sachliche'], Dasein no longer understands the elementary conditions which would alone enable it to go back to the past in a positive manner and make it productively its own" (*Being and Time*, trans. John Macquarrie and Edward Robinson [San Francisco: Harper and Row, 1962], 43). In response to this lack of an objective and positive interpretation, Heidegger proposes a destructive practice of history much like the deconstructive practice Spivak invokes: "If the question of Being is to have its own history made transparent, then this hardened tradition must be loosened up, and the concealments which it has brought about must be dissolved. We understand this task as one in which by taking *the question of Being as our clue*, we are to *destroy* the traditional content of ancient ontology until we arrive at those primordial experiences in which we achieved our first ways of determining the nature of Being—the ways which have guided us ever since" (44). " 'Behind' the phenomena of phenomenology there is essentially nothing else; on the other hand, what is to

become a phenomenon can be hidden. And just because the phenomena are prox- imally and for the most part *not* given, there is need for phenomenology. Covered- up-ness is the counter-concept to 'phenomenon'" (60). "But this very entity, Da- sein, is in itself 'historical,' so that its ownmost ontological elucidation necessarily becomes an 'historiological' Interpretation" (63).

6 "If the peasant insurgent was the victim and the unsung hero of the first wave of resistance against territorial imperialism in India, it is well known that, for reasons of collusion between pre-existing structures of patriarchy and transnational capital- ism it is the urban sub-proletarian female who is the paradigmatic subject of the current configuration of the International Division of Labor" (*IOW* 218).

7 For an examination of the question of the subject operating in the Subaltern Studies group, see Rosalind O'Hanlon, "Recovering the Subject: Subaltern Studies and His- tories of Resistance in Colonial South Asia," *Modern Asian Studies* 22 (1988): 189– 224.

8 Spivak, in her *Socialist Review* interview, also emends her conception of "strategic essentialism" in order to rescue it from Western academics who use the concept as a cover for uncritical essentialism ("Gayatri Spivak on the Politics of the Subaltern," interview by Howard Winant, *Socialist Review* 20, no. 3 (July–September 1990): 93.

9 See Michel Foucault and Gilles Deleuze, "Intellectuals and Power: A Conversation between Michel Foucault and Gilles Deleuze," in *Language, Counter-Memory, Prac- tice: Selected Essays and Interviews*, trans. Donald Bouchard and Sherry Simon (Ithaca, N.Y.: Cornell University Press, 1977), 205–17.

10 Ibid., 206–7.

11 Ibid., 207.

12 Karl Marx, *The Eighteenth Brumaire of Louis Bonaparte*, in *Surveys from Exile: Political Writings, Volume II*, ed. David Fernbach (New York: Vintage, 1974), 143– 249.

13 Interview, 89.

14 "We recognize of course that subordination cannot be understood except as one of the constitutive terms in a binary relationship of which the other is dominance, for subaltern groups are always subject to the activity of ruling groups, even when they rebel and rise up" (*SSS* 35).

15 Jean-François Lyotard, *The Differend: Phrases in Dispute*, trans. Georges Van Den Abbeele (Minneapolis: University of Minnesota Press, 1988).

16 "Within the two contending versions of freedom, the constitution of the female subject in life is the place of the *différend*" (*CPCR* 296).

17 This criticism, operating throughout *A Critique of Postcolonial Reason*, is articulated in Spivak's "Poststructuralism, Marginality, Postcoloniality, and Value," in *Contem- porary Postcolonial Theory*, ed. Padmini Mongia (London: Arnold, 1996), 198–222.

18 "To confront this group is not only to represent (vertreten) them globally in the absence of infrastructural support, but also to learn to represent (darstellen) ourselves" (*CPCR* 276).

19 Asha Varadharajan pursues this question in the following passage:

> Spivak rightly rejects the positivistic tendency to view the concrete as somehow indestructible and static, but fails to see that her own attempt to elicit the constitutive contradictions of subaltern consciousness might discover, not a *definition* of subaltern consciousness that encompasses its buried reality, but an active demonstration of the manner in which the subaltern disarticulates its determinations. The identity of the subaltern, in other words, exists in the subaltern's resistance to its identifications. Spivak seems to believe that because nothing is given immediately to experience or to representation, it must be deemed inaccessible" (*Exotic Parodies: Subjectivity in Adorno, Said, and Spivak* [Minneapolis: University of Minnesota Press, 1995], 93).

20 Spivak points out the terminological confusion perpetuated by the British when they refer to widow sacrifice as *sati*, a term that actually refers to the state of being a good wife (*CPCR* 303).

21 Leerom Medovoi, Shankar Raman, and Benjamin Robinson, "Can the Subaltern Vote?" *Socialist Review* 20, no. 3 (July–September): 133–49.

22 Varadharajan, following up on Adorno's critique of the particular, draws attention to the complicity between the particular and the whole: "Spivak envisages a focus on the particular that fractures or defers the whole, one that does not admit that the particular might be capable of invoking (dare I say referring to?) a whole it cannot articulate" (*Exotic Parodies*, 98).

23 Spivak's example of the hegemonic struggle over the opposing constructions of the Rani—the imperialist and patriarchal—also shows this process, with the vast heterogeneity of "Indian" political culture being reduced under the sign of nativist patriarchal nationalism to the exclusion of any other articulations of Indian identity. The lesson to be drawn from this condition, however—in light of Laclau and Mouffe's argument—is that such an equivalent reduction was the necessary precondition for the revolutionary rupture that led to Indian independence from Britain.

24 This is the paradigmatic moment in Žižek's social analysis, according to which "the Law's *external* relationship to its transgression is *internalized* into the Law's relationship to its own traumatic founding gesture" (*The Indivisible Remainder* [London: Verso, 1995], 155).

25 See also Jacob Torfing, *New Theories of Discourse: Laclau, Mouffe, and Žižek* (Oxford: Blackwell Publishers, 1999). While Torfing provides a detailed exegesis of the difficult arguments of Laclau and Mouffe, his book's limitations are signaled in the

title, the overemphasis of discourse or the symbolic at the expense of the dialectical level of the real as embodied by the symptom. What is lacking, in other words, is the level of the individual as the dialectical display of the relationship between the universal and the particular. See below for my elaboration of this third moment.

26 See, in particular, Stephen Heath, *Questions of Cinema* (Bloomington: Indiana University Press, 1981).

27 Ernesto Laclau, *Emancipation(s)* (London: Verso, 1996), 28.

28 Žižek elaborates on this notion as follows:

> The opposition between fundamentalism and postmodern pluralist identity politics is ultimately a fake, concealing a deeper solidarity (or, to put it in Hegelese, speculative identity): a multiculturalist can easily find even the most "fundamentalist" ethnic identity attractive, but only in so far as it is the identity of the supposedly authentic Other (say, in the USA, Native American tribal identity): a fundamentalist group can easily adopt, in its social functioning, the postmodern strategies of identity politics, presenting itself as one of the threatened minorities, simply striving to maintain its specific way of life and cultural identity. The line of separation between multiculturalist identity politics and fundamentalism is thus purely formal; it often depends merely on the different perspective from which the observer views a movement for maintaining a group identity. (*TS* 210)

29 Here is Žižek's version of Spivak's claim, discussed above, that the ethical position of the leftist in relation to the "other" is ultimately pathetic.

30 For another take on Hegel's limits, see Susan Buck-Morss, "Hegel and Haiti," *Critical Inquiry* 26, no. 4 (summer 2000): 821–65.

31 Walter Mignolo, *Local Cultures/Global Designs* (Princeton, N.J.: Princeton University Press, 1998), 175.

32 Laclau and Mouffe make a similar point: "The hegemonic form of politics only becomes dominant at the beginning of modern times, when the reproduction of the different social areas takes place in permanently changing conditions which constantly require the construction of new systems of differences" (*HSS* 138).

33 Walter Mignolo, *The Darker Side of the Renaissance: Literacy, Territoriality, and Colonization* (Ann Arbor: University of Michigan Press, 1995).

34 Homi Bhabha, "Signs Taken for Wonders," in *The Location of Culture* (London: Routledge, 1994), 116.

35 Cherríe Moraga (*The Last Generation* [Boston: South End Press, 1993]) writes:

> I call myself a Chicana writer. Not a Mexican-American writer, not an Hispanic writer, not a half-breed writer. To be a Chicana is not merely to name

one's racial/cultural identity, but also to name a politic, a politic that refuses assimilation into the U.S. mainstream. It acknowledges our mestizaje—Indian, Spanish, and Africano. After a decade of "hispanicization" (a term superimposed upon us by Reagan-era bureaucrats), the term Chicano assumes even greater radicalism. With the misnomer "Hispanic," Anglo America proffers the Spanish surnamed the illusion of blending into the "melting pot" like any other white immigrant group. But the Latino is neither wholly immigrant nor wholly white; and here in this country, "Indian" and "dark" don't melt. (56–57)

36   According to Rodolfo F. Acuña, many Anglo-Americans "seem to want Mexicans to identify not as Mexicans but as Americans, yet at the same time they insist on labeling all Mexicans—whether US-born, legal immigrants, or undocumented—as 'illegal aliens,' a term that is today's euphemism for 'wetbacks' or 'greasers' " (*Anything but Mexican: Chicanos in Contemporary Los Angeles* [London: Verso, 1996], 2).

37   The term "Mexican-American," of course, is no less politically charged than "Chicano," but the assimilationist politics inherent in the hyphen distinguishes this term from the consciously oppositional "Chicano."

38   The musical group Ilegales plays on this "outlaw" identity as a mode of self-representation.

39   This is not a question of which type of poem is more authentically Chicano, because the whole status of the Chicano figure serves to undo claims of authenticity of all kinds (which is not to say that claims of authenticity are not made within the Chicano community). Spivak points to another danger inherent in the uses and appropriations of multicultural and "Third World" literatures: "Isn't it 'Eurocentric' to choose only such writers who write in the consciousness of marginality and christen them 'Third World'?" (*PMPV* 202).

40   Gloria Anzaldúa, *Borderlands/La Frontera: The New Mestiza* (Spinsters/aunt lute, 1987), 3.

41   The same is true for the function of Chicano Spanish in the identity-construction of Mexico. Anzaldúa writes: " '*Pocho*, cultural traitor, you're speaking the oppressor's language by speaking English, you're ruining the Spanish language,' I have been accused by various Latinos and Latinas. Chicano Spanish is considered by the purist and by most Latinos deficient, a mutilation of Spanish. But Chicano Spanish is a border tongue which developed naturally. Change, *evolución, enriquecimiento de palabras nuevas por invención o adopción* have created variants of Chicano Spanish, *un nuevo lengauje. Un lenguaje que corresponde a un modo de vivir.* Chicano Spanish is not incorrect, it is a living language" (*Borderlands*, 55). This can be seen also in Octavio Paz's infamous essay, "The *Pachuco* and Other Extremes," in *The Labyrinth of Solitude* (New York: Grove Press, 1961).

42 The relationship between the Chicano Movement and Chicano poetry is crucial. Gonzales himself was primarily an activist, not a poet, and founded the Denver-based Crusade for Justice. For a parallel study on a figure who straddled the poetic and political worlds of the Black Arts Movement and the Black Power movement, see Komozi Woodard, *A Nation within a Nation: Amiri Baraka* (*LeRoi Jones*) *and Black Power Politics* (Chapel Hill: University of North Carolina Press, 1999).

43 For a definitive examination of the history of the term "Chicano," see Tino Villanueva, prologue to *Chicanos: Antología histórica y literaria* (Mexico City: Fondo de Cultura Económica, 1980). In discussing the conversion of the word from an insult to a badge of honor, Villanueva writes: "Adviértase que aquí *chicano*, por lo visto, no parece tener ningún valor despectivo, sino que, como sugiere [José] Limón, se utilizaba como un autoapelativo por un determinado *in-group* que se resistía a aceptar las normas culturales norteamericanas" (15).

44 Alurista, "El Plan Espiritual de Aztlán," in *Aztlán: Essays on the Chicano Homeland*, ed. Rudolfo A. Anaya and Francisco Lomelí (Albuquerque: El Norte Publications, 1989), 1.

45 Ibid., 3.

46 Alurista, *Nationchild Plumaroja* (San Diego: Toltecas en Aztlán, 1972), n.p.

47 Alfred Arteaga, *Chicano Poetics: Heterotexts and Hybridities* (Cambridge: Cambridge University Press, 1997), 99.

48 For a detailed study of this process, see Jacques Lafaye, *Quetzalcóatl and Guadalupe* (Chicago: University of Chicago Press, 1974).

49 For discussions of romanticism in Alurista's poetics, see Tomás Ybarra-Frausto, "Alurista's Poetics: The Oral, the Bilingual, the Pre-Columbian," in *Modern Chicano Writers*, ed. Joseph Sommers and Tomás Ybarra-Frausto (Englewood Cliffs, N.J.: Prentice-Hall, 1979); and Juan Rodríguez, "La búsqueda de dentidad y sus motivos en la literatura chicana," in *The Identification and Analysis of Chicano Literature*, ed. Francisco Jiménez (New York: Bilingual Press, 1979).

50 The use of code switching is one of the most dramatic markers of Chicano poetry. Code switching refers to the blending, within the same sentence, of the grammatical structures of two or more languages or dialects. For the Chicano, these languages can include any combination of linguistic codes at hand, including formal Spanish, formal English, varieties of colloquial forms of both languages, and Náhuatl, the language of the Aztecs that still functions as the dominant native language of Mexico. See Rosaura Sánchez, *Chicano Discourse: Socio-Historic Perspectives* (Rowley, Mass.: Newbury House, 1983). Juan Bruce-Novoa prefers the term "interlingualism": "The mixing of two languages I call interlingualism, because the two languages are put into a state of tension which produces a third, an 'inter' possibility of language. 'Bilingualism' implies moving from one language code to another; 'inter-

lingualism' implies the constant tension of the two at once" ("The Other Voice of Silence: Tino Villanuaeva," in *Modern Chicano Writers*, ed. Joseph Sommers and Tómas Ybarra-Frausto (New York: Prentice-Hall, 1979), 133.

51 See Cordelia Candelaria, *Chicano Poetry: A Critical Introduction* (Westport, Conn.: Greenwood Press, 1986), 100.

52 Ignacio M. García, *Chicanismo: The Forging of a Militant Ethos among Mexican Americans* (Tucson: University of Arizona Press, 1997), 97.

53 Rafael Pérez-Torres, *Movements in Chicano Poetry: Against Myths, against Margins* (Cambridge: Cambridge University Press, 1995), 62.

54 Alurista, "Myth, Identity, and Struggle in Three Chicano Novels: Aztlán . . . Anaya, Méndez, and Acosta," in *European Perspectives on Hispanic Literature of the United States* (Houston: Arte Publico Press, 1988), 84.

55 Pérez-Torres, *Movements in Chicano Poetry*, 96.

56 It would be interesting to read Bhabha in terms of his positioning of himself against the "bad Hegel" of dialectical sublation (see, for example, *LC* 61).

57 García Canclini quotes artist Felipe Ehrenberg as saying: "Sometimes one can be more of a Mexican artist in the United States than in Mexico" (interview with author, Mexico City, 6 June 1988).

58 Laclau, *Emancipation(s)*, 65.

59 How exactly Spivak imagines this "two-way dialogue" to take place, given the grounds of her conception of the radical Alterity of the subaltern and the problems inherent in any practice of "speaking," remains to be seen.

60 Pérez-Torres, *Movements in Chicano Poetry*, 226.

61 Spivak writes: "As this [multicultural] material begins to be absorbed into the discipline, the long-established but supple, heterogeneous and hierarchical power-lines of institutional 'dissemination of knowledge' continue to determine and over-determine their condition of representability. It is at the moment of infiltration or insertion, sufficiently under threat by custodians of a fantasmatic high Western culture, that the greatest caution must be exercised" (*PMPV* 200–201).

62 Slavoj Žižek, "Multiculturalism, or, the Cultural Logic of Multinational Capitalism," *New Left Review* 225 (September/October 1997): 46.

63 Aijaz Ahmad, "The Politics of Literary Postcoloniality," in *Contemporary Postcolonial Theory: A Reader*, ed. Padmini Mongia (London: Arnold, 1996): 276–93.

64 Cited in *Culture Clash: Life, Death, and Revolutionary Comedy* (New York: Theater Communications Group, 1998), xiii.

65 Alurista, cited in *Chicano Authors: Inquiry by Interviews*, Juan Bruce-Novoa (Austin: University of Texas Press, 1980), 276. Italicized comments were originally in Spanish, but were translated into English by Bruce-Novoa.

BIBLIOGRAPHY

Acuña, Rodolfo F. *Anything but Mexican: Chicanos in Contemporary Los Angeles.* London: Verso, 1996.

Ahmad, Aijaz. *Lenin and Philosophy.* London: New Left Books, 1971.

——. *Philosophy and the Spontaneous Philosophy of the Scientists and Other Essays.* Edited by Gregory Elliott. New York: Verso, 1990.

——. "The Politics of Literary Postcoloniality." In *Contemporary Postcolonial Theory: A Reader.* Edited by Padmini Mongia. London: Arnold, 1996.

Althusser, Louis. *For Marx.* Translated by Ben Brewster. London: Verso, 1990.

Althusser, Louis, and Etienne Balibar. *Reading Capital.* Translated by Ben Brewster. New York: Monthly Review Press, 1971.

Althusser, Louis, Etienne Balibar, Roger Establet, Pierre Macherey, and Jacques Rancière. *Lire le Capital.* 2 volumes. Paris: F. Maspero, 1965.

Alurista. *Chicano Authors: Inquiry by Interviews*, by Juan Bruce-Novoa. Austin: University of Texas Press, 1980.

——. "Myth, Identity, and Struggle in Three Chicano Novels: Aztlán . . . Anaya, Méndez, and Acosta." In *European Perspectives on Hispanic Literature of the United States.* Houston: Arte Publico Press, 1988.

——. *Nationchild Plumaroja.* San Diego: Toltecas en Aztlán, 1972.

——. "El Plan Espiritual de Aztlán." In *Aztlán: Essays on the Chicano Homeland*, edited by Rudolfo A. Anaya and Francisco Lomelí. Albuquerque: El Norte Publications, 1989.

Anzaldúa, Gloria. *Borderlands/La Frontera: The New Mestiza.* San Francisco: Spinsters/aunt lute, 1987.

Arteaga, Alfred. *Chicano Poetics: Heterotexts and Hybridities.* Cambridge: Cambridge University Press, 1997.

Ashbery, John. "Syringa." In *Houseboat Days.* New York: Viking Press, 1977.

Auerbach, Eric. *Mimesis.* Princeton, N.J.: Princeton University Press, 1953.

Benhabib, Seyla. *Critique, Norm, and Utopia: A Study of the Foundations of Critical Theory.* New York: Columbia University Press, 1986.

Bhabha, Homi. *The Location of Culture.* London: Routledge, 1994.

Boer, Roland. *Jameson and Jeroboam.* Atlanta: Scholars Press, 1996.

Bruce-Novoa, Juan. "The Other Voice of Silence: Tino Villanuaeva." In *Modern Chicano Writers*, edited by Joseph Sommers and Tómas Ybarra-Frausto. New York: Prentice-Hall, 1979.

Buck-Morss, Susan. "Hegel and Haiti." *Critical Inquiry* 26, no. 4 (summer 2000): 821–65.

Burnham, Clint. *The Jamesonian Unconscious: The Aesthetics of Marxist Theory*. Durham, N.C.: Duke University Press, 1995.

Butler, Judith P. *Bodies That Matter: On the Discursive Limits of "Sex."* New York: Routledge, 1993.

——. *Gender Trouble: Feminism and the Subversion of Identity*. New York: Routledge, 1990.

Butler, Judith, Ernesto Laclau, and Slavoj Žižek. *Contingency, Hegemony, Universality: Contemporary Dialogues on the Left*. London: Verso, 2000.

Callinicos, Alex. *Althusser's Marxism*. London: Pluto, 1976.

——. *Is There a Future for Marxism?* London: Macmillan, 1982.

Candelaria, Cordelia. *Chicano Poetry: A Critical Introduction*. Westport, Conn.: Greenwood Press, 1986.

——. "Code-Switching as Metaphor in Chicano Poetry." In *European Perspectives on Hispanic Literature of the United States*. Houston: Arte Público Press, 1988.

Caruth, Cathy. "The Force of Example: Kant's Symbols." *Yale French Studies* 74 (1988): 17–37.

Cassirer, Ernst. *Kant's Life and Thought*. Translated by James Haden. New Haven, Conn.: Yale University Press, 1981.

Clark, Michael. "Imagining the Real: Jameson's Use of Lacan." *New Orleans Review* 11, no. 1 (spring 1984): 67–72.

Cohen, Ted, and Paul Guyer, eds. *Essays in Kant's Aesthetics*. Chicago: University of Chicago Press, 1982.

Culture Clash: Life, Death, and Revolutionary Comedy. New York: Theater Communications Group, 1998.

Cutler, Anthony, et al. *Marx's Capital and Capitalism Today*. London: Routledge and Kegan Paul, 1977.

Deleuze, Gilles. *Kant's Critical Philosophy: The Doctrine of the Faculties*. Translated by Hugh Tomlinson and Barbara Habberjam. London: Athlone Press, 1984.

Deleuze, Gilles, and Félix Guattari. *Kafka: Toward a Minor Literature*. Translated by Dana Polan. Minneapolis: University of Minnesota Press, 1986.

Derrida, Jacques. "Economimesis." *diacritics* 11, no. 2 (June 1981): 21–22.

——. "The Pit and the Pyramid." In *Margins of Philosophy*, translated by Alan Bass. Chicago: University of Chicago Press, 1982.

——. "White Mythology." In *The Margins of Philosophy*, translated by Alan Bass. Chicago: University of Chicago Press, 1982.

Dews, Peter. *Logics of Disintegration: Post-Structuralist Thought and the Claims of Critical Theory*. London: Verso, 1987.

Dowling, William C. *Jameson, Althusser, Marx: An Introduction to the Political Unconscious*. Ithaca, N.Y.: Cornell University Press, 1984.

Eagleton, Terry. *Against the Grain: Selected Essays, 1975–1985*. London: Verso, 1986.

———. *Criticism and Ideology*. London: Verso, 1976.

———. *The Ideology of the Aesthetic*. Oxford: Basil Blackwell, 1990.

Eco, Umberto. *The Role of the Reader*. Bloomington: Indiana University Press, 1979.

Ehrenberg, Felipe. Interview by García Canclini, Mexico City, 6 June 1988.

Elson, Diane, ed. *Value: The Representation of Labor in Capitalism*. London: CSE Books, 1979.

Fichte, Johann Gottlieb. *Science of Knowledge*. Edited and translated by Peter Heath and John Lachs. Cambridge: Cambridge University Press, 1982.

Findlay, J. N. *Kant and the Transcendental Object: A Hermeneutic Study*. Oxford: Clarendon Press, 1981.

Flieger, Jerry Anne. "The Prison-House of Ideology: Critic as Inmate." *diacritics* 12, no. 3 (fall 1992): 50.

Foucault, Michel, and Gilles Deleuze. "Intellectuals and Power: A Conversation between Michel Foucault and Gilles Deleuze." In *Language, Counter-Memory, Practice: Selected Essays and Interviews*, translated by Donald Bouchard and Sherry Simon. Ithaca, N.Y.: Cornell University Press, 1977.

Freud, Sigmund. *The Interpretation of Dreams*. Translated by James Strachey. New York: Basic Books, 1955.

García, Ignacio M. *Chicanismo: The Forging of a Militant Ethos among Mexican Americans*. Tucson: University of Arizona Press, 1977.

García Canclini, Néstor. "Cultural Reconversion." In *On Edge: The Crisis of Contemporary Latin American Culture*, edited by George Yudice, Juan Flores, and Jean Franco. Minneapolis: University of Minnesota Press, 1992.

———. *Hybrid Cultures: Strategies for Entering and Leaving Modernity*. Minneapolis: University of Minnesota Press, 1995.

Garibay, Angel María. *Llave del Náhuatl*. Mexico City: Porrua, 1970.

Glucksmann, André. "A Ventriloquist Marxism." *New Left Review* 72 (March–April 1972): 68–92.

Gomez-Peña, Guillermo. *The New World Border*. San Francisco: City Lights Books, 1996.

Gonzales, Rodolfo "Corky." *I Am Joaquín. Message to Aztlán: Selected Writings of Rodolfo "Corky" Gonzales*. Edited by Antonio Esquibel. Houston: Arte Público Press, 2001.

Guha, Ranajit, ed. *Selected Subaltern Studies*. New York: Oxford University Press, 1988.

Guyer, Paul. *Kant and the Claims of Taste*. 2d ed. Cambridge: Cambridge University Press, 1997.

Hammel, Eckhard. "Hegel und die Dingproduktion: Ein Einblick in Lacans Hegel-Rezeption." *Hegel-Studien* 23 (1988): 227–44.

Hardimon, Michael O. *Hegel's Social Philosophy: The Project of Reconciliation.* Cambridge: Cambridge University Press, 1994.

Hartley, George. "Jameson's Perelman: Reification and the Material Signifier." *Poetics Journal 7* (September 1987): 52–62.

——. *Textual Politics and the Language Poets.* Bloomington: Indiana University Press, 1989.

Heath, Stephen. *Questions of Cinema.* Bloomington: Indiana University Press, 1981.

Hegel, Georg Wilhelm Friedrich. *The Difference between the Fichtean and Schellingian Systems of Philosophy.* Translated by H. S. Harris and Walter Cerf. Albany: State University of New York Press, 1977.

——. *Elements of the Philosophy of Right.* Edited by Allen W. Wood. Cambridge: Cambridge University Press, 1991.

——. *Logic.* Translated by William Wallace. Oxford: Clarendon Press, 1975.

——. *Phenomenology of Spirit.* Translated by A. V. Miller. Oxford: Clarendon Press, 1977.

——. *Philosophy of Mind.* Translated by A. V. Miller. Oxford: Clarendon Press, 1971.

——. *Philosophy of Nature.* Translated by A. V. Miller. Oxford: Clarendon Press, 1970.

——. *Science of Logic.* Translated by A. V. Miller. New York: Humanities Press, 1969.

Heidegger, Martin. *Being and Time.* Translated by John Macquarrie and Edward Robinson. San Francisco: Harper and Row, 1962.

——. *Hegel's Concept of Experience.* New York: Harper and Row, 1970.

——. *Kant and the Problem of Metaphysics.* Translated by James S. Churchill. Bloomington: Indiana University Press, 1962.

——. *Nietzsche.* Translated by David Farrell Krell. San Francisco: Harper and Row, 1979.

——. *Poetry, Language, Thought.* Translated by Albert Hofstadter. New York: Harper and Row, 1971.

Homer, Sean. *Fredric Jameson: Marxism, Hermeneutics, Postmodernism.*

Jameson, Fredric. *Brecht and Method.* London: Verso, 1998.

——. "Cognitive Mapping." In *Marxism and the Interpretation of Culture,* edited by Cary Nelson and Lawrence Grossberg. Urbana: University of Illinois Press, 1988.

——. *Fables of Aggression: Wyngham Lewis, the Modernist as Fascist.* Berkeley: University of California Press, 1979.

——. *The Geo-Political Aesthetic.* Bloomington: Indiana University Press, 1992.

——. *Ideologies of Theory.* 2 vols. Minneapolis: University of Minnesota Press, 1988.

——. *Late Marxism: Adorno, or, the Persistence of the Dialectic.* London: Verso, 1990.

——. *The Political Unconscious.* Ithaca, N.Y.: Cornell University Press, 1981.

——. "Postmodernism, or, the Cultural Logic of Late Capitalism." *New Left Review* 146 (July–August 1984): 52–92.

——. *Postmodernism, or, The Cultural Logic of Late Capitalism.* Durham, N.C.: Duke University Press, 1991.

——. *The Seeds of Time.* New York: Columbia University Press, 1994.

——. *Signatures of the Visible*. New York: Routledge, 1990.

Kafka, Franz. *Collected Stories*. New York: Schocken Books, 1988.

Kant, Immanuel. *Critique of Judgment*. Translated with analytical indexes by James Creed Meredith. Oxford: Clarendon Press, 1952.

——. *Critique of Practical Reason*. Translated by Lewis White Beck. New York: Liberal Arts Press, 1956.

——. *Critique of Pure Reason*. Translated by Norman Kemp Smith. New York: Modern Library, 1958.

——. *First Introduction to the Critique of Judgement*. Translated by James Haden. Indianapolis: Bobbs-Merrill, 1965.

——. *Gesammelte Schriften: Herausgegeben von de Königlich preussischen Akademie der Wissenschaften*. Berlin: W. de Gruyter, 1969.

——. *Kritik der Urteilskraft*. Hamburg: F. Meiner, 1959.

——. *Perpetual Peace and Other Essays on Politics, History, and Morals*. Translated by Ted Humphrey. Indianapolis: Hackett Publishing Company, 1983.

Kaplan, E. Ann, and Michael Sprinker, eds. *The Althusserian Legacy*. New York: Verso, 1993.

Kaufman, Robert. "Red Kant, or the Persistence of the Third Critique in Adorno and Jameson." *Critical Inquiry* 26, no. 4 (summer 2000): 682–724.

Kellner, Douglas, ed. *Postmodernism/Jameson/Critique*. Washington, D.C.: Maisonneuve Press, 1989.

Kemal, Salim. *Kant's Aesthetic Theory*. New York: St. Martin's Press, 1992.

Lacan, Jacques. *The Four Fundamental Concepts of Psycho-Analysis*. New York: W. W. Norton, 1981.

——. *The Seminar of Jacques Lacan: Book I*. Translated by John Forrester. New York: W. W. Norton, 1988.

Laclau, Ernesto. *Emancipation(s)*. London: Verso, 1996.

——. *New Reflections on the Revolution of Our Time*. New York: Verso, 1990.

Laclau, Ernesto, and Chantal Mouffe. *Hegemony and Socialist Strategy*. London: Verso, 1985.

Lafaye, Jacques. *Quetzalcóatl and Guadalupe*. Chicago: University of Chicago Press, 1974.

Lenin, Vladimir Ilyich. "Marxism and Revisionism." *Collected Works*. Volume 15. Moscow: Foreign Languages Publishing House, 1960–.

Lewis, Thomas E. "Reference and Dissemination: Althusser after Derrida." *diacritics* (winter 1985): 37–56.

Lukács, Georg. *Essays on Realism*. Edited by Rodney Livingstone. Translated by David Fernbach. London: Lawrence and Wishart, 1980.

——. *The Historical Novel*. Translated by Hannah and Stanley Mitchell. London: Merlin Press, 1962.

——. *History and Class Consciousness*. Cambridge, Mass.: MIT Press, 1971.

——. *Studies in European Realism*. Translated by Edith Bone. New York: Grosset and Dunlap, 1964.

——. *The Young Hegel*. Translated by Rodney Livingstone. Cambridge, Mass.: MIT, 1976.

Lyotard, Jean-François. *The Differend: Phrases in Dispute*. Translated by Georges Van Den Abbeele. Minneapolis: University of Minnesota Press, 1988.

Mandel, Ernest. *Late Capitalism*. Translated by Rodney Livingstone. Cambridge, Mass.: MIT, 1972.

Marcuse, Herbert. *Hegel's Ontology and the Theory of Historicity*. Translated by Seyla Benhabib. Cambridge, Mass.: MIT, 1987.

Marin, Louis. *Utopics: Spatial Play*. Translated by Robert A. Vollrath. Atlantic Highlands, N.J.: Humanities Press, 1984.

Marx, Karl. *Capital: A Critique of Political Economy*. Translated by Ben Fowkes. 3 vols. New York: Penguin, 1981.

——. *Contribution to the Critique of Hegel's Philosophy of Right: Early Writings*. Translated and edited by T. B. Bottomore. New York: McGraw-Hill, 1964.

——. *The Eighteenth Brumaire of Louis Bonaparte*. In *Surveys from Exile: Political Writings, Volume II*, edited by David Fernbach. New York: Vintage, 1974.

——. *Grundrisse*. Translated by Martin Nicolaus. New York: Penguin, 1973.

Marx, Karl, and Friedrich Engels. *The German Ideology*. Edited by R. Pascal. Parts 1 and 3. New York: International Publishers, 1947.

——. *Werke*. 39 vols. Berlin: Dietz Verlag, 1969.

McCumber, John. *The Company of Words. Hegel, Language, and Systematic Philosophy*. Evanston, Ill.: Northwestern University Press, 1993.

Medovoi, Leerom, Shankar Raman, and Benjamin Robinson. "Can the Subaltern Vote?" *Socialist Review* 20, no. 3 (July–September): 133–49.

Mignolo, Walter. *The Darker Side of the Renaissance: Literacy, Territoriality, and Colonization*. Ann Arbor: University of Michigan Press, 1995.

——. *Local Cultures/Global Designs*. Princeton, N.J.: Princeton University Press, 1998.

Moraga, Cherríe. *The Last Generation*. Boston: South End Press, 1993.

Nietzsche, Friedrich. *The Birth of Tragedy and the Case of Wagner*. Translated by Walter Kaufmann. New York: Vintage Books, 1967.

O'Hanlon, Rosalind. "Recovering the Subject: Subaltern Studies and Histories of Resistance in Colonial South Asia." *Modern Asian Studies* 22 (1988): 189–224.

Paz, Octavio. "The *Pachuco* and Other Extremes." In *The Labyrinth of Solitude*. New York: Grove Press, 1961.

Pérez-Torres, Rafael. *Movements in Chicano Poetry: Against Myths, against Margins*. Cambridge: Cambridge University Press, 1995.

Plato. *The Republic of Plato*. Translated by Allen Bloom. New York: Basic Books, 1968.

Prakash, Gyan. "Subaltern Studies as Postcolonial Criticism." *American Historical Review* 99, no. 5 (December 1994): 1475–90.

Rodríguez, Juan. "La búsqueda de dentidad y sus motivos en la literatura chicana." In *The Identification and Analysis of Chicano Literature*, edited by Francisco Jiménez. New York: Bilingual Press, 1979.

Rose, Gillian. *Hegel contra Sociology*. London: Athlone, 1981.

Sallis, John. *Being and Logos: The Way of Platonic Dialogue*. Atlantic Highlands, N.J.: Humanities Press International, 1986.

———. *Crossings: Nietzsche and the Space of Tragedy*. Chicago: University of Chicago Press, 1991.

———. *The Gathering of Reason*. Athens: Ohio University Press, 1980.

Sánchez, Rosaura. *Chicano Discourse: Socio-Historic Perspectives*. Rowley, Mass.: Newbury House, 1983.

Shepherdson, Charles. "History and the Real: Foucault with Lacan." *Postmodern Culture* 5, no. 2 (January 1995) (http://www.iath.virginia.edu/pmc/text-only/issue.195/shepherd.195).

Spivak, Gayatri Chakravorty. "Can the Subaltern Speak?" In *Marxism and the Interpretation of Culture*, edited by Cary Nelson and Lawrence Grossberg. Urbana: University of Illinois Press, 1988.

———. *A Critique of Postcolonial Reason: Toward a History of the Vanishing Present*. Cambridge, Mass.: Harvard University Press, 1999.

———. "Gayatri Spivak on the Politics of the Subaltern." Interview by Howard Winant. *Socialist Review* 20, no. 3 (July–September 1990): 81–97.

———. *In Other Worlds*. New York: Routledge, 1987.

———. "Poststructuralism, Marginality, Postcoloniality, and Value." In *Contemporary Postcolonial Theory*, edited by Padmini Mongia. London: Arnold, 1996.

———. "The Rani of Sirmur: An Essay in Reading the Archives." *History and Theory* 24 (1985): 247–72.

Sprinker, Michael. *Imaginary Relations: Aesthetics and Ideology in the Theory of Historical Materialism*. London: Verso, 1987.

Torfing, Jacob. *New Theories of Discourse: Laclau, Mouffe, and Žižek*. Oxford: Blackwell Publishers, 1999.

Varadharajan, Asha. *Exotic Parodies: Subjectivity in Adorno, Said, and Spivak*. Minneapolis: University of Minnesota Press, 1995.

Vilar, Pierre. "Marxist History, a History in the Making: Towards a Dialogue with Althusser." In *Althusser: A Critical Reader*, edited by Gregory Elliott. Oxford, U.K.: Blackwell Publishers, 1994.

Villanueva, Tino. Prologue to *Chicanos: Antología histórica y literaria*. Mexico City: Fondo de Cultura Económica, 1980.

Warminski, Andrej. "Pre-positional By-play." *Glyph* 3 (1978): 183–91.

West, Cornel. "Ethics and Action in Fredric Jameson's Marxist Hermeneutics." In *Postmodernism and Politics*, edited by Jonathan Arac. Minneapolis: University of Minnesota Press, 1986.

Williams, Raymond. *Marxism and Literature*. Oxford: Oxford University Press, 1977.

Wood, Allen W. *Hegel's Ethical Thought*. Cambridge: Cambridge University Press, 1990.

——. "Hegel's Ethics." In *The Cambridge Companion to Hegel*, edited by Frederick L. Beiser. Cambridge: Cambridge University Press, 1993.

Woodard, Komozi. *A Nation within a Nation: Amiri Baraka (LeRoi Jones) and Black Power Politics*. Chapel Hill: University of North Carolina Press, 1999.

Ybarra-Frausto, Tomás. "Alurista's Poetics: The Oral, the Bilingual, the Pre-Columbian." In *Modern Chicano Writers*, edited by Joseph Sommers and Tomás Ybarra-Frausto. Englewood Cliffs, N.J.: Prentice-Hall, 1979.

Yúdice, George. "We Are *Not* the World." *Social Text* 31/32 (1992): 202–16.

Zammito, John H. *The Genesis of Kant's Critique of Judgment*. Chicago: University of Chicago Press, 1992.

Žižek, Slavoj. *Enjoy Your Symptom*. New York: Routledge, 1992.

——. *For They Know Not What They Do*. London: Verso, 1991.

——. *The Indivisible Remainder: An Essay on Schelling and Related Matters*. London: Verso, 1996.

——. *Looking Awry: An Introduction to Jacques Lacan through Popular Culture*. Cambridge, Mass.: MIT Press, 1992.

——. *The Metastases of Enjoyment: Six Essays on Woman and Causality*. New York: Verso, 1996.

——. "Multiculturalism, or, the Cultural Logic of Multinational Capitalism." *New Left Review* 225 (September/October 1997): 28–51.

——. *The Sublime Object of Ideology*. London: Verso, 1991.

——. *Tarrying with the Negative: Kant, Hegel, and the Critique of Ideology*. Durham, N.C.: Duke University Press, 1993.

——. *The Ticklish Subject*. London: Verso, 1999.

Zupancic, Alenka. *Ethics of the Real: Kant, Lacan*. New York: Verso, 2000.

INDEX

Absence, 37, 90, 102, 139, 189, 199, 201, 234, 240; determinate, 90

Absent cause, 90, 94, 135, 139, 156, 157, 161, 172, 212; and effect, 75

Absolute, 56, 58, 70, 167, 168; as subject, 56, 58, 75–78

Abyss, 1, 4, 9, 11, 15, 16, 19, 23, 26, 57, 212, 218, 227, 243, 254, 294. *See also* Representation: abyss of

Accord of faculties, 34, 41, 42, 46

Act, psychoanalytic, 226–32. *See also* Psychoanalysis

Actual, 77, 79–80, 171, 208; and rational, 53–54, 78–83

Actualization, 73

Acuña, Rodolfo F., 316 n. 36

Adorno, Theodor, 307–8 n. 8

Aesthetic attributes, 40, 43, 44

Aesthetic idea, 39–40, 43

Aestheticism, 148

Aesthetics, 31, 186, 195, 286

Alienation, 89, 132, 139, 146, 148, 167, 169, 170, 244; theory of, 121

Allegory, 64, 129, 130–36, 142, 145, 148, 175–76, 221

Althusser, Louis, 3, 6, 7, 8, 9, 12, 17, 21, 22, 84–95, 102, 105, 121, 122–24, 128, 156, 157, 161, 179, 183–207, 210, 271, 272, 296–97 n. 10, 297–98 n. 2, 302 n. 1, 303 n. 5, 304 n. 11, 305–6 n. 21, 309 n. 7; Generality II, 100; on ideology, 17, 18, 137, 225–26, 234; on internal distantiation, 193; on interpellation, *see* Interpellation; *Lenin and Philosophy*, 191; "A Letter on Art," 191, 193; on Marx, 16–17, 84–95; on *El Nost Milan*, 184, 186–89; "The 'Piccolo Teatro': Ber-

tolazzi and Brecht," 184, 191, 193; *Reading Capital*, 84, 93, 101, 160, 183, 188–89, 191–92, 195, 197–206, 224; on structural causality, *see* Causality: structural

Alurista, 277–80, 292–93, 317 n. 49, 318 n. 65; "A Child to Be Born," 278–80; "El Plan Espiritual de Aztlán," 278

America, 227, 259, 271, 290, 291

Amerindians, 277, 279

Analogy, 39, 47, 48, 168

Anglo-Americans, 19, 260–61, 265, 274, 277, 279, 280, 286, 290

Antagonism, 4, 206, 259–68

Antiessentialism, 91. *See also* Essentialism

Antigone, 231

Antinomy, 141

Anti-purposiveness, 36–37, 190

Anzaldúa, Gloria, 275, 316 n. 41

Apollonian, vs. Dionysian, 207, 208, 209, 211, 214

Aporia, 141, 144, 256, 258, 266, 213

Appearance, 14, 31, 170, 172, 176, 208, 213; vs. essence, 4, 135, 139, 162–63, 166–67, 170, 173

Art, 40, 42–45, 83, 141, 148, 192, 193, 216, 218

Art drives, 209

Articulation, 52, 82, 205–6, 211, 253; defined, 259

Ashbery, John, 1; "Syringa," 15

Auerbach, Erich, 130–31

Avant-garde, 148

Axiomatic, 178–79, 180

Aztecs, 279

Aztlán, 276, 278–82, 284, 291

Balzac, Honoré de, 142, 174, 177–80; *La Rabouilleuse*, 177; *La Vieille Fille*. 142–45, 149, 177

Base-superstructure, 87, 140–41

Beautiful, 30, 31–34, 36, 38, 39, 41, 42, 45, 163, 216, 217

Beauty, as symbol of good, 39

Becoming, dialectical, 59

Begriff, 240. *See also* Concept

Being, 213; and not-being, 216

Benjamin, Walter, 148

Bertolazzi, 186–88

Beyond, 50, 167, 168, 169, 172

Bhabha, Homi, 273–85, 318 n. 56

Big Other, 12, 14, 15. *See also* Other; Symbolic: order

Binary opposition, 133, 153, 266

Black Arts Movement, 317 n. 42

Body, 11, 69, 237

Borderland, 275, 281

Bourgeoisie, 97, 175, 178, 246, 248

Brecht, Bertolt, 186–88

Bruce-Novoa, Juan, 317–18 n. 50, 318 n. 65

Buck-Morss, Susan, 315 n. 30

Burke, Edmund, 224

Burke, Kenneth, 158

Callinicos, Alex, 302 n. 1

Camera obscura, 183

Canclini, Néstor García, 282, 285–88, 318 n. 57

Capital, 139, 184, 292

Capitalism, 103, 107, 137–40, 144, 151, 227–28; global, 235, 240–43, 246, 249–51, 254, 269; late, 18, 129, 134, 135, 136, 219–26, 234, 288–94; monopoly, 138–39; multinational, 129, 138, 139–40, 141, 149, 280, 289, 291

Caruth, Cathy, 51

Cassirer, Ernst, 299 n. 9

Catachresis, 245, 269

Causality, 29, 45, 46, 165, 174, 302 n. 2; expressive, 87–91, 123; metonymic, 187; structural, 17, 84–85, 87–91, 101, 103, 113, 118–20, 123, 160, 183, 185–97, 302 n. 1, 303 n. 6, 305 n. 20; teleological, 46–47; transitive, 87

Cause: absent, 90, 94, 135, 139, 156, 157, 161, 172, 212; and effect, 75

Chamorro, Violetta, 257–58

Chiasmus, 96, 99

Chicanismo, 257, 276

Chicanos, 19, 260–61, 274, 286, 316 n. 39, 317 n. 43; defined, 277

Chicano Movement, 276–93, 317 n. 42

Christ, 131–32, 169

Church, Roman Catholic, 88, 279, 286

Circulation, 227

Class, 129, 175; consciousness, 129, 156, 247–48; discourse, 133, 134, 173; interest, 247–48; relations, 156; struggle, 226

Clinton, Bill, 260

Code, 135, 137

Code-switching, 280, 289, 291, 317 n. 50

Cognitive mapping, 18, 21, 22, 126, 130, 135, 136–40, 225, 233–34, 236, 238, 289–90

Colonialism, 224, 249, 252, 282. *See also* Neo-colonialism; Postcolonialism

Commodity, 95, 103, 104, 106, 107, 108, 110, 112, 116, 120, 121, 175

Commodity-body, 104, 105

Communism, 120, 150, 231, 260

Concept, 4, 6, 26, 33, 37, 40, 42, 43, 45, 48, 84, 113, 183–84, 187–97, 207, 210, 218, 240; constitutive, 30; empty, 218, 240, 260; of reason, 29, 34; regulative, 29, 30, 41; of understanding, 33, 34, 163

Concrete, 50, 99

Condensation, 177

Consciousness, 246; false, 204; spectatorial, 185, 188; subaltern, 243–44

Contingency, 41, 46, 48, 82

Contradiction, 121, 140, 141, 143, 144, 150, 158, 176, 178, 180; internal, 273

Copula, 70, 195

Counternarratives, 283–84

Counter-nationalism, 276–82

Counter-syncretism, 279

Cultural dominant, 134, 271, 291

Culture, 129, 282
Culture Clash, 292
Cultural studies, 228
Cutler, Anthony, 305 n. 20

Darstellung, 19, 21, 25, 26, 33, 34, 37, 58–61,
    78, 84–126, 183, 212, 220, 258; theatrical,
    183–95; three senses of, 86; vs. Vertretung,
    121, 247–52, 258, 266, 305 n. 17, 314 n. 18;
    vs. Vorstellung, 4, 16, 59, 93–94, 182, 188–
    89, 194, 195, 258, 267. *See also* Presenta-
    tion; Representation; Vertreten;
    Vorstellung
Dasien, 63, 66, 195, 207, 209
Decolonization, 255, 236
Deconstruction, 241, 254, 257, 291; politics
    of, 283
Defamiliarization, 60
Deleuze, Gilles, 30, 46, 121, 199, 245–46, 248–
    50, 258, 266, 270, 288
Democracy, 11, 170, 213, 228, 259–60
Derrida, Jacques, 60, 202, 211, 237, 288, 299–
    300 n. 10
Desire, 6, 14, 16, 17, 42, 65, 130, 175, 177, 180
Destitution, subjective, 5, 230, 232. *See also*
    Desubjectivization; Subject; Subjectivity;
    Subjectivization
Desubjectivization, 11, 227. *See also* Subjec-
    tivization; Destitution, subjective
Determinacy, 74
Determination, 49, 56–57, 70, 71, 77, 80, 87
Dialectic, 73, 111, 179, 185, 211, 215, 256, 271; la-
    bor of, 65; representational, 137. *See also*
    Method: dialectical
Dialectics: Hegelian, 84, 96, 97, 135; Marxist,
    99
Différance, 239, 266, 288
Difference, 205, 282; logic of, 205
Differend, 253, 258, 313 n. 16
Differential, 260, 261, 263
Dionysian, vs. Apollonian, 207–9, 211, 214,
    215

Discourse, 240
Discursivity, 45, 50
Disinterestedness, 33, 191
Disneyland, 222–24
Division of labor, 249
Drama, 61
Dream-work, 243–44
Drive, 230, 232
Dussel, Enrique, 271–72

Eagleton, Terry, 195, 196
East India Company, 236
Eco, Umberto, 195
Effect, structural, 119
Effectivity, 87, 121
Eidos, 215–17
El Movimiento, 276–93, 317 n. 42
Embodiment, 13, 14, 15, 19, 44, 48, 51, 70, 73,
    76, 82, 103, 109, 113, 114, 115, 122, 171, 180,
    184, 211–12, 219, 227, 236, 241, 247, 258, 259,
    264, 265, 275. *See also* Versinnlichung
Empiricism, 88, 91, 94, 102, 123, 183, 193, 194,
    195, 204
Engels, Friedrich, 102–3
English-only legislation, 292
Enjoyment, 12, 13, 16, 230
Enlightenment, 208, 266
Entäusserung, 61, 64, 65, 66, 67, 68, 69, 211, 244
Enthusiasm, vs. fanaticism, 213–14
Entstellung, 244
Entzweiung, 71
Epistemological break, 224
Epistemology, 183, 251, 256
Equivalence, 269
Erinnerung, 63, 65, 66
Erscheinungsform, 95, 104, 107, 119, 120
Essence, 88, 172
Essentialism, 205, 245, 261, 266, 280–81, 288
Europe, 271
Excess, 228
Exchange, 107, 117
Exchange-value, 103–4, 110, 112, 119

Existence, 64, 66, 71

Experience, 129, 162, 172, 239; aesthetic, 24, 34, 239; negative, 162, 240

Expressive causality, 87, 88–91, 123

External reflection. *See* Reflection

Externality, 70, 167, 167

Externalization, 61, 64, 65, 66, 67, 68, 69, 211, 244

Fascism, 227, 265

Fantasm, 176–77, 178, 180, 223

Fantasy, 5, 11, 149, 176, 227, 229, 230, 232, 234, 241, 282

Feeling: aesthetic, 39, 41, 42, 191; moral, 25, 41, 42

Feminism, 242, 272

Fetishism of commodities, 61, 89, 95, 101–2, 108, 118–20, 121

Fetishistic disavowal, 214, 233

Feudalism, 144, 149, 150, 173

Fichte, Johann, 9, 50, 56–58, 61, 77, 109; *Science of Knowledge*, 56

Figuration, 14, 15, 17, 21, 59, 64, 75, 86, 126, 128–29, 132, 133, 134, 136, 138, 139, 141–42, 146, 148, 151, 152, 154, 156, 157, 161, 163, 166, 174, 180, 207, 222, 225, 234, 243, 253, 258; tragic, 206–15

Figurativeness, 3, 149

Figure, 129, 136, 182, 195, 207, 241

Finality, 180; relative, 49. *See also* Purposiveness; Zweckmäßigkeit

Findlay, J. N., 299 n. 8

Form: appearance, 95, 104, 107, 119, 120; commodity, 87, 88, 94, 104, 119; dialectic of value, 106, 107, 110, 113, 114–18, 120; equivalent, 108, 115; expanded, 110–11, 115; general, 111–13, 115; money, 113–18; relative, 108, 109, 115; simple, 106, 107–10

Formalism, 62

Forschung, 98

Foucault, Michel, 6, 121, 237, 245–46, 248–50, 258, 266, 270, 288

Frankfurt School, 21

Freedom, 25, 40, 56, 62, 66, 79, 80, 82, 161, 170, 171

Freud, Sigmund, 6, 17, 127, 147, 153, 219, 253; *The Interpretation of Dreams*, 128, 243

Frye, Northrop, 130, 132–33

Gap, 17, 85, 200

García, Ignacio M., 280

Gedächtnis, 65–66, 67. *See also* Memory

Gedanke, 66, 78, 136

Geist, 7, 44

General equivalent, 111, 123

Genius, 40, 42–45, 210

Globalization, 267, 271, 288, 289. *See also* Capitalism

God, 51, 58, 167, 169, 211; as proposition, 75–78

Gonzales, Rodolfo "Corky," 276–77, 280, 317 n. 42

Goux, Jean-Joseph, 305 n. 17

Greimas, 142, 148

Ground, 41, 156, 174, 195, 273

Guattari, Felix, 199

Guha, Ranajit, 250

Guyer, Paul, 300 n. 12

Hailing, 8. *See also* Interpellation

Hegel, Georg Wilhelm Friedrich, 6, 11, 14, 19, 21, 26, 53–83, 85, 88, 89, 91, 95, 122, 123, 124, 128, 129, 164–71, 173, 178, 182, 194, 205, 212, 226, 231, 233, 258, 264, 269–70, 272, 273, 291, 301 nn. 1–5, 301 n. 8, 303 n. 5; *The Difference between the Fichtean and Schellingian Systems of Philosophy*, 56; *Encyclopedia*, 62, 75, 78; *Lectures on the Philosophy of Religion*, 53; *Phenomenology of Spirit*, 4, 50, 65, 70, 75–78, 96, 295 n. 7, 296 n. 8, 296 n. 11; *Science of Knowledge*, 56; *The Philosophy of Right*, 53, 78–83; *Science of Logic*, 69–74, 75, 91, 139, 162

Hegemony, 15, 19, 173, 183, 206, 255, 259–68, 272, 288, 315 n. 32

Heidegger, Martin, 60, 215, 237, 310 n. 22, 310–11 n. 23, 312 n. 5

Heterogeneity, 245–46, 255–56, 258, 266, 271

Hindess, Barry, 305 n. 20

Hirst, Paul, 305 n. 20

History, 54, 97–98, 100, 128, 130, 132, 134–35, 152, 156–67, 173, 174, 176, 210, 226, 236, 256–57, 262

Homer, Sean, 308 n. 9

Horizon, 198–203

Hume, David, 29

Hurley, James S., 311 n. 27

Husserl, Edmund, 61

Hybridity, 274, 279, 282–88

Hyperdiscourse, 291

Hyperspace, 218–20

Hypotyposis, 33, 34, 39

Hysteria, 12, 229, 233

Hysterical conversion, 14, 15, 16, 19

Hysterical sublime, 173, 218, 224–26

Hysterical theater, 14, 15, 16, 18, 231

Hystericization, 12, 13

Idea, 6, 24, 25, 35, 37, 39, 62, 169, 189, 213; aesthetic, 39–40, 43; of reason, 40

Idealism, German, 22, 96, 97

Identification, 13, 155, 186, 209, 238, 239, 269. *See also* Pathos; Symptom

Identity, 74, 109, 205, 250, 261–63, 276; Chicano, 276, 279; lack of, 74, 79; national, 276, 282–88, 292; speculative, 73, 269

Ideologeme, 133, 134, 173, 174

Ideological apparatus, 7, 174

Ideological closure, 148, 163

Ideological containment, 20

Ideological investment, 132, 145, 146

Ideological State Apparatuses (ISA), 205

Ideology, 7, 8, 9; critique, 14–15, 22; of form, 133, 134; national, 274; structuralist, 155, 159, 161; subject-position, 7, 8, 9, 85, 95, 121, 128, 152, 165, 182, 186, 191, 192–93, 198, 200, 204, 211, 214, 223, 225, 232, 236, 246,

248, 249, 256, 259–60, 262, 265, 270, 274, 277, 291

Illegal aliens, 268, 274–75

Image, 5, 35, 41, 48, 50, 59, 61, 63, 64, 75, 82, 164, 183, 194–95, 210, 213, 216, 217, 231, 243, 248, 258

Imaginary, 2, 7, 17, 152–55, 161, 176, 206, 225, 294; resolution, 140. *See also* Althusser, Louis; Lacan, Jacques

Imagination, 26, 27, 28, 31, 34, 35, 37, 39, 42, 43, 44, 62, 63–65, 164, 172

Imitation, 216, 218

Immanence, 91, 163, 198, 212

Immediacy, 75, 77, 195; abstract, 112

Immigrants, 265, 266, 268, 275, 293, 294

Imperialism, 138, 240, 253, 256; British, 237–38, 250

Impossibility, 19, 37, 38, 73, 74, 79, 86, 109, 114, 115, 239, 254–56, 259, 263

Inadequation, 109, 115

Incommensurability, 4, 23, 171, 195, 274, 276

Indeterminacy, 66, 70, 168

India, 236–43; Indian nationalist discourse, 252

Infrastructure, 87, 140–41

Intelligence, 64, 66, 67

Intelligibility, 43

Interest, 31, 40, 246

Interpellation, 3, 7, 8, 9, 11, 13, 17, 18, 123–24, 128, 182, 191, 229, 234, 308 n. 2, 308 n. 4, 309 n. 6

Interpretation, 130–36, 158

Intrinsic finality, 49. *See also* Purposiveness

Intuition, 26, 27, 28, 30, 31, 33, 34, 35, 37, 38, 39, 43, 48, 49, 59, 62, 63, 65–66, 67, 82, 83, 99, 163, 189, 220; intellectual, 6, 49, 50, 51, 65, 162

Intuitive intellect, 15, 189

Intuitive understanding, 16, 41, 48, 49

Inversion, 95

ISA, 205

Itinerary, 238, 242; defined, 252; of the trace, 251–54

Jakobson, Roman, 309 n. 10

Jameson, Fredric, 3, 6, 20, 21, 127–81, 233–34, 271, 306–7 n. 2, 307 nn. 5–6, 309 n. 9; on aesthetic of cognitive mapping, 137; on collective subject, 127, 148, 163; on *Dog Day Afternoon*, 129; *Fables of Aggression*, 139, 145, 174; *Ideologies of Theory*, 148; "Imaginary and Symbolic in Lacan," 152; "Of Islands and Trenches: Neutralization and the Production of Utopian Discourse," 148; on political unconscious, 3, 15, 17, 21, 126, 127, 128, 129, 130, 133, 135, 140, 141–42, 144, 148, 151, 162, 163, 164, 174–83; *The Political Unconscious*, 127, 130, 156, 173–83, 306 n. 1; on postmodernism, 22, 134, 291, 307 n. 7; "Postmodernism, or, the Cultural Logic of Late Capitalism," 136; on the sublime, 18, 23, 171–73, 218–26, 235, 240, 311 n. 25

Jouissance, 12, 13, 16, 230

Judaism, 169

Judgment, 25, 26–27, 35, 37, 69–74, 218; aesthetic, 27, 30, 32, 33, 39, 45, 163, 189–90, 193; apodeictic, 81; determining, 27; infinite, 9, 69–71, 78, 80; moral, 39, 163; reflective, 27, 45, 168, 189–90; of taste, 30, 31, 33; teleological, 27, 30, 32, 40, 45, 189, 225

Kafka, Franz, 18, 197–206; "The Great Wall of China," 197–206

Kahlo, Frida, 286

Kant, Immanuel, 6, 20, 21, 22–52, 62, 85, 122, 128, 131, 169, 182, 192, 193, 194, 209, 218, 237, 297 n. 1, 299 nn. 9–10; on aesthetic attributes, 43; on Aesthetic Idea, 43; *Critique of Judgment*, 23, 25, 26, 29, 30, 40, 45, 48, 213; *Critique of Pure Reason*, 25, 27, 28, 29, 49, 56; *Critique of Teleological Judgment*, 40, 164; on the sublime, 16, 22, 24, 25, 32, 36, 162–65, 224, 237

Kaufmann, Walter, 208

Kemal, Salim, 298 n. 4

Kernel, 168, 230, 297 n. 12

King's stupid body, 82, 171

Klein, Melanie, 154

Knowledge, 25, 155, 161, 162, 191–92, 246

Kramer, Lawrence, 295 n. 1

Kristeva, Julia, 61

Kunsttriebe, 209

Labor, 100, 101, 105–7, 108, 109, 110, 111, 120, 121

Labor-power, 103, 113

Labor-time, 102, 105, 106, 113, 114

Lacan, Jacques, 6, 9, 11, 12, 128, 145, 152–55, 157, 161, 174, 264, 296 n. 8, 302 n. 9; *The Four Fundamental Concepts of Psychoanalysis*, 159; and Hegel, 65, 165, 166, 182, 270; on the Imaginary, 17; on the Real, 17, 159; on the Symbolic, 17

Lack, 16, 115

Laclau, Ernesto, 19, 256, 259–68, 272, 291; *Emancipation(s)*, 263, 286–87; *Hegemony and Socialist Strategy*, 204–6

Lafaye, Jacques, 317 n. 48

Language, 43, 44, 51, 59, 67, 82, 154, 212, 291

Late Marxism, 21

Latin America, 271, 287

Left, 230, 257–58, 266, 268, 270, 273

Leftover, 12, 70, 73

Lévi-Strauss, Claude, 140–41, 142, 149, 162

Lewis, Thomas E., 195–97, 309 n. 9

Lewis, Wyndham, 145; *Tarr*, 147

Libidinal apparatus, 132, 135, 144–48, 151, 177

Libidinal investment, 177

Limit, internal-immanent, 3, 4, 44, 49, 51, 52

Los Angeles, 219–26

Lukács, Georg, 21, 22, 176, 179

Lynch, Kevin, 137

Lyotard, Jean-François, 253

Lyric, 209–10

Macherey, Pierre, 195

Mandel, Ernest, 289, 302 n. 3, 304 n. 11; *Late Capitalism*, 137

Marcuse, Herbert, 301 n. 4

Margins, 15

Marin, Louis, 142, 149; *Utopics*, 223

Marx, Karl, 3, 6, 20, 21, 85, 89, 91, 113, 117, 121, 183, 194, 196–97, 227, 258, 303 n. 4; *Capital*, 87, 98, 101–21, 186–87, 192, 194; *Critique of Hegel's Philosophy of Right*, 95; on Darstellung as presentation of value, 101–3; on Darstellung as scientific method, 95–101; *1844 Economic and Philosophic Manuscripts*, 89; *The Eighteenth Brumaire of Louis Bonaparte*, 247–48, 257; *The German Ideology*, 96; *Grundrisse*, 99–101, 115–17, 183

Marxism, 18, 19, 21, 22, 23, 85, 130, 132, 152, 182, 198, 205, 234, 235, 272, 288, 297 n. 1, 297 n. 2, 302 n. 3

Master Signifier, 9, 122, 181, 211, 227, 228, 260, 263–65

Master-slave dialectic, 65, 270

Materialism, 95, 155

Materialization, 105

McCumber, John, 65

Mediation, 69, 75, 77

Medovoi, Leerom, 257–58

Memory, 65, 220

Mestizaje, 282, 286

Metaphor, 195–206, 210, 261

Method, dialectical, 84, 136

Metonymy, 195–206, 210, 261

Mexican-Americans, 19, 260, 275, 276, 316 n. 37

Mexicans, 273–74, 286, 316 n. 36

Mexico, 274, 275, 277, 290, 291

Mignolo, Walter, 271–72

Migrant, 287

Miller, A. V., 59, 60

Misrecognition, 95

Modernism, 135, 221

Modernity, 284, 285

Monarch, 9, 11, 69, 80, 81

Montoya, Richard, 292

Moraga, Cherríe, 315 n. 35

Moral love, 254, 256

More, Thomas, Sir, 149; *Utopia*, 149–51

Mouffe, Chantal, 4–5, 19, 256, 259–68, 272, 291; *Hegemony and Socialist Strategy*, 204–6

Movement: dialectical, 55, 65, 66; negative, 59

Multiculturalism, 254, 267, 290, 318 n. 61

Multinationalism, 129, 138, 139–40, 141, 149, 280, 289, 291

Name, 69, 76, 121, 124, 305 n. 19; empty, 74

Name of the Father, 228, 229

Narcissism, 219

Narrative, 141, 161, 174, 175–77, 219, 220–21, 235, 238–43, 256–58, 289; master, 135, 177

Narrativization, 128

National allegory, 135, 139

Nation, 273–94; American, 274, 281

Nationalism, 238, 250–51, 265, 273–94

Native Americans, 277, 279

Natural symbolism, 38–42

Necessity, 62, 65, 72, 135, 156, 162, 174

Negation, 49, 62, 76, 82, 98; determinate, 195; dialectical, 50; self-, 61

Negative, 50, 54, 55, 60, 77; labor of, 54

Negative pleasure, 38

Negativity, 10, 13, 74, 76, 83, 161, 167, 181, 195, 261, 269; abstract, 17; absolute, 5, 70, 79, 82, 124, 170, 173; concrete, 68; immanent, 122, 265; radical, 5, 9, 11, 15, 82, 169, 171, 180, 207, 211, 213–14, 219, 227, 255, 258, 259, 294; space of, 4; subject as, 68, 211

Neocolonialism, 246, 294. *See also* Colonialism; Postcolonialism

Neutralization, 151, 220

Nicaragua, 257–58, 259

Nietzsche, Friedrich, 18, 153, 197, 206–15, 309 n. 13, 309–10 n. 19, 310 n. 20; *The Birth of Tragedy*, 207, 214; reversal of Socrates, 216, 218

Nonidentity, 54. *See also* Identity
North American Free Trade Agreement, 290
Notion, 50, 54, 59, 65, 70, 71, 72, 74, 77, 78, 79, 80, 81, 82, 139, 265, 289. *See also* Concept
Noumena, 49, 168, 237; and phenomena, 165, 166, 215–16

Object, 27, 28, 35, 164, 177; excluded, 275; of knowledge, 235, 236; sublime, 37
Objectification, 16, 132
Objectification of labor, 106, 119
Objet petit a, 12
Obsession, 229–30
Oedipus complex, 154
One, 113, 115, 123, 170, 181, 212
Orientalism, 287
Other, 15, 19, 154, 155, 167, 169, 170, 229–34, 237, 264, 271, 277
Ortega, Daniel, 257–58, 259
Otro, lo, vs. el otro, 271–72, 287, 291
Overdetermination, 88, 99, 101, 146, 243–44, 251
Owl of Minerva, 54–55, 166, 185

Pain, 34, 37, 38
Panopticon, 221
Part-whole, 135
Particular, 282; and universal, 68, 71, 75, 82, 263, 264, 266–67
Pascal, Blaise, 190–91, 213, 227, 239
Pastiche, 220
Pathos, 238–39, 269, 270, 315 n. 29
Patristic, 130–32, 133
Paz, Octavio, 316 n. 41
Pérez-Torres, Rafael, 280–81, 288
Performance, 182
Performativity, 18–19, 66–69, 182, 215, 219
Pervert, 230
Petit objet a, 155
Phantasie, 64–65
Phenomena, 49; and noumena, 165, 166, 215–16

Picture thinking, 78. *See also* Vorstellung
Plato, 195, 208, 209–10, 218; *Phaedrus*, 311 n. 24; *Republic*, 195, 215–18
Play, 43
Pleasure, 34, 38; negative, 35, 37
Pluralism, 270
Poetics, 64, 276–81, 288, 291
Poetry, 40, 207, 212, 276–81, 282, 288, 289, 317 n. 42, 317 n. 50
Point de capiton, 263
Political economy, 85, 99, 113
Political unconscious. *See* Jameson, Fredric
Politics, 266–68, 282, 287, 288
Positing the presuppositions, 162, 166, 175, 178–79
Possibility, space of, 86
Post-Althusserians, 6, 263
Postcolonialism, 282–85
Post-Kantianism, 195
Post-Marxism, 122, 123, 136
Postmodernism, 18, 20, 22, 23, 126, 135, 173, 182, 218, 234, 266, 283; sublime, 3, 17, 22, 225, 238
Postmodernity, 139, 173
Poststructuralism, 6, 135, 159, 244–45, 288, 291
Poulantzas, Nicos, 272
Practice: material, 7, 8; theoretical, 99
Prakash, Gyan, 312 n. 2
Precapitalism, 121
Predicate, 9, 53, 269
Predication, 168, 247
Presence, 189, 195, 199
Presentation, 4, 5, 16, 19, 21, 25, 26, 28, 30, 32–35, 43, 47, 48, 49, 50, 54–56, 58, 74, 78, 79, 84–126, 183, 237; analogical, 47; of Idea, 24, 46; negative, 113, 162, 165, 168, 172, 213, 237; vs. representation, 26, 115, 121. *See also* Darstellung; Representation; Sublime; Vorstellung
Presupposition, 77, 97
Principle, regulative, 47

Problematic, 85, 88, 91, 192

Production, 121, 183, 200; commodity, 90; forces of, 227; mode of, 85, 87, 88, 90, 103, 120, 129, 133, 134, 137–38, 160–62, 173, 175, 226, 235, 243; relations of 124, 247

Proletariat, 135, 176, 267

Proposition, 53, 61, 75–78, 109; speculative, 11, 21, 53, 66, 68, 70, 74, 78, 83, 195, 268, 269, 273, 293, 302 n. 9, 302 n. 11

Psychoanalysis, 5, 130, 152, 228–31; act, 230–33; ethic, 18

Purposiveness, 23, 27, 28–38, 45–48, 51, 190; objective, 32, 33, 46, 189–90; without purpose, 32, 163; subjective, 28, 30–32, 190. See also Anti-purposiveness; Zweckmäßigkeit; Zweckwidrigkeit

Quilting point, 263

Raman, Shankar, 257–58

Ranciere, Jacques, 293

Rani of Sirmur, 236–41

Rational, and actual, 53–54, 78–83

Reagan, Ronald, 171, 227, 259–60

Real, 5, 10, 11, 12, 17, 141, 149, 151, 152, 155–56, 157, 160–72, 173, 174, 175, 178–81, 209, 215, 225, 233, 262, 265; answer of, 12; little piece of, 11, 69; vs. reality, 159, 230

Reality, objective, 25, 163

Reason, 11, 25, 28, 35, 37, 38, 40, 45, 46, 48, 62, 66, 218; speculative, 41, 54; transcendent use of, 164

Recollection, 63, 65, 66

Redoubling, 168, 170

Referent, 155, 195

Reflection, 31, 39, 41, 46, 47, 49, 77, 169, 174, 180; determining, 166, 168, 170–71; external, 139, 163, 165, 166, 167–70, 180–81; judgment of, 72; positing, 164, 166–67, 168, 172, 176; redoubled, 168, 170

Reification, 61, 221

Reinvestment, 135, 138, 148, 154

Relation, social, 119, 121

Religion, 54, 82, 88, 119, 130, 138

Rendered sensible, 24. See also Versinnlichung

Representation, 8, 17, 18, 19, 21, 24, 29, 30, 31, 37, 39, 43–44, 54–56, 85, 99, 150, 151, 152, 179–80, 210, 217, 220, 223, 245, 251; abyss of, 2, 5, 294; beyond of, 3, 5, 6, 16, 18, 35, 49, 120–22, 162, 168, 169, 170, 195, 230, 234, 237, 241, 247–52, 255, 257–58, 262; breakdown of, 14, 15, 35, 168, 237, 246; cultural, 15, 183, 234, 235–94; limits of, 16, 115, 156, 161, 169, 238–42; vs. presentation, 26, 115, 121; and the sublime, 23. See also Darstellung; Vertreten; Vorstellung

Respect, 35, 37

Retroactivity, 5, 6, 67, 69, 82, 86, 100, 106, 120, 126, 147, 159, 162, 165, 166

Revolution, cultural, 134, 173, 175

Rivera, Diego, 286

Robinson, Benjamin, 257–58

Romanticism, 42, 135, 143–44, 149, 279

Rose, Gillian, 53–54, 70, 78, 82

Sallis, John, 297 n. 1; Being and Logos, 215–16; Crossings: Nietzsche and the Space of Tragedy, 208

Sánchez, Rosaura, 317 n. 50

Sartre, Jean-Paul, 21

Sati, 252–54, 312 n. 2

Schein, 120, 207, 209, 211, 212, 215

Schelling, Friedrich, 50, 56, 65, 77

Schema, 34, 38, 39, 40, 41, 42, 128

Schizophrenia, 154

Science, 60, 85, 192–93, 225, 234

Screen, 263

Sedimented form, 134, 173

Semiotic, 154; system, 142

Sensible, 25, 49

Sensible and supersensible (intelligible), 4, 23, 26, 37, 40, 41, 63, 163

Sentence, 21, 75, 76, 253–54

Shepherdson, Charles, 310 n. 21

Sign, 34, 59, 64–66, 67, 68, 75, 82; Bhabha on, 282–85

Signification, 59–66, 67, 128, 260, 291

Signified, 145, 195, 284

Signifier, 122, 145, 154, 195, 221, 284; empty, 26, 259, 264, 266; floating, 259, 260

Signifying chain, 154, 155

Signifying process, 12

Siguenza, Herbert, 292

Simulacrum, 215, 224

Social, 4, 9, 19, 175–76, 180, 202, 205, 211, 228, 261, 262, 265

Social formation, 192, 272

Socialist Review, 257

Society, 133–34, 261, 262, 265, 273

Socrates, 182, 214–18

Socratic philosophy, 6

Soul, 165

Space, 221; decolonized, 236, 255; empty, 264, 266; late-capitalist, 140; negative, 44; utopian, 219

Speaking, 236, 245–46, 249, 275

Spectator, 210, 211, 219, 224; consciousness of, 185, 188; tragic, 206–15

Speculation, 53, 82

Speculative philosophy, 60

Speculative proposition, 11, 21, 53, 66, 68, 70, 74, 78, 83, 195, 268, 269, 273, 293, 302 n. 9, 302 n. 11

Speculative reversal, 13

Spirit, 60, 62, 66, 70, 80, 96

Spivak, Gayatri Chakravorty, 20, 21, 121–22, 235–59, 266, 287, 288, 290, 293, 304 n. 13, 305 n. 17, 312 nn. 3–5, 313 n. 6, 313 n. 17, 314 n. 19, 314 n. 23, 315 n. 29, 316 n. 39, 318 n. 59, 318 n. 61; abyss of heterogeneity, 236; "Can the Subaltern Speak?" 235, 236, 249; *A Critique of Postcolonial Reason*, 235, 236; on history writing, 236; on miming, 239, 254; "Poststructuralism, Marginality,

Postcoloniality and Value," 269; on strategic essentialism, 245, 313 n. 8; on subaltern, 3, 19, 235–59; on the sublime, 235–36, 238, 239–40, 256

Split, internal, 168, 282, 285

Sprinker, Michael, 93, 187–93, 308 n. 3; *Imaginary Relations*, 187

Stalinism, 188, 230, 231, 260

State, 54, 78, 80

State apparatus, 10

Stellung, 61

Strehler, 188

Structural causality, 17, 84–85, 87–91, 101, 103, 113, 118–20, 123, 160, 183, 185–97, 302 n. 1, 303 n. 6, 305 n. 20

Structure, 90–91, 94, 113, 123, 124, 185, 271–72

Structure-in-dominance, 183

Subaltern, 250, 267, 313 n. 14

Subaltern Studies group, 243, 250

Subject, 4, 6, 7, 9, 15, 18, 23, 30, 56, 61, 66, 76, 77, 82, 115, 121, 124, 135, 139, 153, 154, 156, 170, 176, 193, 207, 209–10, 211, 219, 222, 226, 227, 228, 232, 235–36, 243–47, 253, 255, 269, 284, 313 n. 7; colonial, 237, 252; dialectic of, 114–18; externalization of, 68; Fichtean, 9; Hegelian, 5; hystericization of, 12, 13; as impossible, 70, 235; as negativity, 68, 211; and object, 65, 193; of structural causality, 124–26, 206; vs. subjectivization, 17, 167, 170; subject-predicate, 27, 70, 71–73, 77, 79, 96, 109, 293; as substance, 74, 80, 170, 181, 228, 237; of the West, 245–47

Subject-effect, 124, 245

Subjective destitution, 232

Subjectivity, 9, 18, 182, 183, 211, 228–34, 259, 276; empty, 67; radical, 226, 228

Subjectivization, 9, 10, 11, 12, 13, 124, 170, 181, 193, 202, 207, 211, 214, 219, 227, 228, 229, 232, 234, 264–65. *See also* Subject

Subject-position, 7, 8, 9, 14, 193, 204, 270

Sublation, 62, 73

Sublime, 4, 16, 44, 49, 161, 169; defined, 35; Hegelian, 16, 17, 18, 161, 165–71; hysterical, 173, 218, 224–26; Kantian, 5, 15, 17, 18, 22, 161–66, 168, 170, 171, 172, 189, 220, 224, 256; as negative presentation, 34–38, 168, 189; object, 19, 169, 173, 235; postmodern, 3, 17, 22, 225, 238; thing, 11, 171; unrepresentable, 140. *See also* Hegel, Georg Wilhelm Friedrich; Jameson, Fredric; Kant, Immanuel; Spivak, Gayatri Chakravorty; Žižek, Slavoj

Subreption, 225; objective, 29, 32, 33, 35, 46

Substance, 4, 5, 9, 15, 74, 110, 170, 181, 228, 272, 276

Subtext, 158–60

Superego, 13

Supersensibility, 25, 35, 45, 46, 48, 51; substrate, 24, 41

Surplus-value, 103, 184

Suture, 259, 262, 263, 271

Syllogism, 71

Symbol, 51, 52, 59, 64, 131, 135; Bhabha on, 282–85

Symbolic, 2, 5, 11, 45, 47, 64, 135, 137, 152, 155, 161; act, 133, 144, 157, 158, 159, 161, 162, 163, 165, 172, 179–80, 225, 228, 229, 231–32, 234, 261, 264, 265; death, 6, 232; mandate, 12, 13, 171, 230, 234, 256; order, 13, 14, 19, 232, 263, 270–71; resolution, 133, 144, 148, 178; structure, 10. *See also* Lacan, Jacques

Symbolism, 38, 51, 209, 260

Symbolization, 10, 14, 68–69, 154, 166, 227, 230

Symptom, 13, 14, 15, 19, 133, 264, 266; identification with, 267–73, 274, 293–94; Mexican as, 273–94

Symptomatic reading, 84, 102, 124, 184, 186, 200

Syncretism, 279

Synthesis, 149

System, 61, 62, 135, 258; character, 140–44, 175, 181

Taste, 41–42, 163

Tautology, 112

Teatro Campesino, 276

Technic of nature, 32

Teleology, 33, 40, 45–48, 164, 168

Temporality, 51, 285

Terrain, change of, 125, 305–6 n. 21

Terror, in French Revolution, 11, 170, 211, 226, 227, 259

Text, 134, 141, 150, 161, 172, 173, 175, 177–80

Textuality, 157–58

Theater, 18, 92–95, 182, 183–95, 219, 230; authorless, 184–88

Thetic, 61

Thing, 3, 4, 5, 9, 11, 16, 65, 67, 68, 69, 77, 82, 206, 207, 230, 275–76; in-itself, 168; stupid, 11, 17, 183, 226, 227; sublime, 11, 171; traumatic, 13

Thought, 66, 78; dialectical, 136

Time, 48, 220, 221

Time-lag, 284–85

Tito, Marshal, 231

Torfing, Jacob, 314–15 n. 25

Totality, 29, 35, 37, 65, 87, 115, 134, 139, 162, 199, 206, 221, 227, 260, 273

Totalization, 211, 261, 283

Tragedy, space of, 210, 211

Transcendence, 198, 225

Transfiguration, 208

Trauma, 208, 230, 234

Treaty of Guadalupe-Hidalgo, 19

Tropic-concept, 193–97, 208, 211

True, 59, 76

Truth, 65, 78, 155, 161, 163, 215, 239, 265

Unconscious, 128, 135, 139, 145, 154, 177; political, *see* Jameson, Fredric

Understanding, 24, 26, 28, 34, 37, 38, 41, 49, 54, 62, 70, 75, 77, 78, 79, 82, 162, 163, 164, 190, 218; archetypal, 51; concept of, 32, 38; discursive, 16, 21, 23, 25, 40, 44, 48–52, 189; intuitive, 16, 41, 48, 49

Undocumented workers, 265, 266, 269

United States, 227, 259, 260, 271, 290, 291

Universal, 274, 282, 283–84, 288–89; abstract, 77; and individual, 71; and particular, 68, 71, 75, 82, 263, 264, 266–67

Universality, 64, 269; abstract, 57

Unrepresentability, 254, 255

Urteil, 71

Use-value, 102, 103, 104, 110, 111, 113, 115, 121

Utopia, 136

Utopian texts, 150, 178

Utopic discourse, 142, 149

Value, 90, 106, 114, 115, 121, 184; theory of, 84, 101

Value-body, 108–9

Value-form, 106, 107, 110, 113, 114–18, 120

Varadharajan, Asha, 314 n. 19, 314 n. 22

Verarbeitung, 100

Verklärung, 208

Versinnlichung, 33, 34, 37, 39, 85, 129, 211

Vertreten, 82, 121–22, 247–52, 305 n. 17, 315 n. 19

Vicious circle, 11, 17, 172–73, 183, 214, 226, 230

Vilar, Pierre, 303 n. 6

Villanueva, Tino, 317 n. 43

Visible and intelligible. *See* Noumena; Phenomena

Void, 12, 124

Vorstellung, 19, 21, 26, 34, 50, 54, 58, 63–67, 71, 75, 83, 85, 129, 168, 210, 213, 247, 258; vs. Darstellung, 4, 16, 59, 93–94, 182, 188–89, 194, 195, 258, 267. *See also* Darstellung; Representation

West, Cornel, 307 n. 5

Westin Bonaventure Hotel, 218–26, 238

Will, 96, 171, 244, 252–54

Wish-fulfillment, 127, 130, 148, 176, 177–78, 243–44

Woman, 253, 256

Ybarra-Frausto, Tómas, 317 n. 49

Yugoslavia, 231

Žižek, Slavoj, 5, 6, 7, 11, 12, 13–14, 16, 17, 18, 19, 20, 21, 95, 114–18, 122, 174, 213, 226, 228–34, 281, 287, 288–89, 296 n. 8, 306 n. 1, 311 n. 27, 314 n. 25, 315 n. 28, 315 n. 29; on Hegel, 9, 66–69, 73, 79, 165–71, 303 n. 5; on the sublime, 35, 38; *The Sublime Object of Ideology*, 69–70, 265–66; on the symptom, 19, 263–73, 293–94; *The Ticklish Subject*, 272

Zweckmäßigkeit, 27, 28, 36

Zweckwidrigkeit, 36–37, 190

George Hartley is Associate Professor of English at Ohio University.

He is the author of *Textual Politics and the Language Poets.*

Library of Congress Cataloging-in-Publication Data

Hartley, George.

The abyss of representation : Marxism and the postmodern

sublime / George Hartley.

p. cm. — (Post-contemporary interventions)

Includes bibliographical references and index.

ISBN 0-8223-3127-6 (cloth : alk. paper)

ISBN 0-8223-3114-4 (pbk. : alk. paper)

1. Sublime, The—History. 2. Representation (Philosophy)—

History. 3. Idealism—History. 4. Postmodernism—History.

5. Marx, Karl, 1818–1883. I. Title. II. Series.

BH301.S7 H37 2003

121'.4'—dc21   2002153877